THE PELICAN FREUD LIBRARY
VOLUME 15

•

HISTORICAL AND EXPOSITORY WORKS ON PSYCHOANALYSIS

HISTORY OF THE
PSYCHOANALYTIC MOVEMENT,
AN AUTOBIOGRAPHICAL STUDY,
OUTLINE OF PSYCHOANALYSIS
AND OTHER WORKS

Sigmund Freud

•

*Translated from the German
under the general editorship of James Strachey*

*The present volume
edited by Albert Dickson*

PENGUIN BOOKS

Penguin Books Ltd, Harmondsworth, Middlesex, England
Viking Penguin Inc., 40 West 23rd Street, New York, New York 10010, U.S.A.
Penguin Books Australia Ltd, Ringwood, Victoria, Australia
Penguin Books Canada Limited, 2801 John Street, Markham, Ontario, Canada L3R 1B4
Penguin Books (N.Z.) Ltd, 182–190 Wairau Road, Auckland 10, New Zealand

Historical and Expository Works on Psychoanalysis:
History of the Psychoanalytic Movement,
An Autobiographical Study,
An Outline of Psychoanalysis
and other works

Present English translations first published in *The Standard Edition of the Complete
Psychological Works of Sigmund Freud* by the Hogarth Press and the Institute of
Psycho-Analysis, London, as follows:

'The Claims of Psychoanalysis to Scientific Interest', Volume XIII (1955);
'On the History of the Psychoanalytic Movement', Volume XIV (1957);
'Two Encyclopaedia Articles', Volume XVIII (1955); 'A Short Account
of Psychoanalysis', 'The Resistances to Psychoanalysis', Volume XIX
(1961); *An Autobiographical Study*, 'Postscript to *An Autobiographical Study*',
The Question of Lay Analysis, 'Postscript to *The Question of Lay Analysis*',
Volume XX (1959); 'Dr Reik and the Problem of Quackery', Volume
XXI (1961); *An Outline of Psychoanalysis*, Volume XXIII (1964).

'Sigmund Freud: A Sketch of his Life and Ideas' first published in *Two Short
Accounts of Psycho-Analysis* in Pelican Books 1962

This collection, *Historical and Expository Works on Psychoanalysis*,
first published in Pelican Books 1986

Translation and Editorial Matter copyright © the Estate of Angela Richards
and the Institute of Psycho-Analysis, 1955, 1957, 1959, 1961, 1962, 1964

Additional Editorial Matter copyright © Albert Dickson, 1986
All rights reserved

Made and printed in Great Britain by
Richard Clay (The Chaucer Press) Ltd, Bungay, Suffolk
Typeset in Lasercomp Bembo

CONTENTS

VOLUME 15
HISTORICAL AND EXPOSITORY WORKS
ON PSYCHOANALYSIS

CONTENTS

INTRODUCTION TO THE
PELICAN FREUD LIBRARY

The Pelican Freud Library is intended to meet the needs of the
general reader by providing all Freud's major writings in
translation together with an appropriate linking commentary.
It is the first time that such an edition has been produced in
paperback in the English language. It does not supplant *The
Standard Edition of the Complete Psychological Works of Sigmund
Freud*, translated from the German under the general editorship
of James Strachey in collaboration with Anna Freud, assisted
by Alix Strachey and Alan Tyson, editorial assistant Angela
Richards (Hogarth Press, 24 volumes, 1953–74). The *Standard
Edition* remains the fullest and most authoritative collection
published in any language. It does, however, provide a large
enough selection to meet the requirements of all but the most
specialist reader – in particular it aims to cater for students of
sociology, anthropology, criminology, medicine, aesthetics
and education, all of them fields in which Freud's ideas have
established their relevance.

The texts are reprinted unabridged, with corrections, from
the *Standard Edition*. The editorial commentary – introductions,
footnotes, internal cross-references, bibliographies and indexes
– is also based upon the *Standard Edition*, but it has been
abridged and where necessary adapted to suit the less specialized
scope and purposes of the *Pelican Freud Library*. Some corrections have been made and some new material added.

Selection of Material

This is not a complete edition of Freud's psychological works
– still less of his works as a whole, which included important

contributions to neurology and neuropathology dating from the early part of his professional life. Of the psychological writings, virtually all the major works have been included. The arrangement is by subject-matter, so that the main contributions to any particular theme will be found in one volume. Within each volume the works are, for the main part, in chronological sequence. The aim has been to cover the whole field of Freud's observations and his theory of psychoanalysis: that is to say, in the first place, the structure and dynamics of human mental activity; secondly, psychopathology and the mechanism of mental disorder; and thirdly, the application of psychoanalytic theory to wider spheres than the disorders of individuals which Freud originally, and indeed for the greater part of his life, investigated – to the psychology of groups, to social institutions and to religion, art and literature.

In his 'Sigmund Freud: A Sketch of his Life and Ideas' (p. 11 ff. below), James Strachey includes an account of Freud's discoveries as well as defining his principal theories and tracing their development.

Writings excluded from the Edition

The works that have been excluded are: (1) The neurological writings and most of those very early works from the period before the idea of psychoanalysis had taken form. (2) Writings on the actual technique of treatment. These were written specifically for practitioners of psychoanalysis and for analysts in training and their interest is correspondingly specialized. Freud never in fact produced a complete text on psychoanalytic treatment and the papers on technique only deal with selected points of difficulty or theoretical interest. (3) Writings which cover the same ground as other major works which have been included; for example, since the *Library* includes the *Introductory Lectures on Psychoanalysis* and the *New Lectures*, it was decided to leave out several of the shorter expository works in which Freud surveys the whole subject. Similarly, because the *Interpretation of Dreams* is included, the shorter writings on this topic have been omitted. (4) Freud's private correspondence, much of which has now been published in translation.[1] This is not to imply that such letters are without interest or importance though they have not yet received full critical treatment. (5) The numerous short writings such as reviews of books, prefaces to other authors' works, obituary notices and little *pièces d'occasion* – all of which lose interest to a large extent when separated from the books or occasions to which they refer and which would often demand long editorial explanations to make them comprehensible.

All of these excluded writings (with the exception of the works on neurology and the private letters) can be found in the *Standard Edition*.

Editorial Commentary

The bibliographical information, included at the beginning of the Editor's Note or Introduction to each work, gives the title of the German (or other) original, the date and place of its first publication and the position, where applicable, of the work in Freud's *Gesammelte Werke*, the most complete edition at present available of the works in German (published by S. Fischer Verlag, Frankfurt am Main). Details of the first translation of each work into English are also included, together with the *Standard Edition* reference. Other editions are listed only if they contain significant changes. (Full details of all German editions published in Freud's lifetime and of all English editions prior to the *Standard Edition* are included in the *Standard Edition*.)

The date of original publication of each work has been added to the half-title page, with the date of composition included in square brackets wherever it is different from the former date.

Further background information is given in introductory notes and in footnotes to the text. Apart from dealing with the time and circumstances of composition, these notes aim to

1. [See the list, p. 23 *n.* below, and the details in the Bibliography, p. 445 ff.]

make it possible to follow the inception and development of important psychoanalytic concepts by means of systematic cross-references. Most of these references are to other works included in the *Pelican Freud Library*. A secondary purpose is to date additions and alterations made by Freud in successive revisions of the text and in certain cases to provide the earlier versions. No attempt has been made to do this as comprehensively as in the *Standard Edition*, but variants are given whenever they indicate a definite change of view. Square brackets are used throughout to distinguish editorial additions from Freud's text and his own footnotes.

It will be clear from this account that an overwhelming debt is due to the late James Strachey, the general editor and chief translator of the *Standard Edition*. He indeed was mainly responsible for the idea of a *Pelican Freud Library*, and for the original plan of contents. Miss Anna Freud and Mrs Alix Strachey, both now deceased, gave advice of the greatest value. The late Mr Ernst Freud and the Publications Committee of the Institute of Psycho-Analysis also helped in the preparations for this edition.

SIGMUND FREUD

A SKETCH OF HIS LIFE AND IDEAS

SIGMUND FREUD was born on 6 May 1856 in Freiberg, a small town in Moravia, which was at that time a part of Austria-Hungary. In an external sense the eighty-three years of his life were on the whole uneventful and call for no lengthy history.

He came of a middle-class Jewish family and was the eldest child of his father's second wife. His position in the family was a little unusual, for there were already two grown-up sons by his father's first wife. These were more than twenty years older than he was and one of them was already married, with a little boy; so that Freud was in fact born an uncle. This nephew played at least as important a part in his very earliest years as his own younger brothers and sisters, of whom seven were born after him.

His father was a wool-merchant and soon after Freud's birth found himself in increasing commercial difficulties. He therefore decided, when Freud was just three years old, to leave Freiberg, and a year later the whole family settled in Vienna, with the exception of the two elder half-brothers and their children, who established themselves instead in Manchester. At more than one stage in his life Freud played with the idea of joining them in England, but nothing was to come of this for nearly eighty years.

In Vienna during the whole of Freud's childhood the family lived in the most straitened conditions; but it is much to his father's credit that he gave invariable priority to the charge of Freud's education, for the boy was obviously intelligent and was a hard worker as well. The result was that he won a place

11

in the *Gymnasium* at the early age of nine, and for the last six of the eight years he spent at the school he was regularly top of his class. When at the age of seventeen he passed out of school his career was still undecided; his education so far had been of the most general kind, and, though he seemed in any case destined for the university, several faculties lay open to him.

Freud insisted more than once that at no time in his life did he feel 'any particular predilection for the career of a doctor. I was moved, rather,' he says, 'by a sort of curiosity, which was, however, directed more towards human concerns than towards natural objects.'[1] Elsewhere he writes: 'I have no knowledge of having had any craving in my early childhood to help suffering humanity . . . In my youth I felt an overpowering need to understand something of the riddles of the world in which we live and perhaps even to contribute something to their solution.'[2] And in yet another passage in which he was discussing the sociological studies of his last years: 'My interest, after making a lifelong *détour* through the natural sciences, medicine, and psychotherapy, returned to the cultural problems which had fascinated me long before, when I was a youth scarcely old enough for thinking.'[3]

What immediately determined Freud's choice of a scientific career was, so he tells us, being present just when he was leaving school at a public reading of an extremely flowery essay on 'Nature', attributed (wrongly, it seems) to Goethe. But if it was to be science, practical considerations narrowed the choice to medicine. And it was as a medical student that Freud enrolled himself at the university in the autumn of 1873 at the age of seventeen. Even so, however, he was in no hurry to obtain a medical degree. For his first year or two he attended lectures on a variety of subjects, but gradually concentrated first on biology and then on physiology. His very first piece of research was in his third year at the university, when he was

1. [*An Autobiographical Study* (1925*d*), near the opening of the work.]
2. ['Postscript to *The Question of Lay Analysis*' (1927*a*).]
3. ['Postscript (1935) to *An Autobiographical Study*' (1935*a*).]

deputed by the Professor of Comparative Anatomy to investigate a detail in the anatomy of the eel, which involved the dissection of some four hundred specimens. Soon afterwards he entered the Physiological Laboratory under Brücke, and worked there happily for six years. It was no doubt from him that he acquired the main outlines of his attitude to physical science in general. During these years Freud worked chiefly on the anatomy of the central nervous system and was already beginning to produce publications. But it was becoming obvious that no livelihood which would be sufficient to meet the needs of the large family at home was to be picked up from these laboratory studies. So at last, in 1881, he decided to take his medical degree, and a year later, most unwillingly, gave up his position under Brücke and began work in the Vienna General Hospital.

What finally determined this change in his life was something more urgent than family considerations: in June 1882 he became engaged to be married, and thenceforward all his efforts were directed towards making marriage possible. His fiancée, Martha Bernays, came of a well-known Jewish family in Hamburg, and though for the moment she was living in Vienna she was very soon obliged to return to her remote North-German home. During the four years that followed, it was only for brief visits that he could have glimpses of her, and the two lovers had to content themselves with an almost daily interchange of letters. Freud now set himself to establishing a position and a reputation in the medical world. He worked in various departments of the hospital, but soon came to concentrate on neuroanatomy and neuropathology. During this period, too, he published the first inquiry into the possible medical uses of cocaine; and it was this that suggested to Koller the drug's employment as a local anaesthetic. He soon formed two immediate plans: one of these was to obtain an appointment as *Privatdozent*, a post not unlike that of a university lecturer in England, the other was to gain a travelling bursary which would enable him to spend some time in Paris, where the reigning figure was the great Charcot. Both of these aims, if they were realized, would, he felt, bring him real advantages, and in 1885, after a hard struggle, he achieved them both.

The months which Freud spent under Charcot at the Salpêtrière (the famous Paris hospital for nervous diseases) brought another change in the course of his life and this time a revolutionary one. So far his work had been concerned entirely with physical science and he was still carrying out histological studies on the brain while he was in Paris. Charcot's interests were at that period concentrated mainly on hysteria and hypnotism. In the world from which Freud came these subjects were regarded as barely respectable, but he became absorbed in them, and, though Charcot himself looked at them purely as branches of neuropathology, for Freud they meant the first beginnings of the investigation of the mind.

On his return to Vienna in the spring of 1886 Freud set up in private practice as a consultant in nervous diseases, and his long-delayed marriage followed soon afterwards. He did not, however, at once abandon all his neuropathological work: for several more years he studied in particular the cerebral palsies of children, on which he became a leading authority. At this period, too, he produced an important monograph on aphasia. But he was becoming more and more engaged in the treatment of the neuroses. After experimenting in vain with electrotherapy, he turned to hypnotic suggestion, and in 1888 visited Nancy to learn the technique used with such apparent success there by Liébeault and Bernheim. This still proved unsatisfactory and he was driven to yet another line of approach. He knew that a friend of his, Dr Josef Breuer, a Vienna consultant considerably his senior, had some ten years earlier cured a girl suffering from hysteria by a quite new procedure. He now persuaded Breuer to take up the method once more, and he himself applied it to several fresh cases with promising results. The method was based on the assumption that hysteria was the product of a psychical trauma which had been forgotten by the patient; and the treatment consisted in inducing her in a hypnotic state to recall the forgotten trauma to the accompaniment of appropriate emotions. Before very long

Freud began to make changes both in the procedure and in the underlying theory; this led eventually to a breach with Breuer, and to the ultimate development by Freud of the whole system of ideas to which he soon gave the name of psychoanalysis.

From this moment onwards – from 1895, perhaps – to the very end of his life, the whole of Freud's intellectual existence revolved around this development, its far-reaching implications, and its theoretical and practical repercussions. It would, of course, be impossible to give in a few sentences any consecutive account of Freud's discoveries and ideas, but an attempt will be made presently to indicate in a disconnected fashion some of the main changes he has brought about in our habits of thought. Meanwhile we may continue to follow the course of his external life.

His domestic existence in Vienna was essentially devoid of episode: his home and his consulting rooms were in the same house from 1891 till his departure for London forty-seven years later. His happy marriage and his growing family – three sons and three daughters – provided a solid counterweight to the difficulties which, to begin with at least, surrounded his professional career. It was not only the nature of his discoveries that created prejudice against him in medical circles; just as great, perhaps, was the effect of the intense anti-semitic feeling which dominated the official world of Vienna: his appointment to a university professorship was constantly held back by political influence.

One particular feature of these early years calls for mention on account of its consequences. This was Freud's friendship with Wilhelm Fliess, a brilliant but unbalanced Berlin physician, who specialized in the ear and throat, but whose wider interests extended over human biology and the effects of periodic phenomena in vital processes. For fifteen years, from 1887 to 1902, Freud corresponded with him regularly, reported the development of his ideas, forwarded him long drafts outlining his future writings, and, most important of all, sent him an essay of some forty thousand words which has been given the name of a 'Project for a Scientific Psychology'. This essay was composed in 1895, at what might be described as the watershed of Freud's career, when he was reluctantly moving from physiology to psychology; it is an attempt to state the facts of psychology in purely neurological terms. This paper and all the rest of Freud's communications to Fliess have, by a lucky chance, survived: they throw a fascinating light on the development of Freud's ideas and show how much of the later findings of psychoanalysis were already present in his mind at this early stage.

Apart from his relations with Fliess, Freud had little outside support to begin with. He gradually gathered a few pupils round him in Vienna, but it was only after some ten years, in about 1906, that a change was inaugurated by the adhesion of a number of Swiss psychiatrists to his views. Chief among these were Bleuler, the head of the Zurich mental hospital, and his assistant Jung. This proved to be the beginning of the first spread of psychoanalysis. An international meeting of psycho-analysts gathered at Salzburg in 1908, and in 1909 Freud and Jung were invited to give a number of lectures in the United States. Freud's writings began to be translated into many languages, and groups of practising analysts sprang up all over the world. But the progress of psychoanalysis was not without its set-backs: the current which its subject-matter stirred up in the mind ran too deep for its easy acceptance. In 1911 one of Freud's prominent Viennese supporters, Alfred Adler, broke away from him, and two or three years later Jung's differences from Freud led to their separation. Almost immediately after this came the First World War and an interruption of the international spread of psychoanalysis. Soon afterwards, too, came the gravest personal tragedies – the death of a daughter and of a favourite grandchild, and the onset of the malignant illness which was to pursue him relentlessly for the last sixteen years of his life. None of these troubles, how-ever, brought any interruption to the development of Freud's observations and inferences. The structure of his ideas con-tinued to expand and to find ever wider applications – particularly in the sociological field. By now he had become generally recognized as a figure of world celebrity, and no honour pleased him more than his election in 1936, the year of his eightieth birthday, as a Corresponding Member of the Royal Society. It was no doubt this fame, supported by the efforts of influential admirers, including, it is said, President Roosevelt, that protected him from the worst excesses of the National Socialists when Hitler invaded Austria in 1938, though they seized and destroyed his publications. Freud's departure from Vienna was nevertheless essential, and in June of that year, accompanied by some of his family, he made the journey to London, and it was there, a year later, on 23 September 1939, that he died.

It has become a journalistic cliché to speak of Freud as one of the revolutionary founders of modern thought and to couple his name with that of Einstein. Most people would however find it almost as hard to summarize the changes introduced by the one as by the other.

Freud's discoveries may be grouped under three headings – an instrument of research, the findings produced by the instrument, and the theoretical hypotheses inferred from the findings – though the three groups were of course mutually interrelated. Behind all of Freud's work, however, we should posit his belief in the universal validity of the law of determinism. As regards physical phenomena this belief was perhaps derived from his experience in Brücke's laboratory and so, ultimately, from the school of Helmholtz; but Freud extended the belief uncompromisingly to the field of mental phenomena, and here he may have been influenced by his teacher, the psychiatrist Meynert, and indirectly by the philosophy of Herbart.

First and foremost, Freud was the discoverer of the first instrument for the scientific examination of the human mind. Creative writers of genius had had fragmentary insight into mental processes, but no systematic method of investigation existed before Freud. It was only gradually that he perfected the instrument, since it was only gradually that the difficulties in the way of such an investigation became apparent. The forgotten trauma in Breuer's explanation of hysteria provided the earliest problem and perhaps the most fundamental of all, for it showed conclusively that there were active parts of the mind not immediately open to inspection either by an onlooker or by the subject himself. These parts of the mind were described by Freud, without regard for metaphysical or terminological disputes, as the unconscious. Their existence was equally demonstrated by the fact of post-hypnotic suggestion, where a person in a fully waking state performs an action which had been suggested to him some time earlier, though he had totally forgotten the suggestion itself. No examination of the mind could thus be considered complete unless it included this unconscious part of it in its scope. How was this to be accomplished? The obvious answer seemed to be: by means of hypnotic suggestion; and this was the instrument used by Breuer and, to begin with, by Freud. But it soon turned out to be an imperfect one, acting irregularly and uncertainly and sometimes not at all. Little by little, accordingly, Freud abandoned the use of suggestion and replaced it by an entirely fresh instrument, which was later known as 'free association'. He adopted the unheard-of plan of simply asking the person whose mind he was investigating to say whatever came into his head. This crucial decision led at once to the most startling results; even in this primitive form Freud's instrument produced fresh insight. For, though things went along swimmingly for a while, sooner or later the flow of associations dried up: the subject would not or could not think of anything more to say. There thus came to light the fact of 'resistance', of a force, separate from the subject's conscious will, which was refusing to collaborate with the investigation. Here was one basis for a very fundamental piece of theory, for a hypothesis of the mind as something dynamic, as consisting in a number of mental forces, some conscious and some unconscious, operating now in harmony now in opposition with one another.

Though these phenomena eventually turned out to be of universal occurrence, they were first observed and studied in neurotic patients, and the earlier years of Freud's work were largely concerned with discovering means by which the 'resistance' of these patients could be overcome and what lay behind it could be brought to light. The solution was only made possible by an extraordinary piece of self-observation on Freud's part – what we should now describe as his self-analysis. We are fortunate in having a contemporary first-hand description of this event in his letters to Fliess which have already been mentioned. This analysis enabled him to discover the nature of the unconscious processes at work in the mind and to understand why there is such a strong resistance to their becoming conscious; it enabled him to devise techniques for overcoming or evading the resistance in his patients; and, most important of all, it enabled him to realize the very great difference between the mode of functioning of these unconscious processes and that of our familiar conscious ones. A word may be said on each of these three points, for in fact they constitute the core of Freud's contributions to our knowledge of the mind.

The unconscious contents of the mind were found to consist wholly in the activity of conative trends – desires or wishes – which derive their energy directly from the primary physical instincts. They function quite regardless of any consideration other than that of obtaining immediate satisfaction, and are thus liable to be out of step with those more conscious elements in the mind which are concerned with adaptation to reality and the avoidance of external dangers. Since, moreover, these primitive trends are to a great extent of a sexual or of a destructive nature, they are bound to come in conflict with the more social and civilized mental forces. Investigations along this path were what led Freud to his discoveries of the long-disguised secrets of the sexual life of children and of the Oedipus complex.

In the second place, his self-analysis led him to an inquiry into the nature of dreams. These turned out to be, like neurotic symptoms, the product of a conflict and a compromise between the primary unconscious impulses and the secondary conscious ones. By analysing them into their elements it was therefore possible to infer their hidden unconscious contents; and, since dreams are common phenomena of almost universal occurrence, their interpretation turned out to be one of the most useful technical contrivances for penetrating the resistances of neurotic patients.

Finally, the painstaking examination of dreams enabled Freud to classify the remarkable differences between what he termed the primary and secondary processes of thought, between events in the unconscious and conscious regions of the mind. In the unconscious, it was found, there is no sort of organization or coordination: each separate impulse seeks satisfaction independently of all the rest; they proceed uninfluenced by one another; contradictions are completely inoperative, and the most opposite impulses flourish side by side. So, too, in the unconscious, associations of ideas proceed along lines without any regard to logic: similarities are treated as identities, negatives are equated with positives. Again, the objects to which the conative trends are attached in the unconscious are extraordinarily changeable – one may be replaced by another along a whole chain of associations that have no rational basis. Freud perceived that the intrusion into conscious thinking of mechanisms that belong properly to the primary process accounts for the oddity not only of dreams but of many other normal and pathological mental events.

It is not much of an exaggeration to say that all the later part of Freud's work lay in an immense extension and elaboration of these early ideas. They were applied to an elucidation of the mechanisms not only of the psychoneuroses and psychoses but also of such normal processes as slips of the tongue, making jokes, artistic creation, political institutions, and religions; they played a part in throwing fresh light on many applied sciences – archaeology, anthropology, criminology, education; they also served to account for the effectiveness of psychoanalytic therapy. Lastly, too, Freud erected on the basis of these elementary observations a theoretical superstructure, what he named a 'metapsychology', of more general concepts. These, however, fascinating as many people will find them, he always insisted were in the nature of provisional hypotheses. Quite late in his life, indeed, influenced by the ambiguity of the term 'unconscious' and its many conflicting uses, he proposed a new structural account of the mind in which the uncoordinated instinctual trends were called the 'id', the organized realistic part the 'ego', and the critical and moralizing function the 'super-ego' – a new account which has certainly made for a clarification of many issues.

This, then, will have given the reader an outline of the external events of Freud's life and some notion of the scope of his discoveries. Is it legitimate to ask for more? to try to penetrate a little further and to inquire what sort of person Freud was? Possibly not. But human curiosity about great men is insatiable, and if it is not gratified with true accounts it will inevitably clutch at mythological ones. In two of Freud's early books (*The Interpretation of Dreams* and *The Psychopathology of Everyday Life*) the presentation of his thesis had forced on him the necessity of bringing up an unusual amount of personal material. Nevertheless, or perhaps for that very reason, he intensely objected to any intrusion into his private life, and he was correspondingly the subject of a wealth of myths. According to the first and most naïve rumours, for instance, he was an abandoned profligate, devoted to the corruption of public morals. Later fantasies have tended in the opposite direction: he has been represented as a harsh moralist, a ruthless disciplinarian, an autocrat, egocentric and unsmiling, and an essentially unhappy man. To anyone who was acquainted with him, even slightly, both these pictures must seem equally preposterous. The second of them was no doubt partly derived from a knowledge of his physical sufferings during his last years; but partly too it may have been due to the unfortunate impression produced by some of his most widespread portraits. He disliked being photographed, at least by professional photographers, and his features on occasion expressed the fact; artists too seem always to have been overwhelmed by the necessity for representing the inventor of psychoanalysis as a ferocious and terrifying figure. Fortunately, however, alternative versions exist of a more amiable and truer kind – snapshots, for instance, taken on a holiday or with his children, such as will be found in his eldest son's memoir of his father (*Glory Reflected*, by Martin Freud [1957]). In many ways, indeed, this delightful and amusing book serves to redress the balance from more official biographies, invaluable as they are, and reveals something of Freud as he was in ordinary life. Some of these portraits show us that in his earlier days he had well-filled features, but in later life, at any rate after the First World War and even before his illness, this was no longer so, and his features, as well as his whole figure (which was of medium height), were chiefly remarkable for the impression they gave of tense energy and alert observation. He was serious but kindly and considerate in his more formal manners, but in other circumstances could be an entertaining talker with a pleasantly ironical sense of humour. It was easy to discover his devoted fondness for his family and to recognize a man who would inspire affection. He had many miscellaneous interests – he was fond of travelling abroad, of country holidays, of mountain walks – and there were other, more engrossing subjects, art, archaeology, literature. Freud was a very well read man in many languages, not only in German. He read English and French fluently, besides having a fair knowledge of Spanish and Italian. It must be remembered, too, that though the later phases of his education were chiefly scientific (it is true that at the University he studied philosophy for a short time) at school he had learnt the classics and never lost his affection for them. We happen to have a letter written by him at the age of seventeen to a school friend.[1] In it he describes his varying success in the different papers of his school-leaving examination: in Latin a passage from Virgil, and in Greek thirty-three lines from, of all things, *Oedipus Rex*.

In short, we might regard Freud as what in England we should consider the best kind of product of a Victorian up-

1. [Emil Fluss. The letter is included in the volume of Freud's correspondence (1960a).]

bringing. His tastes in literature and art would obviously differ from ours, his views on ethics, though decidedly liberal, would not belong to the post-Freudian age. But we should see in him a man who lived a life of full emotion and of much suffering without embitterment. Complete honesty and directness were qualities that stood out in him, and so too did his intellectual readiness to take in and consider any fact, however new or extraordinary, that was presented to him. It was perhaps an inevitable corollary and extension of these qualities, combined with a general benevolence which a surface misanthropy failed to disguise, that led to some features of a surprising kind. In spite of his subtlety of mind he was essentially unsophisticated, and there were sometimes unexpected lapses in his critical faculty – a failure, for instance, to perceive an untrustworthy authority in some subject that was off his own beat such as Egyptology or philology, and, strangest of all in someone whose powers of perception had to be experienced to be believed, an occasional blindness to defects in his acquaintances. But though it may flatter our vanity to declare that Freud was a human being of a kind like our own, that satisfaction can easily be carried too far. There must in fact have been some-thing very extraordinary in the man who was first able to recognize a whole field of mental facts which had hitherto been excluded from normal consciousness, the man who first interpreted dreams, who first accepted the facts of infantile sexuality, who first made the distinction between the primary and secondary processes of thinking – the man who first made the unconscious mind real to us.

JAMES STRACHEY

[Those in search of further information will find it in the three-volume biography of Freud by Ernest Jones, an abridged version of which was published in Pelican in 1964 (reissued 1974), in the important volume of Freud's letters edited by his son and daughter-in-law, Ernst and Lucie Freud (1960a), in several further volumes of his correspondence, with Wilhelm Fliess (1950a), Karl Abraham (1965a), C. G. Jung (1974a), Oskar Pfister (1963a), Lou Andreas-Salomé (1966a), Edoardo Weiss (1970a) and Arnold Zweig (1968a), and above all in the many volumes of Freud's own works.]

CHRONOLOGICAL TABLE

This table traces very roughly some of the main turning-points in Freud's intellectual development and opinions. A few of the chief events in his external life are also included in it.

1856. 6 May. Birth at Freiberg in Moravia.

1860. Family settles in Vienna.

1865. Enters *Gymnasium* (secondary school).

1873. Enters Vienna University as medical student.

1876-82. Works under Brücke at the Institute of Physiology in Vienna.

1877. First publications: papers on anatomy and physiology.

1881. Graduates as Doctor of Medicine.

1882. Engagement to Martha Bernays.

1882-5. Works in Vienna General Hospital, concentrating on cerebral anatomy: numerous publications.

1884-7. Researches into the clinical uses of cocaine.

1885. Appointed *Privatdozent* (University Lecturer) in Neuropathology.

1885 (October)-1886 (February). Studies under Charcot at the Saltpêtrière (hospital for nervous diseases) in Paris. Interest first turns to hysteria and hypnosis.

1886. Marriage to Martha Bernays. Sets up private practice in nervous diseases in Vienna.

1886-93. Continues work on neurology, especially on the cerebral palsies of children at the Kassowitz Institute in Vienna, with numerous publications. Gradual shift of interest from neurology to psychopathology.

1887. Birth of eldest child (Mathilde).

1887-1902. Friendship and correspondence with Wilhelm Fliess in Berlin. Freud's letters to him during this period, published posthumously in 1950, throw much light on the development of his views.

1887. Begins the use of hypnotic suggestion in his practice.

c. 1888. Begins to follow Breuer in using hypnosis for cathartic treatment of hysteria. Gradually drops hypnosis and substitutes free association.

1889. Visits Bernheim at Nancy to study his suggestion technique.

1889. Birth of eldest son (Martin).

1891. Monograph on Aphasia.

24

Birth of second son (Oliver).

1892. Birth of youngest son (Ernst).

1893. Publication of Breuer and Freud 'Preliminary Communication': exposition of trauma theory of hysteria and of cathartic treatment.
Birth of second daughter (Sophie).

1893–8. Researches and short papers on hysteria, obsessions, and anxiety.

1895. Jointly with Breuer, *Studies on Hysteria*: case histories and description by Freud of his technique, including first account of transference.

1893–6. Gradual divergence of views between Freud and Breuer. Freud introduces concepts of defence and repression and of neurosis being a result of a conflict between the ego and the libido.

1895. *Project for a Scientific Psychology*: included in Freud's letters to Fliess and first published in 1950. An abortive attempt to state psychology in neurological terms; but foreshadows much of Freud's later theories.
Birth of youngest child (Anna).

1896. Introduces the term 'psychoanalysis'.
Death of father (aged eighty).

1897. Freud's self-analysis, leading to the abandonment of the trauma theory and the recognition of infantile sexuality and the Oedipus complex.

1900. *The Interpretation of Dreams*, with final chapter giving first full account of Freud's dynamic view of mental processes, of the unconscious, and of the dominance of the 'pleasure principle'.

1901. *The Psychopathology of Everyday Life*. This, together with the book on dreams, made it plain that Freud's theories applied not only to pathological states but also to normal mental life.

1902. Appointed Professor Extraordinarius.

1905. *Three Essays on the Theory of Sexuality*: tracing for the first time the course of development of the sexual instinct in human beings from infancy to maturity.

c. 1906. Jung becomes an adherent of psychoanalysis.

1908. First international meeting of psychoanalysts (at Salzburg).

1909. Freud and Jung invited to the USA to lecture.
Case history of the first analysis of a child (Little Hans, aged five): confirming inferences previously made from adult analyses, especially as to infantile sexuality and the Oedipus and castration complexes.

c. 1910. First emergence of the theory of 'narcissism'.

1911–15. Papers on the technique of psychoanalysis.

1911. Secession of Adler.
Application of psychoanalytic theories to a psychotic case: the autobiography of Dr Schreber.

1912–13. *Totem and Taboo*: application of psychoanalysis to anthropological material.

1914. Secession of Jung.

'On the History of the Psycho-Analytic Movement'. Includes a polemical section on Adler and Jung.

Writes his last major case history, of the 'Wolf Man' (not published till 1918).

1915. Writes a series of twelve 'metapsychological' papers on basic theoretical questions, of which only five have survived.

1915–17. *Introductory Lectures*: giving an extensive general account of the state of Freud's views up to the time of the First World War.

1919. Application of the theory of narcissism to the war neuroses.

1920. Death of second daughter.

Beyond the Pleasure Principle: the first explicit introduction of the concept of the 'compulsion to repeat' and of the theory of the 'death instinct'.

1921. *Group Psychology*. Beginnings of a systematic analytic study of the ego.

1923. *The Ego and the Id*. Largely revised account of the structure and functioning of the mind with the division into an id, an ego, and a super-ego.

1923. First onset of cancer.

1925. Revised views on the sexual development of women.

1926. *Inhibitions, Symptoms, and Anxiety*. Revised views on the problem of anxiety.

1927. *The Future of an Illusion*. A discussion of religion: the first of a number of sociological works to which Freud devoted most of his remaining years.

1930. *Civilization and its Discontents*. This includes Freud's first extensive study of the destructive instinct (regarded as a manifestation of the 'death instinct').

Freud awarded the Goethe Prize by the City of Frankfurt.

Death of mother (aged ninety-five).

1933. Hitler seizes power in Germany: Freud's books publicly burned in Berlin.

1934–8. *Moses and Monotheism*: the last of Freud's works to appear during his lifetime.

1936. Eightieth birthday. Election as Corresponding Member of Royal Society.

1938. Hitler's invasion of Austria. Freud leaves Vienna for London.

An Outline of Psycho-Analysis. A final, unfinished, but profound exposition of psychoanalysis.

1939. 23 September. Death in London.

JAMES STRACHEY

THE CLAIMS
OF PSYCHOANALYSIS
TO SCIENTIFIC INTEREST
(1913)

DAS INTERESSE AN DER PSYCHOANALYSE

(A) GERMAN EDITIONS:

1913   *Scientia*, **14** (31 and 32), 240–50 and 369–84.
1924   *Gesammelte Schriften*, **4**, 313–43.
1943   *Gesammelte Werke*, **8**, 390–420.

(B) ENGLISH TRANSLATION:

'The Claims of Psycho-Analysis to Scientific Interest'

1955   *Standard Edition*, **13**, 163–90. (Tr. James Strachey.)

The present edition is a reprint of the *Standard Edition* version, with a few editorial changes.

This paper was written by Freud at the express request of the Editor of *Scientia*, the well-known Italian scientific periodical. The precise dates of its publication were probably September and November 1913. It is the only at all comprehensive account that he has given of the non-medical applications of psycho-analysis.

THE CLAIMS
OF PSYCHOANALYSIS
TO SCIENTIFIC INTEREST

PART I

THE PSYCHOLOGICAL INTEREST
OF PSYCHOANALYSIS

PSYCHOANALYSIS is a medical procedure which aims at the cure of certain forms of nervous disease (the neuroses) by a psychological technique. In a small volume published in 1910[1] I described the evolution of psychoanalysis from Josef Breuer's[2] cathartic procedure and its relation to the theories of Charcot[3] and Pierre Janet.[4]

We may give as instances of disorders that are accessible to psychoanalytic treatment hysterical convulsions and paralyses as well as the various symptoms of obsessional neurosis (obsessive ideas and actions). All of these are conditions which are occasionally subject to spontaneous recovery and are dependent on the personal influence of the physician in a haphazard fashion which has not yet been explained. Psychoanalysis has no therapeutic effect on the severer forms of mental disorder properly so called. But – for the first time in the history of medicine – psychoanalysis has made it possible to get some

1. *Five Lectures on Psycho-Analysis* [1910a].

2. [1842–1925. Freud wrote about him on the occasion of his death (Freud, 1925g).]

3. [Jean-Martin Charcot (1825–93), Professor of Neuropathology in Paris. See Freud (1893f).]

4. [Pierre Janet (1859–1947), Professor of Psychology at the Collège de France from 1902 to 1936, was also a specialist in nervous and mental disorders. With Charcot at the Salpêtrière, he made important studies of hysteria and hypnosis. Cf. pp. 90 and 214 below.]

insight into the origin and mechanism alike of the neuroses and psychoses.

This medical significance of psychoanalysis would not, however, justify me in bringing it to the notice of a circle of *savants* concerned in the synthesis of the sciences. And such a plan must seem particularly premature so long as a large number of psychiatrists and neurologists are opposed to the new therapeutic method and reject both its postulates and its findings. If, nevertheless, I regard the experiment as a legitimate one, it is because psychoanalysis can also claim to be of interest to others than psychiatrists, since it touches upon various other spheres of knowledge and reveals unexpected relations between them and the pathology of mental life.

Accordingly in my present paper I shall leave the medical interest of psychoanalysis on one side and illustrate what I have just asserted of the young science by a series of examples.

There are a large number of phenomena related to facial and other expressive movements and to speech, as well as many processes of thought (both in normal and sick people), which have hitherto escaped the notice of psychology because they have been regarded as no more than the results of organic disorder or of some abnormal failure in function of the mental apparatus. What I have in mind are 'parapraxes' (slips of the tongue or pen, forgetfulness, etc.), haphazard actions and dreams in normal people, and convulsive attacks, deliria, visions, and obsessive ideas or acts in neurotic subjects. These phenomena (in so far as they were not entirely neglected, as was the case with the parapraxes) were relegated to pathology and an attempt was made to find 'physiological' explanations of them, though these were invariably unsatisfactory. Psychoanalysis, on the contrary, has been able to show that all these things can be explained by means of hypotheses of a purely psychological nature and can be fitted into the chain of psychical events already known to us. Thus on the one hand psychoanalysis has narrowed the region subject to the physiological point of view and on the other hand has brought a large section of pathology into the sphere of psychology. In this instance the normal phenomena provide the more convincing evidence. Psychoanalysis cannot be accused of having applied to normal cases findings arrived at from pathological material. The evidence in the latter and in the former was reached independently and shows that normal processes and what are described as pathological ones follow the same rules.

I shall now discuss in greater detail two of the normal phenomena with which we are here concerned (phenomena, that is, which can be observed in normal people) – namely, parapraxes and dreams.

By parapraxes, then, I understand the occurrence in healthy and normal people of such events as forgetting words and names that are normally familiar to one, forgetting what one intends to do, making slips of the tongue and pen, misreading, mislaying things and being unable to find them, losing things, making mistakes against one's better knowledge, and certain habitual gestures and movements. All of these have on the whole had little attention paid to them by psychology; they have been classed as instances of 'absent-mindedness' and have been attributed to fatigue, to distracted attention or to the contributory effects of certain slight illnesses. Analytic inquiry, however, shows with enough certainty to satisfy every requirement that these latter factors merely operate as facilitating factors and may be absent. Parapraxes are full-blown psychical phenomena and always have a meaning and an intention. They serve definite purposes which, owing to the prevailing psychological situation, cannot be expressed in any other way. These situations as a rule involve a psychical conflict which prevents the underlying intention from finding direct expression and diverts it along indirect paths. A person who is guilty of a parapraxis may notice it or overlook it; the suppressed intention underlying it may well be familiar to him; but he is usually unaware, without analysis, that that intention is responsible for the parapraxis in question. Analyses of parapraxes are often quite easily and quickly made. If a person's attention is drawn to a blunder, the next thought that occurs to him provides its explanation.

Parapraxes are the most convenient material for anyone who wishes to convince himself of the trustworthiness of psycho-analytic explanations. In a small work, first published in book form in 1904, I presented a large number of examples of this kind, and since then I have been able to add to my collection many contributions from other observers.[1]

The commonest motive for suppressing an intention, which has thereafter to be content with finding its expression in a parapraxis, turns out to be the avoidance of unpleasure. Thus, one obstinately forgets a proper name if one nourishes a secret grudge against its owner; one forgets to carry out an intention if one has in fact only formed it unwillingly – only, for instance, under the pressure of some convention; one loses an object, if one has quarrelled with someone of whom the object reminds one – with its original donor, for instance; one gets into the wrong train if one is making a journey unwillingly and would rather be somewhere else. This motive of avoiding unpleasure is seen most clearly where the forgetting of impressions and experiences is concerned – a fact which had already been observed by many writers before psychoanalysis existed. Memory shows its partiality by being ready to prevent the reproduction of impressions with a distressing affect, even though this purpose cannot be achieved in every case.

In other instances the analysis of a parapraxis is less simple and requires less obvious explanations, on account of the in-trusion of a process which we describe as 'displacement'. One may, for instance, forget the name of someone against whom one has no objection; analysis will show, however, that the name has stirred up the memory of someone else, who has the same or a similar-sounding name and whom one has good reason to dislike. This connection has led to the innocent person's name being forgotten; the intention to forget has, as it were, been displaced along some line of association.

---

1. *The Psychopathology of Everyday Life* [Freud, 1901*b*; *P.F.L.*, **5**]. Cf. also works on the subject by Maeder [1906, 1908], Brill [1912], Jones [1911*a*], Rank [1910*b*, 1912*b*], etc. [See also Lecture 2 in Freud's *Introductory Lectures* (1916–17), *P.F.L.*, **1**, 50 ff.]

Nor is the intention to avoid unpleasure the only one which can find its outlet in parapraxes. In many cases analysis reveals other purposes which have been suppressed in the particular situation and which can only make themselves felt, so to say, as background disturbances. Thus a slip of the tongue will often serve to betray opinions which the speaker wishes to conceal from his interlocutor. Slips of the tongue have been understood in this sense by various great writers and employed for this purpose in their works. The loss of precious objects often turns out to be an act of sacrifice intended to avert some expected evil; and many other superstitions too survive in educated people in the form of parapraxes. The mislaying of objects means as a rule getting rid of them; damage is done to one's possessions (ostensibly by accident) so as to make it necessary to acquire something better – and so on.

Nevertheless, in spite of the apparent triviality of these phenomena, the psychoanalytic explanation of parapraxes involves some slight modifications in our view of the world. We find that even normal people are far more frequently moved by contradictory motives than we should have expected. The number of occurrences that can be described as 'accidental' is considerably diminished. It is almost a consolation to be able to exclude the loss of objects from among the chance events of life; our blunders often turn out to be a cover for our secret intentions. But – what is more important – many serious accidents that we should otherwise have ascribed entirely to chance reveal under analysis the participation of the subject's own volition, though without its being clearly admitted by him. The distinction between a chance accident and deliberate self-destruction, which in practice is so often hard to draw, becomes even more dubious when looked at from an analytic point of view.

The explanation of parapraxes owes its theoretical value to the ease with which they can be solved and their frequency in normal people. But the success of psychoanalysis in explaining them is far surpassed in importance by a further achievement made by it, relating to another phenomenon of normal mental life. What I have in mind is the interpretation of *dreams*, which brought psychoanalysis for the first time into the conflict with official science which was to be its destiny. Medical research explains dreams as purely somatic phenomena, without meaning or significance, and regards them as the reaction of a mental organ sunk in a state of sleep to physical stimuli which partially awaken it. Psychoanalysis raises the status of dreams into that of psychical acts possessing meaning and purpose, and having a place in the subject's mental life, and thus disregards their strangeness, incoherence and absurdity. On this view somatic stimuli merely play the part of material that is worked over in the course of the construction of the dream. There is no half-way house between these two views of dreams. What argues against the physiological hypothesis is its unfruitfulness, and what may be argued in favour of the psychoanalytic one is the fact that it has translated and given a meaning to thousands of dreams and has used them to throw light on the intimate details of the human mind.

I devoted a volume published in 1900 to the important subject of dream-interpretation and have had the satisfaction of seeing the theories put forward in it confirmed and amplified by contributions from almost every worker in the field of psychoanalysis.[1] It is generally agreed that dream interpretation is the foundation stone of psychoanalytic work and that its findings constitute the most important contribution made by psychoanalysis to psychology.

I cannot enter here into the technique by which an interpretation of dreams is arrived at, nor can I give the grounds for the conclusions to which the psychoanalytic investigation of dreams has led. I must restrict myself to enunciating some new concepts, reporting my findings and stressing their importance for normal psychology.

1. *The Interpretation of Dreams* (1900a) [*P.F.L.*, **4**]. See also my shorter essay *On Dreams* (1901a) and other writings by Rank [1910c, 1912c], Stekel [1911], Jones [1912a], Silberer [1909, 1912], Brill [1912], Maeder [1912], Abraham [1907], Ferenczi [1910, 1911], etc. [See further Freud's *Introductory Lectures* (1916–17), *P.F.L.*, **1**, 111 ff.]

I. PSYCHOLOGICAL INTEREST

Psychoanalysis, then, has demonstrated the following facts. All dreams have a meaning. Their strangeness is due to distortions that have been made in the expression of their meaning. Their absurdity is deliberate and expresses derision, ridicule and contradiction. Their incoherence is a matter of indifference for their interpretation. The dream as we remember it after waking is described by us as its 'manifest content'. In the process of interpreting this, we are led to the 'latent dream-thoughts', which lie hidden behind the manifest content and which are represented by it. These latent dream-thoughts are no longer strange, incoherent or absurd; they are completely valid constituents of our waking thought. We give the name of 'dream-work' to the process which transforms the latent dream-thoughts into the manifest content of the dream; it is this dream-work that brings about the distortion which makes the dream-thoughts unrecognizable in the content of the dream.

The dream-work is a psychological process the like of which has hitherto been unknown to psychology. It has claims upon our interest in two main directions. In the first place, it brings to our notice novel processes such as 'condensation' (of ideas) and 'displacement' (of psychical emphasis from one idea to another), processes which we have never come across at all in our waking life, or only as the basis of what are known as 'errors in thought'. In the second place, it enables us to detect the operation in the mind of a play of forces which was concealed from our conscious perception. We find that there is a 'censorship', a testing agency, at work in us, which decides whether an idea cropping up in the mind shall be allowed to reach consciousness, and which, so far as lies within its power, ruthlessly excludes anything that might produce or revive unpleasure. And it will be recalled at this point that in our analysis of parapraxes we found traces of this same intention to avoid unpleasure in remembering things and of similar conflicts between mental impulses.

A study of the dream-work forces on us irresistibly a view of mental life which appears to decide the most controversial problems of psychology. The dream-work compels us to assume the existence of an *unconscious* psychical activity which is more comprehensive and more important than the familiar activity that is linked with consciousness. (I shall have some more to say on this point when I come to discuss the *philosophical* interest of psychoanalysis.) It enables us to dissect the psychical apparatus into a number of different agencies or systems, and shows us that in the system of unconscious mental activity processes operate which are of quite another kind from those perceived in consciousness.

The dream-work has only one function – namely to maintain sleep. 'Dreams are the guardians of sleep.' The dream-*thoughts* themselves may serve the purposes of the most various mental functions. The dream-work accomplishes its task by representing a wish that arises from the dream-thoughts as fulfilled in a hallucinatory fashion.

It may safely be said that the psychoanalytic study of dreams has given us our first insight into a 'depth-psychology' whose existence had not hitherto been suspected.[1] Fundamental changes will have to be introduced into normal psychology if it is to be brought into harmony with these new findings.

It is quite impossible to exhaust the psychological interest of dream interpretation within the limits of my present paper. Let us bear in mind that what I have so far stressed is merely that dreams have a meaning and are objects for psychological study, and let us now proceed with our consideration of the new territory which has been annexed by psychology in the domain of pathology.

The psychological novelties inferred from dreams and parapraxes must be applicable as an explanation of other phenomena if we are to believe in the value of these novelties, or, indeed, in their existence. And we do in fact find that psychoanalysis has shown that the hypotheses of unconscious mental activity, of censorship and repression and of distortion and substitution, at which we have arrived from our study of

1. Psychoanalysis does not at present postulate any relation between this psychical topography and anatomical stratification or histological layers.

these normal phenomena, also afford us a first understanding of a number of *pathological* phenomena and, as one might say, put into our hands the key to all the riddles of the psychology of the neuroses. Thus dreams are to be regarded as the normal prototypes of all psychopathological structures. Anyone who understands dreams can also grasp the psychical mechanism of the neuroses and psychoses.

Starting from dreams, the investigations of psychoanalysis have enabled it to construct a psychology of the neuroses which is being continuously built up piece by piece. But what we are here concerned with – the *psychological* interest of psychoanalysis – obliges us to enter more fully into only two sides of this far-reaching subject: the evidence that many pathological phenomena which had hitherto been believed to require physiological explanations are in fact psychical acts, and the evidence that the processes which lead to abnormal consequences can be traced back to psychical motive forces.

I will illustrate the first of these theses by a few examples. Hysterical attacks have long been recognized as signs of increased emotional excitement and equated with outbreaks of affect. Charcot attempted to reduce the multiplicity of their modes of manifestation by means of descriptive formulas; Pierre Janet recognized the unconscious ideas operating behind such attacks; [1] while psychoanalysis has shown that they are mimetic representations of scenes (whether actually experienced or only invented) with which the patient's imagination is occupied without his becoming conscious of them. The meaning of these pantomimes is concealed from the spectators by means of condensations and distortions of the acts which they represent. And this applies equally to what are described as the 'chronic' symptoms of hysterical patients. All of them are mimetic or hallucinatory representations of fantasies which unconsciously dominate the subject's emotional life and which have the meaning of fulfilments of secret and repressed wishes. The tormenting character of these symptoms is due to

1. [See, however, Freud's later comments on Janet's views in his *Autobiographical Study* (1925*d*), p. 214 below.]

the internal conflict into which these patients' minds are driven by the need to combat such unconscious wishes.

In another neurotic disorder, obsessional neurosis, the patients become the victims of distressing and apparently senseless ceremonials which take the form of the rhythmical repetition of the most trivial acts (such as washing or dressing) or of carrying out meaningless injunctions or of obeying mysterious prohibitions. It was nothing less than a triumph of psychoanalytic research when it succeeded in showing that all these obsessive acts, even the most insignificant and trivial of them, have a meaning, and that they are reflections, translated into indifferent terms, of conflicts in the patients' lives, of the struggle between temptations and moral restraints – reflections of the proscribed wish itself and of the punishment and atonement which that wish incurs. In another form of the same disorder the victim suffers from tormenting ideas (obsessions) which force themselves upon him and are accompanied by affects whose character and intensity are often only quite inadequately accounted for by the terms of the obsessive ideas themselves. Analytic investigation has shown in their case that the affects are entirely justified, since they correspond to self-reproaches which are based on something that is at least *psychically* real. But the ideas to which these affects are attached are not the original ones, but have found their way into their present position by a process of displacement – by being substituted for something that has been repressed. If these displacements can be reversed, the way is open to the discovery of the repressed ideas, and the relation between affect and idea is found to be perfectly appropriate.

In another neurotic disorder, dementia praecox (paraphrenia or schizophrenia), a condition which is in fact incurable, the patient is left, in the most severe cases, in a state of apparently complete apathy. Often his sole remaining actions are certain movements and gestures which are repeated monotonously and have been given the name of 'stereotypies'. An analytic investigation of residues of this kind, made by Jung [1908], has shown that they are the remains of perfectly significant mimetic actions, which at one time gave expression to the subject's ruling wishes. The craziest speeches and the queerest poses and attitudes adopted by these patients become intelligible and can be given a place in the chain of their mental processes if they are approached on the basis of psychoanalytic hypotheses.

Similar considerations apply to the deliria and hallucinations, as well as to the delusional systems, exhibited by various psychotic patients. Where hitherto nothing but the most freakish capriciousness has seemed to prevail, psychoanalytic research has introduced law, order and connection, or has at least allowed us to suspect their presence where its work is still incomplete. The most heterogeneous forms of mental disorder are revealed as the results of processes which are at bottom identical and which can be understood and described by means of psychological concepts. What had already been discovered in the formation of dreams is operative everywhere – psychical conflict, the repression of certain instinctual impulses which have been pushed back into the unconscious by other mental forces, reaction formations set up by the repressing forces, and substitutes constructed by the instincts which have been repressed but have not been robbed of all their energy. The accompanying processes of condensation and displacement, so familiar to us in dreams, are also to be found everywhere. The multiplicity of clinical pictures observed by psychiatrists depends upon two other things: the multiplicity of the psychical mechanisms at the disposal of the repressive process and the multiplicity of developmental dispositions which give the repressed impulses an opportunity for breaking through into substitutive structures.

Psychoanalysis points to psychology for the solution of a good half of the problems of psychiatry. It would nevertheless be a serious mistake to suppose that analysis favours or aims at a *purely* psychological view of mental disorders. It cannot overlook the fact that the other half of the problems of psychiatry are concerned with the influence of organic factors (whether mechanical, toxic or infective) on the mental apparatus. Even in the case of the mildest of these disorders, the neuroses, it makes no claim that their origin is purely psycho-genic but traces their aetiology to the influence upon mental life of an unquestionably organic factor to which I shall refer later [p. 47].

The number of detailed psychoanalytic findings which cannot fail to be of importance for general psychology is too great for me to enumerate them here. I will only mention two other points: psychoanalysis unhesitatingly ascribes the primacy in mental life to affective processes, and it reveals an unexpected amount of affective disturbance and blinding of the intellect in normal no less than in sick people.

PART II

THE CLAIMS
OF PSYCHOANALYSIS
TO THE INTEREST OF THE
NON-PSYCHOLOGICAL SCIENCES

(A) THE PHILOLOGICAL INTEREST OF
PSYCHOANALYSIS

I shall no doubt be overstepping common linguistic usage in postulating an interest in psychoanalysis on the part of philologists, that is of experts in *speech*. For in what follows 'speech' must be understood not merely to mean the expression of thought in words but to include the speech of gesture and every other method, such, for instance, as writing, by which mental activity can be expressed. That being so, it may be pointed out that the interpretations made by psychoanalysis are first and foremost translations from an alien method of expression into the one which is familiar to us. When we interpret a dream we are simply translating a particular thought content (the latent dream-thoughts) from the 'language of dreams' into our waking speech. In the course of doing so we learn the peculiarities of this dream language and it is borne in upon us that it forms part of a highly archaic system of expression. Thus, to take an instance, there is no special indication for the negative in the language of dreams. Contraries may stand for each other in the dream's content and may be represented by the same element. Or we may put it like this: concepts are still ambivalent in dream language, and unite within themselves contrary meanings – as is the case, according to the hypotheses of philologists, in the oldest roots of historical languages.[1] Another striking feature of our dream language is

1. Cf. Abel [1884] on the antithetical meaning of primal words, and my review of his paper [1910e].

its extremely frequent use of symbols, which make us able to some extent to translate the content of dreams without reference to the associations of the individual dreamer. Our researches have not yet sufficiently elucidated the essential nature of these symbols. They are in part substitutes and analogies based upon obvious similarities; but in some of these symbols the *tertium comparationis* which is presumably present escapes our conscious knowledge. It is precisely this latter class of symbols which must probably originate from the earliest phases of linguistic development and conceptual construction. In dreams it is above all the sexual organs and sexual activities which are represented symbolically instead of directly. A philologist, Hans Sperber, of Uppsala, has only recently (1912) attempted to prove that words which originally represented sexual activities have, on the basis of analogies of this kind, undergone an extraordinarily far-reaching change in their meaning.

If we reflect that the means of representation in dreams are principally visual images and not words, we shall see that it is even more appropriate to compare dreams with a system of writing than with a language. In fact, the interpretation of dreams is completely analogous to the decipherment of an ancient pictographic script such as Egyptian hieroglyphs. In both cases there are certain elements which are not intended to be interpreted (or read, as the case may be) but are only designed to serve as 'determinatives', that is to establish the meaning of some other element. The ambiguity of various elements of dreams finds a parallel in these ancient systems of writing; and so too does the omission of various relations, which have in both cases to be supplied from the context. If this conception of the method of representation in dreams has not yet been followed up, this, as will be readily understood, must be ascribed to the fact that psychoanalysts are entirely ignorant of the attitude and knowledge with which a philologist would approach such a problem as that presented by dreams.

The language of dreams may be looked upon as the method by which unconscious mental activity expresses itself. But the unconscious speaks more than one dialect. According to the different psychological conditions governing and distinguishing the various forms of neurosis, we find regular modifications in the way in which unconscious mental impulses are expressed. While the gesture language of hysteria agrees on the whole with the picture language of dreams and visions, etc., the thought language of obsessional neurosis and of the paraphrenias (dementia praecox and paranoia) exhibits special idiomatic peculiarities which, in a number of instances, we have been able to understand and interrelate. For instance, what a hysteric expresses by vomiting an obsessional will express by painstaking protective measures against infection, while a paraphrenic will be led to complaints or suspicions that he is being poisoned. These are all of them different representations of the patient's wish to become pregnant which have been repressed into the unconscious, or of his defensive reaction against that wish.

(B) THE PHILOSOPHICAL INTEREST OF PSYCHOANALYSIS

Philosophy, in so far as it is built on psychology, will be unable to avoid taking the psychoanalytic contributions to psychology fully into account and reacting to this new enrichment of our knowledge just as it has to every considerable advance in the specialized sciences. In particular, the setting up of the hypothesis of unconscious mental activities must compel philosophy to decide one way or the other and, if it accepts the idea, to modify its own views on the relation of mind to body so that they may conform to the new knowledge. It is true that philosophy has repeatedly dealt with the problem of the unconscious, but, with few exceptions, philosophers have taken up one or other of the two following positions. Either their unconscious has been something mystical, something intangible and undemonstrable, whose relation to the mind has remained obscure, or they have identified the mental with the conscious and have proceeded to infer from this definition that what is unconscious cannot be mental or a subject for psychology.

These opinions must be put down to the fact that philosophers have formed their judgement on the unconscious without being acquainted with the phenomena of unconscious mental activity, and therefore without any suspicion of how far unconscious phenomena resemble conscious ones or of the respects in which they differ from them. If anyone possessing that knowledge nevertheless holds to the conviction which equates the conscious and the psychical and consequently denies the unconscious the attribute of being psychical, no objection can, of course, be made except that such a distinction turns out to be highly unpractical. For it is easy to describe the unconscious and to follow its developments if it is approached from the direction of its relation to the conscious, with which it has so much in common. On the other hand, there still seems no possibility of approaching it from the direction of physical events. So that it is bound to remain a matter for psychological study.

There is yet another way in which philosophy can derive a stimulus from psychoanalysis, and that is by itself becoming a subject of psychoanalytic research. Philosophical theories and systems have been the work of a small number of men of striking individuality. In no other science does the personality of the scientific worker play anything like so large a part as in philosophy. And now for the first time psychoanalysis enables us to construct a 'psychography' of a personality. (See the sociological section below.) It teaches us to recognize the affective units – the complexes dependent on instincts – whose presence is to be presumed in each individual, and it introduces us to the study of the transformations and end-products arising from these instinctual forces. It reveals the relations of a person's constitutional disposition and the events of his life to the achievements open to him owing to his peculiar gifts. It can conjecture with more or less certainty from an artist's work the intimate personality that lies behind it. In the same way, psychoanalysis can indicate the subjective and individual motives behind philosophical theories which have ostensibly sprung from impartial logical work, and can draw a critic's attention to the weak spots in the system. It is not the business of psychoanalysis, however, to undertake such criticism itself, for, as may be imagined, the fact that a theory is psychologically determined does not in the least invalidate its scientific truth.

(C) THE BIOLOGICAL INTEREST OF PSYCHOANALYSIS

It has not been the fate of psychoanalysis to be greeted (like other young sciences) with the sympathetic encouragement of those who are interested in the advance of knowledge. For a long time it was disregarded, and when at last it could no longer be neglected it became, for emotional reasons, the object of the most violent attacks from people who had not taken the trouble to become acquainted with it. It owed this unfriendly reception to a single circumstance: for at an early stage of its researches psychoanalysis was driven to the conclusion that nervous illnesses are an expression of a disturbance of the sexual function and it was thus led to devote its attention to an investigation of that function – one which had been far too long neglected. But anyone who respects the rule that scientific judgement should not be influenced by emotional attitudes will assign a high degree of biological interest to psychoanalysis on account of these very investigations and will regard the resistances to it as actual evidence in favour of the correctness of its assertions.

Psychoanalysis has done justice to the sexual function in man by making a detailed examination of its importance in mental and practical life – an importance which has been emphasized by many creative writers and by some philosophers, but which has never been recognized by science.[1] But in the first place it was necessary to enlarge the unduly restricted concept of sexuality, an enlargement that was justified by reference to the extensions of sexuality occurring in the so-called perversions and to the behaviour of children. It turned out to

1. [See Freud's *Three Essays on the Theory of Sexuality* (1905*d*), *P.F.L.*, **7**, 31 ff.]

be impossible to maintain any longer that childhood was asexual and was invaded for the first time by a sudden inrush of sexual impulses at the age of puberty. On the contrary, when once the blinkers of partiality and prejudice had been removed, observation had no difficulty in revealing that sexual interests and activities are present in the human child at almost every age and from the very first. The importance of this infantile sexuality is not impaired by the fact that we cannot everywhere draw a clear line between it and a child's asexual activity. It differs, however, from what is described as the 'normal' sexuality of adults. It includes the germs of all those sexual activities which in later life are sharply contrasted with normal sexual life as being perversions, and as such bound to seem incomprehensible and vicious. The normal sexuality of adults emerges from infantile sexuality by a series of developments, combinations, divisions and suppressions, which are scarcely ever achieved with ideal perfection and consequently leave behind predispositions to a retrogression of the function in the form of illness.

Infantile sexuality exhibits two other characteristics which are of importance from a biological point of view. It turns out to be put together from a number of component instincts which seem to be attached to certain regions of the body ('erotogenic zones') and some of which emerge from the beginning in pairs of opposites – instincts with an active and a passive aim. Just as in later life what is loved is not merely the object's sexual organs but his whole body, so from the very first it is not merely the genitals but many other parts of the body which are the seat of sexual excitation and respond to appropriate stimuli with sexual pleasure. This fact is closely related to the second characteristic of infantile sexuality – namely that to start with it is attached to the self-preservative functions of nutrition and excretion, and, in all probability, of muscular excitation and sensory activity.

If we examine sexuality in the adult with the help of psychoanalysis, and consider the life of children in the light of the knowledge thus gained, we perceive that sexuality is not merely a function serving the purposes of reproduction, on a par with digestion, respiration, etc. It is something far more independent, which stands in contrast to all the individual's other activities and is only forced into an alliance with the individual's economy after a complicated course of development involving the imposition of numerous restrictions. Cases, theoretically quite conceivable, in which the interests of these sexual impulses fail to coincide with the self-preservation of the individual seem actually to be presented by the group of neurotic illnesses. For the final formula which psychoanalysis has arrived at on the nature of the neuroses runs thus: The primal conflict which leads to neuroses is one between the sexual instincts and those which maintain the ego. The neuroses represent a more or less partial overpowering of the ego by sexuality after the ego's attempts at suppressing sexuality have failed.

We have found it necessary to hold aloof from biological considerations during our psychoanalytic work and to refrain from using them for heuristic purposes, so that we may not be misled in our impartial judgement of the psychoanalytic facts before us. But after we have completed our psychoanalytic work we shall have to find a point of contact with biology; and we may rightly feel glad if that contact is already assured at one important point or another. The contrast between the ego instincts and the sexual instinct, to which we have been obliged to trace back the origin of the neuroses, is carried into the sphere of biology in the contrast between the instincts which serve the preservation of the individual and those which serve the survival of the species. In biology we come upon the more comprehensive conception of an immortal germ-plasm to which the different transitory individuals are attached like organs that develop successively. It is only this conception which enables us rightly to understand the part played by the sexual instinctual forces in physiology and psychology.

In spite of all our efforts to prevent biological terminology and considerations from dominating psychoanalytic work, we cannot avoid using them even in our descriptions of the phenomena that we study. We cannot help regarding the term 'instinct' as a concept on the frontier between the spheres of psychology and biology. We speak, too, of 'masculine' and 'feminine' mental attributes and impulses, although, strictly speaking, the differences between the sexes can lay claim to no special psychical characterization. What we speak of in ordinary life as 'masculine' or 'feminine' reduces itself from the point of view of psychology to the qualities of 'activity' and 'passivity' – that is, to qualities determined not by the instincts themselves but by their aims. The regular association of these 'active' and 'passive' instincts in mental life reflects the bisexuality of individuals, which is among the clinical postulates of psychoanalysis.

I shall be satisfied if these few remarks have drawn attention to the many respects in which psychoanalysis acts as an intermediary between biology and psychology.

(D) THE INTEREST OF PSYCHOANALYSIS FROM A DEVELOPMENTAL POINT OF VIEW

Not every analysis of psychological phenomena deserves the name of psychoanalysis. The latter implies more than the mere analysis of composite phenomena into simpler ones. It consists in tracing back one psychical structure to another which preceded it in time and out of which it developed. Medical psychoanalytic procedure was not able to eliminate a symptom until it had traced that symptom's origin and development. Thus from the very first psychoanalysis was directed towards tracing developmental processes. It began by discovering the genesis of neurotic symptoms, and was led, as time went on, to turn its attention to other psychical structures and to construct a genetic psychology which would apply to them too.

Psychoanalysis has been obliged to derive the mental life of adults from that of children, and has had to take seriously the old saying that the child is father to the man. It has traced the continuity between the infantile and adult mind, and has also noted the transformations and rearrangements that occur in the process. In most of us there is a gap in our memories covering the first years of our childhood, of which only a few fragmentary recollections survive. Psychoanalysis may be said to have filled in this gap and to have abolished man's infantile amnesia. (See the section on 'Educational Interest' below.)

Some notable discoveries have been made in the course of this investigation of the infantile mind. Thus it has been possible to confirm, what has often already been suspected, the extraordinarily important influence exerted by the impressions of childhood (and particularly by its earliest years) on the whole course of later development. This brings us up against a psychological paradox – which for psychoanalysts alone is no paradox – that it is precisely these most important of all impressions that are not remembered in later years. Psychoanalysis has been able to establish the decisive and indestructible character of these earliest experiences in the clearest possible way in the case of sexual life. *'On revient toujours à ses premiers amours'* is sober truth. The many riddles in the sexual life of adults can only be solved if stress is laid on the infantile factors in love. Theoretical light is thrown on their influence by the consideration that an individual's first experiences in childhood do not occur only by chance but also correspond to the first activities of his innate or constitutional instinctual dispositions.

Another and far more surprising discovery has been that, in spite of all the later development that occurs in the adult, none of the infantile mental formations perish. All the wishes, instinctual impulses, modes of reaction and attitudes of childhood are still demonstrably present in maturity and in appropriate circumstances can emerge once more. They are not destroyed but merely overlaid – to use the spatial mode of description which psychoanalytic psychology has been obliged to adopt. Thus it is part of the nature of the mental past that, unlike the historic past, it is not absorbed by its derivatives; it persists (whether actually or only potentially) alongside what has proceeded from it. The proof of this assertion lies in the fact that the dreams of normal people revive their childhood characters every night and reduce their whole mental life to an infantile level. This same return to psychical infantilism ('regression') appears in the neuroses and psychoses, whose peculiarities may to a great extent be described as psychical archaisms. The strength in which the residues of infancy are still present in the mind shows us the amount of disposition to illness; that disposition may accordingly be regarded as an expression of an inhibition in development. The part of a person's psychical material which has remained infantile and has been repressed as being unserviceable constitutes the core of his unconscious. And we believe we can follow in our patients' life-histories the way in which this unconscious, held back as it is by the forces of repression, lies in wait for a chance to become active and makes use of its opportunities if the later and higher psychical structures fail to master the difficulties of real life.

In the last few years psychoanalytic writers[1] have become aware that the principle that 'ontogeny is a repetition of phylogeny' must be applicable to mental life; and this has led to a fresh extension of psychoanalytic interest.

(E) THE INTEREST OF PSYCHOANALYSIS FROM THE POINT OF VIEW OF THE HISTORY OF CIVILIZATION

The comparison between the childhood of individual men and the early history of societies has already proved its fruitfulness in several directions, even though the study has scarcely more than begun. In this connection the psychoanalytic mode of thought acts like a new instrument of research. The application of its hypotheses to social psychology enables us both to raise fresh problems and to see old ones in a fresh light and contribute towards their solution.

In the first place, it seems quite possible to apply the psychoanalytic views derived from dreams to products of ethnic imagination such as myths and fairy tales.[2] The need to interpret such productions has long been felt; some 'secret

1. Abraham, Spielrein and Jung.
2. Cf. Abraham [1909], Rank [1909, 1911] and Jung [1911–12].

meaning' has been suspected to lie behind them and it has been presumed that that meaning is concealed by changes and transformations. The study made by psychoanalysis of dreams and neuroses has given it the necessary experience to enable it to guess the technical procedures that have governed these distortions. But in a number of instances it can also reveal the hidden motives which have led to this modification in the original meaning of myths. It cannot accept as the first impulse to the construction of myths a theoretical craving for finding an explanation of natural phenomena or for accounting for cult observances and usages which have become unintelligible. It looks for that impulse in the same psychical 'complexes', in the same emotional trends, which it has discovered at the base of dreams and symptoms.

A similar application of its points of view, its hypotheses and its findings has enabled psychoanalysis to throw light on the origins of our great cultural institutions – on religion, morality, justice and philosophy.[1] By examining the primitive psychological situations which were able to provide the motive for creations of this kind, it has been in a position to reject certain attempts at an explanation that were based on too superficial a psychology and to replace them by a more penetrating insight.

Psychoanalysis has established an intimate connection between these psychical achievements of individuals on the one hand and societies on the other by postulating one and the same dynamic source for both of them. It starts out from the basic idea that the principal function of the mental mechanism is to relieve the individual from the tensions created in him by his needs. One part of this task can be achieved by extracting satisfaction from the external world; and for this purpose it is essential to have control over the real world. But the satisfaction of another part of these needs – among them certain affective impulses – is regularly frustrated by reality. This leads to the further task of finding some other means of dealing with

1. For some first attempts in this direction, see Jung (1912) and Freud (1912–13) [*P.F.L.*, **13**, 43 ff.].

the unsatisfied impulses. The whole course of the history of civilization is no more than an account of the various methods adopted by mankind for 'binding' their unsatisfied wishes, which, according to changing conditions (modified, moreover, by technological advances), have been met by reality sometimes with favour and sometimes with frustration.

An investigation of primitive peoples shows mankind caught up, to begin with, in a childish belief in its own omnipotence.[1] A whole number of mental structures can thus be understood as attempts to deny whatever might disturb this feeling of omnipotence and so to prevent emotional life from being affected by reality until the latter could be better controlled and used for purposes of satisfaction. The principle of avoiding unpleasure dominates human actions until it is replaced by the better one of adaptation to the external world. *Pari passu* with men's progressive control over the world goes a development in their *Weltanschauung*, their view of the universe as a whole. They turn away more and more from their original belief in their own omnipotence, rising from an animistic phase through a religious to a scientific one. Myths, religion and morality find their place in this scheme as attempts to seek a compensation for the lack of satisfaction of human wishes.

Our knowledge of the neurotic illnesses of individuals has been of much assistance to our understanding of the great social institutions. For the neuroses themselves have turned out to be attempts to find *individual* solutions for the problems of compensating for unsatisfied wishes, while the institutions seek to provide *social* solutions for these same problems. The recession of the social factor and the predominance of the sexual one turn these neurotic solutions of the psychological problem into caricatures which are of no service except to help us in explaining such important questions.

---

1. Cf. Ferenczi (1913*b*) and Freud (1912–13), Chapter III [*P.F.L.*, **13**, 143 ff.].

(F) The Interest of Psychoanalysis from the Point of View of the Science of Aesthetics

Psychoanalysis throws a satisfactory light upon some of the problems concerning arts and artists; but others escape it entirely. In the exercising of an art it sees once again an activity intended to allay ungratified wishes – in the first place in the creative artist himself and subsequently in his audience or spectators. The motive forces of artists are the same conflicts which drive other people into neurosis and have encouraged society to construct its institutions. Whence it is that the artist derives his creative capacity is not a question for psychology. The artist's first aim is to set himself free and, by communicating his work to other people suffering from the same arrested desires, he offers them the same liberation.[1] He represents his most personal wishful fantasies as fulfilled; but they only become a work of art when they have undergone a transformation which softens what is offensive in them, conceals their personal origin and, by obeying the laws of beauty, bribes other people with a bonus of pleasure. Psychoanalysis has no difficulty in pointing out, alongside the manifest part of artistic enjoyment, another that is latent though far more potent, derived from the hidden sources of instinctual liberation. The connection between the impressions of the artist's childhood and his life-history on the one hand and his works, as reactions to those impressions, on the other is one of the most attractive subjects of analytic examination.[2]

For the rest, most of the problems of artistic creation and appreciation await further study, which will throw the light of analytic knowledge on them and assign them their place in the complex structure presented by the compensation for human

1. Cf. Rank (1907).
2. Cf. Rank (1912a). See also, for the application of psychoanalysis to aesthetic problems, my book on jokes (1905c) [*P.F.L.*, **6**, 138–9, 185–8. Cf. also Freud's studies on Leonardo (1910c) and Michelangelo (1914b), *P.F.L.*, **14**, 143 ff., 249 ff.].

wishes. Art is a conventionally accepted reality in which, thanks to artistic illusion, symbols and substitutes are able to provoke real emotions. Thus art constitutes a region half-way between a reality which frustrates wishes and the wish-fulfilling world of the imagination – a region in which, as it were, primitive man's strivings for omnipotence are still in full force.

(G) THE SOCIOLOGICAL INTEREST OF PSYCHOANALYSIS

It is true that psychoanalysis has taken the individual mind as its subject, but in investigating the individual it could not avoid dealing with the emotional basis of the relation of the individual to society. It has found that the social feelings invariably contain an erotic element – an element which, if it is over-emphasized and then repressed, becomes one of the marks of a particular group of mental disorders. Psychoanalysis has recognized that in general the neuroses are asocial in their nature and that they always aim at driving the individual out of society and at replacing the safe monastic seclusion of earlier days by the isolation of illness. The intense feeling of guilt which dominates so many neuroses has been shown to be a social modification of neurotic anxiety.

On the other hand, psychoanalysis has fully demonstrated the part played by social conditions and requirements in the causation of neurosis. The forces which, operating from the ego, bring about the restriction and repression of instinct owe their origin essentially to compliance with the demands of civilization. A constitution and a set of childhood experiences which, in other cases, would inevitably lead to a neurosis will produce no such result where this compliance is absent or where these demands are not made by the social circle in which the particular individual is placed. The old assertion that the increase in nervous disorders is a product of civilization is at least a half-truth. Young people are brought into contact with the demands of civilization by upbringing and example; and if instinctual repression occurs independently of these two factors, it is a plausible hypothesis to suppose that a primeval and prehistoric demand has at last become part of the organized and inherited endowment of mankind. A child who produces instinctual repressions spontaneously is thus merely repeating a part of the history of civilization. What is today an act of internal restraint was once an external one, imposed, perhaps, by the necessities of the moment; and, in the same way, what is now brought to bear upon every growing individual as an external demand of civilization may some day become an internal disposition to repression.

(H) THE EDUCATIONAL INTEREST OF PSYCHOANALYSIS

The overmastering interest which must be felt in psychoanalysis by the theory of education is based upon a fact which has become evident. Only someone who can feel his way into the minds of children can be capable of educating them; and we grown-up people cannot understand children because we no longer understand our own childhood. Our infantile amnesia proves that we have grown estranged from our childhood. Psychoanalysis has brought to light the wishes, the thought structures and the developmental processes of childhood. All earlier attempts in this direction have been in the highest degree incomplete and misleading because they have entirely overlooked the inestimably important factor of sexuality in its physical and mental manifestations. The incredulous astonishment which meets the most certainly established findings of psychoanalysis on the subject of childhood – the Oedipus complex, self-love (or 'narcissism'), the disposition to perversions, anal erotism, sexual curiosity – is a measure of the gulf which separates our mental life, our judgements of value and, indeed, our processes of thought from those of even normal children.

When educators have become familiar with the findings of psychoanalysis, it will be easier for them to reconcile themselves to certain phases of infantile development and they will, among other things, not be in danger of overestimating the importance of the socially unserviceable or perverse instinctual impulses which emerge in children. On the contrary they will refrain from any attempt at forcibly suppressing such impulses, when they learn that efforts of this kind often produce no less undesirable results than the alternative, which is so much dreaded by educators, of giving free play to children's naughtiness. The forcible suppression of strong instincts by external means never has the effect in a child of these instincts being extinguished or brought under control; it leads to repression, which establishes a predisposition to later nervous illness. Psychoanalysis has frequent opportunities of observing the part played by inopportune and undiscerning severity of upbringing in the production of neuroses, or the price, in loss of efficiency and of capacity for enjoyment, which has to be paid for the normality upon which the educator insists. And psychoanalysis can also show what precious contributions to the formation of character are made by these asocial and perverse instincts in the child, if they are not subjected to repression but are diverted from their original aims to more valuable ones by the process known as 'sublimation'. Our highest virtues have grown up, as reaction formations and sublimations, out of our worst dispositions. Education should scrupulously refrain from burying these precious springs of action and should restrict itself to encouraging the processes by which these energies are led along safe paths. Whatever we can expect in the way of prophylaxis against neurosis in the individual lies in the hands of a psychoanalytically enlightened education.[1]

It has not been my aim in my present paper to lay before a scientifically orientated public an account of the compass and content of psychoanalysis or of its hypotheses, problems and findings. My purpose will have been fulfilled if I have made clear the many spheres of knowledge in which psychoanalysis is of interest and the numerous links which it has begun to forge between them.

1. See the writings of the Zurich pastor, Dr Oskar Pfister [e.g. Pfister, 1913].

ON THE HISTORY OF
THE PSYCHOANALYTIC MOVEMENT
(1914)

EDITOR'S NOTE

ZUR GESCHICHTE DER PSYCHOANALYTISCHEN BEWEGUNG

(A) GERMAN EDITIONS:

1914 *Jahrbuch der Psychoanalyse*, **6**, 207–260.
1918 *S.K.S.N.*, **4**, 1–77. (1922, 2nd ed.)
1924 Leipzig, Vienna and Zurich: Internationaler
      Psychoanalytischer Verlag. (Issued 1923.)
1946 *Gesammelte Werke*, **10**, 44–113.

(B) ENGLISH TRANSLATIONS:
'The History of the Psychoanalytic Movement'

1916 *Psychoanalytic Review*, **3**, 406–54. (Tr. A. A. Brill.)
1917 New York: Nervous & Mental Disease Publishing Co.
      (Monograph Series No. 25.) (Same translator.)
1938 In *The Basic Writings of Sigmund Freud*. New York.
      Modern Library. Pp. 933–77. (Same translator.)
      'On the History of the Psycho-Analytic Movement'
1924 *Collected Papers*, **1**, 287–359. (Tr. Joan Riviere.)
1957 *Standard Edition*, **14**, 1–66. (Modified version of above.)

The present edition is a reprint of the *Standard Edition* version, with several editorial changes.

In the German editions before 1924 the date 'February, 1914' appears at the end of the work. It seems in fact to have been written in January and February of that year. A few alterations of a minor character were made in the 1924 edition and the long footnote on pp. 91–2 was added.

A full account of the situation which led to the writing of this work is given in Chapter V of the second volume of

Ernest Jones's Freud biography (1955, 142 ff.). Here it is enough to summarize the position very shortly. Adler's disagreements with the views of Freud had come to a head in 1910, and Jung's some three years later. In spite of the divergences which separated them from Freud, they had both long persisted, however, in describing their theories as 'psychoanalysis'. The aim of the present paper was to state clearly the fundamental postulates and hypotheses of psychoanalysis, to show that the theories of Adler and Jung were totally incompatible with them, and to draw the inference that it would lead to nothing but general confusion if these contradictory sets of views were all given the same name. And although for many years popular opinion continued to insist that there were 'three schools of psychoanalysis', Freud's argument eventually prevailed. Adler had already chosen the name of 'Individual Psychology' for his theories, and soon afterwards Jung adopted that of 'Analytical Psychology' for his.

In order to make the essential principles of psychoanalysis perfectly plain, Freud traced the history of their development from their pre-analytic beginnings. The first section of the paper covers the period during which he himself was the only person concerned – that is, up till about 1902. The second section takes the story on till about 1910 – the time during which psychoanalytic views first began to extend to wider circles. It is only in the third section that Freud comes to a discussion of the dissident views, first of Adler and then of Jung, and points out the fundamental respects in which they depart from the findings of psychoanalysis. In this last section, and also to some extent in the rest of the paper, we find Freud adopting a far more belligerent tone than in any of his other writings. And in view of his experiences during the preceding three or four years, this unusual mood cannot be considered surprising.

Discussions of the views of Adler and Jung will be found in two other works of Freud contemporary with the present one. The paper on 'Narcissism' (1914c), which was being composed at almost exactly the same time as the 'History', contains some paragraphs of controversy with Jung (*P.F.L.*, **11**, 72–4) and a similar passage about Adler (ibid., 86–7). The case history of the 'Wolf Man' (1918*b*), written in the main at the end of 1914 but not published until 1918, was largely designed as an empirical refutation of Adler and Jung and contains many attacks on their theories. (See, in particular, *P.F.L.*, **9**, 287–8, 343–4 and *n.*, 358–9.) In Freud's later works there are a number of scattered references to these controversies (chiefly in expository or semi-autobiographical writings), but these are always in a drier tone and never very extensive. Special mention must, however, be made of a closely reasoned discussion of Adler's views[1] on the motive forces leading to repression in Freud's paper on beating fantasies (1919*e*), *P.F.L.*, **10**, 189–93.

As regards the purely historical and autobiographical portions of the work, it must be remarked that Freud went over more or less the same ground in his *Autobiographical Study* (1925*d*; p. 183 below), though it supplements the present paper at some points. For a very much fuller treatment of the subject the reader must, of course, be referred to Ernest Jones's three-volume biography of Freud (Jones, 1953–7).

1. Another severe criticism, of some length, of Adler's views will be found in Lecture 34 of the *New Introductory Lectures* (1933*a*), *P.F.L.*, **2**, 174–8.

ON THE HISTORY OF
THE PSYCHOANALYTIC MOVEMENT

Fluctuat nec mergitur
(On the coat of arms of the City of Paris [1])

I

No one need be surprised at the subjective character of the contribution I propose to make here to the history of the psychoanalytic movement, nor need anyone wonder at the part I play in it. For psychoanalysis is my creation; for ten years I was the only person who concerned himself with it, and all the dissatisfaction which the new phenomenon aroused in my contemporaries has been poured out in the form of criticisms on my head. Although it is a long time now since I was the only psychoanalyst, I consider myself justified in maintaining that even today no one can know better than I do what psychoanalysis is, how it differs from other ways of investigating the life of the mind, and precisely what should be called psychoanalysis and what would better be described by some other name. In thus repudiating what seems to me a cool act of usurpation, I am indirectly informing the readers of this *Jahrbuch* of the events that have led to the changes in its editorship and format.[2]

1. [The coat of arms represents a ship, and the device may be rendered 'it is tossed by the waves, but does not sink'. Freud quoted this motto twice in his correspondence with Fliess, in connection with his own state of mind (Letters 119 and 143, Freud, 1950a).]

2. [The *Jahrbuch* had hitherto been under the direction of Bleuler and Freud and edited by Jung. Freud himself now became sole director and the editorship was taken over by Abraham and Hitschmann. Cf. also p. 105f below.]

In 1909, in the lecture-room of an American university, I had my first opportunity of speaking in public about psychoanalysis.[1] The occasion was a momentous one for my work, and moved by this thought I then declared that it was not I who had brought psychoanalysis into existence: the credit for this was due to someone else, to Josef Breuer, whose work had been done at a time when I was still a student engaged in passing my examinations (1880–2). Since I gave those lectures, however, some well-disposed friends have suggested to me a doubt whether my gratitude was not expressed too extravagantly on that occasion. In their view I ought to have done as I had previously been accustomed to do: treated Breuer's 'cathartic procedure' as a preliminary stage of psychoanalysis, and represented psychoanalysis itself as beginning with my discarding the hypnotic technique and introducing free associations. It is of no great importance in any case whether the history of psychoanalysis is reckoned as beginning with the cathartic method or with my modification of it; I refer to this uninteresting point merely because certain opponents of psychoanalysis have a habit of occasionally recollecting that after all the art of psychoanalysis was not invented by me, but by Breuer. This only happens, of course, if their views allow them to find something in it deserving attention; if they set no such limits to their rejection of it, psychoanalysis is always without question my work alone. I have never heard that Breuer's great share in psychoanalysis has earned him a proportionate measure of criticism and abuse. As I have long recognized that to stir up contradiction and arouse bitterness is the inevitable fate of psychoanalysis, I have come to the conclusion that I must be the true originator of all that is particularly characteristic in it. I am happy to be able to add that none of the efforts to minimize my part in creating this much-abused analysis have ever come from Breuer himself or could claim any support from him.

Breuer's discoveries have so often been described that I can

1. In my *Five Lectures* (1910*a*), delivered at Clark University. [See below, p. 88.]

dispense with discussing them in detail here. These were the fundamental fact that the symptoms of hysterical patients are founded upon scenes in their past lives which have made a great impression on them but have been forgotten (traumas); the therapy founded upon this, which consisted in causing them to remember and reproduce these experiences in a state of hypnosis (catharsis); and the fragment of theory inferred from it, which was that these symptoms represented an abnormal employment of amounts of excitation which had not been disposed of (conversion). Whenever Breuer, in his theoretical contribution to the *Studies on Hysteria* (1895) [*P.F.L.*, **3**, 259 ff.], referred to this process of conversion, he always added my name in brackets after it,[1] as though the priority for this first attempt at theoretical evaluation belonged to me. I believe that actually this distinction relates only to the name, and that the conception came to us simultaneously and together.

It is well known, too, that after Breuer made his first discovery of the cathartic method he let it rest for a number of years, and only took it up again at my instigation, on my return from my studies under Charcot.[2] He had a large consulting practice in medicine which made great claims on him; I myself had only unwillingly taken up the profession of medicine, but I had at that time a strong motive for helping people suffering from nervous affections or at least for wishing to understand something about their states. I had embarked upon physical therapy, and had felt absolutely helpless after the disappointing results from my study of Erb's *Elektrotherapie* [1882], which put forward such a number of indications and recommendations. If I did not at the time arrive on my own account at the conclusion which Moebius[3] established later,

1. [There seems to be some mistake here, as Breuer in fact adds Freud's name only once on the fifteen or so occasions that he uses the term 'conversion' (*P.F.L.*, **3**, 282). The first published use of the term was in Freud's paper on 'The Neuro-Psychoses of Defence' (1894*a*).]

2. [Freud worked at the Salpêtrière in Paris during the winter of 1885–6. See his 'Report on my Studies' (1956*a* [1886]).]

3. [Paul J. Moebius (1853–1907) was Lecturer in Neurology at Leipzig University, and specialized in diseases of the nervous system.]

that the successes of electrical treatment in nervous patients are the effects of suggestion, there is no doubt that only the total absence of these promised successes was to blame. Treatment by suggestion during deep hypnosis, which I learned from Liébeault's and Bernheim's highly impressive demonstrations,[1] then seemed to offer a satisfactory substitute for the failure of electrical treatment. But the practice of *investigating* patients in a state of hypnosis, with which Breuer made me acquainted – a practice which combined an automatic mode of operation with the satisfaction of scientific curiosity – was bound to be incomparably more attractive than the monotonous, forcible prohibitions used in treatment by suggestion, prohibitions which stood in the way of all research.

We have recently received a piece of advice, purporting to represent one of the latest developments of psychoanalysis, to the effect that the current conflict and the exciting cause of illness are to be brought into the foreground in analysis. [Cf. p. 124 below.] Now this is exactly what Breuer and I used to do at the beginning of our work with the cathartic method. We led the patient's attention directly to the traumatic scene in which the symptom had arisen, and we endeavoured to discover the mental conflict in that scene and to release the suppressed affect in it. In the course of this we discovered the mental process, characteristic of the neuroses, which I later named 'regression'. The patient's associations moved back from the scene which we were trying to elucidate to earlier experiences, and compelled the analysis, which was supposed to correct the present, to occupy itself with the past. This regression led constantly further backwards; at first it seemed regularly to bring us to puberty; later on, failures and points which still eluded explanation drew the analytic work still further back into years of childhood which had hitherto been inaccessible to

---

1. [Ambroise-Auguste Liébeault (1823–1904), founder of the methodical application of therapy by suggestion, and his pupil and colleague, Hippolyte Bernheim (1840–1919), represented the Nancy School of hypnotism, which was opposed to that of Charcot's Paris School. Freud spent several weeks at Nancy in 1889.]

any kind of exploration. This regressive direction became an important characteristic of analysis. It appeared that psycho-analysis could explain nothing belonging to the present without referring back to something past; indeed, that every pathogenic experience implied a previous experience which, though not in itself pathogenic, had yet endowed the later one with its pathogenic quality. The temptation to confine one's attention to the known present exciting cause was so strong, however, that even in later analyses I gave way to it. In the analysis of the patient I named 'Dora' [1905e], carried out in 1899,[1] I had knowledge of the scene which occasioned the outbreak of the current illness. I tried innumerable times to submit this experience to analysis, but even direct demands always failed to produce from her anything more than the same meagre and incomplete description of it. Not until a long détour, leading back over her earliest childhood, had been made, did a dream present itself which on analysis brought to her mind the hitherto forgotten details of this scene, so that a comprehension and a solution of the current conflict became possible.

This one example shows how very misleading is the advice referred to above, and what a degree of scientific regression is represented by the neglect of regression in analytic technique which is thus recommended to us.

The first difference between Breuer and myself came to light on a question concerning the finer psychical mechanism of hysteria. He gave preference to a theory which was still to some extent physiological, as one might say; he tried to explain the mental splitting in hysterical patients by the absence of communication between various mental states ('states of con-sciousness', as we called them at that time), and he therefore constructed the theory of 'hypnoid states', the products of which were supposed to penetrate into 'waking consciousness' like unassimilated foreign bodies. I had taken the matter less scientifically; everywhere I seemed to discern motives and tendencies analogous to those of everyday life, and I looked upon psychical splitting itself as an effect of a process of re-pelling which at that time I called 'defence', and later, 'repres-

1. [This is a slip for '1900'. See P.F.L., **8**, 34.]

sion'.[1] I made a short-lived attempt to allow the two mechanisms a separate existence side by side, but as observation showed me always and only one thing, it was not long before my 'defence' theory took up its stand opposite his 'hypnoid' one.

I am quite sure, however, that this opposition between our views had nothing to do with the breach in our relations which followed shortly after. This had deeper causes, but it came about in such a way that at first I did not understand it; it was only later that I learnt from many clear indications how to interpret it. It will be remembered that Breuer said of his famous first patient that the element of sexuality was astonishingly undeveloped in her[2] and had contributed nothing to the very rich clinical picture of the case. I have always wondered why the critics did not more often cite this assertion of Breuer's as an argument against my contention of a sexual aetiology in the neuroses, and even today I do not know whether I ought to regard the omission as evidence of tact or of carelessness on their part. Anyone who reads the history of Breuer's case now in the light of the knowledge gained in the last twenty years will at once perceive the symbolism in it – the snakes, the stiffening, the paralysis of the arm – and, on taking into account the situation at the bedside of the young woman's sick father, will easily guess the real interpretation of her symptoms; his opinion of the part played by sexuality in her mental life will therefore be very different from that of her doctor. In his treatment of her case, Breuer was able to make use of a very intense suggestive *rapport* with the patient, which may serve us as a complete prototype of what we call 'transference' today. Now I have strong reasons for suspecting that after all her symptoms had been relieved, Breuer must have discovered from further indications the sexual motivation of this transference, but that the universal nature of this unexpected

1. [In his *Inhibitions, Symptoms and Anxiety* (1926*d*), *P.F.L.*, **10**, 322–4, Freud revived the term 'defence' to express a general concept of which 'repression' would denote a subspecies.]

2. [Cf. Breuer and Freud (1895*d*), *P.F.L.*, **3**, 73.]

phenomenon escaped him, with the result that, as though confronted by an 'untoward event',[1] he broke off all further investigation. He never said this to me in so many words, but he told me enough at different times to justify this reconstruction of what happened. When I later began more and more resolutely to put forward the significance of sexuality in the aetiology of neuroses, he was the first to show the reaction of distaste and repudiation which was later to become so familiar to me, but which at that time I had not yet learnt to recognize as my inevitable fate.[2]

The fact of the emergence of the transference in its crudely sexual form, whether affectionate or hostile, in every treatment of a neurosis, although this is neither desired nor induced by either doctor or patient, has always seemed to me the most irrefragable proof that the source of the driving forces of neurosis lies in sexual life. This argument has never received anything approaching the degree of attention that it merits, for if it had, investigations in this field would leave no other conclusion open. As far as I am concerned, this argument has remained the decisive one, over and above the more specific findings of analytic work.

There was some consolation for the bad reception accorded to my contention of a sexual aetiology in the neuroses even by my more intimate circle of friends – for a vacuum rapidly formed itself about my person – in the thought that I was taking up the fight for a new and original idea. But, one day, certain memories gathered in my mind which disturbed this pleasing notion, but which gave me in exchange a valuable insight into the processes of human creative activity and the nature of human knowledge. The idea for which I was being made responsible had by no means originated with me. It had been imparted to me by three people whose opinion had commanded my deepest respect – by Breuer himself, by

1. [In English in the original. – Cf. *P.F.L.*, **3**, 95 *n*. A fuller account of this will be found in Jones (1953), 246 f.).]

2. [A discussion of Freud's relations with Breuer will be found in the Editor's Introduction to *Studies on Hysteria* (1895*d*), *P.F.L.*, **3**, 39 ff.]

Charcot, and by Chrobak,[1] the gynaecologist at the university, perhaps the most eminent of all our Vienna physicians. These three men had all communicated to me a piece of knowledge which, strictly speaking, they themselves did not possess. Two of them later denied having done so when I reminded them of the fact; the third (the great Charcot) would probably have done the same if it had been granted me to see him again. But these three identical opinions, which I had heard without understanding, had lain dormant in my mind for years, until one day they awoke in the form of an apparently original discovery.[2]

One day, when I was a young house-physician, I was walking across the town with Breuer, when a man came up who evidently wanted to speak to him urgently. I fell behind. As soon as Breuer was free, he told me in his friendly, instructive way that this man was the husband of a patient of his and had brought him some news of her. The wife, he added, was behaving in such a peculiar way in society that she had been brought to him for treatment as a nervous case. He concluded: 'These things are always *secrets d'alcôve*!' I asked him in astonishment what he meant, and he answered by explaining the word *alcôve* ('marriage-bed') to me, for he failed to realize how extraordinary the *matter* of his statement seemed to me.

Some years later, at one of Charcot's evening receptions, I happened to be standing near the great teacher at a moment when he appeared to be telling Brouardel[3] a very interesting story about something that had happened during his day's work. I hardly heard the beginning, but gradually my attention was seized by what he was talking of: a young married couple from a distant country in the East – the woman a severe

1. [Rudolf Chrobak (1843–1910) was Professor of Gynaecology at Vienna from 1880–1908.]

2. [Freud mentioned this at a meeting of the Vienna Psycho-Analytical Society on 1 April 1908. Cf. Nunberg and Federn (1962, 360).]

3. [P. C. H. Brouardel (1837–1906) was appointed Professor of Forensic Medicine in Paris in 1879. Freud mentions him appreciatively in his 'Report on my Studies in Paris and Berlin' (1956a).]

sufferer, the man either impotent or exceedingly awkward. *'Tâchez donc,'* I heard Charcot repeating, *'je vous assure, vous y arriverez.'* [1] Brouardel, who spoke less loudly, must have expressed his astonishment that symptoms like the wife's could have been produced by such circumstances. For Charcot suddenly broke out with great animation: *'Mais, dans des cas pareils c'est toujours la chose génitale, toujours ... toujours ... toujours';* [2] and he crossed his arms over his stomach, hugging himself and jumping up and down on his toes several times in his own characteristically lively way. I know that for a moment I was almost paralysed with amazement and said to myself: 'Well, but if he knows that, why does he never say so?' But the impression was soon forgotten; brain anatomy and the experimental induction of hysterical paralyses absorbed all my interest.

A year later, I had begun my medical career in Vienna as a lecturer in nervous diseases, and in everything relating to the aetiology of the neuroses I was still as ignorant and innocent as one could expect of a promising student trained at a university. One day I had a friendly message from Chrobak, asking me to take a woman patient of his to whom he could not give enough time, owing to his new appointment as a university teacher. I arrived at the patient's house before he did and found that she was suffering from attacks of meaningless anxiety, and could only be soothed by the most precise information about where her doctor was at every moment of the day. When Chrobak arrived he took me aside and told me that the patient's anxiety was due to the fact that although she had been married for eighteen years she was still *virgo intacta*. The husband was absolutely impotent. In such cases, he said, there was nothing for a medical man to do but to shield this domestic misfortune with his own reputation, and put up with it if people shrugged their shoulders and said of him: 'He's no good if he can't cure her after so many years.' The sole prescription for such a

1. ['Go on trying! I promise you, you'll succeed.']
2. ['But in this sort of case it's always a question of the genitals – always, always, always.']

malady, he added, is familiar enough to us, but we cannot order it. It runs:

'R͵ Penis normalis
dosim
repetatur!'

I had never heard of such a prescription, and felt inclined to shake my head over my kind friend's cynicism.

I have not of course disclosed the illustrious parentage of this scandalous idea in order to saddle other people with the responsibility for it. I am well aware that it is one thing to give utterance to an idea once or twice in the form of a passing *aperçu*, and quite another to mean it seriously – to take it literally and pursue it in the face of every contradictory detail, and to win it a place among accepted truths. It is the difference between a casual flirtation and a legal marriage with all its duties and difficulties, *'Épouser les idées de ...'*[1] is no uncommon figure of speech, at any rate in French.

Among the other new factors which were added to the cathartic procedure as a result of my work and which transformed it into psychoanalysis, I may mention in particular the theory of repression and resistance, the recognition of infantile sexuality, and the interpreting and exploiting of dreams as a source of knowledge of the unconscious.

The theory of repression quite certainly came to me independently of any other source; I know of no outside impression which might have suggested it to me, and for a long time I imagined it to be entirely original, until Otto Rank (1910a) showed us a passage in Schopenhauer's *World as Will and Idea* [1819], in which the philosopher seeks to give an explanation of insanity. What he says there about the struggle against accepting a distressing piece of reality coincides with my concept of repression so completely that once again I owe the chance of making a discovery to my not being well-read. Yet others have read the passage and passed it by without making this discovery, and perhaps the same would have happened to

1. ['To espouse an idea.']

72

me if in my young days I had had more taste for reading philosophical works. In later years I have denied myself the very great pleasure of reading the works of Nietzsche, with the deliberate object of not being hampered in working out the impressions received in psychoanalysis by any sort of anticipatory ideas. I had therefore to be prepared – and I am so, gladly – to forgo all claims to priority in the many instances in which laborious psychoanalytic investigation can merely confirm the truths which the philosopher recognized by intuition.[1]

The theory of repression is the corner-stone on which the whole structure of psychoanalysis rests. It is the most essential part of it; and yet it is nothing but a theoretical formulation of a phenomenon which may be observed as often as one pleases if one undertakes an analysis of a neurotic without resorting to hypnosis. In such cases one comes across a resistance which opposes the work of analysis and in order to frustrate it pleads a failure of memory. The use of hypnosis was bound to hide this resistance; the history of psychoanalysis proper, therefore, only begins with the new technique that dispenses with hypnosis. The theoretical consideration of the fact that this resistance coincides with an amnesia leads inevitably to the view of unconscious mental activity which is peculiar to psychoanalysis and which, too, distinguishes it quite clearly from philosophical speculations about the unconscious. It may thus be said that the theory of psychoanalysis is an attempt to account for two striking and unexpected facts of observation which emerge whenever an attempt is made to trace the symptoms of a neurotic back to their sources in his past life: the facts of transference and of resistance. Any line of investigation which recognizes these two facts and takes them as

1. [Other instances of the anticipation of Freud's ideas are discussed by him in his 'Note on the Prehistory of the Technique of Analysis' (1920b). See also the remarks on Popper-Lynkeus below (p. 77). – The possibility that Freud derived the term 'repression' indirectly from the early nineteenth-century philosopher Herbart is discussed by Ernest Jones (1953, 407 ff.). Cf. the Editor's Note to the papers on 'Repression' (1915d), *P.F.L.*, **11**, 141–2, and 'The Unconscious' (1915e), ibid., 162.]

the starting-point of its work has a right to call itself psychoanalysis, even though it arrives at results other than my own. But anyone who takes up other sides of the problem while avoiding these two hypotheses will hardly escape a charge of misappropriation of property by attempted impersonation, if he persists in calling himself a psychoanalyst.

If anyone sought to place the theory of repression and resistance among the *premisses* instead of the *findings* of psychoanalysis, I should oppose him most emphatically. Such premisses of a general psychological and biological nature do exist, and it would be useful to consider them on some other occasion; but the theory of repression is a product of psychoanalytic work, a theoretical inference legitimately drawn from innumerable observations.

Another product of this sort was the hypothesis of infantile sexuality. This, however, was made at a much later date. In the early days of tentative investigation by analysis no such thing was thought of. At first it was merely observed that the effects of present-day experiences had to be traced back to something in the past. But inquirers often find more than they bargain for. One was drawn further and further back into the past; one hoped at last to be able to stop at puberty, the period in which the sexual impulses are traditionally supposed to awake. But in vain; the tracks led still further back into childhood and into its earlier years. On the way, a mistaken idea had to be overcome which might have been almost fatal to the young science. Influenced by Charcot's view of the traumatic origin of hysteria, one was readily inclined to accept as true and aetiologically significant the statements made by patients in which they ascribed their symptoms to passive sexual experiences in the first years of childhood – to put it bluntly, to seduction. When this aetiology broke down under the weight of its own improbability and contradiction in definitely ascertainable circumstances, the result at first was helpless bewilderment. Analysis had led back to these infantile sexual traumas by the right path, and yet they were not true. The firm ground of reality was gone. At that time I would gladly have given up the whole work, just as my esteemed predecessor, Breuer, had done when he made his unwelcome discovery. Perhaps I persevered only because I no longer had any choice and could not then begin again at anything else. At last came the reflection that, after all, one had no right to despair because one has been deceived in one's expectations; one must revise those expectations. If hysterical subjects trace back their symptoms to traumas that are fictitious, then the new fact which emerges is precisely that they create such scenes in *fantasy*, and this psychical reality requires to be taken into account alongside practical reality. This reflection was soon followed by the discovery that these fantasies were intended to cover up the auto-erotic activity of the first years of childhood, to embellish it and raise it to a higher plane. And now, from behind the fantasies, the whole range of a child's sexual life came to light.[1]

With this sexual activity of the first years of childhood the inherited constitution of the individual also came into its own. Disposition and experience are here linked up in an indissoluble aetiological unity. For *disposition* exaggerates impressions which would otherwise have been completely commonplace and have had no effect, so that they become traumas giving rise to stimulations and fixations; while *experiences* awaken factors in the disposition which, without them, might have long remained dormant and perhaps never have developed. The last word on the subject of traumatic aetiology was spoken later by Abraham [1907], when he pointed out that the sexual constitution which is peculiar to children is precisely calculated to provoke sexual experiences of a particular kind – namely traumas.

In the beginning, my statements about infantile sexuality were founded almost exclusively on the findings of analysis in adults which led back into the past. I had no opportunity of direct observations on children. It was therefore a very great triumph when it became possible years later to confirm almost all my inferences by direct observation and the analysis of very

1. [Cf. Freud's account of this in his *Autobiographical Study* (1925*d*), p. 216 ff. and 217 *n*.]

young children – a triumph that lost some of its magnitude as one gradually realized that the nature of the discovery was such that one should really be ashamed of having had to make it. The further one carried these observations on children, the more self-evident the facts became; but the more astonishing, too, did it become that one had taken so much trouble to overlook them.

Such a certain conviction of the existence and importance of infantile sexuality can, however, only be obtained by the method of analysis, by pursuing the symptoms and peculiarities of neurotics back to their ultimate sources, the discovery of which then explains whatever is explicable in them and enables whatever is modifiable to be changed. I can understand that one would arrive at different results if, as C. G. Jung has recently done, one first forms a theoretical conception of the nature of the sexual instinct and then seeks to explain the life of children on that basis. A conception of this kind is bound to be selected arbitrarily or in accordance with irrelevant considerations, and runs the risk of proving inadequate for the field to which one is seeking to apply it. It is true that the analytic method, too, leads to certain ultimate difficulties and obscurities in regard to sexuality and its relation to the total life of the individual. But these problems cannot be got rid of by speculation; they must await solution through other observations or through observations in other fields.

I need say little about the interpretation of dreams. It came as the first-fruits of the technical innovation I had adopted when, following a dim presentiment, I decided to replace hypnosis by free association. My desire for knowledge had not at the start been directed towards understanding dreams. I do not know of any outside influence which drew my interest to them or inspired me with any helpful expectations. Before Breuer and I ceased to meet I only just had time to tell him in a single sentence that I now understood how to translate dreams. Since this was how the discovery came about, it followed that the *symbolism* in the language of dreams was almost the last thing to become accessible to me, for the dreamer's associations help very little towards understanding symbols. I have held fast to the habit of always studying things themselves before looking for information about them in books, and therefore I was able to establish the symbolism of dreams for myself before I was led to it by Scherner's work on the subject [1861]. It was only later that I came to appreciate to its full extent this mode of expression of dreams. This was partly through the influence of the works of Stekel, who at first did such very creditable work but afterwards went totally astray.[1] The close connection between psychoanalytic dream interpretation and the art of interpreting dreams as practised and held in such high esteem in antiquity only became clear to me much later. Later on I found the essential characteristic and most important part of my dream theory – the derivation of dream distortion from an internal conflict, a kind of inner dishonesty – in a writer who was ignorant, it is true, of medicine, though not of philosophy, the famous engineer J. Popper, who published his *Phantasien eines Realisten* [1899] under the name of Lynkeus.[2]

The interpretation of dreams became a solace and a support to me in those arduous first years of analysis, when I had to master the technique, clinical phenomena and therapy of the neuroses all at the same time. At that period I was completely isolated and in the network of problems and accumulation of difficulties I often dreaded losing my bearings and also my confidence. There were often patients with whom an un-accountably long time elapsed before my hypothesis, that a neurosis was bound to become intelligible through analysis, proved true; but these patients' dreams, which might be regarded as analogues of their symptoms, almost always confirmed the hypothesis.

It was only my success in this direction that enabled me to persevere. The result is that I have acquired a habit of gauging the measure of a psychologist's understanding by his attitude

1. [A longer discussion of Stekel's influence is contained in a passage added by Freud in 1925 to the section on symbolism, Chapter VI (E), in *The Interpretation of Dreams* (1900a), *P.F.L.*, **4**, 466–7.]

2. [See Freud's two papers on this, 1923*f* and 1932*c*.]

to dream interpretation; and I have observed with satisfaction that most of the opponents of psychoanalysis avoid this field altogether or else display remarkable clumsiness if they attempt to deal with it. Moreover, I soon saw the necessity of carrying out a self-analysis, and this I did with the help of a series of my own dreams which led me back through all the events of my childhood; and I am still of the opinion today that this kind of analysis may suffice for anyone who is a good dreamer and not too abnormal.[1]

I think that by thus unrolling the story of the development of psychoanalysis I have shown what it is, better than by a systematic description of it. I did not at first perceive the peculiar nature of what I had discovered. I unhesitatingly sacrificed my growing popularity as a doctor, and the increase in attendance during my consulting hours, by making a systematic inquiry into the sexual factors involved in the causation of my patients' neuroses; and this brought me a great many new facts which finally confirmed my conviction of the practical importance of the sexual factor. I innocently addressed a meeting of the Vienna Society for Psychiatry and Neurology with Krafft-Ebing[2] in the chair [cf. Freud, 1896c], expecting that the material losses I had willingly undergone would be made up for by the interest and recognition of my colleagues. I treated my discoveries as ordinary contributions to science and

1. [Freud's contemporary account of important parts of his self-analysis will be found in the Fliess correspondence (1950a), particularly in Letters 70 and 71, written in October 1897. – He did not always take such a favourable view of self-analysis as in the text above. For instance, in a letter to Fliess of 14 November 1897 (1950a, Letter 75), he wrote: 'My self-analysis is still interrupted and I have realized the reason. I can only analyse myself with the help of knowledge obtained objectively (like an outsider). Genuine self-analysis is impossible; otherwise there would be no [neurotic] illness. Since I still find some puzzles in my patients, they are bound to hold me up in my self-analysis.']

2. [R. von Krafft-Ebing (1840–1903) was Professor of Psychiatry at Strasbourg 1872–3, at Graz 1873–89, where he also directed the provincial mental hospital, and at Vienna 1889–1902. He was also distinguished for his work on criminology, neurology and psychopathia sexualis.]

hoped they would be received in the same spirit. But the silence which my communications met with, the void which formed itself about me, the hints that were conveyed to me, gradually made me realize that assertions on the part played by sexuality in the aetiology of the neuroses cannot count upon meeting with the same kind of treatment as other communications. I understood that from now onwards I was one of those who have 'disturbed the sleep of the world', as Hebbel says,[1] and that I could not reckon upon objectivity and tolerance. Since, however, my conviction of the general accuracy of my observations and conclusions grew even stronger, and since neither my confidence in my own judgement nor my moral courage were precisely small, the outcome of the situation could not be in doubt. I made up my mind to believe that it had been my fortune to discover some particularly important facts and connections, and I was prepared to accept the fate that sometimes accompanies such discoveries.

I pictured the future as follows: I should probably succeed in maintaining myself by means of the therapeutic success of the new procedure, but science would ignore me entirely during my lifetime; some decades later, someone else would infallibly come upon the same things – for which the time was not now ripe – would achieve recognition for them and bring me honour as a forerunner whose failure had been inevitable. Meanwhile, like Robinson Crusoe, I settled down as comfortably as possible on my desert island. When I look back to those lonely years, away from the pressures and confusions of today, it seems like a glorious heroic age. My 'splendid isolation' was not without its advantages and charms. I did not have to read any publications, nor listen to any ill-informed opponents; I was not subject to influence from any quarter; there was nothing to hustle me. I learnt to restrain speculative tendencies and to follow the unforgotten advice of my master, Charcot: to look at the same things again and again until they themselves begin to speak. My publications, which I was able

1. [A reference to Kandaules' words to Gyges in Hebbel's *Gyges und sein Ring*, Act V, Scene 1.]

to place with a little trouble, could always lag far behind my knowledge, and could be postponed as long as I pleased, since there was no doubtful 'priority' to be defended. *The Interpretation of Dreams*, for instance, was finished in all essentials at the beginning of 1896[1] but was not written out until the summer of 1899. The analysis of 'Dora' was over at the end of 1899 [1900];[2] the case history was written in the next two weeks, but was not published until 1905. Meanwhile my writings were not reviewed in the medical journals, or, if as an exception they *were* reviewed, they were dismissed with expressions of scornful or pitying superiority. Occasionally a colleague would make some reference to me in one of his publications; it would be very short and not at all flattering – words such as 'eccentric', 'extreme' or 'very peculiar' would be used. It once happened that an assistant at the clinic in Vienna where I gave my university lectures asked me for permission to attend the course. He listened very attentively and said nothing; after the last lecture was over he offered to join me outside. As we walked away, he told me that with his chief's knowledge he had written a book combating my views; he regretted very much, however, that he had not first learnt more about them from my lectures, for in that case he would have written much of it differently. He had indeed inquired at the clinic whether he had not better first read *The Interpretation of Dreams*, but had been advised against doing so – it was not worth the trouble. He then himself compared the structure of my theory, so far as he now understood it, with that of the Catholic Church as regards its internal solidity. In the interests of the salvation of his soul, I shall assume that this remark implied a certain amount of appreciation. But he concluded by saying that it was too late to alter anything in his book, since it was already in print. Nor did my colleague think it necessary later to make any public avowal of his change of views on

1. [See, however, the Editor's Introduction to *The Interpretation of Dreams* (1900a), *P.F.L.*, **4**, 38 ff.]

2. [See footnote on p. 67.]

the subject of psychoanalysis; but preferred, in his capacity as a regular reviewer for a medical journal, to follow its development with flippant comments.[1]

Whatever personal sensitiveness I possessed became blunted during those years, to my advantage. I was saved from becoming embittered, however, by a circumstance which is not always present to help lonely discoverers. Such people are as a rule tormented by the need to account for the lack of sympathy or the aversion of their contemporaries, and feel this attitude as a distressing contradiction of the security of their own sense of conviction. There was no need for me to feel so; for psychoanalytic theory enabled me to understand this attitude in my contemporaries and to see it as a necessary consequence of fundamental analytic premises. If it was true that the set of facts I had discovered were kept from the knowledge of patients themselves by internal resistances of an affective kind, then these resistances would be bound to appear in healthy people too, as soon as some external source confronted them with what was repressed. It was not surprising that they should be able to justify this rejection of my ideas on intellectual grounds though it was actually affective in origin. The same thing happened equally often with patients; the arguments they advanced were the same and were not precisely brilliant. In Falstaff's words, reasons are 'as plenty as blackberries'.[2] The only difference was that with patients one was in a position to bring pressure to bear on them so as to induce them to get insight into their resistances and overcome them, whereas one had to do without this advantage in dealing with people who were ostensibly healthy. How to compel these healthy people to examine the matter in a cool and scientifically objective spirit was an unsolved problem which was best left to time to clear up. In the history of science one can clearly see that often the very proposition which has at first called out nothing but contradiction has later come to be accepted, although no new proofs in support of it have been brought forward.

1. [A sequel to this anecdote will be found on p. 232 below.]
2. [*I Henry IV*, Act II, Scene 4.]

It was hardly to be expected, however, that during the years when I alone represented psychoanalysis I should develop any particular respect for the world's opinion or any bias towards intellectual appeasement.

II

From the year 1902 onwards, a number of young doctors gathered round me with the express intention of learning, practising and spreading the knowledge of psychoanalysis. The stimulus came from a colleague who had himself experienced the beneficial effects of analytic therapy.[1] Regular meetings took place on certain evenings at my house, discussions were held according to certain rules and the participants endeavoured to find their bearings in this new and strange field of research and to interest others in it. One day a young man who had passed through a technical training college introduced himself with a manuscript which showed very unusual comprehension. We persuaded him to go through the *Gymnasium* [secondary school] and the university and to devote himself to the non-medical side of psychoanalysis. The little Society acquired in him a zealous and dependable secretary and I gained in Otto Rank a most loyal helper and co-worker.[2]

The small circle soon expanded, and in the course of the next few years often changed its composition. On the whole I could tell myself that it was hardly inferior, in wealth and variety of talent, to the staff of any clinical teacher one could think of. It included from the beginning the men who were later to play such a considerable, if not always a welcome, part in the history of the psychoanalytic movement. At that time, however, one could not yet guess at these developments. I had

1. [Wilhelm Stekel.]
2. [*Footnote added* 1924:] Now director of the Internationaler Psycho-analytischer Verlag [International Psycho-Analytical Publishing House] and editor of the *Zeitschrift* and *Imago* from their inception [see below, p. 107].

every reason to be satisfied, and I think I did everything possible to impart my own knowledge and experience to the others. There were only two inauspicious circumstances which at last estranged me inwardly from the group. I could not succeed in establishing among its members the friendly relations that ought to obtain between men who are all engaged upon the same difficult work; nor was I able to stifle the disputes about priority for which there were so many opportunities under these conditions of work in common. The difficulties in the way of giving instruction in the practice of psychoanalysis, which are quite particularly great and are responsible for much in the present dissensions, were evident already in this private Vienna Psycho-Analytical Society. I myself did not venture to put forward a still unfinished technique and a theory still in the making with an authority which would probably have enabled the others to avoid some wrong turnings and ultimate disasters. The self-reliance of intellectual workers, their early independence of their teacher, is always gratifying from a psychological point of view; but it is only of advantage to science if those workers fulfil certain personal conditions which are none too common. For psychoanalysis in particular a long and severe discipline and training in self-discipline would have been required. In view of the courage displayed by their devotion to a subject so much frowned upon and so poor in prospects, I was disposed to tolerate much among the members to which I should otherwise have made objection. Besides doctors, the circle included others – men of education who had recognized something important in psychoanalysis: writers, painters and so on. My *Interpretation of Dreams* [1900*a*] and my book on jokes [1905*c*], among others, had shown from the beginning that the theories of psychoanalysis cannot be restricted to the medical field, but are capable of application to a variety of other mental sciences.

In 1907 the situation changed all at once and contrary to all expectations. It appeared that psychoanalysis had unobtrusively awakened interest and gained friends, and that there were even some scientific workers who were ready to acknowledge it. A communication from Bleuler[1] had informed me before this that my works had been studied and made use of in the Burghölzli. In January 1907, the first member of the Zurich clinic came to Vienna – Dr Eitingon.[2] Other visits followed, which led to an animated exchange of ideas. Finally, on the invitation of C. G. Jung, at that time still assistant physician at the Burghölzli, a first meeting took place at Salzburg in the spring of 1908, which brought together friends of psycho-analysis from Vienna, Zurich and other places. One of the results of this first Psycho-Analytical Congress was the founding of a periodical called the *Jahrbuch für psychoanalytische und psychopathologische Forschungen* [see below, p. 106], under the direction of Bleuler and Freud and edited by Jung, which first appeared in 1909. This publication gave expression to an intimate co-operation between Vienna and Zurich.

I have repeatedly acknowledged with gratitude the great services rendered by the Zurich School of Psychiatry in the spread of psychoanalysis, particularly by Bleuler and Jung, and I have no hesitation in doing so again, even in the greatly altered circumstances of the present. True, it was not the support of the Zurich School which first directed the attention of the scientific world to psychoanalysis at that time. What had happened was that the latency period had expired and everywhere psychoanalysis was becoming the object of ever-increasing interest. But in all other places this accession of interest at first produced nothing but a very emphatic re-pudiation, mostly a quite passionate one; whereas in Zurich, on the contrary, agreement on general lines was the dominant note. Moreover, nowhere else did such a compact little group of adherents exist, or could a public clinic be placed at the service of psychoanalytic researches, or was there a clinical teacher who included psychoanalytic theories as an integral part of his psychiatric course. The Zurich group thus became

1. [Eugen Bleuler (1857–1939), the well-known psychiatrist, then head of the Burghölzli, the public mental hospital at Zurich.]

2. [*Footnote added* 1924:] The subsequent founder of the Psycho-Analytic Policlinic in Berlin. [Cf. p. 175 below.]

the nucleus of the small band who were fighting for the re-cognition of analysis. The only opportunity of learning the new art and working at it in practice lay there. Most of my followers and co-workers at the present time came to me by way of Zurich, even those who were geographically much nearer to Vienna than to Switzerland. In relation to Western Europe, which contains the great centres of our culture, the position of Vienna is an outlying one; and its prestige has for many years been affected by strong prejudices. Representatives of all the most important nations congregate in Switzerland, where intellectual activity is so lively; a focus of infection there was bound to be of great importance for the spread of the 'psychical epidemic', as Hoche of Freiburg has called it.[1]

According to the evidence of a colleague who witnessed developments at the Burghölzli, it appears that psychoanalysis awakened interest there very early. In Jung's work on occult phenomena, published in 1902, there was already an allusion to my book on dream-interpretation. From 1903 or 1904, says my informant, psychoanalysis was in the forefront of interest. After personal relations between Vienna and Zurich had been estab-lished, an informal society was also started, in the middle of 1907, in the Burghölzli, where the problems of psychoanalysis were discussed at regular meetings. In the alliance between the Vienna and Zurich Schools the Swiss were by no means mere recipients. They had already produced very creditable scientific work, the results of which were of service to psycho-analysis. The association experiments started by the Wundt School had been interpreted by them in a psychoanalytic sense, and had proved applicable in unexpected ways. By this means it had become possible to arrive at rapid experimental confirma-tion of psychoanalytic observations and to demonstrate directly to students certain connections which an analyst would only have been able to tell them about. The first bridge linking up

1. [Alfred Hoche (1865–1943), Professor of Psychiatry at Freiburg, was particularly vehement and abusive in his attacks on psychoanalysis. He read a paper on it at a medical congress at Baden-Baden with the title 'A Psychical Epidemic among Doctors' (Hoche, 1910).]

experimental psychology with psychoanalysis had been built.

In psychoanalytic treatment, association experiments enable a provisional, qualitative analysis of the case to be made, but they furnish no essential contribution to the technique and can be dispensed with in carrying out analyses. More important, however, was another achievement by the Zurich School, or its leaders, Bleuler and Jung. The former showed that light could be thrown on a large number of purely psychiatric cases by adducing the same processes as have been recognized through psychoanalysis to obtain in dreams and neuroses (Freudian mechanisms); and Jung [1907] successfully applied the analytic method of interpretation to the most alien and obscure phenomena of dementia praecox [schizophrenia], so that their sources in the life-history and interests of the patient came clearly to light. After this it was impossible for psychiatrists to ignore psychoanalysis any longer. Bleuler's great work on schizophrenia (1911), in which the psychoanalytic point of view was placed on an equal footing with the clinical systematic one, completed this success.

I will not omit to point out a divergence which was already at that time noticeable in the direction taken by the work of the two schools. As early as in 1897 [1] I had published the analysis of a case of schizophrenia, which however was of a paranoid character, so that the solution of it could not take away from the impression made by Jung's analyses. But to me the important point had been, not so much the possibility of interpreting the symptoms, as the psychical mechanism of the disease, and above all the agreement of this mechanism with that of hysteria, which had already been discovered. At that time no light had yet been thrown on the differences between the two mechanisms. For I was then already aiming at a libido theory of the neuroses, which was to explain all neurotic and psychotic phenomena as proceeding from abnormal vicissitudes of the libido, that is, as diversions from its normal employment. This point of view was missed by the Swiss

1. [This wrong date appears in all the German editions. The case was published in May 1896. It occupies Section III of Freud's second paper on 'The Neuro-Psychoses of Defence' (1896b).]

investigators. As far as I know, even today Bleuler maintains the view that the various forms of dementia praecox have an organic causation; and at the Salzburg Congress in 1908 Jung, whose book on this disease had appeared in 1907, supported the toxic theory of its causation, which takes no account of the libido theory, although it is true that it does not rule it out. Later on (1912) he came to grief on this same point, by making too much of the material which he had previously refused to employ.

There is a third contribution made by the Swiss School, probably to be ascribed entirely to Jung, which I do not value so highly as others do whose concern with these matters is more remote. I refer to the theory of 'complexes' which grew out of the *Diagnostische Assoziationsstudien* [*Studies in Word-Association*] (1906). It has neither itself produced a psychological theory, nor has it proved capable of easy incorporation into the context of psychoanalytic theory. The word 'complex', on the other hand, has become naturalized, so to speak, in psychoanalytic language; it is a convenient and often indispensable term for summing up a psychological state descriptively.[1] None of the other terms coined by psychoanalysis for its own needs has achieved such widespread popularity or been so misapplied to the detriment of the construction of clearer concepts. Analysts began to speak among themselves of a 'return of a complex' where they meant a 'return of the repressed', or fell into the habit of saying 'I have a complex against him', where the only correct expression would have been 'a resistance against him'.

In the years following 1907, when the Schools of Vienna and Zurich were united, psychoanalysis made the extraordinary surge forward of which the momentum is felt even today; this is shown both by the spread of psychoanalytic literature and by the constant increase in the number of doctors who are practising or studying it, as well as by the frequency of the

1. [Freud seems to have first borrowed the term from Jung in a paper on evidence in legal proceedings (1906c). He himself, however, had used the word in what seems a very similar sense long before, in a footnote to the case of Frau Emmy von N. in *Studies on Hysteria* (1895d), *P.F.L.*, **3**, 126 *n.*]

attacks made on it at congresses and in learned societies. It has penetrated into the most distant lands and has everywhere not merely startled psychiatrists but commanded the attention of the educated public and of scientific workers in other fields. Havelock Ellis, who has followed its development with sympathy though without ever calling himself an adherent, wrote in 1911 in a report for the Australasian Medical Congress: 'Freud's psychoanalysis is now championed and carried out not only in Austria and in Switzerland, but in the United States, in England, in India, in Canada, and, I doubt not, in Australasia.' [1] A physician from Chile (probably a German) spoke at the International Congress at Buenos Aires in 1910 in support of the existence of infantile sexuality and commended highly the effects of psychoanalytic therapy on obsessional symptoms.[2] An English neurologist in Central India (Berkeley-Hill) informed me, through a distinguished colleague who was visiting Europe, that the analyses of Mohammedan Indians which he had carried out showed that the aetiology of their neuroses was no different from what we find in our European patients.

The introduction of psychoanalysis into North America was accompanied by very special marks of honour. In the autumn of 1909, Stanley Hall, the President of Clark University, Worcester, Massachusetts, invited Jung and myself to take part in the celebration of the twentieth anniversary of the foundation of the university by giving a number of lectures in German. To our great surprise, we found the members of that small but highly esteemed university for the study of education and philosophy so unprejudiced that they were acquainted with all the literature of psychoanalysis and had given it a place in their lectures to students. In prudish America it was possible, in academic circles at least, to discuss freely and scientifically everything that in ordinary life is regarded as objectionable. The five lectures which I improvised in Worcester appeared in an English translation in the *American Journal of Psychology* [1910a], and were shortly afterwards published in German

1. Havelock Ellis, 1911.
2. G. Greve, 1910.

under the title *Über Psychoanalyse*. Jung read a paper on diagnostic association experiments [1910*a*] and another on conflicts in the mind of the child [1910*b*]. We were rewarded with the honorary degree of Doctor of Laws. During that week of celebrations at Worcester, psychoanalysis was represented by five men: besides Jung and myself, there were Ferenczi, who had joined me for the journey, Ernest Jones, then at the University of Toronto (Canada) and now in London, and A. A. Brill, who was already practising psychoanalysis in New York.

The most important personal relationship which arose from the meeting at Worcester was that with James J. Putnam, Professor of Neuropathology at Harvard University. Some years before, he had expressed an unfavourable opinion of psychoanalysis, but now he rapidly became reconciled to it and recommended it to his countrymen and his colleagues in a series of lectures which were as rich in content as they were brilliant in form. The esteem he enjoyed throughout America on account of his high moral character and unflinching love of truth was of great service to psychoanalysis and protected it against the denunciations which in all probability would otherwise quickly have overwhelmed it. Later on, yielding too much to the strong ethical and philosophical bent of his nature, Putnam made what seems to me an impossible demand – he expected psychoanalysis to place itself at the service of a particular moral-philosophical conception of the Universe – but he remains the chief pillar of the psychoanalytic movement in his native land.[1]

For the further spread of this movement Brill and Jones deserve the greatest credit: in their writings they drew their countrymen's attention with unremitting assiduity to the easily observable fundamental facts of everyday life, of dreams and neurosis. Brill has contributed still further to this effect by his medical practice and by his translation of my works, and Jones

1. [*Footnote added* 1924:] See Putnam's *Addresses on Psycho-Analysis*, 1921. [Freud contributed a preface to this (1921*a*).] – Putnam died in 1918. [See Freud's obituary of him (1919*b*).]

by his instructive lectures and by his skill in debate at congresses in America.[1] The absence of any deep-rooted scientific tradition in America and the much less stringent rule of official authority there have been of decided advantage to the impetus given by Stanley Hall. It was characteristic of that country that from the beginning professors and superintendents of mental hospitals showed as much interest in analysis as independent practitioners. But it is clear that precisely for this reason the ancient centres of culture, where the greatest resistance has been displayed, must be the scene of the decisive struggle over psychoanalysis.

Among European countries France has hitherto shown itself the least disposed to welcome psychoanalysis, although useful work in French by A. Maeder of Zurich has provided easy access to its theories. The first indications of sympathy came from the provinces: Morichau-Beauchant (Poitiers) was the first Frenchman to adhere publicly to psychoanalysis. Régis[2] and Hesnard (Bordeaux) have recently [1914] attempted to disperse the prejudices of their countrymen against the new ideas by an exhaustive presentation, which, however, is not always understanding and takes special exception to symbolism.[3] In Paris itself, a conviction still seems to reign (to which Janet himself gave eloquent expression at the Congress[4] in London in 1913) that everything good in psychoanalysis is a repetition of Janet's views with insignificant modifications, and that everything else in it is bad. At this Congress itself, indeed, Janet had to submit to a number of corrections by Ernest Jones, who was able to point out to him his insufficient knowledge of the subject.[5] Even though we deny his claims,

1. The publications of both authors have appeared in collected volumes: Brill, 1912, and Ernest Jones, 1913.

2. [E. Régis (1855–1918) was Professor of Psychiatry at Bordeaux from 1905.]

3. [Before 1924 this read 'an exhaustive and understanding presentation which only took exception to symbolism'.]

4. [The International Medical Congress.]

5. [Cf. Janet (1913) and Jones (1915).]

however, we cannot forget the value of his work on the psychology of the neuroses.

In Italy, after several promising starts, no real interest was forthcoming. To Holland analysis found early access through personal connections: Van Emden, Van Ophuijsen, Van Renterghem (*Freud en zijn School* [1913]) and the two Stärckes are actively occupied with it both in practice and theory.[1] In scientific circles in England interest in analysis has developed very slowly, but there is reason to expect that the sense for the practical and the passionate love of justice in the English will ensure it a brilliant future there.

In Sweden, P. Bjerre, who succeeded to Wetterstrand's practice, gave up hypnotic suggestion, at least for the time, in favour of analytic treatment. R. Vogt (Christiania) had already shown an appreciation of psychoanalysis in his *Psykiatriens grundtraek*, published in 1907; so that the first textbook of psychiatry to refer to psychoanalysis was written in Norwegian. In Russia, psychoanalysis has become generally known and has spread widely; almost all my writings, as well as those of other adherents of analysis, have been translated into Russian. But a really penetrating comprehension of analytic theories has not yet been evinced in Russia; so that the contributions of Russian physicians are at present not very notable. The only trained analyst there is M. Wulff who practises in Odessa. It is principally due to L. Jekels that psychoanalysis has been introduced to Polish scientific and literary circles. Hungary, so near geographically to Austria, and so far from it scientifically, has produced only one collaborator, S. Ferenczi, but one that indeed outweighs a whole society.[2]

1. The first official recognition of dream interpretation and psychoanalysis in Europe was extended to them by the psychiatrist Jelgersma, Rector of the University of Leyden, in his rectorial address on 9 February 1914.

2. [*Footnote added* 1923:] It is not my intention, of course, to bring this account, written in 1914, 'up to date' [in English in the original]. I will only add a few remarks to indicate how the picture has altered in the interval, which includes the World War. In Germany a gradual infiltration of analytic theories into clinical psychiatry is taking place, though this is not always

As regards the position of psychoanalysis in Germany, it can only be said that it forms the centre-point of scientific discussions and provokes the most emphatic expressions of disagreement both among doctors and laymen; these are not yet at an end, but are constantly flaring up again, sometimes with greater intensity. No official educational bodies there have up to now recognized psychoanalysis. Successful practitioners who employ it are few; only a few institutions, such as Binswanger's in Kreuzlingen (on Swiss soil) and Marcinowski's in Holstein, have opened their doors to it. One of the most prominent representatives of analysis, Karl Abraham, at one time an assistant of Bleuler's, maintains himself in the critical atmosphere of Berlin. One might wonder that this state of things should have continued unaltered for several years if one did not know that the account I have given only represents external appearances. Too much significance should not be attributed to rejection by the official representatives of science and heads of institutions, and by the followers dependent on them. It is natural that its opponents should give loud expression to their views, while its intimidated adherents keep silence. Some of the latter, whose first contributions to analysis raised favourable

---

admitted. The French translations of my works that have been appearing during the last few years have finally aroused a keen interest in psychoanalysis even in France, though for the moment this is more active in literary circles than in scientific ones. In Italy M. Levi Bianchini (of Nocera Superiore) and Edoardo Weiss (of Trieste) have come forward as translators and champions of psychoanalysis (cf. the *Biblioteca Psicoanalitica Italiana*). A collected edition of my works which is appearing in Madrid (translated by López-Ballesteros) is evidence of the lively interest taken in it in Spanish-speaking countries (Prof. H. Delgado in Lima). As regards England, the prophecy which I have made above seems to be in steady course of fulfilment; a special centre for the study of analysis has been formed at Calcutta in British India. In North America it is still true that the depth of understanding of analysis does not keep pace with its popularity. In Russia, since the Revolution, psychoanalytic work has begun afresh at several centres. In Poland the *Polska Biblioteka Psychoanalityczna* is now appearing. In Hungary a brilliant analytic school is flourishing under the leadership of Ferenczi. (Cf. the Festschrift issued in honour of his fiftieth birthday [which included an appreciation by Freud, 1923*i*].) At the present time the Scandinavian countries are still the least receptive.

expectations, have later withdrawn from the movement under the pressure of circumstances. The movement itself advances surely though silently; it is constantly gaining new adherents among psychiatrists and laymen, it brings in a growing stream of new readers for psychoanalytic literature and for that very reason drives its opponents to ever more violent defensive efforts. At least a dozen times in recent years, in reports of the proceedings of certain congresses and scientific bodies or in reviews of certain publications, I have read that now psychoanalysis is dead, defeated and disposed of once and for all. The best answer to all this would be in the terms of Mark Twain's telegram to the newspaper which had falsely published news of his death: 'Report of my death greatly exaggerated.' After each of these obituaries psychoanalysis regularly gained new adherents and co-workers or acquired new channels of publicity. After all, being declared dead was an advance on being buried in silence.

Hand in hand with this expansion of psychoanalysis in space went an expansion in content; it extended from the field of the neuroses and psychiatry to other fields of knowledge. I shall not treat this aspect of the development of our discipline in much detail, since this has been done with great success by Rank and Sachs [1913] in a volume (one of Löwenfeld's *Grenzfragen*[1]) which deals exhaustively with precisely this side of analytic research. Moreover, this development is still in its infancy; it has been little worked at, consists mostly of tentative beginnings and in part of no more than plans. No reasonable person will see any grounds for reproach in this. An enormous mass of work confronts a small number of workers, most of whom have their main occupation elsewhere and can bring only the qualifications of an amateur to bear on the technical problems of these unfamiliar fields of science. These workers, who derive from psychoanalysis, make no secret of their amateurishness. Their aim is merely to act as sign-posts and stop-gaps for the specialists, and to put the analytic technique and principles at their

1. [*Grenzfragen des Nerven- und Seelenlebens* (Border Problems of Nervous and Mental Life), edited by Leopold Löwenfeld and Hans Kurella.]

disposal against a time when they in turn shall take up the work. That the results achieved are nevertheless not inconsiderable is due partly to the fruitfulness of the analytic method, and partly to the circumstances that there are already a few investigators who are not doctors, and have taken up the application of psychoanalysis to the mental sciences as their profession in life.

Most of these applications of analysis naturally go back to a hint in my earliest analytic writings. The analytic examination of neurotic people and the neurotic symptoms of normal people necessitated the assumption of psychological conditions which could not possibly be limited to the field in which they had been discovered. In this way analysis not only provided us with the explanation of pathological phenomena, but revealed their connection with normal mental life and disclosed unsuspected relationships between psychiatry and the most various other sciences dealing with activities of the mind. Certain typical dreams, for instance, yielded an explanation of some myths and fairy-tales. Riklin [1908] and Abraham [1909] followed this hint and initiated the researches into myths which have found their completion, in a manner complying with even expert standards, in Rank's works on mythology [e.g. 1909, 1911]. Further investigation into dream symbolism led to the heart of the problems of mythology, folklore (Jones [e.g. 1912a, 1912b] and Storfer [1914]) and the abstractions of religion. A deep impression was made on all hearers at one of the psychoanalytical congresses when a follower of Jung's demonstrated the correspondence between schizophrenic fantasies and the cosmogonies of primitive times and races.[1] Mythological material later received further elaboration (which, though open to criticism, was none the less very interesting) at the hands of Jung, in works attempting to correlate the neuroses with religious and mythological fantasies.

Another path led from the investigation of dreams to the

1. [Jan Nelken at the Weimar Congress in 1911. An expanded version of the paper will be found in Nelken, 1912.]

analysis of works of imagination and ultimately to the analysis of their creators – writers and artists themselves. At an early stage it was discovered that dreams invented by writers will often yield to analysis in the same way as genuine ones. (Cf. 'Gradiva' [Jensen, 1903; Freud, 1907a, *P.F.L.*, **14**, 27 ff.].) The conception of unconscious mental activity made it possible to form a preliminary idea of the nature of imaginative creative writing; and the realization, gained in the study of neurotics, of the part played by the instinctual impulses enabled us to perceive the sources of artistic production and confronted us with two problems: how the artist reacts to this instigation and what means he employs to disguise his reactions.[1] Most analysts with general interests have contributed something to the solution of these problems, which are the most fascinating among the applications of psychoanalysis. Naturally, opposition was not lacking in this direction either on the part of people who knew nothing of analysis; it took the same form as it did in the original field of psychoanalytic research – the same misconceptions and vehement rejections. It was only to be expected from the beginning that, whatever the regions into which psychoanalysis might penetrate, it would inevitably experience the same struggles with those already in possession of the field. These attempted invasions, however, have not yet stirred up the attention in some quarters which awaits them in the future. Among the strictly scientific applications of analysis to literature, Rank's exhaustive work on the theme of incest [1912a] easily takes the first place. Its subject is bound to arouse the greatest unpopularity. Up to the present, little work based on psychoanalysis has been done in the sciences of language and history. I myself ventured the first approach to the problems of the psychology of religion by drawing a parallel between religious ritual and the ceremonials of neurotics (1907b).[2]

---

1. Cf. Rank's *Der Künstler* [*The Artist*, 1907], analyses of imaginative writers by Sadger [1909], Reik [1912, etc.], and others, my own small work on a childhood memory of Leonardo da Vinci's [1910c; *P.F.L.*, **14**, 143 ff.], and Abraham's analysis of Segantini [1911].

2. [*P.F.L.*, 13, 27 *ff.*]

Dr Pfister, a pastor in Zurich, has traced back the origin of religious fanaticism to perverse eroticism in his book on the piety of Count von Zinzendorf [1910], as well as in other contributions. In the latest works of the Zurich School, however, we find analysis permeated with religious ideas rather than the opposite outcome that had been in view.

In the four essays with the title *Totem and Taboo*[1] I have made an attempt to deal with the problems of social anthropology in the light of analysis; this line of investigation leads direct to the origins of the most important institutions of our civilization, of the structure of the state, of morality and religion, and, moreover, of the prohibition against incest and of conscience. It is no doubt too early to decide how far the conclusions thus reached will be able to withstand criticism.

The first example of an application of the analytic mode of thought to the problems of aesthetics was contained in my book on jokes.[2] Everything beyond this is still awaiting workers, who may expect a particularly rich harvest in this field. We are entirely without the co-operation of specialists in all these branches of knowledge, and in order to attract them Hanns Sachs, in 1912, founded the periodical *Imago* which is edited by him and Rank. A beginning has been made by Hitschmann and von Winterstein in throwing psychoanalytic light on philosophical systems and personalities, and here there is much need both of extended and of deeper investigation.

The revolutionary discoveries of psychoanalysis in regard to the mental life of children – the part played in it by sexual impulses (von Hug-Hellmuth [1913]), and the fate of those components of sexuality which become unserviceable in the function of reproduction – were bound early to direct attention to education and to stimulate an attempt to bring analytic points of view into the foreground in that field of work. Recognition is due to Dr Pfister for having, with sincere enthusiasm, initiated the application of psychoanalysis in this direction and brought it to the notice of ministers of religion and those concerned with education. (Cf. *The Psycho-Analytic Method*,

1. [(1912–13), ibid., **13**, 43 ff.]
2. [(1905c), ibid., **6**, 138–9, 185–8.]

1913.[1]) He has succeeded in gaining the sympathy and participation of a number of Swiss teachers in this. Other members of his profession are said to share his views but to have preferred nevertheless to remain cautiously in the background. In their retreat from psychoanalysis, a section of Vienna analysts seem to have arrived at a kind of combination of medicine and education.[2]

With this incomplete outline I have attempted to give some idea of the still incalculable wealth of connections which have come to light between medical psychoanalysis and other fields of science. There is material here for a generation of investigators to work at, and I do not doubt that the work will be carried out as soon as the resistances against psychoanalysis are overcome on its original ground.[3]

To write the story of these resistances would, I think, be both fruitless and inopportune at the present time. The story is not very creditable to the scientific men of our day. But I must add at once that it has never occurred to me to pour contempt upon the opponents of psychoanalysis merely because they were opponents – apart from the few unworthy individuals, the adventurers and profiteers, who are always to be found on both sides in time of war. I knew very well how to account for the behaviour of these opponents and, moreover, I had learnt that psychoanalysis brings out the worst in everyone. But I made up my mind not to answer my opponents and, so far as my influence went, to restrain others from polemics. Under the peculiar conditions of the controversy over psychoanalysis it seemed to me very doubtful whether either public or written discussion would avail anything; it was certain which way the majority at congresses and meetings would go, and my faith in the reasonableness and good behaviour of the gentlemen who opposed me was not at any time great. Experience shows that only very few people are capable of remaining polite, to say nothing of objective, in a scientific dispute, and the impression

1. [Freud wrote a preface to this (1913b).]
2. Adler and Furtmüller, *Heilen und Bilden* [*Healing and Educating*], 1914.
3. See my two articles in *Scientia* (1913j) [p. 27 ff. above].

made on me by scientific squabbles has always been odious. Perhaps this attitude on my part has been misunderstood; perhaps I have been thought so good-natured or so easily intimidated that no further notice need be taken of me. This was a mistake; I can be as abusive and enraged as anyone; but I have not the art of expressing the underlying emotions in a form suitable for publication and I therefore prefer to abstain completely.

Perhaps in some respects it would have been better if I had given free rein to my own passions and to those of others round me. We have all heard of the interesting attempt to explain psychoanalysis as a product of the Vienna milieu. As recently as in 1913 Janet was not ashamed to use this argument, although he himself is no doubt proud of being a Parisian, and Paris can scarcely claim to be a city of stricter morals than Vienna.[1] The suggestion is that psychoanalysis, and in particular its assertion that the neuroses are traceable to disturbances in sexual life, could only have originated in a town like Vienna – in an atmosphere of sensuality and immorality foreign to other cities – and that it is simply a reflection, a projection into theory, as it were, of these peculiar Viennese conditions. Now I am certainly no local patriot; but this theory about psychoanalysis always seems to me quite exceptionally senseless – so senseless, in fact, that I have sometimes been inclined to suppose that the reproach of being a citizen of Vienna is only a euphemistic substitute for another reproach which no one would care to put forward openly.[2] If the premises on which the argument rests were the opposite of what they are, then it might be worth giving it a hearing. If there were a town in which the inhabitants imposed exceptional restrictions on themselves as regards sexual satisfaction, and if at the same time they exhibited a marked tendency to severe neurotic disorders, that town might certainly give rise in an observer's mind to the idea that the two circumstances had some connection with each other, and might suggest that one was contingent on the

1. [The last clause of this sentence was added in 1924.]
2. [Presumably Freud's Jewish origin.]

other. But neither of these assumptions is true of Vienna. The Viennese are no more abstinent and no more neurotic than the inhabitants of any other capital city. There is rather less embarrassment – less prudery – in regard to sexual relationships than in the cities of the West and North which are so proud of their chastity. These peculiar characteristics of Vienna would be more likely to mislead the observer on the causation of neurosis than to enlighten him on it.

Vienna has done everything possible, however, to deny her share in the origin of psychoanalysis. In no other place is the hostile indifference of the learned and educated section of the population so evident to the analyst as in Vienna.

It may be that my policy of avoiding wide publicity is to some extent responsible for this. If I had encouraged or allowed the medical societies of Vienna to occupy themselves with psychoanalysis in stormy debates which would have discharged all the passions and brought into the open all the reproaches and invectives that were on its opponents' tongues or in their hearts – then, perhaps, the ban on psychoanalysis would have been overcome by now and it would no longer be a stranger in its native city. As it is, the poet may be right when he makes his Wallenstein say:

> Doch das vergeben mir die Wiener nicht,
> dass ich um ein Spektakel sie betrog.[1]

The task to which I was not equal—that of demonstrating to the opponents of psychoanalysis *suaviter in modo* their injustice and arbitrariness – was undertaken and carried out most creditably by Bleuler in a paper written in 1910, 'Freud's Psycho-Analysis: A Defence and Some Critical Remarks'. It would seem so natural for me to praise this work (which offers criticisms in both directions) that I will hasten to say what I take exception to in it. It seems to me still to display partiality, to be too lenient to the faults of the opponents of psychoanalysis and too severe on the shortcomings of its adherents. This trait

1. [Literally: 'But what the Viennese will not forgive me is having cheated them out of a spectacle.' Schiller, *Die Piccolomini*, Act II, Scene 7.]

in it may possibly explain why the opinion of a psychiatrist of such high repute, such undoubted ability and independence, failed to carry more weight with his colleagues. The author of *Affectivity* (1906*a*), ought not to be surprised if the influence of a work is determined not by the strength of its arguments but by its affective tone. Another part of its influence – its influence on the followers of psychoanalysis – was destroyed later by Bleuler himself, when in 1913 he showed the reverse side of his attitude to psychoanalysis in his 'Criticism of the Freudian Theory'. In that paper he subtracts so much from the structure of psychoanalytic theory that our opponents may well be glad of the help given them by this champion of psychoanalysis. These adverse judgements of Bleuler's, however, are not based on new arguments or better observations. They rely simply on the state of his own knowledge, the inadequacy of which he no longer himself admits, as he did in his earlier works. It seemed therefore that an almost irreparable loss threatened psychoanalysis here. But in his last publication, 'Criticisms of my *Schizophrenia*' (1914), Bleuler rallies his forces in the face of the attacks made on him for having introduced psychoanalysis into his book on schizophrenia, and makes what he himself calls a 'presumptuous claim'. 'But now I will make a presumptuous claim: I consider that up to the present the various schools of psychology have contributed extremely little towards explaining the nature of psychogenic symptoms and diseases, but that depth-psychology offers something towards a psychology which still awaits creation and which physicians are in need of in order to understand their patients and to cure them rationally; and I even believe that in my *Schizophrenia* I have taken a very short step towards that understanding. The first two assertions are certainly correct; the last may be an error.'

Since by 'depth-psychology' he means nothing else but psychoanalysis, we may for the present be content with this acknowledgement.

III

Mach es kurz!
Am Jüngsten Tag ist's nur ein Furz! [1]
GOETHE

Two years after the first private Congress of psychoanalysts the second took place, this time at Nuremberg, in March 1910. In the interval between them, influenced partly by the favourable reception in America, by the increasing hostility in German-speaking countries, and by the unforeseen acquisition of support from Zurich, I had conceived a project which with the help of my friend Ferenczi I carried out at this second Congress. What I had in mind was to organize the psycho-analytic movement, to transfer its centre to Zurich and to give it a chief who would look after its future career. As this scheme has met with much opposition among the adherents of psychoanalysis, I will set out my reasons for it in some detail. I hope that these will justify me, even though it turns out that what I did was in fact not very wise.

I judged that the new movement's association with Vienna was no recommendation but rather a handicap to it. A place in the heart of Europe like Zurich, where an academic teacher had opened the doors of his institution to psychoanalysis, seemed to me much more promising. I also took it that a

1. [Literally: 'Cut it short! On the Day of Judgement it is no more than a fart.' The lines occur in some ironic verses written late in Goethe's life (Grossherzog Wilhelm Ernst Ausgabe, 15, 400–1). Satan is represented in them as bringing up a number of charges against Napoleon, and the words quoted by Freud are God the Father's reply. Freud had many years earlier (on 4 December 1896) quoted the same words in a letter to Fliess, as the suggested motto for a chapter on 'Resistance' (Freud, 1950a, Letter 51). Two possible explanations, not necessarily incompatible, may be offered for Freud's use of the quotation in the present connection. He may be applying the words to the criticisms put forward by the opponents of psychoanalysis, or he may be applying them ironically to himself for wasting his time on such trivialities.]

second handicap lay in my own person, opinion about which was too much confused by the liking or hatred of the different sides: I was either compared to Columbus, Darwin and Kepler, or abused as a general paralytic. I wished, therefore, to withdraw into the background both myself and the city where psychoanalysis first saw the light. Moreover, I was no longer young; I saw that there was a long road ahead, and I felt oppressed by the thought that the duty of being a leader should fall to me so late in life.[1] Yet I felt that there must be someone at the head. I knew only too well the pitfalls that lay in wait for anyone who became engaged in analysis, and hoped that many of them might be avoided if an authority could be set up who would be prepared to instruct and admonish. This position had at first been occupied by myself, owing to my fifteen years' start in experience which nothing could counterbalance. I felt the need of transferring this authority to a younger man, who would then as a matter of course take my place after my death. This man could only be C. G. Jung, since Bleuler was my contemporary in age; in favour of Jung were his exceptional talents, the contributions he had already made to psychoanalysis, his independent position and the impression of assured energy which his personality conveyed. In addition to this, he seemed ready to enter into a friendly relationship with me and for my sake to give up certain racial prejudices which he had previously permitted himself. I had no inkling at that time that in spite of all these advantages the choice was a most unfortunate one, that I had lighted upon a person who was incapable of tolerating the authority of another, but who was still less capable of wielding it himself, and whose energies were relentlessly devoted to the furtherance of his own interests.

I considered it necessary to form an official association because I feared the abuses to which psychoanalysis would be subjected as soon as it became popular. There should be some headquarters whose business it would be to declare: 'All this nonsense is nothing to do with analysis; this is not psychoanalysis.' At the sessions of the local groups (which together

1. [In 1910 Freud was 54.]

would constitute the international association) instruction should be given as to how psychoanalysis was to be conducted and doctors should be trained, whose activities would then receive a kind of guarantee. Moreover, it seemed to me desirable, since official science had pronounced its solemn ban upon psychoanalysis and had declared a boycott against doctors and institutions practising it, that the adherents of psychoanalysis should come together for friendly communication with one another and mutual support.

This and nothing else was what I hoped to achieve by founding the International Psycho-Analytical Association. It was probably more than could be attained. Just as my opponents were to discover that it was not possible to stem the tide of the new movement, so I was to find that it would not proceed in the direction I wished to mark out for it. The proposals made by Ferenczi in Nuremberg were adopted, it is true; Jung was elected President and made Riklin his Secretary; the publication of a bulletin which should link the Central Executive with the local groups was resolved upon. The object of the Association was declared to be 'to foster and further the science of psychoanalysis founded by Freud, both as pure psychology and in its application to medicine and the mental sciences; and to promote mutual support among its members in all endeavours to acquire and to spread psychoanalytic knowledge'. The scheme was strongly opposed only by the Vienna group. Adler, in great excitement, expressed the fear that 'censorship and restrictions on scientific freedom' were intended. Finally the Viennese gave in, after having secured that the seat of the Association should be not Zurich, but the place of residence of the President for the time being, who was to be elected for two years.

At this Congress three local groups were constituted: one in Berlin, under the chairmanship of Abraham; one in Zurich, whose head had become the President of the whole Association; and one in Vienna, the direction of which I made over to Adler. A fourth group, in Budapest, could not be formed until later. Bleuler had not attended the Congress on account of illness, and later he evinced hesitation about joining the Association on general grounds; he let himself be persuaded to do so, it is true, after a personal conversation with me, but resigned again shortly afterwards as a result of disagreements in Zurich. This severed the connection between the Zurich local group and the Burghölzli institution.

One outcome of the Nuremberg Congress was the founding of the *Zentralblatt für Psychoanalyse*, for which purpose Adler and Stekel joined forces. It was obviously intended originally to represent the Opposition: it was meant to win back for Vienna the hegemony threatened by the election of Jung. But when the two founders of the journal, labouring under the difficulties of finding a publisher, assured me of their peaceful intentions and as a guarantee of their sincerity gave me a right of veto, I accepted the direction of it and worked energetically for the new organ; its first number appeared in September 1910.

I will now continue the story of the Psycho-Analytical Congresses. The third Congress took place in September 1911, at Weimar, and was even more successful than the previous ones in its general atmosphere and scientific interest. J. J. Putnam, who was present on this occasion, declared afterwards in America how much pleasure it had given him and expressed his respect for 'the mental attitude' of those who attended it, quoting some words I was said to have used in reference to them: 'They have learnt to tolerate a bit of truth.' (Putnam, 1912.) It is a fact that no one who had attended scientific congresses could have failed to carry away a favourable impression of the Psycho-Analytical Association. I myself had conducted the first two congresses and I had allowed every speaker time for his paper, leaving discussions to take place in private afterwards among the members. Jung, as President, took over the direction at Weimar and reintroduced formal discussions after each paper, which, however, did not give rise to any difficulties as yet.

A very different picture was presented by the fourth Congress, held in Munich two years later, in September 1913. It is still fresh in the memory of all who were present. It was conducted by Jung in a disagreeable and incorrect manner; the speakers were restricted in time and the discussions overwhelmed the papers. By a malicious stroke of chance it happened that that evil genius, Hoche,[1] had settled in the very building in which the meetings were held. Hoche would have had no difficulty in convincing himself of the nonsense which the analysts made of his description of them as a fanatical sect blindly submissive to their leader. The fatiguing and unedifying proceedings ended in the re-election of Jung to the Presidency of the International Psycho-Analytical Association, which he accepted, although two-fifths of those present refused him their support. We dispersed without any desire to meet again.

At about the time of this Congress the strength of the International Psycho-Analytical Association was as follows. The local groups in Vienna, Berlin and Zurich had been formed at the Congress in Nuremberg as early as 1910. In May 1911 a group at Munich under the chairmanship of Dr L. Seif was added. In the same year the first American local group was formed under the chairmanship of A. A. Brill, with the name 'The New York Psychoanalytic Society'. At the Weimar Congress the foundation of a second American group was authorized; it came into existence during the following year under the name of 'The American Psychoanalytic Association', and included members from Canada and the whole of America; Putnam was elected President and Ernest Jones Secretary. Shortly before the Congress in Munich in 1913, the Budapest local group was formed under the chairmanship of Ferenczi. Soon after this the first English group was formed by Ernest Jones, who had returned to London. The membership of these local groups, of which there were now eight, naturally affords no means of estimating the number of unorganized students and adherents of psychoanalysis.

The development of the periodicals devoted to psychoanalysis also deserves a brief mention. The first of these was

1. [See footnote, p. 85.]

a series of monographs entitled *Schriften zur angewandten See-lenkunde*, which have appeared irregularly since 1907 and now number fifteen issues. (The publisher was to begin with Heller in Vienna and later F. Deuticke.) They comprise works by Freud ([1907a, 1910c] Nos. 1 and 7), Riklin [1908], Jung [1908], Abraham ([1909, 1911] Nos. 4 and 11), Rank ([1909, 1911] Nos. 5 and 13), Sadger [1909], Pfister [1910], Max Graf [1911], Jones ([1911b, 1912a] Nos. 10 and 14), Storfer [1911] and von Hug-Hellmuth [1913].[1] When the journal *Imago* (which will be referred to shortly) was founded, this form of publication ceased to have quite the same value. After the meeting at Salzburg in 1908, the *Jahrbuch für psychoanalytische und psychopathologische Forschungen* was founded, which appeared for five years under Jung's editorship and has now re-emerged, under two new editors[2] and with a slight change in its title, as the *Jahrbuch der Psychoanalyse*. It is no longer intended to be, as it has been in recent years, merely a repository for the publication of self-contained works. Instead, it will endeavour, through the activity of its editors, to fulfil the aim of recording all the work done and all the advances made in the sphere of psychoanalysis.[3] The *Zentralblatt für Psychoanalyse*, which, as I have already said, was started by Adler and Stekel after the foundation of the International Psycho-Analytical Association in Nuremberg in 1910, has, during its short existence, had a stormy career. As early as in the tenth number of the first volume [July 1911] an announcement appeared on the front page that, on account of scientific differences of opinion with the director, Dr Alfred Adler had decided to withdraw voluntarily from the editorship. After this Dr Stekel remained the only editor (from the summer of 1911). At the Weimar Congress [September 1911] the *Zentralblatt* was raised to the position of official organ of the International Association and

1. [*Footnote added* 1924:] Since then, further works have appeared, by Sadger ([1914, 1920] Nos. 16 and 18) and Kielholz ([1919] No. 17).

2. [See p. 63 *n.* 2 above.]

3. [*Footnote added* 1924:] It ceased publication at the beginning of the war [after only a single volume (1914) had been issued].

made available to all members in return for an increase in the annual subscription. From the third number of the second volume [1] onwards (winter [December] 1912) Stekel became solely responsible for its contents. His behaviour, of which it is not easy to publish an account, had compelled me to resign the direction and hurriedly to establish a new organ for psychoanalysis – the *Internationale Zeitschrift für ärztliche Psychoanalyse*. The combined efforts of almost all our workers and of Hugo Heller, the new publisher, resulted in the appearance of the first number in January 1913, whereupon it took the place of the *Zentralblatt* as official organ of the International Psycho-Analytical Association.

Meanwhile, early in 1912, a new periodical, *Imago* (published by Heller), designed exclusively for the application of psychoanalysis to the mental sciences, was founded by Dr Hanns Sachs and Dr Otto Rank. *Imago* is now in the middle of its third volume and is read with interest by a continually increasing number of subscribers, some of whom have little connection with medical analysis. [2]

Apart from these four periodical publications (*Schriften zur angewandten Seelenkunde, Jahrbuch, Zeitschrift* and *Imago*) other German and foreign journals publish works which may claim a place in the literature of psychoanalysis. *The Journal of Abnormal Psychology*, directed by Morton Prince, usually contains so many good analytic contributions that it must be regarded as the principal representative of analytic literature in America. In the winter of 1913, White and Jelliffe in New

1. ['Second volume' in all former editions. It should in fact be 'third volume'. The volumes ran from October to September.]

2. [*Footnote added* 1924:] The publication of these two periodicals was transferred in 1919 to the Internationaler Psychoanalytischer Verlag. At the present time (1923) they are both in their ninth volume. (Actually, the *Internationale Zeitschrift* is in the eleventh and *Imago* in the twelfth year of its existence, but, in consequence of events during the war, Volume IV of the *Zeitschrift* covered more than one year, i.e. the years 1916–18, and Volume V of *Imago* the years 1917–18.) With the beginning of Volume VI the word 'ärztliche' ['medical'] was dropped from the title of the *Internationale Zeitschrift*.

York started a new periodical (*The Psychoanalytic Review*) which is devoted exclusively to psychoanalysis, no doubt bearing in mind the fact that most medical men in America who are interested in analysis find the German language a difficulty.[1]

I must now mention two secessions which have taken place among the adherents of psychoanalysis; the first occurred between the founding of the Association in 1910 and the Weimar Congress in 1911; the second took place after this and became manifest at Munich in 1913. The disappointment that they caused me might have been averted if I had paid more attention to the reactions of patients under analytic treatment. I knew very well of course that anyone may take to flight at his first approach to the unwelcome truths of analysis; I had always myself maintained that everyone's understanding of it is limited by his own repressions (or rather, by the resistances which sustain them) so that he cannot go beyond a particular point in his relation to analysis. But I had not expected that anyone who had reached a certain depth in his understanding of analysis could renounce that understanding and lose it. And yet daily experience with patients had shown that total rejection of analytic knowledge may result whenever a specially strong resistance arises at any depth in the mind; one may have succeeded in laboriously bringing a patient to grasp some parts of analytic knowledge and to handle them like possessions of his own, and yet one may see him, under the domination of the very next resistance, throw all he has learnt to the winds and stand on the defensive as he did in the days when he was a carefree beginner. I had to learn that the very same thing can happen with psychoanalysts as with patients in analysis.

It is no easy or enviable task to write the history of these two secessions, partly because I am without any strong personal motive for doing so – I had not expected gratitude nor am I revengeful to any effective degree – and partly because I know that by doing so I shall lay myself open to the invectives of my

1. [*Footnote added* 1924:] In 1920 Ernest Jones undertook the founding of *The International Journal of Psycho-Analysis*, intended for readers in England and America.

not too scrupulous opponents and offer the enemies of analysis the spectacle they so heartily desire – of 'the psychoanalysts tearing one another limb from limb'. After exercising so much self-restraint in not coming to blows with opponents outside analysis, I now see myself compelled to take up arms against its former followers or people who still like to call themselves its followers. I have no choice in the matter, however; only indolence or cowardice could lead one to keep silence, and silence would cause more harm than a frank revelation of the harms that already exist. Anyone who has followed the growth of other scientific movements will know that the same upheavals and dissensions commonly occur in them as well. It may be that elsewhere they are more carefully concealed; but psychoanalysis, which repudiates so many conventional ideals, is more honest in these matters too.

Another very severe drawback is that I cannot entirely avoid throwing some analytic light on these two opposition movements. Analysis is not suited, however, for polemical use; it presupposes the consent of the person who is being analysed and a situation in which there is a superior and a subordinate. Anyone, therefore, who undertakes an analysis for polemical purposes must expect the person analysed to use analysis against him in turn, so that the discussion will reach a state which entirely excludes the possibility of convincing any impartial third person. I shall therefore restrict to a minimum my use of analytic knowledge, and, with it, of indiscretion and aggressiveness towards my opponents; and I may also point out that I am not basing any scientific criticism on these grounds. I am not concerned with the truth that may be contained in the theories which I am rejecting, nor shall I attempt to refute them. I shall leave that task to other qualified workers in the field of psychoanalysis, and it has, indeed, already been partly accomplished. I wish merely to show that these theories controvert the fundamental principles of analysis (and on what points they controvert them) and that for this reason they should not be known by the name of analysis. So I shall avail myself of analysis only in order to explain how these divergences from it could arise among analysts. When I come to the points at which the divergences occurred, I shall have, it is true, to defend the just rights of psychoanalysis with some remarks of a purely critical nature.

The first task confronting psychoanalysis was to explain the neuroses; it used the two facts of resistance and transference as starting-points, and, taking into consideration the third fact of amnesia, accounted for them with its theories of repression, of the sexual motive forces in neurosis and of the unconscious. Psychoanalysis has never claimed to provide a complete theory of human mentality in general, but only expected that what it offered should be applied to supplement and correct the knowledge acquired by other means. Adler's theory, however, goes far beyond this point; it seeks at one stroke to explain the behaviour and character of human beings as well as their neurotic and psychotic illnesses. It is actually more suited to any other field than that of neurosis, although for reasons connected with the history of its development it still places this in the foreground. For many years I had opportunities of studying Dr Adler and have never refused to recognize his unusual ability, combined with a particularly speculative disposition. As an instance of the 'persecution' to which he asserts he has been subjected by me, I can point to the fact that after the Association was founded I made over to him the leadership of the Vienna group. It was not until urgent demands were put forward by all the members of the Society that I let myself be persuaded to take the chair again at its scientific meetings. When I perceived how little gift Adler had precisely for judging unconscious material, my view changed to an expectation that he would succeed in discovering the connections of psychoanalysis with psychology and with the biological foundations of instinctual processes – an expectation which was in some sense justified by the valuable work he had done on 'organ inferiority' [Adler, 1907]. And he did in fact effect something of the kind; but his work conveys an impression 'as if' – to speak in his own 'jargon' [1] – it was intended

1. [The terms 'as if' and 'jargon' figure prominently in Adler's writings.]

to prove that psychoanalysis was wrong in everything and that it had only attributed so much importance to sexual motive forces because of its credulity in accepting the assertions of neurotics. I may even speak publicly of the personal motive for his work, since he himself announced it in the presence of a small circle of members of the Vienna group: 'Do you think it gives me such great pleasure to stand in your shadow my whole life long?' To be sure, I see nothing reprehensible in a younger man freely admitting his ambition, which one would in any case guess was among the incentives for his work. But even though a man is dominated by a motive of this kind he should know how to avoid being what the English, with their fine social tact, call 'unfair' – which in German can only be expressed by a much cruder word. How little Adler has succeeded in this is shown by the profusion of petty outbursts of malice which disfigure his writings and by the indications they contain of an uncontrolled craving for priority. At the Vienna Psycho-Analytical Society we once actually heard him claim priority for the conception of the 'unity of the neuroses' and for the 'dynamic view' of them. This came as a great surprise to me, for I had always believed that these two principles were stated by me before I ever made Adler's acquaintance.

This striving of Adler's for a place in the sun has, however, had one result which is bound to be beneficial to psychoanalysis. When, after irreconcilable scientific disagreements had come to light, I was obliged to bring about Adler's resignation from the editorship of the Zentralblatt, he left the Vienna Society as well, and founded a new one, which at first adopted the tasteful name of 'The Society for Free Psycho-Analysis' ['Verein für freie Psychoanalyse']. But outsiders who are unconnected with analysis are evidently as unskilful in appreciating the differences between the views of two psychoanalysts as we Europeans are in detecting the differences between two Chinese faces. 'Free' psychoanalysis remained in the shadow of 'official', 'orthodox' psychoanalysis and was treated merely as an appendage to the latter. Then Adler took a step for which we are thankful; he severed all connection with psychoanalysis, and gave his theory the name of 'Individual Psychology'. There is room enough on God's earth, and anyone who can has a perfect right to potter about on it without being prevented; but it is not a desirable thing for people who have ceased to understand one another and have grown incompatible with one another to remain under the same roof. Adler's 'Individual Psychology' is now one of the many schools of psychology which are adverse to psychoanalysis and its further development is no concern of ours.[1]

The Adlerian theory was from the very beginning a 'system' – which psychoanalysis was careful to avoid becoming. It is also a remarkably good example of 'secondary revision', such as occurs, for instance, in the process to which dream material is submitted by the action of waking thought. In Adler's case the place of dream material is taken by the new material obtained through psychoanalytic studies; this is then viewed purely from the standpoint of the ego, reduced to the categories with which the ego is familiar, translated, twisted and – exactly as happens in dream formation – is misunderstood.[2] Moreover, the Adlerian theory is characterized less by what it asserts than by what it denies, so that it consists of three sorts of elements of quite dissimilar value: useful contributions to the psychology of the ego, superfluous but admissible translations of the analytic facts into the new 'jargon', and distortions and perversions of these facts when they do not comply with the requirements of the ego.

The elements of the first sort have never been ignored by psychoanalysis, although they did not deserve any special attention from it; it was more concerned to show that every ego trend contains libidinal components. The Adlerian theory emphasizes the counterpart to this, the egoistic constituent in libidinal instinctual impulses. This would have been an appreciable gain if Adler had not on every occasion used this observation in order to deny the libidinal impulses in favour of their egoistic instinctual components. His theory does what

1. [See p. 60 above.]
2. [See *The Interpretation of Dreams* (1900a), P.F.L., **4**, 630–1.]

every patient does and what our conscious thought in general does – namely, makes use of a *rationalization*, as Jones [1908] has called it, in order to conceal the unconscious motive. Adler is so consistent in this that he positively considers that the strongest motive force in the sexual act is the man's intention of showing himself master of the woman – of being 'on top'. I do not know if he has expressed these monstrous notions in his writings.

Psychoanalysis recognized early that every neurotic symptom owes its possibility of existence to a compromise. Every symptom must therefore in some way comply with the demands of the ego which manipulates the repression; it must offer some advantage, it must admit of some useful application, or it would meet with the same fate as the original instinctual impulse itself which has been fended off. The term 'gain from illness' has taken this into account; one is even justified in differentiating the 'primary' gain to the ego, which must be operative at the time of the generation of the symptom, from a 'secondary' part, which supervenes in attachment to other purposes of the ego, if the symptom is to persist.[1] It has also long been known that the withdrawal of this gain from illness, or its disappearance in consequence of some change in real external circumstances, constitutes one of the mechanisms of a cure of the symptom. In the Adlerian doctrine the main emphasis falls on these easily verifiable and clearly intelligible connections, while the fact is altogether overlooked that on countless occasions the ego is merely making a virtue of necessity in submitting, because of its usefulness, to the very disagreeable symptom which is forced upon it – for instance, in accepting anxiety as a means to security. The ego is here playing the ludicrous part of the clown in a circus who by his gestures tries to convince the audience that every change in the

1. [A full discussion of 'gain from illness' will be found in Lecture 24 of the *Introductory Lectures* (1916–17), *P.F.L.*, **1**, 429–33; it is mentioned again in a footnote added in 1923 to the 'Dora' case history (1905*e*), ibid., **8**, 75–6 *n*., where Freud revised his earlier views, and gives what is probably the clearest account of the topic.]

circus ring is being carried out under his orders. But only the youngest of the spectators are deceived by him.

Psychoanalysis is obliged to give its backing to the second constituent of Adler's theory as it would to something of its own. And in fact it is nothing else than psychoanalytic knowledge, which that author extracted from sources open to everyone during ten years of work in common and which he has now labelled as his own by a change in nomenclature. I myself consider 'safeguarding [*Sicherung*]', for instance, a better term than 'protective measure [*Schutzmassregel*]' which is the one I employ; but I cannot discover any difference in their meaning. Again, a host of familiar features come to light in Adler's propositions when one restores the earlier 'fantasied' and 'fantasy' in place of 'feigned [*fingiert*]', 'fictive' and 'fiction'. The identity of these terms would be insisted upon by psychoanalysis even if their author had not taken part in our common work over a period of many years.

The third part of the Adlerian theory, the twisted interpretations and distortions of the disagreeable facts of analysis, are what definitely separate 'Individual Psychology', as it is now to be called, from psychoanalysis. As we know, the principle of Adler's system is that the individual's aim of self-assertion, his 'will to power', is what, in the form of a 'masculine protest', plays a dominating part in the conduct of life, in character formation and in neurosis. This 'masculine protest', the Adlerian motive force, is nothing else, however, but repression detached from its psychological mechanism and, moreover, sexualized in addition – which ill accords with the vaunted ejection of sexuality from its place in mental life.[1] The 'masculine protest' undoubtedly exists, but if it is made into the [sole] motive force of mental life the observed facts are

1. [The term 'masculine protest' was introduced by Adler in a paper to the Nuremberg Congress (Adler, 1910). A detailed criticism of the concept, and of Adler's theory of repression, is given in Freud's paper ' "A Child is Being Beaten"' (1919e), *P.F.L.*, **10**, 189–93. Cf. also Freud's papers 'On Narcissism' (1914c), ibid., **11**, 86–7, and 'A Seventeenth-Century Demonological Neurosis' (1923d), ibid., **14**, 407–8.]

being treated like a spring-board that is left behind after it has been used to jump off from. Let us consider one of the fundamental situations in which desire is felt in infancy: that of a child observing the sexual act between adults. Analysis shows, in the case of people with whose life-story the physician will later be concerned, that at such moments two impulses take possession of the immature spectator. In boys, one is the impulse to put himself in the place of the active man, and the other, the opposing current, is the impulse to identify himself with the passive woman.[1] Between them these two impulses exhaust the pleasurable possibilities of the situation. The first alone can come under the head of the masculine protest, if that concept is to retain any meaning at all. The second, however, the further course of which Adler disregards or which he knows nothing about, is the one that will become the more important in the subsequent neurosis. Adler has so merged himself in the jealous narrowness of the ego that he takes account only of those instinctual impulses which are agreeable to the ego and are encouraged by it; the situation in neurosis, in which the impulses are *opposed* to the ego, is precisely the one that lies beyond his horizon.

In connection with the attempt, which psychoanalysis has made necessary, to correlate the fundamental principle of its theory with the mental life of children, Adler exhibits the most serious departures from actual observation and the most fundamental confusion in his concepts. The biological, social and psychological meanings of 'masculine' and 'feminine' are here hopelessly mixed.[2] It is impossible, and is disproved by observation, that a child, whether male or female, should found the plan of its life on an original depreciation of the female sex and take the wish to be a real man as its 'guiding line'.[3] Children have, to begin with, no idea of the significance of the distinction between the sexes; on the contrary, they start with

1. [Cf. Chapter III of *The Ego and the Id* (1923b), ibid., **11**, 372.]
2. [Cf. a footnote added in 1915 to the *Three Essays* (1905d), *P.F.L.*, **7**, 141 n. 1.]
3. ['*Leitlinie*', a term constantly used by Adler.]

the assumption that the same genital organ (the male one) is possessed by both sexes; they do not begin their sexual researches with the problem of the distinction between the sexes,[1] while the *social* underestimation of women is completely foreign to them. There are women in whose neurosis the wish to be a man has played no part. Whatever in the nature of a masculine protest can be shown to exist is easily traceable to a disturbance in primary narcissism due to threats of castration or to the earliest interferences with sexual activities. All disputes about the psychogenesis of the neuroses must eventually be decided in the field of the neuroses of childhood. Careful dissection of a neurosis in early childhood puts an end to all misapprehensions about the aetiology of the neuroses and to all doubts about the part played by the sexual instincts in them.[2] That is why, in his criticism of Jung's paper 'Psychic Conflicts in a Child' [1910b], Adler [1911a] was obliged to resort to the imputation that the facts of the case had been one-sidedly arranged, 'no doubt by the [child's] father'.

I will not dwell any longer on the biological aspect of the Adlerian theory nor discuss whether either actual 'organ inferiority' [p. 110] or the subjective feeling of it – one does not know which – is really capable of serving as the foundation of Adler's system. I will merely remark in passing that if it were so neurosis would appear as a by-product of every kind of physical decrepitude, whereas observation shows that an impressive majority of ugly, misshapen, crippled and miserable people fail to react to their defects by neurosis. Nor will I deal with the interesting assertion according to which inferiority is to be traced back to the feeling of being a child. It shows the disguise under which the factor of infantilism, which is so strongly emphasized by psychoanalysis, reappears in 'Individual Psychology'. On the other hand, I must point out how all the psychological acquisitions of psychoanalysis have

1. [This statement (which was repeated in a passage added in 1915 to the *Three Essays* (1905d), *P.F.L.*, **7**, 113) was corrected in his later paper on the distinction between the sexes (1925j), ibid., **7**, 336 n. 2.]

2. [This is the main thesis of Freud's 'Wolf Man' analysis (1918b), *P.F.L.*, **9**, 225 ff., which was drafted a few months before the present paper.]

been thrown to the winds by Adler. In his book *Über den nervösen Charakter* [1912] the unconscious is still mentioned as a psychological peculiarity, without, however, any relation to his system. Later, he has consistently declared that it is a matter of indifference to him whether an idea is conscious or unconscious. Adler has never from the first shown any understanding of repression. In an abstract of a paper read by him at the Vienna Society (February 1911) he wrote that it must be pointed out that the evidence in a particular case showed that the patient had never repressed his libido, but had been continually 'safeguarding' himself against it [cf. Adler, 1911c]. Soon afterwards, in a discussion at the Vienna Society, he said: 'If you ask where repression comes from, you are told, "from civilization"; but if you go on to ask where civilization comes from, you are told "from repression". So you see it is all simply playing with words.'[1] A tithe of the acuteness and ingenuity with which Adler has unmasked the defensive devices of the 'nervous character' would have been enough to show him the way out of this pettifogging argument. What is meant is simply that civilization is based on the repressions effected by former generations, and that each fresh generation is required to maintain this civilization by effecting the same repressions. I once heard of a child who thought people were laughing at him, and began to cry, because when he asked where eggs come from he was told 'from hens', and when he went on to ask where hens come from he was told 'from eggs'. But they were not playing with words; on the contrary, they were telling him the truth.

Everything that Adler has to say about dreams, the shibboleth of psychoanalysis, is equally empty and unmeaning. At first he regarded dreams as a turning away from the feminine to the masculine line – which is simply a translation of the wish-fulfilment theory of dreams into the language of the 'masculine protest'. Later he found that the essence of dreams lies in enabling men to accomplish unconsciously what they are denied consciously. Adler [1911b, 215 n.] must also be credited with priority in confusing dreams with latent dream-

1. [Cf. Nunberg and Federn (1974, 142, 171).]

thoughts – a confusion on which the discovery of his 'prospective tendency' rests. Maeder [1912] followed his lead in this later.[1] Here the fact is readily overlooked that every interpretation of a dream which is incomprehensible in its manifest form is based on the very method of dream interpretation whose premisses and conclusions are being disputed. In regard to resistance Adler informs us that it serves the purpose of putting into effect the patient's opposition to the physician. This is certainly true; it is as much as to say that it serves the purpose of resistance. Where it comes from, however, or how it happens that its phenomena are at the disposal of the patient is not further inquired into, as being of no interest to the ego. The detailed mechanism of the symptoms and manifestations of diseases, the explanation of the manifold variety of those diseases and their forms of expression are disregarded *in toto*; for everything alike is pressed into the service of the masculine protest, self-assertion and the aggrandizement of the personality. The system is complete; to produce it has cost an enormous amount of labour in the recasting of interpretations, while it has not furnished a single new observation. I fancy I have made it clear that it has nothing to do with psychoanalysis.

The view of life which is reflected in the Adlerian system is founded exclusively on the aggressive instinct; there is no room in it for love. We might feel surprise that such a cheerless *Weltanshauung* should have met with any attention at all; but we must not forget that human beings, weighed down by the burden of their sexual needs, are ready to accept anything if only the 'overcoming of sexuality' is offered them as a bait.

Adler's secession took place before the Weimar Congress in 1911; after that date the Swiss began theirs. The first signs of it, curiously enough, were a few remarks of Riklin's in some popular articles appearing in Swiss publications, so that the general public learned earlier than those most intimately concerned in the subject that psychoanalysis had got the better of

1. [See a footnote added in 1914 to *The Interpretation of Dreams* (1900a), P.F.L., **4**, 735–6 n. 1.]

some regrettable errors which had previously discredited it. In 1912 Jung boasted, in a letter from America, that his modifications of psychoanalysis had overcome the resistances of many people who had hitherto refused to have anything to do with it. I replied that that was nothing to boast of, and that the more he sacrificed of the hard-won truths of psychoanalysis the more would he see resistances vanishing. [Cf. Freud (1974a, 515 and n. 1, 517.] This modification which the Swiss were so proud of introducing was again nothing else but a pushing into the background of the sexual factor in psychoanalytic theory. I confess that from the beginning I regarded this 'advance' as too far-reaching an adjustment to the demands of actuality.

These two retrograde movements away from psychoanalysis, which I must now compare with each other, show another point in common: for they both court a favourable opinion by putting forward certain lofty ideas, which view things, as it were, *sub specie aeternitatis*. With Adler, this part is played by the relativity of all knowledge and the right of the personality to put an artificial construction on the data of knowledge according to individual taste; with Jung, the appeal is made to the historic right of youth to throw off the fetters in which tyrannical age with its hidebound views seeks to bind it. A few words must be devoted to exposing the fallacy of these ideas.

The relativity of our knowledge is a consideration which may be advanced against every other science just as well as against psychoanalysis. It is derived from familiar reactionary currents of present-day feeling which are hostile to science, and it lays claims to an appearance of superiority to which no one is entitled. None of us can guess what the ultimate judgement of mankind about our theoretical efforts will be. There are instances in which rejection by the first three generations has been corrected by the succeeding one and changed into recognition. After a man has listened carefully to the voice of criticism in himself and has paid some attention to the criticisms of his opponents, there is nothing for him to do but with all his strength to maintain his own convictions which are based on experience. One should be content to conduct one's case honestly, and should not assume the office of judge, which is reserved for the remote future. The stress on arbitrary personal views in scientific matters is bad; it is clearly an attempt to dispute the right of psychoanalysis to be valued as a science – after that value, incidentally, has already been depreciated by what has been said before [on the relative nature of all knowledge]. Anyone who sets a high value on scientific thought will rather seek every possible means and method of circumscribing the factor of fanciful personal predilections as far as possible wherever it still plays too great a part. Moreover, it is opportune to recall that any zeal in defending ourselves is out of place. These arguments of Adler's are not intended seriously. They are only meant for use against his opponents; they do not touch his own theories. Nor have they prevented his followers from hailing him as the Messiah, for whose appearance expectant humanity has been prepared by a number of forerunners. The Messiah is certainly no relative phenomenon.

Jung's argument *ad captandam benevolentiam* [1] rests on the too optimistic assumption that the progress of the human race, of civilization and knowledge, has always pursued an unbroken line; as if there had been no periods of decadence, no reactions and restorations after every revolution, no generations who have taken a backward step and abandoned the gains of their predecessors. His approach to the standpoint of the masses, his abandonment of an innovation which proved unwelcome, make it *a priori* improbable that Jung's corrected version of psychoanalysis can justly claim to be a youthful act of liberation. After all, it is not the age of the doer that decides this but the character of the deed.

Of the two movements under discussion Adler's is indubitably the more important; while radically false, it is marked by consistency and coherence. It is, moreover, in spite of everything, founded upon a theory of the instincts. Jung's modification, on the other hand, loosens the connection of the

1. ['For the purpose of gaining good-will.']

phenomena with instinctual life; and further, as its critics (e.g. Abraham, Ferenczi and Jones) have pointed out, it is so obscure, unintelligible and confused as to make it difficult to take up any position upon it. Wherever one lays hold of anything, one must be prepared to hear that one has misunderstood it, and one cannot see how to arrive at a correct understanding of it. It is put forward in a peculiarly vacillating manner, one moment as 'quite a mild deviation, which does not justify the outcry that has been raised about it' (Jung), and the next moment as a new message of salvation which is to begin a new epoch for psychoanalysis, and, indeed, a new *Weltanschauung* for everyone.

When one thinks of the inconsistencies displayed in the various public and private pronouncements made by the Jungian movement, one is bound to ask oneself how much of this is due to lack of clearness and how much to lack of sincerity. It must be admitted, however, that the exponents of the new theory find themselves in a difficult position. They are now disputing things which they themselves formerly upheld, and they are doing so, moreover, not on the ground of fresh observations which might have taught them something further, but in consequence of fresh interpretations which make the things they see look different to them now from what they did before. For this reason they are unwilling to give up their connection with psychoanalysis, as whose representatives they became known to the world, and prefer to give it out that psychoanalysis has changed. At the Munich Congress I found it necessary to clear up this confusion, and I did so by declaring that I did not recognize the innovations of the Swiss as legitimate continuations and further developments of the psychoanalysis that originated with me. Outside critics (like Furtmüller) had already seen how things were, and Abraham is right in saying that Jung is in full retreat from psychoanalysis. I am of course perfectly ready to allow that everyone has a right to think and to write what he pleases; but he has no right to put it forward as something other than what it really is.

Just as Adler's investigation brought something new to

psychoanalysis – a contribution to the psychology of the ego – and then expected us to pay too high a price for this gift by throwing over all the fundamental theories of analysis, so in the same way Jung and his followers paved the way for their fight against psychoanalysis by presenting it with a new acquisition. They traced in detail (as Pfister did before them) the way in which the material of sexual ideas belonging to the family complex and incestuous object-choice is made use of in representing the highest ethical and religious interests of man – that is, they have illuminated an important instance of the sublimation of the erotic instinctual forces and of their transformation into trends which can no longer be called erotic. This was in complete harmony with all the expectations of psychoanalysis, and would have agreed very well with the view that in dreams and neurosis a regressive dissolution of this sublimation, as of all others, becomes visible. But the world would have risen in indignation and protested that ethics and religion were being sexualized. Now I cannot refrain from thinking teleologically for once and concluding that these discoverers were not equal to meeting such a storm of indignation. Perhaps it even began to rage in their own bosoms. The theological prehistory of so many of the Swiss throws no less light on their attitude to psychoanalysis than does Adler's socialist prehistory on the development of his psychology. One is reminded of Mark Twain's famous story of all the things that happened to his watch and of his concluding words: 'And he used to wonder what became of all the unsuccessful tinkers, and gunsmiths, and shoemakers, and blacksmiths; but nobody could ever tell him.'

Suppose – to make use of a simile – that in a particular social group there lives a *parvenu*, who boasts of being descended from a noble family living in another place. It is pointed out to him, however, that his parents live somewhere in the neighbourhood, and that they are quite humble people. There is only one way of escape from his difficulty and he seizes on it. He can no longer repudiate his parents, but he asserts that they themselves are of noble lineage and have merely come down in the world; and he procures a family-tree from some obliging official source. It seems to me that the Swiss have been obliged to behave in much the same way. If ethics and religion were not allowed to be sexualized but had to be something 'higher' from the start, and if nevertheless the ideas contained in them seemed undeniably to be descended from the Oedipus and family complex, there could be only one way out: it must be that from the very first these complexes themselves do not mean what they seem to be expressing, but bear the higher 'anagogic' meaning (as Silberer [1914] calls it) which made it possible for them to be employed in the abstract trains of thought of ethics and religious mysticism.

I am quite prepared to be told again that I have mis-understood the substance and purpose of the Neo-Zurich theory; but I must protest in advance against any contradictions to my view of it that may be found in the publications of that school being laid at my door instead of theirs. I can find no other way of making the whole range of Jung's innovations intelligible to myself and of grasping all their implications. All the changes that Jung has proposed to make in psychoanalysis flow from his intention to eliminate what is objectionable in the family complexes, so as not to find it again in religion and ethics. For sexual libido an abstract concept has been substi-tuted, of which one may safely say that it remains mystifying and incomprehensible to wise men and fools alike. The Oedi-pus complex has a merely 'symbolic' meaning: the mother in it means the unattainable, which must be renounced in the interests of civilization; the father who is killed in the Oedipus myth is the 'inner' father, from whom one must set oneself free in order to become independent. Other parts of the material of sexual ideas will no doubt be subjected to similar reinterpretations in the course of time. In the place of a conflict between ego-dystonic erotic trends and the self-preservative ones a conflict appears between the 'life-task' and 'psychical inertia'; [1] the neurotic's sense of guilt corresponds to his self-reproach for not properly fulfilling his 'life-task'. In this

1 [Cf. Freud (1915*f*), *P.F.L.*, **10**, 158 and *n.*1.]

way a new religio-ethical system has been created, which, just like the Adlerian system, was bound to reinterpret, distort or jettison the factual findings of analysis. The truth is that these people have picked out a few cultural overtones from the symphony of life and have once more failed to hear the mighty and primordial melody of the instincts.

In order to preserve this system intact it was necessary to turn entirely away from observation and from the technique of psychoanalysis. Occasionally enthusiasm for the cause even permitted a disregard of scientific logic – as when Jung finds that the Oedipus complex is not 'specific' enough for the aetiology of the neuroses, and proceeds to attribute this specific quality to inertia, the most universal characteristic of all matter, animate and inanimate! It is to be noted, by the way, that the 'Oedipus complex' represents only a topic with which the individual's mental forces have to deal, and is not itself a force, like 'psychical inertia'. The study of individual people had shown (and always will show) that the sexual complexes in their original sense are alive in them. On that account the investigation of individuals was pushed into the background [in the new theories] and replaced by conclusions based on evidence derived from anthropological research. The greatest risk of coming up against the original, undisguised meaning of these reinterpreted complexes was to be met with in the early childhood of every individual; consequently in therapy the injunction was laid down that this past history should be dwelt on as little as possible and the main emphasis put on reverting to the current conflict, in which, moreover, the essential thing was on no account to be what was accidental and personal, but what was general – in fact, the non-fulfilment of the life-task. As we know, however, a neurotic's current conflict becomes comprehensible and admits of solution only when it is traced back to his prehistory, when one goes back along the path that his libido took when he fell ill.

The form taken by the Neo-Zurich therapy under these influences can be conveyed in the words of a patient who experienced it himself: 'This time not a trace of attention was given to the past or to the transference. Wherever I thought I recognized the latter it was pronounced to be a pure libidinal symbol. The moral instruction was very fine and I followed it faithfully, but I did not advance a step. It was even more annoying for me than for him, but how could I help it? . . . Instead of freeing me by analysis, every day brought fresh tremendous demands on me, which had to be fulfilled if the neurosis was to be conquered – for instance, inward concentration by means of introversion, religious meditation, resuming life with my wife in loving devotion, etc. It was almost beyond one's strength; it was aiming at a radical transformation of one's whole inner nature. I left the analysis as a poor sinner with intense feelings of contrition and the best resolutions, but at the same time in utter discouragement. Any clergyman would have advised what he recommended, but where was I to find the strength?' The patient, it is true, reported that he had heard that analysis of the past and of the transference must be gone through first; but he had been told that he had already had enough of it. Since this first kind of analysis had not helped him more, the conclusion seems to me justified that the patient had *not* had enough of it. Certainly the subsequent treatment, which no longer had any claim to be called psychoanalysis, did not improve matters. It is remarkable that the members of the Zurich School should have made the long journey round by way of Vienna in order to wind up at the nearby city of Berne, where Dubois [1] cures neuroses by ethical encouragement in a more considerate manner. [2]

The total incompatibility of this new movement with psychoanalysis shows itself too, of course, in Jung's treatment of repression, which is hardly mentioned nowadays in his writings, in his misunderstanding of dreams, which, like Adler

1. [Paul Dubois (1848–1918), Professor of Neuropathology at Berne, had some celebrity during the early part of the century for his method of treating neuroses by 'persuasion'.]

2. I know the objections there are to making use of a patient's reports, and I will therefore expressly state that my informant is a trustworthy person, very well capable of forming a judgement. He gave me this information quite spontaneously and I make use of his communication without asking his consent, since I cannot allow that a psychoanalytic technique has any right to claim the protection of medical discretion.

[cf. p. 117], in complete disregard of dream psychology, he confuses with the latent dream-thoughts, and in his loss of all understanding of the unconscious – in short, in all the points which I should regard as the essence of psychoanalysis. When Jung tells us that the incest complex is merely 'symbolic', that after all it has no 'real' existence, that after all a savage feels no desire towards an old hag but prefers a young and pretty woman, we are tempted to conclude that 'symbolic' and 'without real existence' simply mean something which, in virtue of its manifestations and pathogenic effects, is described by psychoanalysis as 'existing unconsciously' – a description that disposes of the apparent contradiction.

If one bears in mind that dreams are something different from the latent dream-thoughts which they work over, there is nothing surprising in patients dreaming of things with which their minds have been filled during the treatment, whether it be the 'life-task', or 'being on top' or 'underneath'. The dreams of people being analysed can undoubtedly be directed, in the same way as they are by stimuli produced for experimental purposes. One can determine a part of the material which appears in a dream; nothing in the essence or mechanism of dreams is altered by this. Nor do I believe that 'biographical' dreams, as they are called, occur outside analysis.[1] If, on the other hand, one analyses dreams which occurred before treatment, or if one considers the dreamer's own additions to what has been suggested to him in the treatment, or if one avoids setting him any such tasks, then one may convince oneself how far removed it is from the purpose of a dream to produce attempted solutions of the life-task. Dreams are only a form of thinking; one can never reach an understanding of this form by reference to the content of the thoughts; only an appreciation of the dream-work will lead to that understanding.[2]

1. [See *The Interpretation of Dreams* (1900a), *P.F.L.*, 4, 465 and *n.* 3.]
2. [The topic of this paragraph was discussed by Freud at greater length in Section VII of 'Remarks on the Theory and Practice of Dream-Interpretation' (1923c). Cf. also a footnote added in 1925 to Chapter VI (I) of *The Interpretation of Dreams, P.F.L.*, 4, 649 *n.* 2.]

It is not difficult to find a factual refutation of Jung's misconceptions of psychoanalysis and deviations from it. Every analysis conducted in a proper manner, and in particular every analysis of a child, strengthens the convictions upon which the theory of psychoanalysis is founded, and rebuts the reinterpretations made by both Jung's and Adler's systems. In the days before his illumination, Jung himself [1910b; see above, p. 89] carried out and published an analysis of this kind of a child; it remains to be seen whether he will undertake a new interpretation of its results with the help of a different 'one-sided arrangement of the facts', to use the expression employed by Adler in this connection [p. 116 above].

The view that the sexual representation of 'higher' thoughts in dreams and neurosis is nothing but an archaic mode of expression is of course irreconcilable with the fact that in neurosis these sexual complexes prove to be the bearers of the quantities of libido which have been withdrawn from utilization in real life. If it was merely a question of a sexual 'jargon', the economy of the libido could not have been altered in any way by it. Jung admits this himself in his *Darstellung der psychoanalytischen Theorie* [1913] and formulates the task of therapy as the detaching of libidinal cathexes from these complexes. This can never be achieved, however, by directing the patient away from them and urging him to sublimate, but only by exhaustive examination of them and by making them fully and completely conscious. The first piece of reality which the patient must deal with is his illness. Efforts to spare him that task point to the physician's incapacity to help him to overcome his resistances, or else to the physician's dread of the results of the work.

It may be said lastly that by his 'modification' of psychoanalysis Jung has given us a counterpart to the famous Lichtenberg knife.[1] He has changed the hilt, and he has put a new blade into it; yet because the same name is engraved on it we are expected to regard the instrument as the original one.

1. [The *mot* is quoted in Freud's book on jokes (1905c), *P.F.L.*, **6**, 98 *n.*]

I think I have made clear, on the contrary, that the new teaching which aims at replacing psychoanalysis signifies an abandonment of analysis and a secession from it. Some people may be inclined to fear that this secession is bound to have more momentous consequences for analysis than would another, owing to its having been started by men who have played so great a part in the movement and have done so much to advance it. I do not share this apprehension.

Men are strong so long as they represent a strong idea; they become powerless when they oppose it. Psychoanalysis will survive this loss and gain new adherents in place of these. In conclusion, I can only express a wish that fortune may grant an agreeable upward journey to all those who have found their stay in the underworld of psychoanalysis too uncomfortable for their taste. The rest of us, I hope, will be permitted without hindrance to carry through to their conclusion our labours in the depths.

February 1914

TWO ENCYCLOPAEDIA ARTICLES
(1923 [1922])

'PSYCHOANALYSE' UND 'LIBIDOTHEORIE'

(A) GERMAN EDITIONS:

1923 In *Handwörterbuch der Sexualwissenschaft*, ed. M. Marcuse, Bonn, Pp. 296–8 and 377–83.
1940 *Gesammelte Werke*, **13**, 211–33.

(B) ENGLISH TRANSLATIONS:
'Two Encyclopaedia Articles'

1942 *International Journal of Psycho-Analysis*, **23**, 97–107. (Tr. James Strachey.)
1950 *Collected Papers*, **5**, 107–35. (Same translator.)
1955 *Standard Edition*, **18**, 233–59. (Modified version of above.)

The present edition is a reprint of the *Standard Edition* version, with a few editorial modifications.

These articles were written during the summer of 1922, that is to say, before Freud's final re-casting of his views upon the structure of the mind in *The Ego and the Id* (1923*b*; *P.F.L.*, **11**, 339 ff.). But the new views, though unexpressed in these articles, must already have been clearly present in his thoughts while he was writing them, for it was in September 1922, at the Berlin Psycho-Analytical Congress, that he first made public his newly defined conceptions of ego, super-ego and id. These new ideas were taken into account not long afterwards in a somewhat similarly conceived didactic article, written for an American publication (1924*f*; p. 159 ff. below).

TWO ENCYCLOPAEDIA ARTICLES

A. PSYCHOANALYSIS

PSYCHOANALYSIS is the name (1) of a procedure for the investigation of mental processes which are almost inaccessible in any other way, (2) of a method (based upon that investigation) for the treatment of neurotic disorders and (3) of a collection of psychological information obtained along those lines, which is gradually being accumulated into a new scientific discipline.

History. – The best way of understanding psychoanalysis is still by tracing its origin and development. In 1880 and 1881 Dr Josef Breuer of Vienna, a well-known physician and experimental physiologist, was occupied in the treatment of a girl who had fallen ill of a severe hysteria while she was nursing her sick father. The clinical picture was made up of motor paralyses, inhibitions, and disturbances of consciousness. Following a hint given him by the patient herself, who was a person of great intelligence, he put her into a state of hypnosis and contrived that, by describing to him the moods and thoughts that were uppermost in her mind, she returned on each particular occasion to a normal mental condition. By consistently repeating the same laborious process, he succeeded in freeing her from all her inhibitions and paralyses, so that in the end he found his trouble rewarded by a great therapeutic success as well as by an unexpected insight into the nature of the puzzling neurosis. Nevertheless, Breuer refrained from following up his discovery or from publishing anything about the case until some ten years later, when the personal influence of the present writer (Freud, who had returned to Vienna in

1886 after studying in the school of Charcot) prevailed on him to take up the subject afresh and embark upon a joint study of it. These two, Breuer and Freud, published a preliminary paper 'On the Psychical Mechanism of Hysterical Phenomena' in 1893,[1] and in 1895 a volume entitled *Studies on Hysteria* (which reached its fourth edition in 1922), in which they described their therapeutic procedure as '*cathartic*'.[2]

Catharsis. – The investigations which lay at the root of Breuer and Freud's studies led to two chief results, and these have not been shaken by subsequent experience: first, that hysterical symptoms have sense and meaning, being substitutes for normal mental acts; and secondly, that the uncovering of this unknown meaning is accompanied by the removal of the symptoms – so that in this case scientific research and therapeutic effort coincide. The observations were carried out upon a series of patients who were treated in the same manner as Breuer's first patient, that is to say, put into a state of deep hypnosis; and the results seemed brilliant, until later their weak side became evident. The theoretical ideas put forward at that time by Breuer and Freud were influenced by Charcot's theories on traumatic hysteria and could find support in the findings of his pupil Pierre Janet, which, though they were published earlier than the *Studies*, were in fact subsequent to Breuer's first case. From the very beginning the factor of *affect* was brought into the foreground: hysterical symptoms, the authors maintained, came into existence when a mental process with a heavy charge of affect was in any way prevented from being levelled out along the normal path leading to consciousness and movement (i.e. was prevented from being '*abreacted*'); as a result of this the affect, which was in a sense '*strangulated*', was diverted along wrong paths and flowed off into the somatic innervation (a process named '*conversion*'). The occasions upon which 'pathogenic ideas' of this kind arose were described by Breuer and Freud as '*psychical traumas*', and, since these often dated back to the very remote past, it was possible

1. [*P.F.L.*, **3**, 51 ff.]
2. [Ibid., **3**, 103, 167 *n*.]

for the authors to say that hysterics suffered mainly from reminiscences (which had not been dealt with). Under the treatment, therefore, '*catharsis*' came about when the path to consciousness was opened and there was a normal discharge of affect. It will be seen that an essential part of this theory was the assumption of the existence of *unconscious* mental processes. Janet too had made use of unconscious acts in mental life; but, as he insisted in his later polemics against psychoanalysis, to him the phrase was no more than a make-shift expression, a '*manière de parler*', and he intended to suggest no new point of view by it.

In a theoretical section of the *Studies* Breuer brought forward some speculative ideas about the processes of excitation in the mind. These ideas determined the direction of future lines of thought and even today have not received sufficient appreciation. But they brought his contributions to this branch of science to an end, and soon afterwards he withdrew from the common work.

The Transition to Psychoanalysis. – Contrasts between the views of the two authors had been visible even in the *Studies*. Breuer supposed that the pathogenic ideas produced their traumatic effect because they arose during '*hypnoid states*', in which mental functioning was subject to special limitations. The present writer rejected this explanation and inclined to the belief that an idea became pathogenic if its content was in opposition to the predominant trend of the subject's mental life so that it provoked him into '*defence*'. (Janet had attributed to hysterical patients a constitutional incapacity for holding together the contents of their minds; and it was at this point that his path diverged from that of Breuer and Freud.) Moreover, the two innovations which led the present writer to move away from the cathartic method had already been mentioned in the *Studies*. After Breuer's withdrawal they became the starting-point of fresh developments.

Abandonment of Hypnosis. – The first of these innovations was based on practical experience and led to a change in technique. The second consisted in an advance in the clinical

understanding of neuroses. It soon appeared that the therapeutic hopes which had been placed upon cathartic treatment
in hypnosis were to some extent unfulfilled. It was true that
the disappearance of the symptoms went hand-in-hand with
the catharsis, but total success turned out to be entirely dependent upon the patient's relation to the physician and thus resembled the effect of 'suggestion'. If that relation was disturbed, all
the symptoms reappeared, just as though they had never been
cleared up. In addition to this, the small number of people
who could be put into a deep state of hypnosis involved a very
considerable limitation, from the medical standpoint, of the
applicability of the cathartic procedure. For these reasons the
present writer decided to give up the use of hypnosis. But at
the same time the impressions he had derived from hypnosis
afforded him the means of replacing it.

Free Association. – The effect of the hypnotic condition upon
the patient had been so greatly to increase his ability to make
associations that he was able straight away to find the path –
inaccessible to his conscious reflection – which led from the
symptom to the thoughts and memories connected with it.
The abandonment of hypnosis seemed to make the situation
hopeless, until the writer recalled a remark of Bernheim's to
the effect that things that had been experienced in a state of
somnambulism were only *apparently* forgotten and that they
could be brought into recollection at any time if the physician
insisted forcibly enough that the patient knew them. The writer
therefore endeavoured to insist on his *unhypnotized* patients
giving him their associations, so that from the material thus
provided he might find the path leading to what had been
forgotten or fended off. He noticed later that the insistence
was unnecessary and that copious ideas almost always arose in
the patient's mind, but that they were held back from being
communicated and even from becoming conscious by certain
objections put by the patient in his own way. It was to be
expected – though this was still unproved and not until later
confirmed by wide experience – that everything that occurred
to a patient setting out from a particular starting-point must

also stand in an internal connection with that starting-point; hence arose the technique of educating the patient to give up the whole of his critical attitude and of making use of the material which was thus brought to light for the purpose of uncovering the connections that were being sought. A strong belief in the strict determination of mental events certainly played a part in the choice of this technique as a substitute for hypnosis.

The 'Fundamental Technical Rule' of this procedure of 'free association' has from that time on been maintained in psychoanalytic work. The treatment is begun by the patient being required to put himself in the position of an attentive and dispassionate self-observer, merely to read off all the time the surface of his consciousness, and on the one hand to make a duty of the most complete honesty while on the other not to hold back any idea from communication, even if (1) he feels that it is too disagreeable or if (2) he judges that it is nonsensical or (3) too unimportant or (4) irrelevant to what is being looked for. It is uniformly found that precisely those ideas which provoke these last-mentioned reactions are of particular value in discovering the forgotten material.

Psychoanalysis as an Interpretative Art. – The new technique altered the picture of the treatment so greatly, brought the physician into such a new relation to the patient and produced so many surprising results that it seemed justifiable to distinguish the procedure from the cathartic method by giving it a new name. The present writer gave this method of treatment, which could now be extended to many other forms of neurotic disorder, the name of *psychoanalysis*.[1] Now, in the first resort, this psychoanalysis was an art of *interpretation* and it set itself the task of carrying deeper the first of Breuer's great discoveries – namely, that neurotic symptoms are significant substitutes for other mental acts which have been omitted. It was now a question of regarding the material produced by the patients' associations as though it hinted at a hidden meaning and of

1. [The term 'psychoanalysis' was first used in Freud's paper 'Heredity and the Aetiology of the Neuroses' (1896*a*).]

discovering that meaning from it. Experience soon showed that the attitude which the analytic physician could most advantageously adopt was to surrender himself to his own unconscious mental activity, in a state of *evenly suspended attention*, to avoid so far as possible reflection and the construction of conscious expectations, not to try to fix anything that he heard particularly in his memory, and by these means to catch the drift of the patient's unconscious with his own unconscious. It was then found that, except under conditions that were too unfavourable, the patient's associations emerged like allusions, as it were, to one particular theme and that it was only necessary for the physician to go a step further in order to guess the material which was concealed from the patient himself and to be able to communicate it to him. It is true that this work of interpretation was not to be brought under strict rules and left a great deal of play to the physician's tact and skill; but, with impartiality and practice, it was usually possible to obtain trustworthy results – that is to say, results which were confirmed by being repeated in similar cases. At a time when so little was as yet known of the unconscious, the structure of the neuroses and the pathological processes underlying them, it was a matter for satisfaction that a technique of this kind should be available, even if it had no better theoretical basis. Moreover, it is still employed in analyses at the present day in the same manner, though with a sense of greater assurance and with a better understanding of its limitations.

The Interpretation of Parapraxes and Haphazard Acts. – It was a triumph for the interpretative art of psychoanalysis when it succeeded in demonstrating that certain common mental acts of normal people, for which no one had hitherto attempted to put forward a psychological explanation, were to be regarded in the same light as the symptoms of neurotics: that is to say, they had a *meaning*, which was unknown to the subject but which could easily be discovered by analytic means. The phenomena in question were such events as the temporary forgetting of familiar words and names, forgetting to carry out prescribed tasks, everyday slips of the tongue and of the pen, misreadings, losses and mislayings of objects, certain errors, instances of apparently accidental self-injury, and finally habitual movements carried out seemingly without intention or in play, tunes hummed 'thoughtlessly', and so on. All of these were shorn of their physiological explanation, if any such had ever been attempted, were shown to be strictly determined and were revealed as an expression of the subject's suppressed intentions or as a result of a clash between two intentions one of which was permanently or temporarily unconscious. The importance of this contribution to psychology was of many kinds. The range of mental determinism was extended by it in an unforeseen manner; the supposed gulf between normal and pathological mental events was narrowed; in many cases a useful insight was afforded into the play of mental forces that must be suspected to lie behind the phenomena. Finally, a class of material was brought to light which is calculated better than any other to stimulate a belief in the existence of unconscious mental acts even in people to whom the hypothesis of something at once mental and unconscious seems strange and even absurd. The study of one's own parapraxes and haphazard acts, for which most people have ample opportunities, is even today the best preparation for an approach to psychoanalysis. In analytic treatment, the interpretation of parapraxes retains a place as a means of uncovering the unconscious, alongside the immeasurably more important interpretation of associations.

The Interpretation of Dreams. – A new approach to the depths of mental life was opened when the technique of free association was applied to dreams, whether one's own or those of patients in analysis. In fact, the greater and better part of what we know of the processes in the unconscious levels of the mind is derived from the interpretation of dreams. Psychoanalysis has restored to dreams the importance which was generally ascribed to them in ancient times, but it treats them differently. It does not rely upon the cleverness of the dream interpreter but for the most part hands the task over to the dreamer himself by asking him for his associations to the separate elements of the dream. By pursuing these associations further we obtain knowledge of thoughts which coincide entirely with the dream but which can be recognized – up to a certain point – as genuine and completely intelligible portions of waking mental activity. Thus the recollected dream emerges as the *manifest dream-content*, in contrast to the *latent dream-thoughts* discovered by interpretation. The process which has transformed the latter into the former, that is to say into 'the dream', and which is undone by the work of interpretation, may be called the *'dream-work'*.

We also describe the latent dream-thoughts, on account of their connection with waking life, as *'residues of the [previous] day'*. By the operation of the dream-work (to which it would be quite incorrect to ascribe any 'creative' character) the latent dream-thoughts are *condensed* in a remarkable way, are *distorted* by the *displacement* of psychical intensities and are arranged with a view to being *represented in visual pictures*; and, besides all this, before the manifest dream is arrived at, they are submitted to a process of *secondary revision* which seeks to give the new product something in the nature of sense and coherence. Strictly speaking, this last process does not form a part of the dream-work.[1]

The Dynamic Theory of Dream Formation. – An understanding of the dynamics of dream formation did not involve any very great difficulties. The motive power for the formation of dreams is not provided by the latent dream-thoughts or day's residues, but by an unconscious impulse, repressed during the day, with which the day's residues have been able to establish contact and which contrives to make a *wish-fulfilment* for itself out of the material of the latent thoughts. Thus every dream is on the one hand the fulfilment of a wish on the part of the unconscious and on the other hand (in so far as it succeeds in guarding the state of sleep against being disturbed) the fulfilment of the normal wish to sleep which set the sleep going. If we disregard the unconscious contribution to the formation of the dream and limit the dream to its latent thoughts, it can

1. [In *The Interpretation of Dreams*, P.F.L., **4**, 630, secondary revision is regarded as part of the dream-work.]

represent anything with which waking life has been concerned – a reflection, a warning, an intention, a preparation for the immediate future or, once again, the satisfaction of an unfulfilled wish. The unrecognizability, strangeness and absurdity of the manifest dream are partly the result of the translation of the thoughts into a different, so to say *archaic*, method of expression, but partly the effect of a restrictive, critically disapproving agency in the mind, which does not entirely cease to function during sleep. It is plausible to suppose that the '*dream censorship*', which we regard as being responsible in the first instance for the distortion of the dream-thoughts into the manifest dream, is an expression of the same mental forces which during the daytime had held back or *repressed* the unconscious wishful impulse.

It has been worth while to enter in some detail into the explanation of dreams, since analytic work has shown that the dynamics of the formation of dreams are the same as those of the formation of symptoms. In both cases we find a struggle between two trends, of which one is unconscious and ordinarily repressed and strives towards satisfaction – that is, wish-fulfilment – while the other, belonging probably to the conscious ego, is disapproving and repressive. The outcome of this conflict is a *compromise formation* (the dream or the symptom) in which both trends have found an incomplete expression. The theoretical importance of this conformity between dreams and symptoms is illuminating. Since dreams are not pathological phenomena, the fact shows that the mental mechanisms which produce the symptoms of illness are equally present in normal mental life, that the same uniform law embraces both the normal and the abnormal and that the findings of research into neurotics or psychotics cannot be without significance for our understanding of the healthy mind.

Symbolism. – In the course of investigating the form of expression brought about by the dream-work, the surprising fact emerged that certain objects, arrangements and relations are represented, in a sense indirectly, by 'symbols', which are used by the dreamer without his understanding them and to which as a rule he offers no associations. Their translation has to be provided by the analyst, who can himself only discover it empirically by experimentally fitting it into the context. It was later found that linguistic usage, mythology and folklore afford the most ample analogies to dream symbols. Symbols, which raise the most interesting and hitherto unsolved problems, seem to be a fragment of extremely ancient inherited mental equipment. The use of a common symbolism extends far beyond the use of a common language.

The Aetiological Significance of Sexual Life. – The second novelty which emerged after the hypnotic technique had been replaced by free associations was of a clinical nature. It was discovered in the course of the prolonged search for the traumatic experiences from which hysterical symptoms appeared to be derived. The more carefully the search was pursued the more extensive seemed to be the network of aetiologically significant impressions, but the further back, too, did they reach into the patient's puberty or childhood. At the same time they assumed a uniform character and eventually it became inevitable to bow before the evidence and recognize that at the root of the formation of every symptom there were to be found traumatic experiences from early sexual life. Thus a sexual trauma stepped into the place of an ordinary trauma and the latter was seen to owe its aetiological significance to an associative or symbolic connection with the former, which had preceded it. An investigation of cases of common nervousness (falling into the two classes of *neurasthenia* and *anxiety neurosis*) which was simultaneously undertaken led to the conclusion that these disorders could be traced to *contemporary* abuses in the patients' sexual life and could be removed if these were brought to an end. It was thus easy to infer that neuroses in general are an expression of disturbances in sexual life, the so-called *actual neuroses* [1] being the consequences (by chemical agency) of *contemporary* injuries and the *psychoneuroses* the consequences (by psychical modification) of *bygone* injuries to a biological function which had hitherto been gravely neglected

1. [See p. 209 *n.* 1 below.]

by science. None of the theses of psychoanalysis has met with such tenacious scepticism or such embittered resistance as this assertion of the preponderating aetiological significance of sexual life in the neuroses. It should, however, be expressly remarked that, in its development up to the present day, psychoanalysis has found no reason to retreat from this opinion.

Infantile Sexuality. – As a result of its aetiological researches, psychoanalysis found itself in the position of dealing with a subject the very existence of which had scarcely been suspected previously. Science had become accustomed to consider sexual life as beginning with puberty and regarded manifestations of sexuality in children as rare signs of abnormal precocity and degeneracy. But now psychoanalysis revealed a wealth of phenomena, remarkable, yet of regular occurrence, which made it necessary to date back the beginning of the sexual function in children almost to the commencement of extra-uterine existence; and it was asked with astonishment how all this could have come to be overlooked. The first glimpses of sexuality in children had indeed been obtained through the analytic examination of adults and were consequently saddled with all the doubts and sources of error that could be attributed to such a belated retrospect; but subsequently (from 1908 onwards) a beginning was made with the analysis of children themselves and with the unembarrassed observation of their behaviour, and in this way direct confirmation was reached for the whole factual basis of the new view.

Sexuality in children showed a different picture in many respects from that in adults, and, surprisingly enough, it exhibited numerous traces of what, in adults, were condemned as 'perversions'. It became necessary to enlarge the concept of what was sexual, till it covered more than the impulsion towards the union of the two sexes in the sexual act or towards provoking particular pleasurable sensations in the genitals. But this enlargement was rewarded by the new possibility of grasping infantile, normal and perverse sexual life as a single whole.

The analytic researches carried out by the writer fell, to

begin with, into the error of greatly overestimating the importance of *seduction* as a source of sexual manifestations in children and as a root for the formation of neurotic symptoms. This misapprehension was corrected when it became possible to appreciate the extraordinarily large part played in the mental life of neurotics by the activities of *fantasy*, which clearly carried more weight in neurosis than did external reality. Behind these fantasies there came to light the material which allows us to draw the picture which follows of the development of the sexual function.

The Development of the Libido. – The sexual instinct, the dynamic manifestation of which in mental life we shall call '*libido*', is made up of component instincts into which it may once more break up and which are only gradually united into well-defined organizations. The sources of these component instincts are the organs of the body and in particular certain specially marked *erotogenic zones*; but contributions are made to libido from every important functional process in the body. At first the individual component instincts strive for satisfaction independently of one another, but in the course of development they become more and more convergent and concentrated. The first (pregenital) stage of organization to be discerned is the *oral* one, in which – in conformity with the suckling's predominant interest – the oral zone plays the leading part. This is followed by the *sadistic-anal* organization, in which the *anal* zone and the component instinct of *sadism* are particularly prominent; at this stage the difference between the sexes is represented by the contrast between active and passive. The third and final stage of organization is that in which the majority of the component instincts converge under the *primacy of the genital zones*. As a rule this development is passed through swiftly and unobtrusively; but some individual portions of the instincts remain behind at the prodromal stages of the process and thus give rise to *fixations* of libido, which are important as constituting predispositions for subsequent irruptions of repressed impulses and which stand in a definite relation to the later development of neuroses and perversions. (See the article on 'The Libido Theory' below.)

The Process of Finding an Object, and the Oedipus Complex. –In the first instance the oral component instinct finds satisfaction by attaching itself to the sating of the desire for nourishment; and its object is the mother's breast. It then detaches itself, becomes independent and at the same time *auto-erotic*, that is it finds an object in the child's own body. Others of the component instincts also start by being auto-erotic and are not until later diverted on to an external object. It is a particularly important fact that the component instincts belonging to the genital zone habitually pass through a period of intense auto-erotic satisfaction. The component instincts are not all equally serviceable in the final genital organization of libido; some of them (for instance, the anal components) are consequently left aside and suppressed, or undergo complicated transformations.

In the very earliest years of childhood (approximately between the ages of two and five) a convergence of the sexual impulses occurs of which, in the case of boys, the object is the mother. This choice of an object, in conjunction with a corresponding attitude of rivalry and hostility towards the father, provides the content of what is known as the *Oedipus complex*, which in every human being is of the greatest importance in determining the final shape of his erotic life. It has been found to be characteristic of a normal individual that he learns to master his Oedipus complex, whereas the neurotic subject remains involved in it.

The Diphasic Onset of Sexual Development. – Towards the end of the fifth year this early period of sexual life normally comes to an end. It is succeeded by a period of more or less complete *latency*, during which ethical restraints are built up, to act as defences against the desires of the Oedipus complex. In the subsequent period of *puberty*, the Oedipus complex is revivified in the unconscious and embarks upon further modifications. It is only at puberty that the sexual instincts develop to their full intensity; but the direction of that development, as well as all the predispositions for it, have already been determined by the early efflorescence of sexuality during childhood which preceded it. This diphasic development of the sexual function – in two stages, interrupted by the latency period – appears to be a biological peculiarity of the human species and to contain the determining factor for the origin of neuroses.

The Theory of Repression. – These theoretical considerations, taken together with the immediate impressions derived from analytic work, lead to a view of the neuroses which may be described in the roughest outline as follows. The neuroses are the expression of conflicts between the ego and such of the sexual impulses as seem to the ego incompatible with its integrity or with its ethical standards. Since these impulses are not *ego-syntonic*, the ego has *repressed* them: that is to say, it has withdrawn its interest from them and has shut them off from becoming conscious as well as from obtaining satisfaction by motor discharge. If in the course of analytic work one attempts to make these repressed impulses conscious, one becomes aware of the repressive forces in the form of *resistance*. But the achievement of repression fails particularly readily in the case of the sexual instincts. Their dammed–up libido finds other ways out from the unconscious: for it *regresses* to earlier phases of development and earlier attitudes towards objects, and, at weak points in the libidinal development where there are infantile fixations, it breaks through into consciousness and obtains discharge. What results is a *symptom* and consequently in its essence a substitutive sexual satisfaction. Nevertheless the symptom cannot entirely escape from the repressive forces of the ego and must therefore submit to modifications and displacements – exactly as happens with dreams – by means of which its characteristic of being a sexual satisfaction becomes unrecognizable. Consequently symptoms are in the nature of compromises between the repressed sexual instincts and the repressing ego instincts; they represent a wish–fulfilment for both partners to the conflict simultaneously, but one which is incomplete for each of them. This is quite strictly true of the symptoms of hysteria, while in the symptoms of obsessional neurosis there is often a stronger emphasis upon the side of the repressing function owing to the erection of reaction formations, which are assurances against sexual satisfaction.

Transference. – If further proof were needed of the truth that the motive forces behind the formation of neurotic symptoms are of a sexual nature, it would be found in the fact that in the course of analytic treatment a special emotional relation is regularly formed between the patient and the physician. This goes far beyond rational limits. It varies between the most affectionate devotion and the most obstinate enmity and derives all of its characteristics from earlier erotic attitudes of the patient's which have become unconscious. This *transference* alike in its positive and in its negative form is used as a weapon by the resistance; but in the hands of the physician it becomes the most powerful therapeutic instrument and it plays a part scarcely to be overestimated in the dynamics of the process of cure.

The Corner-Stones of Psychoanalytic Theory. – The assumption that there are unconscious mental processes, the recognition of the theory of resistance and repression, the appreciation of the importance of sexuality and of the Oedipus complex – these constitute the principal subject-matter of psychoanalysis and the foundations of its theory. No one who cannot accept them all should count himself a psychoanalyst.

Later History of Psychoanalysis. – Psychoanalysis was carried approximately thus far by the work of the writer of this article, who for more than ten years was its sole representative. In 1906 the Swiss psychiatrists Bleuler and C. G. Jung began to play a lively part in analysis; in 1908 a first conference of its supporters took place at Salzburg; and the young science soon found itself the centre of interest both among psychiatrists and laymen. Its reception in Germany, with her morbid craving for authority, was not precisely to the credit of German science and moved even so cool a partisan as Bleuler to an energetic protest. Yet no condemnation or dismissal at official congresses served to hold up the internal growth or external expansion of psychoanalysis. In the course of the next ten years it extended far beyond the frontiers of Europe and became especially popular in the United States of America, and this was due in no small degree to the advocacy and collaboration of Putnam (Boston), Ernest Jones (Toronto; later London), Flournoy (Geneva), Ferenczi (Budapest), Abraham (Berlin), and many others besides. The anathema which was imposed upon psychoanalysis led its supporters to combine in an international organization which in the present year (1922) is holding its eighth private Congress in Berlin and now includes local groups in Vienna, Budapest, Berlin, Holland, Zurich, London, New York, Calcutta and Moscow. This development was not interrupted even by the World War. In 1918–19 Dr Anton von Freund of Budapest founded the Internationaler Psychoanalytischer Verlag, which publishes journals and books concerned with psychoanalysis, and in 1920 Dr M. Eitingon opened in Berlin the first psychoanalytic clinic for the treatment of neurotics without private means.[1] Translations of the writer's principal works, which are now in preparation, into French, Italian and Spanish, testify to a growing interest in psychoanalysis in the Latin world as well.

Between 1911 and 1913 two movements of divergence from psychoanalysis took place, evidently with the object of mitigating its repellent features. One of these (sponsored by C. G. Jung), in an endeavour to conform to ethical standards, divested the Oedipus complex of its real significance by giving it only a *symbolic* value, and in practice neglected the uncovering of the forgotten and, as we may call it, 'prehistoric' period of childhood. The other (originated by Alfred Adler in Vienna) reproduced many factors from psychoanalysis under other names – repression, for instance, appeared in a sexualized version as the 'masculine protest'.[2] But in other respects it turned away from the unconscious and the sexual instincts, and endeavoured to trace back the development of character and of the neuroses to the 'will to power', which by means of overcompensation strives to check the dangers arising from

1. [Cf. p. 175 below.]
2. [See p. 114 n. 1 above.]

'organ inferiority'. Neither of these movements, with their systematic structures, had any permanent influence on psychoanalysis. In the case of Adler's theories it soon became clear that they had very little in common with psychoanalysis, which they were designed to replace.

More Recent Advances in Psychoanalysis. – Since psychoanalysis has become the field of work for such a large number of observers it has made advances, both in extent and depth; but unfortunately these can receive only the briefest mention in the present article.

Narcissism. – The most important theoretical advance has certainly been the application of the libido theory to the repressing ego. The ego itself came to be regarded as a reservoir of what was described as narcissistic libido, from which the libidinal cathexes of objects flowed out and into which they could be once more withdrawn. By the help of this conception it became possible to embark upon the analysis of the ego and to make a clinical distinction of the psychoneuroses into *transference neuroses* and *narcissistic* disorders. In the former (hysteria and obsessional neurosis) the subject has at his disposal a quantity of libido striving to be transferred on to extraneous objects, and use is made of this in carrying out analytic treatment; on the other hand, the narcissistic disorders (dementia praecox, paranoia, melancholia) are characterized by a withdrawal of the libido from objects and they are therefore scarcely accessible to analytic therapy. But their therapeutic inaccessibility has not prevented analysis from making the most fruitful beginnings in the deeper study of these illnesses, which are counted among the psychoses.

Development of Technique. – After the analyst's curiosity had, as it were, been gratified by the elaboration of the technique of interpretation, it was inevitable that interest should turn to the problem of discovering the most effective way of influencing the patient. It soon became evident that the physician's immediate task was to assist the patient in getting to know, and afterwards in overcoming, the resistances which emerged in him during treatment and of which, to begin with, he himself was unaware. And it was found at the same time that the essential part of the process of cure lay in the overcoming of these resistances and that unless this was achieved no permanent mental change could be brought about in the patient. Since the analyst's efforts have in this way been directed upon the patient's resistance, analytic technique has attained a certainty and delicacy rivalling that of surgery. Consequently, everyone is strongly advised against undertaking psychoanalytic treatments without a strict training, and a physician who ventures upon them on the strength of his medical qualification is in no respect better than a layman.

Psychoanalysis as a Therapeutic Procedure. – Psychoanalysis has never set itself up as a panacea and has never claimed to perform miracles. In one of the most difficult spheres of medical activity it is the only possible method of treatment for certain illnesses and for others it is the method which yields the best or the most permanent results – though never without a corresponding expenditure of time and trouble. A physician who is not wholly absorbed in the work of giving help will find his labours amply repaid by obtaining an unhoped-for insight into the complications of mental life and the interrelations between the mental and the physical. Where at present it cannot offer help but only theoretical understanding, it may perhaps be preparing the way for some later, more direct means of influencing neurotic disorders. Its province is above all the two transference neuroses, hysteria and obsessional neurosis, in which it has contributed to the discovery of their internal structure and operative mechanisms; and, beyond them, all kinds of phobias, inhibitions, deformities of character, sexual perversions and difficulties in erotic life. Some analysts (Jelliffe, Groddeck, Felix Deutsch) have reported too that the analytic treatment of gross organic diseases is not unpromising, since a mental factor not infrequently contributes to the origin and continuance of such illnesses. Since psychoanalysis demands a certain amount of psychical plasticity from its patients, some kind of age-limit must be laid down in their selection; and since it necessitates the devotion of long and intense attention to the individual patient, it would be uneconomical to squander such expenditure upon completely worthless persons who happen to be neurotic. Experience upon material in clinics can alone show what modifications may be necessary in order to make psycho-analytic treatment accessible to wider strata of the popula-tion or to adapt it to weaker intelligences.

Comparison between Psychoanalysis and Hypnotic and Suggestive Methods. – Psychoanalytic procedure differs from all methods making use of suggestion, persuasion, etc., in that it does not seek to suppress by means of authority any mental phenomenon that may occur in the patient. It endeavours to trace the causation of the phenomenon and to remove it by bringing about a permanent modification in the conditions that led to it. In psychoanalysis the suggestive influence which is inevitably exercised by the physician is diverted on to the task assigned to the patient of overcoming his resistances, that is, of carrying forward the curative process. Any danger of falsifying the products of a patient's memory by suggestion can be avoided by prudent handling of the technique; but in general the arousing of resistances is a guarantee against the misleading effects of suggestive influence. It may be laid down that the aim of the treatment is to remove the patient's re-sistances and to pass his repressions in review and thus to bring about the most far-reaching unification and strengthening of his ego, to enable him to save the mental energy which he is expending upon internal conflicts, to make the best of him that his inherited capacities will allow and so to make him as efficient and as capable of enjoyment as is possible. The removal of the symptoms of the illness is not specifically aimed at, but is achieved, as it were, as a by-product if the analysis is properly carried through. The analyst respects the patient's individuality and does not seek to remould him in accordance with his own – that is, according to the physician's – personal ideals; he is glad to avoid giving advice and instead to arouse the patient's power of initiative.

Its Relation to Psychiatry. – Psychiatry is at present essentially a descriptive and classificatory science whose orientation is still towards the somatic rather than the psychological and which is without the possibility of giving explanations of the phenomena which it observes. Psychoanalysis does not, however, stand in opposition to it, as the almost unanimous behaviour of the psychiatrists might lead one to believe. On the contrary, as a *depth-psychology*, a psychology of those processes in mental life which are withdrawn from consciousness, it is called upon to provide psychiatry with an indispensable groundwork and to free it from its present limitations. We can foresee that the future will give birth to a scientific psychiatry, to which psychoanalysis has served as an introduction.

Criticisms and Misunderstandings of Psychoanalysis. – Most of what is brought up against psychoanalysis, even in scientific works, is based upon insufficient information which in its turn seems to be determined by emotional resistances. Thus it is a mistake to accuse psychoanalysis of 'pan-sexualism' and to allege that it derives all mental occurrences from sexuality and traces them all back to it. On the contrary, psychoanalysis has from the very first distinguished the sexual instincts from others which it has provisionally termed 'ego instincts'. It has never dreamt of trying to explain everything, and even the neuroses it has traced back not to sexuality alone but to the conflict between the sexual impulses and the ego. In psychoanalysis (unlike the works of C. G. Jung) the term '*libido*' does not mean psychical energy in general but the motive force of the sexual instincts. Some assertions, such as that every dream is the fulfilment of a sexual wish, have never been maintained by it at all. The charge of one-sidedness made against psycho-analysis, which, as *the science of the unconscious mind*, has its own definite and restricted field of work, is as inapplicable as it would be if it were made against chemistry. To believe that psychoanalysis seeks a cure for neurotic disorders by giving a free rein to sexuality is a serious misunderstanding which can only be excused by ignorance. The making conscious of re-pressed sexual desires in analysis makes it possible, on the contrary, to obtain a mastery over them which the previous repression had been unable to achieve. It can more truly be said that analysis sets the neurotic free from the chains of his sexuality. Moreover, it is quite unscientific to judge analysis by whether it is calculated to undermine religion, authority and morals; for, like all sciences, it is entirely non-tendentious and has only a single aim – namely to arrive at a consistent view of one portion of reality. Finally, one can only characterize as simple-minded the fear which is sometimes expressed that all the highest goods of humanity, as they are called – research, art, love, ethical and social sense – will lose their value or their dignity because psychoanalysis is in a position to demonstrate their origin in elementary and animal instinctual impulses.

The Non-Medical Applications and Correlations of Psychoanalysis. – Any estimate of psychoanalysis would be incomplete if it failed to make clear that, alone among the medical disciplines, it has the most extensive relations with the mental sciences, and that it is in a position to play a part of the same importance in the studies of religious and cultural history and in the sciences of mythology and literature as it is in psychiatry. This may seem strange when we reflect that originally its only object was the understanding and improvement of neurotic symptoms. But it is easy to indicate the starting-point of the bridge that leads over to the mental sciences. The analysis of dreams gave us an insight into the unconscious processes of the mind and showed us that the mechanisms which produce pathological symptoms are also operative in the normal mind. Thus psychoanalysis became a *depth-psychology* and capable as such of being applied to the mental sciences, and it was able to answer a good number of questions with which the academic psychology of consciousness was helpless to deal. At quite an early stage problems of human *phylogenesis* arose. It became clear that pathological function was often nothing more than a *regression* to an earlier stage in the development of normal function. C. G. Jung was the first to draw explicit attention to the striking similarity between the disordered fantasies of sufferers from dementia praecox and the myths of primitive peoples; while the present writer pointed out that the two wishes which combine to form the Oedipus complex coincide precisely with the two principal prohibitions imposed by *totemism* (not to kill the tribal ancestor and not to marry any woman belonging to one's own clan) and drew far-reaching conclusions from this fact. The significance of the Oedipus complex began to grow to gigantic proportions and it looked as though social order, morals, justice and religion had arisen together in the primaeval ages of mankind as reaction formations against the Oedipus complex. Otto Rank [1911, 1912a] threw a brilliant light upon mythology and the history of literature by the application of psychoanalytic views, as did Theodor Reik [1919] upon the history of morals and religions, while Dr Pfister [1913], of Zurich, aroused the interest of pastoral workers and teachers, and demonstrated the importance of the psychoanalytic standpoint for education. Further discussion of these applications of psychoanalysis would be out of place here, and it is enough to say that the limits of their influence are not yet in sight.

Psychoanalysis an Empirical Science – Psychoanalysis is not, like philosophies, a system starting out from a few sharply defined basic concepts, seeking to grasp the whole universe with the help of these and, once it is completed, having no room for fresh discoveries or better understanding. On the contrary, it keeps close to the facts in its field of study, seeks to solve the immediate problems of observation, gropes its way forward by the help of experience, is always incomplete and always ready to correct or modify its theories. There is no incongruity (any more than in the case of physics or chemistry) if its most general concepts lack clarity and if its postulates are provisional; it leaves their more precise definition to the results of future work.

B. THE LIBIDO THEORY

LIBIDO is a term used in the theory of the instincts for describing the dynamic manifestation of sexuality. It was already used in this sense by Moll (1898)[1] and was introduced into psychoanalysis by the present writer. What follows is limited to a description of the developments which the theory of the instincts has passed through in psychoanalysis – developments which are still proceeding.

Contrast between Sexual Instincts and Ego Instincts. – Psychoanalysis early became aware that all mental occurrences must be regarded as built on the basis of an interplay of the forces of the elementary instincts. This, however, led to a difficult predicament, since psychology included no theory of the instincts. No one could say what an instinct really was, the question was left entirely to individual caprice, and every psychologist was in the habit of postulating any instincts in any number that he chose. The first sphere of phenomena to be studied by psychoanalysis comprised what are known as the transference neuroses (hysteria and obsessional neurosis). It was found that their symptoms came about by sexual instinctual impulses being rejected (repressed) by the subject's personality (his ego) and then finding expression by circuitous paths through the unconscious. These facts could be met by drawing a contrast between the sexual instincts and ego instincts (*instincts of self-preservation*), which was in line with the popular saying that hunger and love are what make the world go round: libido was the manifestation of the force of love in the same sense as was hunger of the self-preservative instinct. The nature of the ego instincts remained for the time being undefined and, like all the other characteristics of the ego, inaccessible to analysis. There was no means of deciding whether,

1. [Freud himself had in fact used the term 'libido' in his correspondence with Fliess as early as 18 August 1894 (1950a) and in his first paper on anxiety neurosis (1895b), *P.F.L.*, **10**, 48.]

and if so what, qualitative differences were to be assumed to exist between the two classes of instincts.

Primal Libido. – C. G. Jung attempted to resolve this obscurity along speculative lines by assuming that there was only a single primal libido which could be either sexualized or desexualized and which therefore coincided in its essence with mental energy in general. This innovation was methodologically disputable, caused a great deal of confusion, reduced the term 'libido' to the level of a superfluous synonym and was still in practice confronted with the necessity for distinguishing between sexual and asexual libido. The difference between the sexual instincts and instincts with other aims was not to be got rid of by means of a new definition.

Sublimation. – An attentive examination of the sexual trends, which alone were accessible to psychoanalysis, had meanwhile led to some remarkable detailed findings. What is described as the sexual instinct turns out to be of a highly composite nature and is liable to disintegrate once more into its component instincts. Each component instinct is unalterably characterized by its *source*, that is, by the region or zone of the body from which its excitation is derived. Each has furthermore as distinguishable features an *object* and an *aim*. The aim is always discharge accompanied by satisfaction, but it is capable of being changed from activity to passivity. The object is less closely attached to the instinct than was at first supposed; it is easily exchanged for another one, and, moreover, an instinct which had an external object can be turned round upon the subject's own self. The separate instincts can either remain independent of one another or – in what is still an inexplicable manner – can be combined and merged into one another to perform work in common. They are also able to replace one another and to transfer their libidinal cathexis to one another, so that the satisfaction of one instinct can take the place of the satisfaction of others. The most important vicissitude which an instinct can undergo seems to be *sublimation*; here both object and aim are changed, so that what was originally a sexual instinct finds satisfaction in some achievement which is no longer sexual but has a higher social or ethical valuation. These different features do not as yet combine to form an integral picture.

Narcissism. – A decisive advance was made when the analysis of dementia praecox and other psychotic disorders was ventured upon and thus the examination was begun of the ego itself, which had so far been known only as the agency of repression and opposition. It was found that the pathogenic process in dementia praecox is the withdrawal of the libido from objects and its introduction into the ego, while the clamorous symptoms of the disease arise from the vain struggles of the libido to find a pathway back to objects. It thus turned out to be possible for object-libido to change into cathexis of the ego and *vice versa*. Further reflection showed that this process must be presumed to occur on the largest scale and that the ego is to be regarded as a great reservoir of libido from which libido is sent out *to* objects and which is always ready to absorb libido flowing back *from* objects. Thus the instincts of self-preservation were also of a libidinal nature: they were sexual instincts which, instead of external objects, had taken the subject's own ego as an object. Clinical experience had made us familiar with people who behaved in a striking fashion as though they were in love with themselves and this perversion had been given the name of *narcissism*. The libido of the self-preservative instincts was now described as *narcissistic libido* and it was recognized that a high degree of this self-love constituted the primary and normal state of things. The earlier formula laid down for the transference neuroses consequently required to be modified, though not corrected. It was better, instead of speaking of a conflict between sexual instincts and ego instincts, to speak of a conflict between object-libido and ego-libido, or, since the nature of these instincts was the same, between the object-cathexes and the ego.

Apparent Approach to Jung's Views. – It thus seemed on the face of it as though the slow process of psychoanalytic research was following in the steps of Jung's speculation about a primal libido, especially because the transformation of object-libido into narcissism necessarily carried along with it a certain degree of desexualization, or abandonment of the specifically sexual aims. Nevertheless, it has to be borne in mind that the fact that the self-preservative instincts of the ego are recognized as libidinal does not necessarily prove that there are no other instincts operating in the ego.

The Herd Instinct. – It has been maintained in many quarters that there is a special innate and not further analysable 'herd instinct', which determines the social behaviour of human beings and impels individuals to come together into larger communities. Psychoanalysis finds itself in contradiction to this view. Even if the social instinct is innate, it may without any difficulty be traced back to what were originally libidinal object–cathexes and may have developed in the childhood of the individual as a reaction formation against hostile attitudes of rivalry. It is based on a peculiar kind of identification with other people.

Aim-inhibited Sexual Impulses. – The social instincts belong to a class of instinctual impulses which need not be described as sublimated, though they are closely related to these. They have not abandoned their directly sexual aims, but they are held back by internal resistances from attaining them; they rest content with certain approximations to satisfaction and for that very reason lead to especially firm and permanent attachments between human beings. To this class belong in particular the affectionate relations between parents and children, which were originally fully sexual, feelings of friendship, and the emotional ties in marriage which had their origin in sexual attraction.

Recognition of Two Classes of Instincts in Mental Life. – Though psychoanalysis endeavours as a rule to develop its theories as independently as possible from those of other sciences, it is nevertheless obliged to seek a basis for the theory of the instincts in biology. On the ground of a far-reaching consideration of the processes which go to make up life and which lead to death, it becomes probable that we should recognize the existence of two classes of instincts, corresponding to the contrary processes of construction and dissolution in the organism. On this view, the one set of instincts, which work essentially in silence, would be those which follow the aim of leading the living creature to death and therefore deserve to be called the '*death instincts*'; these would be directed outwards as the result of the combination of numbers of unicellular elementary organisms, and would manifest themselves as *destructive* or *aggressive* impulses. The other set of instincts would be those which are better known to us in analysis – the libidinal, sexual or life instincts, which are best comprised under the name of *Eros*; their purpose would be to form living substance into ever greater unities, so that life may be prolonged and brought to higher development. The erotic instincts and the death instincts would be present in living beings in regular mixtures or fusions; but 'defusions'[1] would also be liable to occur. Life would consist in the manifestations of the conflict or interaction between the two classes of instincts; death would mean for the individual the victory of the destructive instincts, but reproduction would mean for him the victory of Eros.

The Nature of the Instincts. – This view would enable us to characterize instincts as tendencies inherent in living substance towards restoring an earlier state of things: that is to say, they would be historically determined and of a conservative nature and, as it were, the expression of an inertia or elasticity present in what is organic. Both classes of instincts, Eros as well as the death instinct, would, on this view, have been in operation and working against each other from the first origin of life.

---

1. [This seems to be the earliest appearance of this term, which is discussed at greater length in Chapter IV of *The Ego and the Id* (1923*b*), P.F.L., **11**, 381–2.]

A SHORT ACCOUNT OF
PSYCHOANALYSIS
(1924 [1923])

KURZER ABRISS DER PSYCHOANALYSE

(A) German Editions:

1928   *Gesammelte Schriften*, **11**, 183–200.
1940   *Gesammelte Werke*, **13**, 403–27.

(B) English Translations:

'Psychoanalysis: Exploring the Hidden Recesses of the Mind'

1924   In *These Eventful Years: The Twentieth Century in the Making, as Told by Many of its Makers*, Vol. II, Chap. LXXIII, 511–23, London and New York: Encyclopaedia Britannica Publishing Co. (Tr. A. A. Brill.)

1961   *Standard Edition*, **19**, 189–209. (Tr. James Strachey.)

The present edition is a reprint of the *Standard Edition* version, with a few editorial changes.

We learn from Ernest Jones (1957, 114) that this was written by Freud, at the request of the American publishers, in October and November 1923. This work is to be distinguished from the article written some two years later for the *Encyclopaedia Britannica* itself (1926*f*).

A SHORT ACCOUNT OF
PSYCHOANALYSIS

I

PSYCHOANALYSIS may be said to have been born with the twentieth century; for the publication in which it emerged before the world as something new – my *Interpretation of Dreams* – bears the date '1900'.[1] But, as may well be supposed, it did not drop from the skies ready-made. It had its starting-point in older ideas, which it developed further; it sprang from earlier suggestions, which it elaborated. Any history of it must therefore begin with an account of the influences which determined its origin and should not overlook the times and circumstances that preceded its creation.

Psychoanalysis grew up in a narrowly restricted field. At the outset, it had only a single aim – that of understanding something of the nature of what were known as the 'functional' nervous diseases, with a view to overcoming the impotence which had so far characterized their medical treatment. The neurologists of that period had been brought up to have a high respect for chemico-physical and pathologico-anatomical facts; and they were latterly under the influence of the findings of Hitzig and Fritsch, of Ferrier, Goltz[2] and others, who seemed to have established an intimate and possibly exclusive connection between certain functions and particular parts of the

---

1. [It was actually published at the beginning of November 1899.]

2. [Eduard Hitzig (1838–1907) was Professor of Psychiatry at Halle University. – Gustav Fritsch (1838–1927) was Head of the Histology Department at Berlin University. – Sir David Ferrier, F.R.S. (1843–1928) was Professor of Neuropathology at King's College, London. – Friedrich L. Goltz (1834–1902) was Professor of Physiology at Strasbourg University.]

brain. They did not know what to make of the psychical factor and could not understand it. They left it to the philosophers, the mystics and – the quacks; and they considered it unscientific to have anything to do with it. Accordingly they could find no approach to the secrets of neuroses, and in particular of the enigmatic 'hysteria', which was, indeed, the prototype of the whole species. As late as in 1885, when I was studying at the Salpêtrière, I found that people were content to account for hysterical paralyses by a formula which asserted that they were founded on slight functional disturbances of the same parts of the brain which, when they were severely damaged, led to the corresponding organic paralyses.

Of course this lack of understanding affected the *treatment* of these pathological conditions badly as well. In general this consisted in measures designed to 'harden' the patient – in the prescription of medicines and in attempts, mostly very ill-contrived and executed in an unfriendly manner, at bringing mental influences to bear on him by threats, jeers and warnings and by exhorting him to make up his mind to 'pull himself together'. Electrical treatment was given out as being a specific cure for nervous conditions; but anyone who has endeavoured to carry out Erb's [1882] detailed instructions must marvel at the space that fantasy can occupy even in what professes to be an exact science. The decisive turn was taken in the eighties, when the phenomena of hypnotism made one more attempt to find admission to medical science – this time with more success than so often before, thanks to the work of Liébeault, Bernheim,[1] Heidenhain[2] and Forel.[3] The essential thing was that the genuineness of these phenomena was recognized. Once this had been admitted, two fundamental and unforgettable lessons could not fail to be drawn from hypnotism. First, one

---

1. [Cf. p. 66 *n*. 1 above.]

2. [Rudolf P. H. Heidenhain (1834–97) was Professor of Physiology and Histology at Breslau University.]

3. [August Forel (1848–1931) was Professor of Psychiatry at Zurich University. Freud wrote a favourable review of his book on hypnotism (Freud, 1889a).]

was given convincing proof that striking somatic changes could after all be brought about solely by mental influences, which in this case one had oneself set in motion. Secondly, one received the clearest impression – especially from the behaviour of subjects *after* hypnosis – of the existence of mental processes that one could only describe as 'unconscious'. The 'unconscious' had, it is true, long been under discussion among philosophers as a theoretical concept; but now for the first time, in the phenomena of hypnotism, it became something actual, tangible and subject to experiment. Apart from all this, hypnotic phenomena showed an unmistakable similarity to the manifestations of some neuroses.

It is not easy to overestimate the importance of the part played by hypnotism in the history of the origin of psychoanalysis. From a theoretical as well as from a therapeutic point of view, psychoanalysis has at its command a legacy which it has inherited from hypnotism.

Hypnosis also proved a valuable aid in the study of the neuroses – once again, first and foremost, of hysteria. Charcot's experiments created a great impression. He suspected that certain paralyses which appeared after a trauma (an accident) were of a hysterical nature, and he showed that, by suggesting a trauma under hypnosis, he was able to provoke paralyses of the same sort artificially. The expectation was thus raised that traumatic influences might in all cases play a part in the production of hysterical symptoms. Charcot himself made no further efforts towards a psychological understanding of hysteria; but his pupil, Pierre Janet, took up the question and was able to show, with the help of hypnosis, that the symptoms of hysteria were firmly dependent on certain unconscious thoughts (*idées fixes*). Janet attributed to hysteria a supposed constitutional incapacity for holding mental processes together – an incapacity which led to a disintegration (dissociation) of mental life.

Psychoanalysis, however, was not in any way based on these researches of Janet's. The decisive factor in its case was the experience of a Viennese physician, Dr Josef Breuer. In 1881, independently of any outside influence, he was able with the help of hypnosis to study and restore to health a highly gifted girl who suffered from hysteria. [Cf. *P.F.L.*, **3**, 73.] Breuer's findings were not given to the public until fifteen years later, after he had taken the present writer (Freud) into collaboration. This case of Breuer's retains its unique significance for our understanding of the neuroses to this day; so that we cannot avoid dwelling on it a little longer. It is essential to realize clearly in what its peculiarity consisted. The girl had fallen ill while she was nursing her father, to whom she was tenderly attached. Breuer was able to establish that all her symptoms were related to this period of nursing and could be explained by it. Thus it had for the first time become possible to obtain a complete view of a case of this puzzling neurosis, and all its symptoms had turned out to have a meaning. Further, it was a universal feature of the symptoms that they had arisen in situations involving an impulse to an action which, however, had not been carried out but had for other reasons been suppressed. The symptoms had, in fact, appeared *in place of* the actions that were not performed. Thus, to explain the aetiology of hysterical symptoms, we were led to the subject's emotional life (to affectivity) and to the interplay of mental forces (to dynamics); and since then these two lines of approach have never been dropped.

The precipitating causes of the symptoms were compared by Breuer to Charcot's traumas. Now it was a remarkable fact that all these traumatic precipitating causes, and all the mental impulses starting from them, were lost to the patient's memory, as though they had never happened; while their products – the symptoms – persisted unaltered, as though, so far as they were concerned, there was no such thing as the effacing effect of time. Here, therefore, we had a fresh proof of the existence of mental processes which were unconscious but for that very reason especially powerful – processes which we had first come to know in post-hypnotic suggestion. The therapeutic procedure adopted by Breuer was to induce the patient, under hypnosis, to remember the forgotten traumas and to react to them with powerful expressions of affect. When this had been done, the symptoms, which had till then taken the place of these expressions of emotion, disappeared. Thus one and the same procedure served simultaneously the purposes of investigating and of getting rid of the ailment; and this unusual conjunction was later retained in psychoanalysis.

After the present writer had, during the early nineties, confirmed Breuer's results in a considerable number of patients, the two, Breuer and Freud, together decided on a publication, *Studies on Hysteria* (1895*d*), which contained their findings and an attempt at a theory based on them. This asserted that hysterical symptoms arose when the affect of a mental process cathected with a strong affect was forcibly prevented from being worked over consciously in the normal way and was thus diverted into a wrong path. In cases of hysteria, according to this theory, the affect passed over into an unusual somatic innervation ('conversion'), but could be given another direction and got rid of ('abreacted'), if the experience were revived under hypnosis. The authors gave this procedure the name of 'catharsis' (purging, setting free of a strangulated affect).

The cathartic method was the immediate precursor of psychoanalysis; and, in spite of every extension of experience and of every modification of theory, is still contained within it as its nucleus. But it was no more than a new medical procedure for influencing certain nervous diseases, and nothing suggested that it might become a subject for the most general interest and for the most violent contradiction.

II

Soon after the publication of *Studies on Hysteria* the partnership between Breuer and Freud came to an end. Breuer, who was in reality a consultant in internal medicine, gave up treating nervous patients, and Freud devoted himself to the further perfection of the instrument left over to him by his elder collaborator. The technical novelties which he introduced and the discoveries which he made changed the cathartic method into psychoanalysis. The most momentous step, no doubt, was his determination to do without the assistance of hypnosis in his technical procedure. He did so for two reasons: first, because, in spite of a course of instruction with Bernheim at Nancy, he did not succeed in inducing hypnosis in a sufficient number of cases, and secondly, because he was dissatisfied with the therapeutic results of catharsis based on hypnosis. It is true that these results were striking and appeared after a treatment of short duration, but they turned out not to be permanent and to depend too much on the patient's personal relations with the physician. The abandonment of hypnosis made a breach in the course of development of the procedure up to then, and it meant a fresh start.

Hypnosis had, however, performed the service of restoring to the patient's memory what he had forgotten. It was necessary to find some other technique to replace it; and the idea occurred to Freud of substituting for it the method of 'free association'. That is to say, he pledged his patients to refrain from any conscious reflection and to abandon themselves, in a state of quiet concentration, to following the ideas which occurred to them spontaneously (involuntarily) – 'to skim off the surface of their consciousness'. They were to communicate these ideas to the physician even if they felt objections to doing so, if, for instance, the thoughts seemed too disagreeable, too senseless, too unimportant or irrelevant. The choice of free association as a means of investigating the forgotten unconscious material seems so strange that a word in justification of it will not be out of place. Freud was led to it by an expectation that the so-called 'free' association would prove in fact to be unfree, since, when all conscious intellectual purposes had been suppressed, the ideas that emerged would be seen to be determined by the unconscious material. This expectation was justified by experience. When the 'fundamental rule of psychoanalysis' which has just been stated was obeyed, the course of free association produced a plentiful store of ideas which could put one on the track of what the patient had forgotten. To be sure, this material did not bring up what had actually been forgotten, but it brought up such plain and numerous hints at it that, with the help of a certain amount of supplementing and interpreting, the doctor was able to guess (to reconstruct) the forgotten material from it. Thus free association together with the art of interpretation performed the same function as had previously been performed by hypnotism.

It looked as though our work had been made much more difficult and complicated; but the inestimable gain was that an insight was now obtained into an interplay of forces which had been concealed from the observer by the hypnotic state. It became evident that the work of uncovering what had been pathogenically forgotten had to struggle against a constant and very intense resistance. The critical objections which the patient raised in order to avoid communicating the ideas which occurred to him, and against which the fundamental rule of psychoanalysis was directed, had themselves already been manifestations of this resistance. A consideration of the phenomena of resistance led to one of the corner-stones of the psychoanalytic theory of the neuroses – the theory of repression. It was plausible to suppose that the same forces which were now struggling against the pathogenic material being made conscious had at an earlier time made the same efforts with success. A gap in the aetiology of neurotic symptoms was thus filled. The impressions and mental impulses, for which the symptoms were now serving as substitutes, had not been forgotten without reason or on account of a constitutional incapacity for synthesis (as Janet supposed); they had, through the influence of other mental forces, met with a repression the success and evidence of which was precisely their being debarred from consciousness and excluded from memory. It was only in consequence of this repression that they had become pathogenic – that is, had succeeded in manifesting themselves along unusual paths as symptoms.

A conflict between two groups of mental trends had to be looked on as the ground for repression and accordingly as the cause of every neurotic illness. And here experience taught us a new and surprising fact about the nature of the forces that were struggling against each other. Repression invariably proceeded from the sick person's conscious personality (his ego) and took its stand on aesthetic and ethical motives; the impulses that were subjected to repression were those of selfishness and cruelty, which can be summed up in general as evil, but above all sexual wishful impulses, often of the crudest and most forbidden kind. Thus the symptoms were a substitute for forbidden satisfactions and the illness seemed to correspond to an incomplete subjugation of the immoral side of human beings.

Advance in knowledge made ever clearer the enormous part played in mental life by sexual wishful impulses, and led to a detailed study of the nature and development of the sexual instinct.[1] But we also came upon another purely empirical finding, in the discovery that the experiences and conflicts of the first years of childhood play an unsuspectedly important part in the individual's development and leave behind them ineffaceable dispositions bearing upon the period of maturity. This led to the revelation of something that had hitherto been fundamentally overlooked by science – infantile sexuality, which, from the tenderest age onwards, is manifested both in physical reactions and in mental attitudes. In order to bring together this sexuality of children with what is described as the normal sexuality of adults and the abnormal sexual life of perverts, the concept of what was sexual had itself to be corrected and widened in a manner which could be justified by the evolution of the sexual instinct.

After hypnosis was replaced by the technique of free association, Breuer's cathartic procedure turned into psychoanalysis, which for more than a decade was developed by the author (Freud) alone. During that time psychoanalysis gradually acquired a theory which appeared to give a satisfactory account of the origin, meaning and purpose of neurotic symptoms and provided a rational basis for medical attempts at curing the complaint. I will once again enumerate the factors

1. Freud, *Three Essays on the Theory of Sexuality* (1905d) [*P.F.L.*, **7**, 31 ff.].

that go to make up this theory. They are: emphasis on instinctual life (affectivity), on mental dynamics, on the fact that even the apparently most obscure and arbitrary mental phenomena invariably have a meaning and a causation, the theory of psychical conflict and of the pathogenic nature of repression, the view that symptoms are substitutive satisfactions, the recognition of the aetiological importance of sexual life, and in particular of the beginnings of infantile sexuality. From a philosophical standpoint this theory was bound to adopt the view that the mental does not coincide with the conscious, that mental processes are in themselves unconscious and are only made conscious by the functioning of special organs (agencies or systems). By way of completing this list, I will add that among the affective attitudes of childhood the complicated emotional relation of children to their parents – what is known as the Oedipus complex – came into prominence. It became ever clearer that this was the nucleus of every case of neurosis, and in the patient's behaviour towards his analyst certain phenomena of his emotional transference emerged which came to be of great importance for theory and technique alike.

In the form which it thus assumed, the psychoanalytic theory of the neuroses already contained a number of things which ran counter to accepted opinions and inclinations and which were calculated to provoke astonishment, repugnance and scepticism in outsiders: for instance, the attitude of psychoanalysis to the problem of the unconscious, its recognition of an infantile sexuality and the stress it laid on the sexual factor in mental life generally. But more was to follow.

III

In order to reach even half-way to an understanding of how, in a hysterical girl, a forbidden sexual wish can change into a painful symptom, it had been necessary to make far-reaching and complicated hypotheses about the structure and functioning of the mental apparatus. There was an evident contradiction here between expenditure of effort and result. If the conditions postulated by psychoanalysis really existed, they were of a fundamental nature and must be able to find expression in other phenomena besides hysterical ones. But if this inference were correct, psychoanalysis would have ceased to be of interest only to neurologists; it could claim the attention of everyone to whom psychological research was of any importance. Its findings would not only have to be taken into account in the field of pathological mental life but could not be overlooked either in coming to an understanding of normal functioning.

Evidence of its being of use for throwing light on other than pathological mental activity was early forthcoming in connection with two kinds of phenomena: with the very frequent parapraxes that occur in everyday life – such as forgetting things, slips of the tongue, and mislaying objects – and with the dreams dreamt by healthy and psychically normal people. Small failures of functioning, like the temporary forgetting of normally familiar proper names, slips of the tongue and of the pen, and so on, had hitherto not been considered worthy of any explanation at all or were supposed to be accounted for by conditions of fatigue, by distraction of the attention, etc. The present writer then showed from many examples, in his book *The Psychopathology of Everyday Life* (1901*b*), that events of this kind have a meaning, and arise owing to a conscious intention being interfered with by another, suppressed or actually unconscious one. As a rule, quick reflection or a short analysis is enough to reveal the interfering influence. Owing to the frequency of such parapraxes as slips of the tongue, it became easy for anyone to convince himself from his own experience of the existence of mental processes which are not conscious, but which are nevertheless operative and which at least find expression as inhibitions and modifications of other, intended acts.

The analysis of dreams led further: it was brought to public notice by the present writer as early as in 1900 in *The Interpretation of Dreams*. This showed that dreams are constructed in just the same way as neurotic symptoms. Like them, they may appear strange and senseless; but, if we examine them by a technique which differs little from the free association used in psychoanalysis, we are led from their manifest content to a secret meaning, to the latent dream-thoughts. This latent meaning is always a wishful impulse which is represented as fulfilled at the moment of the dream. But, except in young children and under the pressure of imperative physical needs, this secret wish can never be expressed recognizably. It has first to submit to a distortion, which is the work of restrictive, censoring forces in the dreamer's ego. In this way the manifest dream, as it is remembered in waking life, comes about. It is distorted, to the pitch of being unrecognizable, by concessions made to the dream censorship; but it can be revealed once more by analysis as an expression of a situation of satisfaction or as the fulfilment of a wish. It is a compromise between two conflicting groups of mental trends, just as we have found to be the case with hysterical symptoms. The formula which, at bottom, best meets the essence of the dream is this: a dream is a (disguised) fulfilment of a (repressed) wish. The study of the process which transforms the latent dream-wish into the manifest content of the dream – a process known as the 'dream-work' – has taught us the best part of what we know of unconscious mental life.

Now a dream is not a morbid symptom but a product of the normal mind. The wishes which it represents as fulfilled are the same as those which are repressed in neuroses. Dreams owe the possibility of their genesis merely to the favourable circumstance that during the state of sleep, which paralyses man's power of movement, repression is mitigated into the dream censorship. If, however, the process of dream formation oversteps certain limits, the dreamer brings it to a stop and wakes up in a fright. Thus it is proved that the same forces and the same processes taking place between them operate in normal as in pathological mental life. From the date of *The Interpretation of Dreams* psychoanalysis had a twofold significance. It was not only a new method of treating the neuroses but it was also a new psychology; it claimed the attention not only of nerve specialists but also of all those who were students of a mental science.

The reception given it in the scientific world was, however, no friendly one. For some ten years no one took any notice of Freud's works. About the year 1907 attention was drawn to psychoanalysis by a group of Swiss psychiatrists (Bleuler and Jung, in Zurich), and a storm of indignation, which was not precisely fastidious in its methods and arguments, thereupon broke out, particularly in Germany. In this, psychoanalysis was sharing the fate of many novelties which, after a certain lapse of time, have found general recognition. Nevertheless, it lay in its nature that it should inevitably arouse particularly violent opposition. It wounded the prejudices of civilized humanity at some specially sensitive spots. It subjected every individual, as it were, to the analytic reaction, by uncovering what had by universal agreement been repressed into the unconscious; and in this way it forced its contemporaries to behave like patients who, under analytic treatment, above all else bring their resistances to the fore. It must also be admitted that it was no easy thing to become convinced of the correctness of the psychoanalytic theories, nor to obtain instruction in the practice of analysis.

The general hostility, however, did not succeed in preventing psychoanalysis from continuous expansion during the next decade in two directions; on the map, for interest in it was constantly cropping up in new countries, and in the field of the mental sciences, for it was constantly finding applications in new branches of knowledge. In 1909 President G. Stanley Hall invited Freud and Jung to give a series of lectures at Clark University in Worcester, Mass., of which he was the head and where they were given a friendly reception. [Cf. Freud, 1910a.] Since then psychoanalysis has remained popular in America, although precisely in that country its name has been coupled with much superficiality and some abuses. As early as in 1911, Havelock Ellis was able to report that analysis was studied and practised, not only in Austria and Switzerland, but also in the United States, in

England, India, Canada, and, no doubt, in Australia too.

It was in this period of struggle and of first blossoming, moreover, that the periodicals devoted exclusively to psychoanalysis were inaugurated. These were the *Jahrbuch für psychoanalytische und psychopathologische Forschungen* (1909–14), directed by Bleuler and Freud and edited by Jung, which ceased publication at the outbreak of the World War, the *Zentralblatt für Psychoanalyse* (1911), edited by Adler and Stekel, which was soon replaced by the *Internationale Zeitschrift für Psychoanalyse* (1913, today in its tenth volume); further, since 1912, *Imago*, founded by Rank and Sachs, a periodical for the application of psychoanalysis to the mental sciences. The great interest taken in the subject by Anglo-American doctors was shown in 1913 by the founding of the still active *Psychoanalytic Review* by White and Jelliffe. Later, in 1920, *The International Journal of Psycho-Analysis*, intended specially for readers in England, made its appearance under the editorship of Ernest Jones. The Internationaler Psychoanalytischer Verlag and the corresponding English undertaking, The International Psycho-Analytical Press, brought out a continuous series of analytic publications under the name of the Internationale Psychoanalytische Bibliothek. The literature of psychoanalysis is, of course, not to be found only in these periodicals, which are for the most part supported by psychoanalytic societies; it appears far and wide in a great number of places, in scientific and in literary publications. Among the periodicals of the Latin world which pay special attention to psychoanalysis the *Rivista de Psiquiatria*, edited by H. Delgado in Lima (Peru), may be specially mentioned.

An essential difference between this second decade of psychoanalysis and the first lay in the fact that the present writer was no longer its sole representative. A constantly growing circle of pupils and followers had collected around him, who devoted themselves first to the diffusion of the theories of psychoanalysis and then extended them, supplemented them and carried them deeper. In the course of years, several of these supporters, as was inevitable, seceded, took their own paths, or turned themselves into an opposition which seemed to threaten the continuity of the development of psychoanalysis. Between 1911 and 1913 C. G. Jung in Zurich and Alfred Adler in Vienna produced some stir by their attempts at giving new interpretations to the facts of analysis and their efforts at a diversion from the analytic standpoint. But it soon appeared that these secessions had effected no lasting damage. What temporary success they achieved was easily accounted for by the readiness of the mass of people to have themselves set free from the pressure of the demands of psychoanalysis by whatever path might be opened to them. The great majority of co-workers remained firm and continued their work along the lines indicated to them. We shall come on their names repeatedly in the short account below of the findings of psychoanalysis in the many and various fields of its application.

IV

The noisy rejection of psychoanalysis by the medical world could not deter its supporters from developing it, to begin with, along its original lines into a specialized pathology and treatment of the neuroses – a task which has not been completely accomplished even today. Its undeniable therapeutic success, which far exceeded any that had previously been achieved, constantly spurred them on to fresh efforts; while the difficulties which came to light as the material was examined more deeply led to profound alterations in the technique of analysis and to important corrections in its theoretical hypotheses and postulates.

In the course of this development, the technique of psychoanalysis has become as definite and as delicate as that of any other specialized branch of medicine. A failure to understand this fact has led to many abuses (particularly in England and America) because people who have acquired only a literary knowledge of psychoanalysis from reading consider themselves capable of undertaking analytic treatments without having received any special training. The consequences of such behaviour are damaging both to the science and to the patients and have brought much discredit upon psychoanalysis. The foundation of a first psychoanalytic out-patient clinic (by Max Eitingon in Berlin in 1920) has therefore become a step of high practical importance. This institute seeks on the one hand to make analytic treatment accessible to wide circles of the population and on the other hand undertakes the education of doctors to be practical analysts by a course of training which includes as a condition that the learner shall agree to be analysed himself.

Among the hypothetical concepts which enable the doctor to deal with the analytic material, the first to be mentioned is that of 'libido'. Libido means in psychoanalysis in the first instance the force (thought of as quantitatively variable and measurable) of the sexual instincts directed towards an object – 'sexual' in the extended sense required by analytic theory. Further study showed that it was necessary to set alongside this 'object-libido' a 'narcissistic' or 'ego-libido', directed to the subject's own ego; and the interaction of these two forces has enabled us to account for a great number of normal and abnormal processes in mental life. A rough distinction was soon made between what are known as the 'transference neuroses' and the narcissistic disorders. The former (hysteria and obsessional neurosis) are the objects proper of psychoanalytic treatment, while the others, the narcissistic neuroses, though they can, it is true, be examined by the help of analysis, offer fundamental difficulties to therapeutic influence. It is true that the libido theory of psychoanalysis is by no means complete and that its relation to a general theory of the instincts is not yet clear, for psychoanalysis is a young science, quite unfinished and in a stage of rapid development. Here, however, it should be emphatically pointed out how erroneous the charge of pan-sexualism is which is so often levelled at psychoanalysis. It seeks to show that psychoanalytic theory knows of no mental motive forces other than purely sexual ones and in doing so exploits popular prejudices by using the word 'sexual' not in its analytic but in its vulgar sense.

The psychoanalytic view would also have to include in narcissistic disorders all the ailments described in psychiatry as 'functional psychoses'. It could not be doubted that neuroses and psychoses are not separated by a hard and fast line, any more than health and neurosis; and it was plausible to explain the mysterious psychotic phenomena by the discoveries achieved on the neuroses, which had hitherto been equally incomprehensible. The present writer had himself, during the period of his isolation, made a case of paranoid illness partly intelligible by an analytic investigation and had pointed out in this unquestionable psychosis the same contents (complexes) and a similar interplay of forces as in the simple neuroses.[1] Bleuler [1906b] followed out the indications of what he called 'Freudian mechanisms' in a whole number of psychoses, and Jung won high opinions as an analyst at a single blow when, in 1907, he explained the most eccentric symptoms in the end-stages of dementia praecox from the individual life-histories of the patients. The comprehensive study of schizophrenia by Bleuler (1911) probably demonstrated once and for all the justification of a psychoanalytic angle of approach for the understanding of these psychoses.

In this way psychiatry became the first field to which psychoanalysis was applied and it has remained so ever since. The same research workers who have done most to deepen analytic knowledge of the neuroses, such as Karl Abraham in Berlin and Sándor Ferenczi in Budapest (to name only the most prominent), have also played a leading part in throwing analytic light on the psychoses. The conviction of the unity and intimate connection of all the disorders that present themselves as neurotic and psychotic phenomena is becoming more and more firmly established despite all the efforts of the psychiatrists. People are beginning to understand – best of all, perhaps, in America – that the psychoanalytic study of the neuroses is

1. [See Section III of Freud's second paper on the neuropsychoses of defence (1896b).]

the only preparation for an understanding of the psychoses, and that psychoanalysis is destined to make possible a scientific psychiatry of the future which will not need to content itself with describing curious clinical pictures and unintelligible sequences of events and with tracing the influence of gross anatomical and toxic traumas upon a mental apparatus which is inaccessible to our knowledge.

V

But the importance of psychoanalysis for psychiatry would never have drawn the attention of the intellectual world to it or won it a place in *The History of our Times*.[1] This result was brought about by the relation of psychoanalysis to normal, not to pathological, mental life. Originally, analytic research had indeed no other aim than to establish the determinants of the onset (the genesis) of a few morbid mental states. In the course of its efforts, however, it succeeded in bringing to light facts of fundamental importance, in actually creating a new psychology, so that it became obvious that the validity of such findings could not possibly be restricted to the sphere of pathology. We have seen already when it was that the decisive proof was produced of the correctness of this conclusion. It was when dreams were successfully interpreted by analytic technique – dreams, which are a part of the mental life of normal people and which yet may in fact be regarded as pathological products that can regularly appear under healthy conditions.

If the psychological discoveries gained from the study of dreams were firmly kept in view, only one further step was needed before psychoanalysis could be proclaimed as the theory of the deeper mental processes not directly accessible to consciousness – as a 'depth-psychology' – and before it could be applied to almost all the mental sciences. This step lay in the transition from the mental activity of individual men to the

1. [In English in the original – a probable allusion to the title of the publication for which this paper was written.]

psychical functions of human communities and peoples – that is, from individual to group psychology; and many surprising analogies forced this transition upon us. It had been found, for instance, that in the deep strata of unconscious mental activity contraries are not distinguished from each other but are expressed by the same element. But already in 1884 Karl Abel the philologist had put forward the view (in his 'Über den Gegensinn der Urworte'[1]) that the oldest languages known to us treat contraries in the same way. Thus Ancient Egyptian, for example, had in the first instance only one word for 'strong' and 'weak', and not till later were the two sides of the antithesis distinguished by slight modifications. Even in the most modern languages clear relics of such antithetical meanings are to be found. So in German '*Boden*' ['garret' or 'ground'] means the highest as well as the lowest thing in the house; similarly in Latin '*altus*' means 'high' and 'deep'. Thus the equivalence of contraries in dreams is a universal archaic trait in human thinking.

To take an instance from another field, it is impossible to escape the impression of the perfect correspondence which can be discovered between the obsessive actions of certain obsessional patients and the religious observances of believers all over the world.[2] Some cases of obsessional neurosis actually behave like a caricature of a private religion, so that it is tempting to liken the official religions to an obsessional neurosis that has been mitigated by becoming universalized. This comparison, which is no doubt highly objectionable to all believers, has nevertheless proved most fruitful psychologically. For psychoanalysis soon discovered in the case of obsessional neurosis what the forces are that struggle with one another in it till their conflicts find a remarkable expression in the ceremonial of obsessive actions. Nothing similar was suspected in the case of religious ceremonial until, by tracing back religious feeling to the relation with the father as its deepest root, it

1. ['The Antithetical Meaning of Primal Words'; cf. Freud (1910e).]
2. [Cf. Freud, 'Obsessive Actions and Religious Practices' (1907b), *P.F.L.*, **13**, 27 ff.]

became possible to point to an analogous dynamic situation in that case too.[1] This instance, moreover, may warn the reader that even in its application to non-medical fields psychoanalysis cannot avoid wounding cherished prejudices, touching upon deeply rooted sensibilities and thus provoking enmities which have an essentially emotional basis.

If we may assume that the most general features of unconscious mental life (conflicts between instinctual impulses, repressions and substitutive satisfactions) are present everywhere, and if there is a depth-psychology which leads to a knowledge of those features, then we may reasonably expect that the application of psychoanalysis to the most varied spheres of human mental activity will everywhere bring to light important and hitherto unattainable results. In an exceedingly valuable study, Otto Rank and Hanns Sachs (1913) have tried to bring together what the work of psychoanalysts had been able to achieve up to that time towards fulfilling these expectations. Lack of space prevents me from attempting to complete their enumeration here. I can only select for mention the most important findings with the addition of a few details.

If we leave little-known internal urges out of account, we may say that the main motive force towards the cultural development of man has been real external exigency, which has withheld from him the easy satisfaction of his natural needs and exposed him to immense dangers. This external frustration drove him into a struggle with reality, which ended partly in adaptation to it and partly in control over it; but it also drove him into working and living in common with those of his kind, and this already involved a renunciation of a number of instinctual impulses which could not be satisfied socially. With the further advances of civilization the demands of repression also grew. Civilization is after all built entirely on renunciation of instinct, and every individual on his journey from childhood to maturity has in his own person to recapitulate this development of humanity to a state of judicious resignation. Psychoanalysis has shown that it is predominantly, though not

1. [Cf. *Totem and Taboo* (1912–13), ibid., **13**, 43 ff.]

exclusively, sexual instinctual impulses that have succumbed to this cultural suppression. One portion of them, however, exhibit the valuable characteristic of allowing themselves to be diverted from their immediate aims and of thus placing their energy at the disposal of cultural development in the form of 'sublimated' trends. But another portion persist in the unconscious as unsatisfied wishes and press for some, even if it is distorted, satisfaction.

We have seen that one part of human mental activity is directed towards obtaining control over the real external world. Psychoanalysis now tells us further that another, particularly highly prized, part of creative mental work serves for the fulfilment of wishes – for the substitutive satisfaction of the repressed wishes which, from the days of childhood, live in the spirit of each of us, unsatisfied. Among these creations, whose connection with an incomprehensible unconscious was always suspected, are myths and works of imaginative writing and of art, and the researches of psychoanalysts have in fact thrown a flood of light on the fields of mythology, the science of literature, and the psychology of artists. It is enough to mention Otto Rank's work [1907] as an example. We have shown that myths and fairy tales can be interpreted like dreams, we have traced the convoluted paths that lead from the urge of the unconscious wish to its realization in a work of art, we have learnt to understand the emotional effect of a work of art on the observer, and in the case of the artist himself we have made clear his internal kinship with the neurotic as well as his distinction from him, and we have pointed out the connection between his innate disposition, his chance experiences and his achievements. The aesthetic appreciation of works of art and the elucidation of the artistic gift are, it is true, not among the tasks set to psychoanalysis. But it seems that psychoanalysis is in a position to speak the decisive word in all questions that touch upon the imaginative life of man.

And now, as a third point, psychoanalysis has shown us, to our growing astonishment, the enormously important part played by what is known as the 'Oedipus complex' – that is, the emotional relation of a child to its two parents – in the mental life of human beings. Our astonishment diminishes when we realize that the Oedipus complex is the psychical correlate of two fundamental biological facts: the long period of the human child's dependence, and the remarkable way in which its sexual life reaches a first climax in the third to fifth years of life, and then, after a period of inhibition, sets in again at puberty. And here, the discovery was made that a third and extremely serious part of human intellectual activity, the part which has created the great institutions of religion, law, ethics, and all forms of civic life, has as its fundamental aim the enabling of the individual to master his Oedipus complex and to divert his libido from its infantile attachments into the social ones that are ultimately desired. The applications of psychoanalysis to the science of religion and sociology (e.g. by the present writer [1912–13], Theodor Reik [1919] and Oskar Pfister [1913]), which have led to these findings, are still young and insufficiently appreciated; but it cannot be doubted that further studies will only confirm the certainty of these important conclusions.

By way, as it were, of postscript, I must also mention that educationists, too, cannot avoid making use of the hints which they have received from the analytic exploration of the mental life of children; and further that voices have been raised among therapists (e.g. Groddeck and Jelliffe), maintaining that the psychoanalytic treatment of serious organic complaints shows promising results, since in many of these affections some part is played by a psychical factor on which it is possible to bring influence to bear.

Thus we may express our expectation that psychoanalysis, whose development and achievements hitherto have been briefly and inadequately related in these pages, will enter into the cultural development of the next decades as a significant ferment, and will help to deepen our understanding of the world and to fight against some things in life which are recognized as injurious. It must not be forgotten, however, that psychoanalysis alone cannot offer a complete picture of the world. If we accept the distinction which I have recently proposed of dividing the mental apparatus into an ego, turned towards the external world and equipped with consciousness, and an unconscious id, dominated by its instinctual needs, then psychoanalysis is to be described as a psychology of the id (and of its effects upon the ego). In each field of knowledge, therefore, it can make only *contributions*, which require to be completed from the psychology of the ego.[1] If these contributions often contain the essence of the facts, this only corresponds to the important part which, it may be claimed, is played in our lives by the mental unconscious that has so long remained unknown.

1. [Freud seems, in this passage, to be imposing unusual restrictions on the scope of psychoanalysis.]

AN AUTOBIOGRAPHICAL STUDY
(1925 [1924])

EDITOR'S NOTE

SELBSTDARSTELLUNG

(A) German Editions:

1925　In Grote's *Die Medizin der Gegenwart in Selbstdar-stellungen*, **4**, 1–52. (Leipzig: Meiner.)

1928　*Gesammelte Schriften*, **11**, 119–82.

1934　In book form, with title *Selbstdarstellung*. Leipzig, Vienna and Zurich: Internationaler Psychoanalytischer Verlag. (1936, 2nd ed., with new footnotes and 'Nachschrift 1935'.)

1948　*Gesammelte Werke*, **14**, 33–96. (With new footnotes from 2nd ed., but without additional matter.)

'Nachschrift 1935'

1935　*Almanach 1936*, 9–14.

1936　In *Selbstdarstellung*, 2nd ed.

1950　*Gesammelte Werke*, **16**, 31–4.

(B) English Translations:
An Autobiographical Study

1927　In *The Problem of Lay-Analyses*. New York: Brentano. Pp. 189–316. (Tr. James Strachey.)

1935　London: Hogarth Press and Institute of Psycho-Analysis. (Revised from 2nd German ed., with new footnotes and 'Postscript (1935)'.) New York: Norton. (As London edition, but with different title.)

1959　*Standard Edition*, **20**, 1–74. (Modified version of above.)

The present edition is a corrected reprint of the *Standard Edition* version, with some editorial modifications.

As Freud explains in his 'Postscript' (see below), the English translation of this work, when it was first published in America in 1927, was included in the same volume as his discussion of 'lay analysis'; but the *Autobiographical Study* was not mentioned either on the title-page or on the outer cover of the book. When the work was taken over by a new American publisher eight years later, he suggested to Freud that it should be revised and brought up to date. Thus the new material appeared in English before its publication in German.

We learn from Ernest Jones (1957, 123) that the main work was written in August and September 1924, and actually appeared in February 1925; the 'Postscript' was completed by May 1935.

This work is commonly, and quite misleadingly, referred to as Freud's 'Autobiography'. The title of the series to which it was originally contributed – *Die Medizin der Gegenwart in Selbstdarstellungen* (which might be translated 'Contemporary Medicine in Self-Portrayals') – shows clearly enough that the aim of its editors (it was published in four volumes, 1923–5, with contributions from some twenty-seven leading medical authorities) was to present an account of the recent history of medical science from the pens of those who had played a chief part in making it. Thus Freud's study is essentially an account of his personal share in the development of psychoanalysis. As he himself points out in the opening paragraph, he was inevitably going over much of the ground which he had already traversed in his paper 'On the History of the Psycho-Analytic Movement' (1914*d*); cf. p. 57 ff. Nevertheless, as a comparison between the two works will show, his present mood was a very different one. The controversies that embittered the earlier paper had now faded into insignificance and he was able to give a cool and entirely objective account of the evolution of his scientific views.

Those who wish for the story of his personal life must once
more be referred to the three volumes of Ernest Jones's biography.

AN AUTOBIOGRAPHICAL STUDY

I

SEVERAL of the contributors to this series of 'Autobiographical Studies' have begun by expressing their misgivings at the unusual difficulties of the task they have undertaken. The difficulties in my case are, I think, even greater; for I have already more than once published papers upon the same lines as the present one, papers which, from the nature of the subject, have dealt more with personal considerations than is usual or than would otherwise have been necessary.

I gave my first account of the development and subject matter of psychoanalysis in five lectures which I delivered in 1909 before Clark University at Worcester, Mass., where I had been invited to attend the celebration of the twentieth anniversary of the foundation of that body.[1] Only recently I gave way to the temptation of making a contribution of a similar kind to an American collective publication dealing with the opening years of the twentieth century, since its editors had shown their recognition of the importance of psychoanalysis by allotting a special chapter to it.[2] Between these two dates appeared a paper, 'On the History of the Psychoanalytic Movement',[3] which, in fact, contains the essence of

---

1. The lectures were first published (in English) in the *American Journal of Psychology* (1910); the original German was issued under the title of *Über Psychoanalyse* [1910a].

2. *These Eventful Years* (New York, 1924). My essay, translated by Dr A. A. Brill, forms chapter lxxiii of the second volume [1924f; cf. p. 159 ff. above].

3. [Freud (1914d); cf. p. 57 ff. above.]

all that I can say on the present occasion. Since I must not contradict myself and since I have no wish to repeat myself exactly, I must endeavour to construct a narrative in which subjective and objective attitudes, biographical and historical interests, are combined in a new proportion.

I was born on 6 May 1856, at Freiberg in Moravia, a small town in what is now Czechoslovakia. My parents were Jews, and I have remained a Jew myself. I have reason to believe that my father's family were settled for a long time on the Rhine (at Cologne), that, as a result of a persecution of the Jews during the fourteenth or fifteenth century, they fled eastwards, and that, in the course of the nineteenth century, they migrated back from Lithuania through Galicia into German Austria. When I was a child of four I came to Vienna, and I went through the whole of my education there. At the *Gymnasium* [grammar school] I was at the top of my class for seven years; I enjoyed special privileges there, and had scarcely ever to be examined in class. Although we lived in very limited circumstances, my father insisted that, in my choice of a profession, I should follow my own inclinations alone. Neither at that time, nor indeed in my later life, did I feel any particular predilection for the career of a doctor.[1] I was moved, rather, by a sort of curiosity, which was, however, directed more towards human concerns than towards natural objects; nor had I grasped the importance of observation as one of the best means of gratifying it. My deep engrossment in the Bible story[2] (almost as soon as I had learnt the art of reading) had, as I recognized much later, an enduring effect upon the direction of my interest. Under the powerful influence of a school friendship with a boy rather my senior who grew up to be a well-known politician, I developed a wish to study law like him and to engage in social activities. At the same time, the theories of Darwin, which were then of topical interest, strongly attracted me,

1. [This is enlarged upon in Freud's Postscript to *The Question of Lay Analysis* (1927a); see p. 35 ff. below.]

2. [This sentence and the following one were added in 1935.]

for they held out hopes of an extraordinary advance in our understanding of the world; and it was hearing Goethe's beautiful essay on Nature read aloud at a popular lecture by Professor Carl Brühl[1] just before I left school that decided me to become a medical student.

When, in 1873, I first joined the University, I experienced some appreciable disappointments. Above all, I found that I was expected to feel myself inferior and an alien because I was a Jew. I refused absolutely to do the first of these things. I have never been able to see why I should feel ashamed of my descent or, as people were beginning to say, of my 'race'. I put up, without much regret, with my non-acceptance into the community; for it seemed to me that in spite of this exclusion an active fellow-worker could not fail to find some nook or cranny in the framework of humanity. These first impressions at the University, however, had one consequence which was afterwards to prove important; for at an early age I was made familiar with the fate of being in the Opposition and of being put under the ban of the 'compact majority'.[2] The foundations were thus laid for a certain degree of independence of judgement.

I was compelled, moreover, during my first years at the University, to make the discovery that the peculiarities and limitations of my gifts denied me all success in many of the departments of science into which my youthful eagerness had plunged me. Thus I learned the truth of Mephistopheles' warning:

Vergebens, dass ihr ringsum wissenschaftlich schweift,
Ein jeder lernt nur, was er lernen kann.[3]

At length, in Ernst Brücke's[4] physiological laboratory, I

1. [This name was inserted in 1935. According to Pestalozzi (1956) the essay 'Fragment über die Natur' was in fact written by the Swiss author, G. C. Tobler. Goethe included it by a paramnesia among his own works.]
2. [The reference is to Ibsen's *Enemy of the People*.]
3. ['It is in vain that you range around from science to science: each man learns only what he can learn.' – Goethe, *Faust*, Part I, Scene 4.]
4. [Ernst Wilhelm von Brücke (1819–92), Professor of Physiology.]

found rest and full satisfaction – and men, too, whom I could respect and take as my models: the great Brücke himself, and his assistants, Sigmund Exner[1] and Ernst Fleischl von Marxow.[2] With the last of these, a brilliant man, I was privileged to be upon terms of friendship. Brücke gave me a problem to work out in the histology of the nervous system; I succeeded in solving it to his satisfaction and in carrying the work further on my own account. I worked at this Institute, with short interruptions, from 1876 to 1882, and it was generally thought that I was marked out to fill the next post of Assistant that might fall vacant there.[3] The various branches of medicine proper, apart from psychiatry, had no attraction for me. I was decidedly negligent in pursing my medical studies, and it was not until 1881 that I took my somewhat belated degree as a Doctor of Medicine.

The turning-point came in 1882, when my teacher, for whom I felt the highest possible esteem, corrected my father's generous improvidence by strongly advising me, in view of my bad financial position, to abandon my theoretical career. I followed his advice, left the physiological laboratory and entered the General Hospital as an *Aspirant* [Clinical Assistant]. I was soon afterwards promoted to being a *Sekundararzt* [Junior or House Physician], and worked in various departments of the hospital, among others for more than six months under Meynert,[4] by whose work and personality I had been greatly struck while I was still a student.

In a certain sense I nevertheless remained faithful to the line of work upon which I had originally started. The subject which Brücke had proposed for my investigations had been the spinal cord of one of the lowest of the fishes (*Ammocoetes Pet-*

---

1. [Sigmund Exner (1846–1926) succeeded Brücke as Professor of Physiology.]

2. [Ernst Fleischl von Marxow (1840–91) was distinguished both as physicist and physiologist.]

3. [There are many references to this period in *The Interpretation of Dreams* (1900*a*). See, in particular, *P.F.L.*, **4**, 619 ff.]

4. [Theodor Meynert (1833–92), Professor of Psychiatry.]

romyzon);[1] and I now passed on to the human central nervous system. Just at this time Flechsig's[2] discoveries of the non-simultaneity of the formation of the medullary sheaths were throwing a revealing light upon the intricate course of its tracts. The fact that I began by choosing the medulla oblongata as the one and only subject of my work was another sign of the continuity of my development. In complete contrast to the diffuse character of my studies during my earlier years at the University, I was now developing an inclination to concentrate my work exclusively upon a single subject or problem. This inclination has persisted and has since led to my being accused of one-sidedness.

I now became as active a worker in the Institute of Cerebral Anatomy as I had previously been in the physiological one. Some short papers upon the course of the tracts and the nuclear origins in the medulla oblongata [Freud, 1885*d*, 1886*b*, 1886*c*] date from these hospital years, and some notice was taken of my findings by Edinger.[3] One day Meynert, who had given me access to the laboratory even during the times when I was not actually working under him, proposed that I should definitely devote myself to the anatomy of the brain, and promised to hand over his lecturing work to me, as he felt he was too old to manage the newer methods. This I declined, in alarm at the magnitude of the task; it is possible, too, that I had guessed already that this great man was by no means kindly disposed towards me.

From the material point of view, brain anatomy was certainly no better than physiology, and, with an eye to pecuniary considerations, I began to study nervous diseases. There were, at that time, few specialists in that branch of medicine in Vienna, the material for its study was distributed over a number of different departments of the hospital, there was no satis-

1. [Freud, 1877*a* and 1878*a*.]

2. [Paul Flechsig (1847–1929) was Professor of Psychiatry at Leipzig University.]

3. [Ludwig Edinger (1855–1918), the well-known Berlin Professor of Neuro-Anatomy.]

factory opportunity of learning the subject, and one was forced to be one's own teacher. Even Nothnagel,[1] who had been appointed a short time before, on account of his book upon cerebral localization [1879], did not single out neuropathology from among the other subdivisions of medicine. In the distance shone the great name of Charcot;[2] so I formed a plan of first obtaining an appointment as University Lecturer on Nervous Diseases in Vienna and of then going to Paris to continue my studies.

In the course of the following years, while I continued to work as a junior physician, I published a number of clinical observations on organic diseases of the nervous system. I gradually became familiar with the ground; I was able to localize the site of a lesion in the medulla oblongata so accurately that the pathological anatomist had no further information to add; I was the first person in Vienna to send a case for autopsy with a diagnosis of polyneuritis acuta.

The fame of my diagnoses and of their *post-mortem* confirmation brought me an influx of American physicians, to whom I lectured upon the patients in my department in a sort of pidgin English. About the neuroses I understood nothing. On one occasion I introduced to my audience a neurotic suffering from a persistent headache as a case of chronic localized meningitis; they all quite rightly rose in revolt and deserted me, and my premature activities as a teacher came to an end. By way of excuse I may add that this happened at a time when greater authorities than myself in Vienna were in the habit of diagnosing neurasthenia as cerebral tumour.

In the spring of 1885 I was appointed Lecturer in Neuropathology on the ground of my histological and clinical publications. Soon afterwards, as the result of a warm testimonial from Brücke, I was awarded a travelling bursary of considerable value.[3] In the autumn of the same year I made the journey to Paris.

1. [Hermann Nothnagel (1841–1905), Professor of Medicine.]
2. [See above, p. 29 n. 3.]
3. [The amount was 600 florins, worth something under £50 or $250 at

I became a student at the Salpêtrière, but, as one of the crowd of foreign visitors, I had little attention paid me to begin with. One day in my hearing Charcot expressed his regret that since the war he had heard nothing from the German translator of his lectures; he went on to say that he would be glad if someone would undertake to translate the new volume of his lectures into German. I wrote to him and offered to do so; I can still remember a phrase in the letter, to the effect that I suffered only from '*l'aphasie motrice*' and not from '*l'aphasie sensorielle du français*'. Charcot accepted the offer, I was admitted to the circle of his personal acquaintances, and from that time forward I took a full part in all that went on at the Clinic.

As I write these lines, a number of papers and newspaper articles have reached me from France, which give evidence of a violent objection to the acceptance of psychoanalysis, and which often make the most inaccurate assertions in regard to my relations with the French School. I read, for instance, that I made use of my visit to Paris to familiarize myself with the theories of Pierre Janet and then made off with my booty. I should therefore like to say explicitly that during the whole of my visit to the Salpêtrière Janet's name was never so much as mentioned.

What impressed me most of all while I was with Charcot were his latest investigations upon hysteria, some of which were carried out under my own eyes. He had proved, for instance, the genuineness of hysterical phenomena and their conformity to laws ('*introite et hic dii sunt*'),[1] the frequent occurrence of hysteria in men, the production of hysterical

---

the time. Freud's official report on his visits to Paris and Berlin has now become available (Freud, 1956a [1886]).]

1. [In a letter to Fliess of 4 December 1896 (Freud, 1950a, Letter 51), Freud quoted these words as a 'proud motto' for a chapter on the psychology of hysteria in a book that he was planning (but never wrote). The phrase is more usually quoted as: '*Introite, nam et hic dii sunt*'. ('Enter, for here too are gods.')]

paralyses and contractures by hypnotic suggestion and the fact that such artificial products showed, down to their smallest details, the same features as spontaneous attacks, which were often brought on traumatically. Many of Charcot's demonstrations began by provoking in me and in other visitors a sense of astonishment and an inclination to scepticism, which we tried to justify by an appeal to one of the theories of the day. He was always friendly and patient in dealing with such doubts, but he was also most decided; it was in one of these discussions that (speaking of theory) he remarked, '*Ça n'empêche pas d'exister*', a *mot* which left an indelible mark upon my mind.[1]

No doubt not the whole of what Charcot taught us at that time holds good today: some of it has become doubtful, some has definitely failed to withstand the test of time. But enough is left over that has found a permanent place in the storehouse of science. Before leaving Paris I discussed with the great man a plan for a comparative study of hysterical and organic paralyses. I wished to establish the thesis that in hysteria paralyses and anaesthesias of the various parts of the body are demarcated according to the popular idea of their limits and not according to anatomical facts. He agreed with this view, but it was easy to see that in reality he took no special interest in penetrating more deeply into the psychology of the neuroses.[2] When all is said and done, it was from pathological anatomy that his work had started.

Before I returned to Vienna I stopped for a few weeks in Berlin, in order to gain a little knowledge of the general disorders of childhood. Kassowitz,[3] who was at the head of a public institute in Vienna for the treatment of children's diseases, had promised to put me in charge of a department for the nervous diseases of children. In Berlin I was given assistance

1. [A footnote by Freud to one of his translations of Charcot (Freud, 1892 94, 210) shows that this remark was addressed to him himself.]

2. [Some seven years later Freud published his paper on the subject, in French (1893c).]

3. [Max Kassowitz (1842–1913), the Vienna paediatrician.]

and a friendly reception by Baginsky.[1] In the course of the next few years I published, from the Kassowitz Institute, several monographs of considerable size on unilateral and bilateral cerebral palsies in children [Freud, 1891*a*, 1893*b*]. And for that reason, at a later date (in 1897), Nothnagel made me responsible for dealing with the same subject in his great *Handbuch der allgemeinen und speziellen Therapie* [Freud, 1897*a*].

In the autumn of 1886 I settled down in Vienna as a physician, and married the girl who had been waiting for me in a distant city for more than four years. I may here go back a little and explain how it was the fault of my *fiancée* that I was not already famous at that youthful age.[2] A side interest, though it was a deep one, had led me in 1884 to obtain from Merck[3] some of what was then the little-known alkaloid cocaine and to study its physiological action. While I was in the middle of this work, an opportunity arose for making a journey to visit my *fiancée*, from whom I had been parted for two years. I hastily wound up my investigation of cocaine and contented myself in my monograph on the subject [1884*e*] with prophesying that further uses for it would soon be found. I suggested, however, to my friend Königstein,[4] the ophthalmologist, that he should investigate the question of how far the anaesthetizing properties of cocaine were applicable in diseases of the eye. When I returned from my holiday I found that not he, but another of my friends, Carl Koller[5] (now in New York), whom I had also spoken to about cocaine, had made the decisive experiments upon animals' eyes and had demonstrated them at the Ophthalmological Congress at Heidelberg. Koller is therefore rightly regarded as the dis-

1. [Adolf Baginsky (1843–1918) was the editor of a paediatric journal to which Freud contributed neurological abstracts.]

2. [This episode is discussed at length in Chapter VI of Jones, 1953.]

3. [A chemical firm in Darmstadt.]

4. [Leopold Königstein (1850–1924), Professor of Ophthalmology, was a lifelong friend of Freud's.]

5. [Carl Koller (1857–1944) was house surgeon at the Vienna General Hospital at the time of this discovery. He later became a successful ophthalmic surgeon in New York.]

coverer of local anaesthesia by cocaine, which has become so important in minor surgery; but I bore my *fiancée* no grudge for the interruption.[1]

I will now return to the year 1886, the time of my settling down in Vienna as a specialist in nervous diseases. The duty devolved upon me of giving a report before the Gesellschaft der Aerzte [Society of Medicine] upon what I had seen and learnt with Charcot. But I met with a bad reception. Persons of authority, such as the chairman (Bamberger, the physician), declared that what I said was incredible. Meynert challenged me to find some cases in Vienna similar to those which I had described and to present them before the Society. I tried to do so; but the senior physicians in whose departments I found any such cases refused to allow me to observe them or to work at them. One of them, an old surgeon, actually broke out with the exclamation: 'But, my dear sir, how can you talk such nonsense? *Hysteron* (*sic*) means the uterus. So how can a man be hysterical?' I objected in vain that what I wanted was not to have my diagnosis approved, but to have the case put at my disposal. At length, outside the hospital, I came upon a case of classical hysterical hemi-anaesthesia in a man, and demonstrated it before the Gesellschaft der Aerzte [1886d]. This time I was applauded, but no further interest was taken in me. The impression that the high authorities had rejected my innovations remained unshaken; and, with my hysteria in men and my production of hysterical paralyses by suggestion, I found myself forced into the Opposition. As I was soon afterwards excluded from the laboratory of cerebral anatomy[2] and for terms on end had nowhere to deliver my lectures, I withdrew from academic life and ceased to attend the learned societies. It is a whole generation since I have visited the Gesellschaft der Aerzte.

1. [In 1924 this read '*mein damaliges Versäumnis* (my omission at the time)'. This was changed in 1935 to '*die damalige Störung* (the interruption at the time)'.]

2. [Freud's relations with Meynert are discussed among the associations to one of his dreams in *The Interpretation of Dreams* (1900a), P.F.L., **4**, 568–9; cf. also ibid., 253.]

Anyone who wants to make a living from the treatment of nervous patients must clearly be able to do something to help them. My therapeutic arsenal contained only two weapons, electrotherapy and hypnotism, for prescribing a visit to a hydropathic establishment after a single consultation was an inadequate source of income. My knowledge of electrotherapy was derived from W. Erb's textbook [1882], which provided detailed instructions for the treatment of all the symptoms of nervous diseases. Unluckily I was soon driven to see that following these instructions was of no help whatever and that what I had taken for an epitome of exact observations was merely the construction of fantasy. The realization that the work of the greatest name in German neuropathology had no more relation to reality than some 'Egyptian' dream-book, such as is sold in cheap bookshops, was painful, but it helped to rid me of another shred of the innocent faith in authority from which I was not yet free. So I put my electrical apparatus aside, even before Moebius had saved the situation by explaining that the successes of electric treatment in nervous disorders (in so far as there were any) were the effect of suggestion on the part of the physician.

With hypnotism the case was better. While I was still a student I had attended a public exhibition given by Hansen the 'magnetist',[1] and had noticed that one of the subjects experimented upon had become deathly pale at the onset of cataleptic rigidity and had remained so as long as that condition lasted. This firmly convinced me of the genuineness of the phenomena of hypnosis. Scientific support was soon afterwards given to this view by Heidenhain[2]; but that did not restrain the professors of psychiatry from declaring for a long time to come that hypnotism was not only fraudulent but dangerous and from regarding hypnotists with contempt. In Paris I had seen hypnotism used freely as a method for producing symptoms in patients and then removing them again. And

1. [Carl Hansen (1833–97), the Danish mesmerist, whose popular demonstrations did much to reawaken interest in hypnosis.]

2. [See p. 162 n. 2 above.]

now the news reached us that a school had arisen at Nancy which made an extensive and remarkably successful use of suggestion, with or without hypnosis, for therapeutic purposes. It thus came about, as a matter of course, that in the first years of my activity as a physician my principal instrument of work, apart from haphazard and unsystematic psychotherapeutic methods, was hypnotic suggestion.

This implied, of course, that I abandoned the treatment of organic nervous diseases; but that was of little importance. For on the one hand the prospects in the treatment of such disorders were in any case never promising, while, on the other hand, in the private practice of a physician working in a large town, the quantity of such patients was nothing compared to the crowds of neurotics, whose number seemed further multiplied by the way in which they hurried, with their troubles unsolved, from one physician to another. And, apart from this, there was something positively seductive in working with hypnotism. For the first time there was a sense of having overcome one's helplessness; and it was highly flattering to enjoy the reputation of being a miracle-worker. It was not until later that I was to discover the drawbacks of the procedure. At the moment there were only two points to complain of: first, that I could not succeed in hypnotizing every patient, and secondly, that I was unable to put individual patients into as deep a state of hypnosis as I should have wished. With the idea of perfecting my hypnotic technique, I made a journey to Nancy in the summer of 1889 and spent several weeks there. I witnessed the moving spectacle of old Liébeault working among the poor women and children of the labouring classes. I was a spectator of Bernheim's astonishing experiments upon his hospital patients, and I received the profoundest impression of the possibility that there could be powerful mental processes which nevertheless remained hidden from the consciousness of men. Thinking it would be instructive, I had persuaded one of my patients to follow me to Nancy. This patient was a very highly gifted hysteric, a woman of good birth, who had been handed over to me because no one knew what to do with her. By hypnotic influence I had made it possible for her to lead a tolerable existence and I was always able to take her out of the misery of her condition. But she always relapsed again after a short time, and in my ignorance I attributed this to the fact that her hypnosis had never reached the stage of somnambulism with amnesia. Bernheim now attempted several times to bring this about, but he too failed. He frankly admitted to me that his great therapeutic successes by means of suggestion were only achieved in his hospital practice and not with his private patients. I had many stimulating conversations with him, and undertook to translate into German his two works upon suggestion and its therapeutic effects.[1]

During the period from 1886 to 1891 I did little scientific work, and published scarcely anything. I was occupied with establishing myself in my new profession and with assuring my own material existence as well as that of a rapidly increasing family. In 1891 there appeared the first of my studies on the cerebral palsies of children, which was written in collaboration with my friend and assistant, Dr Oskar Rie [Freud, 1891a]. An invitation which I received in the same year to contribute to an encyclopaedia of medicine[2] led me to investigate the theory of aphasia. This was at the time dominated by the views of Wernicke and Lichtheim, which laid stress exclusively upon localization. The fruit of this inquiry was a small critical and speculative book, *Zur Auffassung der Aphasien* [1891b].

But I must now show how it happened that scientific research once more became the chief interest of my life.

II

I must supplement what I have just said by explaining that from the very first I made use of hypnosis in *another* manner, apart from hypnotic suggestion. I used it for questioning the patient upon the origin of his symptom, which in his waking

1. [This must be a mistake, since the first of Freud's translations of Bernheim was published before his visit to Nancy (Freud, 1888–9). The second appeared in 1892.]

2. [Villaret's *Handwörterbuch*, to which Freud contributed some unsigned and not certainly identifiable articles (1888b and 1891c).]

state he could often describe only very imperfectly or not at all. Not only did this method seem more effective than mere suggestive commands or prohibitions, but it also satisfied the curiosity of the physician, who, after all, had a right to learn something of the origin of the phenomenon which he was striving to remove by the monotonous procedure of suggestion.

The manner in which I arrived at this other procedure was as follows. While I was still working in Brücke's laboratory I had made the acquaintance of Dr Josef Breuer, who was one of the most respected family physicians in Vienna, but who also had a scientific past, since he had produced several works of permanent value upon the physiology of respiration and upon the organ of equilibrium. He was a man of striking intelligence and fourteen years older than myself. Our relations soon became more intimate and he became my friend and helper in my difficult circumstances. We grew accustomed to share all our scientific interests with each other. In this relationship the gain was naturally mine. The development of psychoanalysis afterwards cost me his friendship. It was not easy for me to pay such a price, but I could not escape it.

Even before I went to Paris, Breuer had told me about a case of hysteria which, between 1880 and 1882, he had treated in a peculiar manner which had allowed him to penetrate deeply into the causation and significance of hysterical symptoms. This was at a time, therefore, when Janet's works still belonged to the future. He repeatedly read me pieces of the case history, and I had an impression that it accomplished more towards an understanding of neuroses than any previous observation. I determined to inform Charcot of these discoveries when I reached Paris, and I actually did so. But the great man showed no interest in my first outline of the subject, so that I never returned to it and allowed it to pass from my mind.

When I was back in Vienna I turned once more to Breuer's observation and made him tell me more about it. The patient had been a young girl of unusual education and gifts, who had fallen ill while she was nursing her father, of whom she was devotedly fond. When Breuer took over her case it presented a variegated picture of paralyses with contractures, inhibitions and states of mental confusion. A chance observation showed her physician that she could be relieved of these clouded states of consciousness if she was induced to express in words the affective fantasy by which she was at the moment dominated. From this discovery, Breuer arrived at a new method of treatment. He put her into deep hypnosis and made her tell him each time what it was that was oppressing her mind. After the attacks of depressive confusion had been overcome in this way, he employed the same procedure for removing her inhibitions and physical disorders. In her waking state the girl could no more describe than other patients how her symptoms had arisen, and she could discover no link between them and any experiences of her life. In hypnosis she immediately discovered the missing connection. It turned out that all her symptoms went back to moving events which she had experienced while nursing her father; that is to say, her symptoms had a meaning and were residues or reminiscences of those emotional situations. It was found in most instances that there had been some thought or impulse which she had had to suppress while she was by her father's sick-bed, and that, in place of it, as a substitute for it, the symptom had afterwards appeared. But as a rule the symptom was not the precipitate of a single such 'traumatic' scene, but the result of a summation of a number of similar situations. When the patient recalled a situation of this kind in a hallucinatory way under hypnosis and carried through to its conclusion, with a free expression of emotion, the mental act which she had originally suppressed, the symptom was abolished and did not return. By this procedure Breuer succeeded, after long and painful efforts, in relieving his patient of all her symptoms.

The patient had recovered and had remained well and, in fact, had become capable of doing serious work. But over the final stage of this hypnotic treatment there rested a veil of obscurity, which Breuer never raised for me; and I could not understand why he had so long kept secret what seemed to me an invaluable discovery instead of making science the richer by it. The immediate question, however, was whether it was possible to generalize from what he had found in a single case. The state of things which he had discovered seemed to me to be of so fundamental a nature that I could not believe it could fail to be present in any case of hysteria if it had been proved to occur in a single one. But the question could only be decided by experience. I therefore began to repeat Breuer's investigations with my own patients and eventually, especially after my visit to Bernheim in 1889 had taught me the limitations of hypnotic suggestion, I worked at nothing else. After observing for several years that his findings were invariably confirmed in every case of hysteria that was accessible to such treatment, and after having accumulated a considerable amount of material in the shape of observations analogous to his, I proposed to him that we should issue a joint publication. At first he objected vehemently, but in the end he gave way, especially since, in the meantime, Janet's works had anticipated some of his results, such as the tracing back of hysterical symptoms to events in the patient's life, and their removal by means of hypnotic reproduction *in statu nascendi*. In 1893 we issued a preliminary communication, 'On the Psychical Mechanism of Hysterical Phenomena', and in 1895 there followed our book, *Studies on Hysteria*. [Cf. p. 132 above.]

If the account I have so far given has led the reader to expect that the *Studies on Hysteria* must, in all essentials of their material content, be the product of Breuer's mind, that is precisely what I myself have always maintained and what it has been my aim to repeat here. As regards the *theory* put forward in the book, I was partly responsible, but to an extent which it is today no longer possible to determine.[1] That theory was in any case unpretentious and hardly went beyond the direct description of the observations. It did not seek to establish the nature of hysteria but merely to throw light upon the origin of its symptoms. Thus it laid stress upon the significance of the

1. [The subject of this paragraph and the next is discussed at some length in the Editor's Introduction to *Studies on Hysteria*, *P.F.L.*, **3**, 39 ff.]

life of the emotions and upon the importance of distinguishing between mental acts which are unconscious and those which are conscious (or rather capable of being conscious); it introduced a dynamic factor, by supposing that a symptom arises through the damming-up of an affect, and an economic factor, by regarding that same symptom as the product of the transformation of an amount of energy which would otherwise have been employed in some other way. (This latter process was described as *conversion*.) Breuer spoke of our method as *cathartic*; its therapeutic aim was explained as being to provide that the quota of affect used for maintaining the symptom, which had got on to the wrong lines and had, as it were, become strangulated there, should be directed on to the normal path along which it could obtain discharge (or *abreaction*). The practical results of the cathartic procedure were excellent. Its defects, which became evident later, were those of all forms of hypnotic treatment. There are still a number of psychotherapists who have not gone beyond catharsis as Breuer understood it and who still speak in its favour. Its value as an abridged method of treatment was shown afresh by Simmel [1918] in his treatment of war neuroses in the German army during the Great War. The theory of catharsis had not much to say on the subject of sexuality. In the case histories which I contributed to the *Studies* sexual factors played a certain part, but scarcely more attention was paid to them than to other emotional excitations. Breuer wrote of the girl, who has since become famous as his first patient, that her sexual side was extraordinarily undeveloped.[1] It would have been difficult to guess from the *Studies on Hysteria* what an importance sexuality has in the aetiology of the neuroses.

The stage of development which now followed, the transition from catharsis to psychoanalysis proper, has been described by me several times already in such detail that I shall find it difficult to bring forward any new facts. The event which formed the opening of this period was Breuer's retirement from our common work, so that I became the sole

1. [Cf. *P.F.L.*, **3**, 73.]

administrator of his legacy. There had been differences of opinion between us at quite an early stage, but they had not been a ground for our separating. In answering the question of when it is that a mental process becomes pathogenic – that is, when it is that it becomes impossible for it to be dealt with normally – Breuer preferred what might be called a physiological theory: he thought that the processes which could not find a normal outcome were such as had originated during unusual, 'hypnoid', mental states. This opened the further question of the origin of these hypnoid states. I, on the other hand, was inclined to suspect the existence of an interplay of forces and the operation of intentions and purposes such as are to be observed in normal life. Thus it was a case of 'hypnoid hysteria' versus 'neuroses of defence'. But such differences as this would scarcely have alienated him from the subject if there had not been other factors at work. One of these was undoubtedly that his work as a physician and family doctor took up much of his time, and that he could not, like me, devote his whole strength to the work of catharsis. Again, he was affected by the reception which our book had received both in Vienna and in Germany. His self-confidence and powers of resistance were not developed so fully as the rest of his mental organization. When, for instance, the *Studies* met with a severe rebuff from Strümpell,[1] I was able to laugh at the lack of comprehension which his criticism showed, but Breuer felt hurt and grew discouraged. But what contributed chiefly to his decision was that my own further work led in a direction to which he found it impossible to reconcile himself.

The theory which we had attempted to construct in the *Studies* remained, as I have said, very incomplete; and in particular we had scarcely touched on the problem of aetiology, on the question of the ground in which the pathogenic process takes root. I now learned from my rapidly increasing experience that it was not *any* kind of emotional excitation that was in action behind the phenomena of neurosis but habitually

1. [Adolf von Strümpell (1853–1925), the well-known German neurologist, reviewed the book very critically. Cf. Strümpell (1896).]

one of a sexual nature, whether it was a current sexual conflict or the effect of earlier sexual experiences. I was not prepared for this conclusion and my expectations played no part in it, for I had begun my investigation of neurotics quite unsuspectingly. While I was writing my 'History of the Psycho-Analytic Movement' in 1914, there recurred to my mind some remarks that had been made to me by Breuer, Charcot, and Chrobak, which might have led me to this discovery earlier.[1] But at the time I heard them I did not understand what these authorities meant; indeed they had told me more than they knew themselves or were prepared to defend. What I heard from them lay dormant and inactive within me, until the chance of my cathartic experiments brought it out as an apparently original discovery. Nor was I then aware that in deriving hysteria from sexuality I was going back to the very beginnings of medicine and following up a thought of Plato's. It was not until later that I learnt this from an essay by Havelock Ellis.[2]

Under the influence of my surprising discovery, I now took a momentous step. I went beyond the domain of hysteria and began to investigate the sexual life of the so-called neurasthenics who used to visit me in numbers during my consultation hours. This experiment cost me, it is true, my popularity as a doctor, but it brought me convictions which today, almost thirty years later, have lost none of their force. There was a great deal of equivocation and mystery-making to be overcome, but, once that had been done, it turned out that in all of these patients grave abuses of the sexual function were present. Considering how extremely widespread are these abuses on the one hand and neurasthenia on the other, a frequent coincidence between the two would not have proved much; but there was more in it than that one bald fact. Closer observation suggested to me that it was possible to pick out from the confused jumble of clinical pictures covered by the name of neurasthenia two

1. [Cf. p. 69f. above.]

2. [In a letter to Fliess of 3 January 1899 (Freud, 1950a, Letter 101), Freud mentioned that the article by Ellis (1898) 'begins with Plato and ends with Freud'.]

fundamentally different types, which might appear in any degree of mixture but which were nevertheless to be observed in their pure forms. In the one type the central phenomenon was the anxiety attack with its equivalents, rudimentary forms and chronic substitutive symptoms; I consequently gave it the name of *anxiety neurosis*, and limited the term *neurasthenia* to the other type.[1] Now it was easy to establish the fact that each of these types had a different abnormality of sexual life as its corresponding aetiological factor: in the former, *coitus interruptus*, unconsummated excitation and sexual abstinence, and in the latter, excessive masturbation and too numerous nocturnal emissions. In a few specially instructive cases, which had shown a surprising alteration in the clinical picture from one type to the other, it could be proved that there had been a corresponding change in the underlying sexual régime. If it was possible to put an end to the abuse and allow its place to be taken by normal sexual activity, a striking improvement in the condition was the reward.

I was thus led into regarding the neuroses as being without exception disturbances of the sexual function, the so-called '*actual neuroses*' being the direct toxic expression of such disturbances and the *psychoneuroses* their mental expression. My medical conscience felt pleased at my having arrived at this conclusion. I hoped that I had filled up a gap in medical science, which, in dealing with a function of such great biological importance, had failed to take into account any injuries beyond those caused by infection or by gross anatomical lesions. The medical aspect of the matter was, moreover, supported by the fact that sexuality was not something purely mental. It had a somatic side as well, and it was possible to assign special chemical processes to it and to attribute sexual excitation to the presence of some particular, though at present unknown, substances.[2] There must also have been some good reason why the true spontaneous

1. [Freud (1895*b*), *P.F.L.*, **10**, 31 ff.]

2. [Cf. *Three Essays* (1905*d*), ibid., **7**, 136 ff. and 137 *n*. 1; also Editor's Note, ibid., 35–6.]

neuroses resembled no group of diseases more closely than the phenomena of intoxication and abstinence, which are produced by the administration or privation of certain toxic substances, or than exophthalmic goitre, which is known to depend upon the product of the thyroid gland.

Since that time I have had no opportunity of returning to the investigation of the 'actual' neuroses;[1] nor has this part of my work been continued by anyone else. If I look back today at my early findings, they strike me as being the first rough outlines of what is probably a far more complicated subject. But on the whole they seem to me still to hold good. I should have been very glad if I had been able, later on, to make a psychoanalytic examination of some more cases of simple juvenile neurasthenia, but unluckily the occasion did not arise. To avoid misconceptions, I should like to make it clear that I am far from denying the existence of mental conflicts and of neurotic complexes in neurasthenia. All that I am asserting is that the symptoms of these patients are not mentally determined or removable by analysis, but that they must be regarded as direct toxic consequences of disturbed sexual chemical processes.

During the years that followed the publication of the *Studies*, having reached these conclusions upon the part played by sexuality in the aetiology of the neuroses, I read some papers on the subject before various medical societies, but was only met with incredulity and contradiction. Breuer did what he could for some time longer to throw the great weight of his personal influence into the scales in my favour, but he effected nothing and it was easy to see that he too shrank from recognizing the sexual aetiology of the neuroses. He might have crushed me or at least disconcerted me by pointing to his own

1. [The 'actual' neuroses, i.e. those with a purely contemporary and physical aetiology (neurasthenia and anxiety neurosis), were much discussed by Freud during the Breuer period, but not often mentioned in his later writings. See, for example, the paper on narcissism (1914*c*), *P.F.L.*, **11**, 76–8, the *Introductory Lectures* (1916–17), ibid., **1**, 433–8, and *Inhibitions, Symptoms and Anxiety* (1926*d*), ibid., **10**, 264, 298–9, 320. Cf. also ibid., **10**, 80 *n*., 114 *n*., and p. 140 above.]

first patient, in whose case sexual factors had ostensibly played no part whatever. But he never did so, and I could not understand why this was, until I came to interpret the case correctly and to reconstruct, from some remarks which he had made, the conclusion of his treatment of it. After the work of catharsis had seemed to be completed, the girl had suddenly developed a condition of 'transference love'; he had not connected this with her illness, and had therefore retired in dismay.[1] It was obviously painful to him to be reminded of this apparent *contretemps*. His attitude towards me oscillated for some time between appreciation and sharp criticism; then accidental difficulties arose, as they never fail to do in a strained situation, and we parted.

Another result of my taking up the study of nervous disorders in general was that I altered the technique of catharsis. I abandoned hypnotism and sought to replace it by some other method, because I was anxious not to be restricted to treating hysteriform conditions. Increasing experience had also given rise to two grave doubts in my mind as to the use of hypnotism even as a means to catharsis. The first was that even the most brilliant results were liable to be suddenly wiped away if my personal relation with the patient became disturbed. It was true that they would be re-established if a reconciliation could be effected; but such an occurrence proved that the personal emotional relation between doctor and patient was after all stronger than the whole cathartic process, and it was precisely that factor which escaped every effort at control. And one day I had an experience which showed me in the crudest light what I had long suspected. It related to one of my most acquiescent patients, with whom hypnotism had enabled me to bring about the most marvellous results, and whom I was engaged in relieving of her suffering by tracing back her attacks of pain to their origins. As she woke up on one occasion, she threw her arms round my neck. The unexpected entrance of a servant relieved us from a painful discussion, but from that time

1. [The full story is told by Ernest Jones (1953, 246 ff.). Cf. also *P.F.L.*, **3**, 95 *n*.]

onwards there was a tacit understanding between us that the hypnotic treatment should be discontinued. I was modest enough not to attribute the event to my own irresistible personal attraction, and I felt that I had now grasped the nature of the mysterious element that was at work behind hypnotism. In order to exclude it, or at all events to isolate it, it was necessary to abandon hypnotism.

But hypnotism had been of immense help in the cathartic treatment, by widening the field of the patient's consciousness and putting within his reach knowledge which he did not possess in his waking life. It seemed no easy task to find a substitute for it. While I was in this perplexity there came to my help the recollection of an experiment which I had often witnessed while I was with Bernheim. When the subject awoke from the state of somnambulism, he seemed to have lost all memory of what had happened while he was in that state. But Bernheim maintained that the memory was present all the same; and if he insisted on the subject remembering, if he asseverated that the subject knew it all and had only to say it, and if at the same time he laid his hand on the subject's forehead, then the forgotten memories used in fact to return, hesitatingly at first, but eventually in a flood and with complete clarity. I determined that I would act in the same way. My patients, I reflected, must in fact 'know' all the things which had hitherto only been made accessible to them in hypnosis; and assurances and encouragement on my part, assisted perhaps by the touch of my hand, would, I thought, have the power of forcing the forgotten facts and connections into consciousness. No doubt this seemed a more laborious process than putting the patients into hypnosis, but it might prove highly instructive. So I abandoned hypnotism, only retaining my practice of requiring the patient to lie upon a sofa while I sat behind him, seeing him, but not seen myself.

III

My expectations were fulfilled; I was set free from hypnotism. But along with the change in technique the work of catharsis took on a new complexion. Hypnosis had screened from view an interplay of forces which now came in sight and the understanding of which gave a solid foundation to my theory.

How had it come about that the patients had forgotten so many of the facts of their external and internal lives but could nevertheless recollect them if a particular technique was applied? Observation supplied an exhaustive answer to these questions. Everything that had been forgotten had in some way or other been distressing; it had been either alarming or painful or shameful by the standards of the subject's personality. It was impossible not to conclude that that was precisely why it had been forgotten – that is, why it had not remained conscious. In order to make it conscious again in spite of this, it was necessary to overcome something that fought against one in the patient; it was necessary to make efforts on one's own part so as to urge and compel him to remember. The amount of effort required of the physician varied in different cases; it increased in direct proportion to the difficulty of what had to be remembered. The expenditure of force on the part of the physician was evidently the measure of a *resistance* on the part of the patient. It was only necessary to translate into words what I myself had observed, and I was in possession of the theory of *repression*.

It was now easy to reconstruct the pathogenic process. Let us keep to a simple example, in which a particular impulsion had arisen in the subject's mind but was opposed by other powerful impulsions. We should have expected the mental *conflict* which now arose to take the following course. The two dynamic quantities – for our present purposes let us call them 'the instinct' and 'the resistance' – would struggle with each other for some time in the fullest light of consciousness, until the instinct was repudiated and the cathexis of energy withdrawn from its impulsion. This would have been the normal solution. In a neurosis, however (for reasons which were still unknown), the conflict found a different outcome. The ego drew back, as it were, on its first collision with the objectionable instinctual impulse; it debarred the impulse from access to consciousness and to direct motor discharge, but at the same time the impulse retained its full cathexis of energy. I named this process *repression*; it was a novelty, and nothing like it had ever before been recognized in mental life. It was obviously a primary mechanism of defence, comparable to an attempt at flight, and was only a forerunner of the later-developed normal condemning judgement. The first act of repression involved further consequences. In the first place the ego was obliged to protect itself against the constant threat of a renewed advance on the part of the repressed impulse by making a permanent expenditure of energy, an *anticathexis*, and it thus impoverished itself. On the other hand, the repressed impulse, which was now *unconscious*, was able to find means of discharge and of substitutive satisfaction by circuitous routes, and thus to bring the whole purpose of the repression to nothing. In the case of conversion hysteria the circuitous route led to the somatic innervation; the repressed impulse broke its way through at some, point or other and produced *symptoms*. The symptoms were thus results of a compromise, for although they were substitutive satisfactions they were nevertheless distorted and deflected from their aim owing to the resistance of the ego.

The theory of repression became the corner-stone of our understanding of the neuroses. A different view had now to be taken of the task of therapy. Its aim was no longer to 'abreact' an affect which had got on to the wrong lines but to uncover repressions and replace them by acts of judgement which might result either in the accepting or in the condemning of what had formerly been repudiated.[1] I showed my recognition of the new situation by no longer calling my method of investigation and treatment *catharsis* but *psychoanalysis*.

It is possible to take repression as a centre and to bring all the

1. [Cf. Freud's paper on 'Repression' (1915*d*), *P.F.L.*, **11**, 145.]

elements of psychoanalytic theory into relation with it. But before doing so I have a further comment of a polemical nature to make. According to Janet's view a hysterical woman was a wretched creature who, on account of a constitutional weakness, was unable to hold her mental acts together, and it was for that reason that she fell a victim to a splitting of her mind and to a restriction of the field of her consciousness. The outcome of psychoanalytic investigations, on the other hand, showed that these phenomena were the result of dynamic factors – of mental conflict and of repression. This distinction seems to me to be far-reaching enough to put an end to the glib repetition of the view that whatever is of value in psychoanalysis is merely borrowed from the ideas of Janet. The reader will have learned from my account that historically psychoanalysis is completely independent of Janet's discoveries, just as in its content it diverges from them and goes far beyond them. Janet's works would never have had the implications which have made psychoanalysis of such importance to the mental sciences and have made it attract such universal interest. I always treated Janet himself with respect, since his discoveries coincided to a considerable extent with those of Breuer, which had been made earlier but were published later than his. But when in the course of time psychoanalysis became a subject of discussion in France, Janet behaved ill, showed ignorance of the facts and used ugly arguments. And finally he revealed himself to my eyes and destroyed the value of his own work by declaring that when he had spoken of 'unconscious' mental acts he had meant nothing by the phrase – it had been no more than a *façon de parler*.

But the study of pathogenic repressions and of other phenomena which have still to be mentioned compelled psychoanalysis to take the concept of the 'unconscious' seriously. Psychoanalysis regarded everything mental as being in the first instance unconscious; the further quality of 'consciousness' might also be present, or again it might be absent. This of course provoked a denial from the philosophers, for whom 'conscious' and 'mental' were identical, and who protested that they could not conceive of such an absurdity as the 'unconscious mental'. There was no help for it, however, and this idiosyncrasy of the philosophers could only be disregarded with a shrug. Experience (gained from pathological material, of which the philosophers were ignorant) of the frequency and power of impulses of which one knew nothing directly, and whose existence had to be inferred like some fact in the external world, left no alternative open. It could be pointed out, incidentally, that this was only treating one's own mental life as one had always treated other people's. One did not hesitate to ascribe mental processes to other people, although one had no immediate consciousness of them and could only infer them from their words and actions. But what held good for other people must be applicable to oneself. Anyone who tried to push the argument further and to conclude from it that one's own hidden processes belonged actually to a second *consciousness* would be faced with the concept of a consciousness of which one knew nothing, of an 'unconscious consciousness' – and this would scarcely be preferable to the assumption of an 'unconscious mental'. If on the other hand one declared, like some other philosophers, that one was prepared to take pathological phenomena into account, but that the processes underlying them ought not to be described as mental but as 'psychoid', the difference of opinion would degenerate into an unfruitful dispute about words, though even so expediency would decide in favour of keeping the expression 'unconscious mental'. The further question as to the ultimate nature of this unconscious is no more sensible or profitable than the older one as to the nature of the conscious.

It would be more difficult to explain concisely how it came about that psychoanalysis made a further distinction in the unconscious, and separated it into a *preconscious* and an unconscious proper. It will be sufficient to say that it appeared a legitimate course to supplement the theories that were a direct expression of experience with hypotheses that were designed to facilitate the handling of the material and related to matters which could not be a subject of immediate observation. The very same procedure is adopted by the older sciences. The subdivision of the unconscious is part of an attempt to picture the apparatus of the mind as being built up of a number of *agencies* or *systems* whose relations to one another are expressed in spatial terms, without, however, implying any connection with the actual anatomy of the brain. (I have described this as the *topographical* method of approach.) Such ideas as these are part of a speculative superstructure of psychoanalysis, any portion of which can be abandoned or changed without loss or regret the moment its inadequacy has been proved. [See p. 242 f. below.] But there is still plenty to be described that lies closer to actual experience.

I have already mentioned that my investigation of the precipitating and underlying causes of the neuroses led me more and more frequently to conflicts between the subject's sexual impulses and his resistances to sexuality. In my search for the pathogenic situations in which the repressions of sexuality had set in and in which the symptoms, as substitutes for what was repressed, had had their origin, I was carried further and further back into the patient's life and ended by reaching the first years of his childhood. What poets and students of human nature had always asserted turned out to be true: the impressions of that early period of life, though they were for the most part buried in amnesia, left ineradicable traces upon the individual's growth and in particular laid down the disposition to any nervous disorder that was to follow. But since these experiences of childhood were always concerned with sexual excitations and the reaction against them, I found myself faced by the fact of *infantile sexuality* – once again a novelty and a contradiction of one of the strongest of human prejudices. Childhood was looked upon as 'innocent' and free from the lusts of sex, and the fight with the demon of 'sensuality' was not thought to begin until the troubled age of puberty. Such occasional sexual activities as it had been impossible to overlook in children were put down as signs of degeneracy or premature depravity or as a curious freak of nature. Few of the findings of psychoanalysis have met with such universal contradiction or have aroused such an outburst of indignation as the assertion that the sexual function starts at the beginning of life and reveals its presence by important signs even in childhood. And yet no other finding of analysis can be demonstrated so easily and so completely.

Before going further into the question of infantile sexuality I must mention an error into which I fell for a while and which might well have had fatal consequences for the whole of my work. Under the influence of the technical procedure which I used at that time, the majority of my patients re-produced from their childhood scenes in which they were sexually seduced by some grown-up person. With female patients the part of seducer was almost always assigned to their father. I believed these stories, and consequently supposed that I had discovered the roots of the subsequent neurosis in these experiences of sexual seduction in childhood. My con-fidence was strengthened by a few cases in which relations of this kind with a father, uncle, or elder brother had continued up to an age at which memory was to be trusted. If the reader feels inclined to shake his head at my credulity, I cannot altogether blame him; though I may plead that this was at a time when I was intentionally keeping my critical faculty in abeyance so as to preserve an unprejudiced and receptive atti-tude towards the many novelties which were coming to my notice every day. When, however, I was at last obliged to recognize that these scenes of seduction had never taken place, and that they were only fantasies which my patients had made up or which I myself had perhaps forced on them, I was for some time completely at a loss.[1] My confidence alike in my technique and in its results suffered a severe blow; it could not

1. [Freud mentioned the discovery of this mistake in a letter to Fliess of 21 September 1897 (Freud, 1950a, Letter 69). Apart from an allusion in the *Three Essays* (1905d), *P.F.L.*, **7**, 108 f., the first explicit statement of Freud's change of view occurs in a paper on sexuality in the aetiology of the neuroses (1906a), ibid., **10**, 75–6. A similar account to the present one is given on p. 74f. above. For Freud's later views on the matter, see the paper on 'Female Sexuality' (1931b), ibid., **7**, 386, and the *New Introductory Lectures* (1933a), ibid., **2**, 154.]

be disputed that I had arrived at these scenes by a technical method which I considered correct, and their subject-matter was unquestionably related to the symptoms from which my investigation had started. When I had pulled myself together, I was able to draw the right conclusions from my discovery: namely, that the neurotic symptoms were not related directly to actual events but to wishful fantasies, and that as far as the neurosis was concerned psychical reality was of more importance than material reality. I do not believe even now that I forced the seduction fantasies on my patients, that I 'suggested' them. I had in fact stumbled for the first time upon the *Oedipus complex*, which was later to assume such an overwhelming importance, but which I did not recognize as yet in its disguise of fantasy. Moreover, seduction during childhood retained a certain share, though a humbler one, in the aetiology of neuroses. But the seducers turned out as a rule to have been older children.

It will be seen, then, that my mistake was of the same kind as would be made by someone who believed that the legendary story of the early kings of Rome (as told by Livy) was historical truth instead of what it is in fact — a reaction against the memory of times and circumstances that were insignificant and occasionally, perhaps, inglorious. When the mistake had been cleared up, the path to the study of the sexual life of children lay open. It thus became possible to apply psychoanalysis to another field of science and to use its data as a means of discovering a new piece of biological knowledge.

The sexual function, as I found, is in existence from the very beginning of the individual's life, though at first it is attached to the other vital functions and does not become independent of them until later; it has to pass through a long and complicated process of development before it becomes what we are familiar with as the normal sexual life of the adult. It begins by manifesting itself in the activity of a whole number of *component instincts*. These are dependent upon *erotogenic zones* in the body; some of them make their appearance in pairs of opposite impulses (such as sadism and masochism or the impulses to look and to be looked at); they operate independently of one another in a search for pleasure, and they find their object for the most part in the subject's own body. Thus at first the sexual function is non-centralized and predominantly *auto-erotic*. Later, syntheses begin to appear in it; a first stage of organization is reached under the dominance of the *oral* components, an *anal-sadistic* stage follows, and it is only after the third stage has at last been reached that the primacy of the *genitals* is established and that the sexual function begins to serve the ends of reproduction. In the course of this process of development a number of elements of the various component instincts turn out to be unserviceable for this last end and are therefore left on one side or turned to other uses, while others are diverted from their aims and carried over into the genital organization. I gave the name of *libido* to the energy of the sexual instincts and to that form of energy alone. I was next driven to suppose that the libido does not always pass through its prescribed course of development smoothly. As a result either of the excessive strength of certain of the components or of experiences involving premature satisfaction, *fixations* of the libido may occur at various points in the course of its development. If subsequently a repression takes place, the libido flows back to these points (a process described as *regression*), and it is from them that the energy breaks through in the form of a symptom. Later on it further became clear that the localization of the point of fixation is what determines the *choice of neurosis*, that is, the form in which the subsequent illness makes its appearance.

The process of arriving at an *object*, which plays such an important part in mental life, takes place alongside of the organization of the libido. After the stage of *auto-erotism*, the first love-object in the case of both sexes is the mother; and it seems probable that to begin with a child does not distinguish its mother's organ of nutrition from its own body. Later, but still in the first years of infancy, the relation known as the *Oedipus complex* becomes established: boys concentrate their sexual wishes upon their mother and develop hostile impulses against their father as being a rival, while girls adopt an an-alogous attitude.[1] All of the different variations and conse-quences of the Oedipus complex are important; and the innately bisexual constitution of human beings makes itself felt and increases the number of simultaneously active tendencies. Children do not become clear for quite a long time about the differences between the sexes; and during this period of *sexual researches* they produce typical *sexual theories* which, being circumscribed by the incompleteness of their authors' own physical development, are a mixture of truth and error and fail to solve the problems of sexual life (the riddle of the Sphinx – that is, the question of where babies come from). We see, then, that a child's first object-choice is an *incestuous* one. The whole course of development that I have described is run through rapidly. For the most remarkable feature of the sexual life of man is its *diphasic* onset, its onset in two waves, with an interval between them. It reaches a first climax in the fourth or fifth year of a child's life. But thereafter this early efflorescence of sexuality passes off; the sexual impulses which have shown such liveliness are overcome by repression, and a *period of latency* follows, which lasts until puberty and during which the *reaction-formations* of morality, shame and disgust are built up. Of all living creatures man alone seems to show this

1. [*Footnote added* 1935:] The information about infantile sexuality was obtained from the study of men and the theory deduced from it was con-cerned with male children. It was natural enough to expect to find a complete parallel between the two sexes; but this turned out not to hold. Further investigations and reflections revealed profound differences between the sexual development of men and women. The first sexual object of a baby girl (just as of a baby boy) is her mother; and before a woman can reach the end of her normal development she has to change not only her sexual object but also her leading genital zone. From this circumstance difficulties arise and possibilities of inhibition which are not present in the case of men. [Freud had in fact begun to express doubts about the symmetry of the sexual development of the two sexes before the publication of the present work, notably in 'The Dissolution of the Oedipus Complex' (1924*d*), *P.F.L.*, **7**, 313 ff.; his new views were developed more fully in another paper, written only a little later than this one, on the effects of the distinction between the sexes (1925*j*), ibid., **7**, 323 ff.]

diphasic onset of sexual growth, and it may perhaps be the biological determinant of his predisposition to neuroses.[1] At puberty the impulses and object-relations of a child's early years become reanimated, and amongst them the emotional ties of its Oedipus complex. In the sexual life of puberty there is a struggle between the urges of early years and the inhibitions of the latency period. Before this, and while the child is at the highest point of its infantile sexual development, a genital organization of a sort is established; but only the male genitals play a part in it, and the female ones remain undiscovered. (I have described this as the period of *phallic* primacy.) At this stage the contrast between the sexes is not stated in terms of 'male' or 'female' but of 'possessing a penis' or 'castrated'. The *castration complex* which arises in this connection is of the profoundest importance in the formation alike of character and of neuroses.

In order to make this condensed account of my discoveries upon the sexual life of man more intelligible, I have brought together conclusions which I reached at different dates and incorporated by way of supplement or correction in the successive editions of my *Three Essays on the Theory of Sexuality* (1905*d*). I hope it will have been easy to gather the nature of my extension (on which so much stress has been laid and which has excited so much opposition) of the concept of sexuality. That extension is of a twofold kind. In the first place sexuality is divorced from its too close connection with the genitals and is regarded as a more comprehensive bodily function, having pleasure as its goal and only secondarily coming to serve the ends of reproduction. In the second place the sexual impulses are regarded as including all of those merely affectionate and friendly impulses to which usage applies the exceedingly ambiguous word 'love'. I do not, however, con-

---

1. [*Footnote added* 1935:] The period of latency is a physiological phenomenon. It can, however, only give rise to a complete interruption of sexual life in cultural organizations which have made the suppression of infantile sexuality a part of their system. This is not the case with the majority of primitive peoples.

sider that these extensions are innovations but rather restorations: they signify the removal of inexpedient limitations of the concept into which we had allowed ourselves to be led.

The detaching of sexuality from the genitals has the advantage of allowing us to bring the sexual activities of children and of perverts into the same scope as those of normal adults. The sexual activities of children have hitherto been entirely neglected and though those of perverts have been recognized it has been with moral indignation and without understanding. Looked at from the psychoanalytic standpoint, even the most eccentric and repellent perversions are explicable as manifestations of component instincts of sexuality which have freed themselves from the primacy of the genitals and are now in pursuit of pleasure on their own account as they were in the very early days of the libido's development. The most important of these perversions, homosexuality, scarcely deserves the name. It can be traced back to the constitutional bisexuality of all human beings and to the after-effects of the phallic primacy. Psychoanalysis enables us to point to some trace or other of a homosexual object-choice in everyone. If I have described children as 'polymorphously perverse',[1] I was only using a terminology that was generally current; no moral judgement was implied by the phrase. Psychoanalysis has no concern whatever with such judgements of value.

The second of my alleged extensions of the concept of sexuality finds its justification in the fact revealed by psychoanalytic investigation that all of these affectionate impulses were originally of a completely sexual nature but have become *inhibited in their aim* or *sublimated*. The manner in which the sexual instincts can thus be influenced and diverted enables them to be employed for cultural activities of every kind, to which indeed they bring the most important contributions.

My surprising discoveries as to the sexuality of children were made in the first instance through the analysis of adults. But later (from about 1908 onwards) it became possible to

1. [*P.F.L.*, **7**, 109.]

confirm them fully and in every detail by direct observations upon children.[1] Indeed, it is so easy to convince oneself of the regular sexual activities of children that one cannot help asking in astonishment how the human race can have succeeded in overlooking the facts and in maintaining for so long the wishful legend of the asexuality of childhood. This surprising circumstance must be connected with the amnesia which, with the majority of adults, hides their own infancy.

IV

The theories of resistance and of repression, of the unconscious, of the aetiological significance of sexual life and of the importance of infantile experiences – these form the principal constituents of the theoretical structure of psychoanalysis. In these pages, unfortunately, I have been able to describe only the separate elements and not their interconnections and their bearing upon one another. But I am obliged now to turn to the alterations which gradually took place in the technique of the analytic method.

The means which I first adopted for overcoming the patient's resistance, by insistence and encouragement, had been indispensable for the purpose of giving me a first general survey of what was to be expected. But in the long run it proved to be too much of a strain on both sides, and further, it seemed open to certain obvious criticisms. It therefore gave place to another method which was in one sense its opposite. Instead of urging the patient to say something upon some particular subject, I now asked him to abandon himself to a process of *free association* – that is, to say whatever came into his head, while ceasing to give any conscious direction to his thoughts. It was essential, however, that he should bind himself to report literally everything that occurred to his self-perception and not to give way to critical objections which sought to put certain associations on one side on the ground that they were not sufficiently important or that they were irrelevant or that they were

1. [Cf. the analysis of 'Little Hans' (1909*b*), *P.F.L.*, **8**, 165 ff.]

altogether meaningless. There was no necessity to repeat explicitly the demand for candour on the patient's part in reporting his thoughts, for it was the precondition of the whole analytic treatment.

It may seem surprising that this method of free association, carried out subject to the observation of the *fundamental rule of psychoanalysis*, should have achieved what was expected of it, namely the bringing into consciousness of the repressed material which was held back by resistances. We must, however, bear in mind that free association is not really free. The patient remains under the influence of the analytic situation even though he is not directing his mental activities on to a particular subject. We shall be justified in assuming that nothing will occur to him that has not some reference to that situation. His resistance against reproducing the repressed material will now be expressed in two ways. Firstly it will be shown by critical objections; and it was to deal with these that the fundamental rule of psychoanalysis was invented. But if the patient observes that rule and so overcomes his reticences, the resistance will find another means of expression. It will so arrange it that the repressed material itself will never occur to the patient but only something which approximates to it in an allusive way; and the greater the resistance, the more remote from the actual idea that the analyst is in search of will be the substitutive association which the patient has to report. The analyst, who listens composedly but without any constrained effort to the stream of associations and who, from his experience, has a general notion of what to expect, can make use of the material brought to light by the patient according to two possibilities. If the resistance is slight he will be able from the patient's allusions to infer the unconscious material itself; or if the resistance is stronger he will be able to recognize its character from the associations, as they seem to become more remote from the topic in hand, and will explain it to the patient. Uncovering the resistance, however, is the first step towards overcoming it. Thus the work of analysis involves an *art of interpretation*, the successful handling of which may require tact and practice but which is not hard to acquire. But it is not only in the saving of labour that the method of free association has an advantage over the earlier method. It exposes the patient to the least possible amount of compulsion, it never allows of contact being lost with the actual current situation, it guarantees to a great extent that no factor in the structure of the neurosis will be overlooked and that nothing will be introduced into it by the expectations of the analyst. It is left to the patient in all essentials to determine the course of the analysis and the arrangement of the material; any systematic handling of particular symptoms or complexes thus becomes impossible. In complete contrast to what happened with hypnotism and with the urging method, interrelated material makes its appearance at different times and at different points in the treatment. To a spectator, therefore – though in fact there must be none – an analytic treatment would seem completely obscure.

Another advantage of the method is that it need never break down. It must theoretically always be possible to have an association, provided that no conditions are made as to its character. Yet there is one case in which in fact a breakdown occurs with absolute regularity; from its very uniqueness, however, this case too can be interpreted.

I now come to the description of a factor which adds an essential feature to my picture of analysis and which can claim, alike technically and theoretically, to be regarded as of the first importance. In every analytic treatment there arises, without the physician's agency, an intense emotional relationship between the patient and the analyst which is not to be accounted for by the actual situation. It can be of a positive or of a negative character and can vary between the extremes of a passionate, completely sensual love and the unbridled expression of an embittered defiance and hatred. This *transference* – to give it its short name – soon replaces in the patient's mind the desire to be cured, and, so long as it is affectionate and moderate, becomes the agent of the physician's influence and neither more nor less than the mainspring of the joint work of analysis. Later on, when it has become passionate or has been converted into hostility, it becomes the principal tool of the resistance. It may then happen that it will paralyse the patient's powers of associating and endanger the success of the treatment. Yet it would be senseless to try to evade it; for an analysis without transference is an impossibility. It must not be supposed, however, that transference is created by analysis and does not occur apart from it. Transference is merely uncovered and isolated by analysis. It is a universal phenomenon of the human mind, it decides the success of all medical influence, and in fact dominates the whole of each person's relations to his human environment. We can easily recognize it as the same dynamic factor which the hypnotists have named 'suggestibility', which is the agent of hypnotic *rapport* and whose incalculable behaviour led to difficulties with the cathartic method as well. When there is no inclination to a transference of emotion such as this, or when it has become entirely negative, as happens in dementia praecox or paranoia, then there is also no possibility of influencing the patient by psychological means.

It is perfectly true that psychoanalysis, like other psycho-therapeutic methods, employs the instrument of suggestion (or transference). But the difference is this: that in analysis it is not allowed to play the decisive part in determining the therapeutic results. It is used instead to induce the patient to perform a piece of psychical work – the overcoming of his transference-resistances – which involves a permanent alteration in his mental economy. The transference is made conscious to the patient by the analyst, and it is resolved by convincing him that in his transference attitude he is *re-experiencing* emotional relations which had their origin in his earliest object attachments during the repressed period of his childhood. In this way the transference is changed from the strongest weapon of the resistance into the best instrument of the analytic treatment. Nevertheless its handling remains the most difficult as well as the most important part of the technique of analysis.

With the help of the method of free association and of the related art of interpretation, psychoanalysis succeeded in achieving one thing which appeared to be of no practical importance but which in fact necessarily led to a totally fresh attitude and a fresh scale of values in scientific thought. It became possible to prove that *dreams* have a meaning, and to discover it. In classical antiquity great importance was attached to dreams as foretelling the future; but modern science would have nothing to do with them, it handed them over to superstition, declaring them to be purely 'somatic' processes – a kind of twitching of a mind that is otherwise asleep. It seemed quite inconceivable that anyone who had done serious scientific work could make his appearance as an 'interpreter of dreams'. But by disregarding the excommunication pronounced upon dreams, by treating them as unexplained neurotic symptoms, as delusional or obsessional ideas, by neglecting their apparent content and by making their separate component images into subjects for free association, psychoanalysis arrived at a different conclusion. The numerous associations produced by the dreamer led to the discovery of a thought structure which could no longer be described as absurd or confused, which ranked as a completely valid psychical product, and of which the *manifest* dream was no more than a distorted, abbreviated, and misunderstood translation, and for the most part a translation into visual images. These *latent dream-thoughts* contained the meaning of the dream, while its manifest content was simply a make-believe, a façade, which could serve as a starting-point for the associations but not for the interpretation.

There were now a whole series of questions to be answered, among the most important of them being whether the formation of dreams had a motive, under what conditions it took place, by what methods the dream-thoughts (which are invariably full of sense) become converted into the dream (which is often senseless), and others besides. I attempted to solve all of these problems in *The Interpretation of Dreams*, which I published in the year 1900. I can only find space here for the briefest abstract of my investigation. When the latent dream-thoughts that are revealed by the analysis of a dream are examined, one of them is found to stand out from among the rest, which are intelligible and well known to the dreamer. These latter thoughts are residues of waking life (the *day's residues*, as they are called technically); but the isolated thought is found to be a wishful impulse, often of a very repellent kind, which is foreign to the waking life of the dreamer and is consequently disavowed by him with surprise or indignation. This impulse is the actual constructor of the dream: it provides the energy for its production and makes use of the day's residues as material. The dream which thus originates represents a situation of satisfaction for the impulse, it is the fulfilment of its wish. It would not be possible for this process to take place without being favoured by the presence of something in the nature of a state of sleep. The necessary mental precondition of sleep is the concentration of the ego upon the wish to sleep and the withdrawal of psychical energy from all the interests of life. Since at the same time all the paths of approach to motility are blocked, the ego is also able to reduce the expenditure [of energy] by which at other times it maintains the repressions. The unconscious impulse makes use of this nocturnal relaxation of repression in order to push its way into consciousness with the dream. But the repressive resistance of the ego is not abolished in sleep but merely reduced. Some of it remains in the shape of a *censorship of dreams* and forbids the unconscious impulse to express itself in the forms which it would properly assume. In consequence of the severity of the censorship of dreams, the latent dream-thoughts are obliged to submit to being altered and softened so as to make the forbidden meaning of the dream unrecognizable. This is the explanation of *dream distortion*, which accounts for the most striking characteristics of the manifest dream. We are therefore justified in asserting that *a dream is the (disguised) fulfilment of a (repressed) wish*. It will now be seen that dreams are constructed like a neurotic symptom: they are compromises between the demands of a repressed impulse and the resistance of a censoring force in the ego. Since they have a similar origin they are equally unintelligible and stand in equal need of interpretation.

There is no difficulty in discovering the general function of dreaming. It serves the purpose of fending off, by a kind of soothing action, external or internal stimuli which would tend to arouse the sleeper, and thus of securing sleep against interruption. External stimuli are fended off by being given a new interpretation and by being woven into some harmless situation; internal stimuli, caused by instinctual demands, are given free play by the sleeper and allowed to find satisfaction in the formation of dreams, so long as the latent dream-thoughts submit to the control of the censorship. But if they threaten to break free and the meaning of the dream becomes too plain, the sleeper cuts short the dream and wakes in a fright. (Dreams of this class are known as *anxiety dreams*.) A similar failure in the function of dreaming occurs if an external stimulus becomes too strong to be fended off. (This is the class of *arousal dreams*.) I have given the name of *dream-work* to the process which, with the co-operation of the censorship, converts the latent thoughts into the manifest content of the dream. It consists of a peculiar way of treating the preconscious material of thought, so that its component parts become *condensed*, its psychical emphasis becomes *displaced*, and the whole of it is translated into visual images or *dramatized*, and completed by a deceptive *secondary revision*. The dream-work is an excellent example of the processes occurring in the deeper, unconscious layers of the mind, which differ considerably from the familiar normal processes of thought. It also displays a number of archaic characteristics, such as the use of a *symbolism* (in this case of a predominantly sexual kind) which it has since also been possible to discover in other spheres of mental activity.

We have explained that the unconscious instinctual impulse of the dream connects itself with a residue of the day, with some interest of waking life which has not been disposed of; it thus gives the dream which it constructs a double value for the work of analysis. For on the one hand a dream that has been analysed reveals itself as the fulfilment of a repressed wish; but on the other hand it may be a continuation of some preconscious activity of the day before and may contain every kind of subject-matter and give expression to an intention, a warning, a reflection, or once more to the fulfilment of a

AN AUTOBIOGRAPHICAL STUDY

wish. Analysis exploits the dream in both directions, as a means of obtaining knowledge alike of the patient's conscious and of his unconscious processes. It also profits from the fact that dreams have access to the forgotten material of childhood, and so it happens that infantile amnesia is for the most part overcome in connection with the interpretation of dreams. In this respect dreams achieve a part of what was previously the task of hypnotism. On the other hand, I have never maintained the assertion which has so often been ascribed to me that dream interpretation shows that all dreams have a sexual content or are derived from sexual motive forces. It is easy to see that hunger, thirst, or the need to excrete, can produce dreams of satisfaction just as well as any repressed sexual or egoistic impulse. The case of young children affords us a convenient test of the validity of our theory of dreams. In them the various psychical systems are not yet sharply divided and the repressions have not yet grown deep, so that we often come upon dreams which are nothing more than undisguised fulfilments of wishful impulses left over from waking life. Under the influence of imperative needs, adults may also produce dreams of this infantile type.[1]

In the same way that psychoanalysis makes use of dream interpretation, it also profits by the study of the numerous little slips and mistakes which people make – symptomatic actions, as they are called. I investigated this subject in a series of papers which were published for the first time in book form in 1904 under the title of The Psychopathology of Everyday Life [Freud, 1901b; P.F.L., 5]. In this widely circulated work I have pointed out that these phenomena are not accidental, that they require more than physiological explanations, that they have a meaning and can be interpreted, and that one is justified in inferring from them the presence of restrained or repressed

1. [Footnote added 1935:] When it is considered how frequently the function of dreaming miscarries, the dream may aptly be characterized as an attempt at the fulfilment of a wish. Aristotle's old definition of the dream as mental life during sleep still holds good. There was a reason for my choosing as the title of my book not The Dream but The Interpretation of Dreams.

impulses and intentions. But what constitutes the enormous importance of dream interpretation, as well as of this latter study, is not the assistance they give to the work of analysis but another of their attributes. Previously psychoanalysis had only been concerned with solving pathological phenomena and in order to explain them it had often been driven into making assumptions whose comprehensiveness was out of all proportion to the importance of the actual material under consideration. But when it came to dreams, it was no longer dealing with a pathological symptom, but with a phenomenon of normal mental life which might occur in any healthy person. If dreams turned out to be constructed like symptoms, if their explanation required the same assumptions – the repression of impulses, substitutive formation, compromise formation, the dividing of the conscious and the unconscious into various psychical systems – then psychoanalysis was no longer an auxiliary science in the field of psychopathology, it was rather the starting-point of a new and deeper science of the mind which would be equally indispensable for the understanding of the normal. Its postulates and findings could be carried over to other regions of mental happening; a path lay open to it that led far afield, into spheres of universal interest.

V

I must interrupt my account of the internal growth of psychoanalysis and turn to its external history. What I have so far described of its discoveries has related for the most part to the results of my own work; but I have also filled in my story with material from later dates and have not distinguished between my own contributions and those of my pupils and followers.

For more than ten years after my separation from Breuer I had no followers. I was completely isolated. In Vienna I was shunned; abroad no notice was taken of me. My *Interpretation of Dreams*, published in 1900, was scarcely reviewed in the technical journals. In my paper 'On the History of the Psycho-Analytic Movement' [1914*d*] I mentioned as an instance of the attitude adopted by psychiatric circles in Vienna a conversation with an assistant at the clinic [at which I lectured], who had written a book against my theories but had never read my *Interpretation of Dreams*. He had been told at the clinic that it was not worth while. The man in question, who has since become a professor, has gone so far as to repudiate my report of the conversation and to throw doubts in general upon the accuracy of my recollection. I can only say that I stand by every word of the account I then gave. [Cf. p. 80 above.]

As soon as I realized the inevitable nature of what I had come up against, my sensitiveness greatly diminished. Moreover, my isolation gradually came to an end. To begin with, a small circle of pupils gathered round me in Vienna; and then, after 1906, came the news that the psychiatrists at Zurich, E. Bleuler, his assistant C. G. Jung, and others, were taking a lively interest in psychoanalysis. We got into personal touch with one another, and at Easter 1908 the friends of the young science met at Salzburg, agreed upon the regular repetition of similar informal congresses and arranged for the publication of a journal which was edited by Jung and was given the title of *Jahrbuch für psychoanalytische und psychopathologische Forschungen*. It was brought out under the direction of Bleuler and myself and ceased publication at the beginning of the [first] World War. At the same time that the Swiss psychiatrists joined the movement, interest in psychoanalysis began to be aroused all over Germany as well; it became the subject of a large number of written comments and of lively discussions at scientific congresses. But its reception was nowhere friendly or even benevolently non-committal. After the briefest acquaintance with psychoanalysis German science was united in rejecting it.

Even today it is of course impossible for me to foresee the final judgement of posterity upon the value of psychoanalysis for psychiatry, psychology, and the mental sciences in general. But I fancy that, when the history of the phase we have lived through comes to be written, German science will not have cause to be proud of those who represented it. I am not thinking of the fact that they rejected psychoanalysis or of the decisive way in which they did so; both of these things were easily intelligible, they were only to be expected and at any rate they threw no discredit on the character of the opponents of analysis. But for the degree of arrogance which they displayed, for their conscienceless contempt of logic, and for the coarseness and bad taste of their attacks there could be no excuse. It may be said that it is childish of me to give free rein to such feelings as these now, after fifteen years have passed; nor would I do so unless I had something more to add. Years later, during the World War, when a chorus of enemies were bringing against the German nation the charge of barbarism, a charge which sums up all that I have written above, it none the less hurt deeply to feel that my own experience would not allow me to contradict it.[1]

One of my opponents boasted of silencing his patients as soon as they began to talk of anything sexual and evidently thought that this technique gave him a right to judge the part played by sexuality in the aetiology of the neuroses. Apart from emotional resistances, which were so easily explicable by the psychoanalytic theory that it was impossible to be misled by them, it seemed to me that the main obstacle to agreement lay in the fact that my opponents regarded psychoanalysis as a product of my speculative imagination and were unwilling to believe in the long, patient and unbiased work which had gone to its making. Since in their opinion analysis had nothing to do with observation or experience, they believed that they themselves were justified in rejecting it without experience. Others again, who did not feel so strongly convinced of this, repeated in their resistance the classical manoeuvre of not looking through the microscope so as to avoid seeing what they had denied. It is remarkable, indeed, how incorrectly most people act when they are obliged to form a judgement of their own on some new subject. For years I have been told by 'benevolent' critics – and I hear the same thing even today – that

1. [Cf. a paragraph in 'Thoughts for the Times on War and Death', written during the war (1915b), P.F.L., **12**, 65–6.]

psychoanalysis is right up to such-and-such a point but that there it begins to exaggerate and to generalize without justification. And I know that, though nothing is more difficult than to decide where such a point lies, these critics had been completely ignorant of the whole subject only a few weeks or days earlier.

The result of the official anathema against psychoanalysis was that the analysts began to come closer together. At the second Congress, held at Nuremberg in 1910, they formed themselves, on the proposal of Ferenczi, into an 'International Psycho-Analytical Association' divided into a number of local societies but under a common President. The Association survived the Great War and still exists, consisting today of branch societies in Austria, Germany, Hungary, Switzerland, Great Britain, Holland, Russia, and India, as well as two in the United States. I arranged that C. G. Jung should be appointed as the first President, which turned out later to have been a most unfortunate step. At the same time a second journal devoted to psychoanalysis was started, the *Zentralblatt für Psychoanalyse*, edited by Adler and Stekel, and a little later a third, *Imago*, edited by two non-medical analysts, H. Sachs and O. Rank, and intended to deal with the application of analysis to the mental sciences. Soon afterwards Bleuler [1910] published a paper in defence of psychoanalysis. Though it was a relief to find honesty and straightforward logic for once taking part in the dispute, yet I could not feel completely satisfied by Bleuler's essay. He strove too eagerly after an appearance of impartiality; nor is it a matter of chance that it is to him that our science owes the valuable concept of *ambivalence*. In later papers Bleuler adopted such a critical attitude towards the theoretical structure of analysis and rejected or threw doubts upon such essential parts of it that I could not help asking myself in astonishment what could be left of it for him to admire. Yet not only has he subsequently uttered the strongest pleas in favour of 'depth-psychology' but he based his comprehensive study of schizophrenia [Bleuler, 1911] upon it. Nevertheless, Bleuler did not for long remain a member of the International Psycho-Analytical Association; he resigned from it as a result of misunderstandings with Jung, and the Burghölzli[1] was lost to analysis.

Official disapproval could not hinder the spread of psychoanalysis either in Germany or in other countries. I have elsewhere [p. 90 ff. above] followed the stages of its growth and given the names of those who were its first representatives. In 1909 G. Stanley Hall invited Jung and me to America to go to Clark University, Worcester, Mass., of which he was President, and to spend a week giving lectures (in German) at the celebration of the twentieth anniversary of that body's foundation. Hall was justly esteemed as a psychologist and educationist, and had introduced psychoanalysis into his courses several years earlier; there was a touch of the 'king-maker' about him, a pleasure in setting up authorities and in then deposing them. We also met James J. Putnam there, the Harvard neurologist, who in spite of his age was an enthusiastic supporter of psychoanalysis and threw the whole weight of a personality that was universally respected into the defence of the cultural value of analysis and the purity of its aims. He was an estimable man, in whom, as a reaction against a predisposition to obsessional neurosis, an ethical bias predominated; and the only thing in him that was disquieting was his inclination to attach psychoanalysis to a particular philosophical system and to make it the servant of moral aims.[2] Another event of this time which made a lasting impression on me was a meeting with William James the philosopher. I shall never forget one little scene that occurred as we were on a walk together. He stopped suddenly, handed me a bag he was carrying and asked me to walk on, saying that he would catch me up as soon as he had got through an attack of angina pectoris which was just coming on. He died of that disease a year later; and I have always wished that I might be as fearless as he was in the face of approaching death.

At that time I was only fifty-three. I felt young and healthy, and my short visit to the New World encouraged my self-

1. [See p. 84 and *n*. 1 above.]
2. [See p. 89 and *n*. 1 above.]

respect in every way. In Europe I felt as though I were despised; but over there I found myself received by the foremost men as an equal. As I stepped on to the platform at Worcester to deliver my *Five Lectures on Psycho-Analysis* [1910*a*] it seemed like the realization of some incredible day-dream: psychoanalysis was no longer a product of delusion, it had become a valuable part of reality. It has not lost ground in America since our visit; it is extremely popular among the lay public and is recognized by a number of official psychiatrists as an important element in medical training. Unfortunately, however, it has suffered a great deal from being watered down. Moreover, many abuses which have no relation to it find a cover under its name, and there are few opportunities for any thorough training in technique or theory. In America, too, it has come in conflict with behaviourism, a theory which is naïve enough to boast that it has put the whole problem of psychology completely out of court.

In Europe during the years 1911–13 two secessionist movements from psychoanalysis took place, led by men who had previously played a considerable part in the young science, Alfred Adler and C. G. Jung. Both movements seemed most threatening and quickly obtained a large following. But their strength lay, not in their own content, but in the temptation which they offered of being freed from what were felt as the repellent findings of psychoanalysis even though its actual material was no longer rejected. Jung attempted to give to the facts of analysis a fresh interpretation of an abstract, impersonal and non-historical character, and thus hoped to escape the need for recognizing the importance of infantile sexuality and of the Oedipus complex as well as the necessity for any analysis of childhood. Adler seemed to depart still further from psychoanalysis; he entirely repudiated the importance of sexuality, traced back the formation both of character and of the neuroses solely to men's desire for power and to their need to compensate for their constitutional inferiorities, and threw all the psychological discoveries of psychoanalysis to the winds. But what he had rejected forced its way back into his closed system under other names; his ' masculine protest'[1] is nothing else than repression unjustifiably sexualized. The criticism with which the two heretics were met was a mild one; I only insisted that both Adler and Jung should cease to describe their theories as 'psychoanalysis'. After a lapse of ten years it can be asserted that both of these attempts against psychoanalysis have blown over without doing any harm.

If a community is based on agreement upon a few cardinal points, it is obvious that people who have abandoned that common ground will cease to belong to it. Yet the secession of former pupils has often been brought up against me as a sign of my intolerance or has been regarded as evidence of some special fatality that hangs over me. It is a sufficient answer to point out that in contrast to those who have left me, like Jung, Adler, Stekel and a few besides, there are a great number of men, like Abraham, Eitingon, Ferenczi, Rank, Jones, Brill, Sachs, Pfister, van Emden, Reik, and others, who have worked with me for some fifteen years in loyal collaboration and for the most part in uninterrupted friendship. I have only mentioned the oldest of my pupils, who have already made a distinguished name for themselves in the literature of psychoanalysis; if I have passed over others, that is not to be taken as a slight, and indeed among those who are young and have joined me lately talents are to be found on which great hopes may be set. But I think I can say in my defence that an intolerant man, dominated by an arrogant belief in his own infallibility, would never have been able to maintain his hold upon so large a number of intellectually eminent people, especially if he had at his command as few practical attractions as I had.

The World War, which broke up so many other organizations, could do nothing against our 'International'. The first meeting after the war took place in 1920, at The Hague, on neutral ground. It was moving to see how hospitably the Dutch welcomed the starving and impoverished subjects of the Central European states; and I believe this was the first occasion in a ruined world on which Englishmen and Germans sat at

1. [See p. 114 and *n.* 1 above.]

the same table for the friendly discussion of scientific interests. Both in Germany and in the countries of Western Europe the war had actually stimulated interest in psychoanalysis. The observation of war neuroses had at last opened the eyes of the medical profession to the importance of psychogenesis in neurotic disturbances, and some of our psychological conceptions, such as the 'gain from illness' and the 'flight into illness',[1] quickly became popular. The last Congress before the German collapse, which was held at Budapest in 1918, was attended by official representatives of the allied governments of the Central European powers, and they agreed to the establishment of psychoanalytic centres for the treatment of war neuroses. But this point was never reached. Similarly too the comprehensive plans made by one of our leading members, Dr Anton von Freund, for establishing in Budapest a centre for analytic study and treatment came to grief as a result of the political upheavals that followed soon afterwards and of the premature death of their irreplaceable author. At a later date some of his ideas were put into execution by Max Eitingon, who in 1920 founded a psychoanalytical clinic in Berlin. During the brief period of Bolshevik rule in Hungary, Ferenczi was still able to carry on a successful course of instruction as the official representative of psychoanalysis at the University of Budapest. After the war our opponents were pleased to announce that events had produced a conclusive argument against the validity of the theses of analysis. The war neuroses, they said, had proved that sexual factors were unnecessary to the aetiology of neurotic disorders. But their triumph was frivolous and premature. For on the one hand no one had been able to carry out a thorough analysis of a case of war neurosis, so that in fact nothing whatever was known for certain as to their motivation and no conclusions could be drawn from this uncertainty; while on the other hand psychoanalysis had long before arrived at the concept of narcissism and of narcissistic neuroses, in which the subject's libido is attached to his own ego instead of to an object.[2] Though on other occasions, there-

1. [See p. 113 *n*. above.]
2. [Cf. Freud's introduction to a book on the war neuroses (1919*d*).]

fore, the charge was brought against psychoanalysis of having made an unjustifiable extension of the concept of sexuality, yet, when it became convenient for controversial ends, this crime was forgotten and we were once more held down to the narrowest meaning of the word.

If the preliminary cathartic period is left on one side, the history of psychoanalysis falls from my point of view into two phases. In the first of these I stood alone and had to do all the work myself: this was from 1895–6 until 1906 or 1907. In the second phase, lasting from then until the present time, the contributions of my pupils and collaborators have been growing more and more in importance, so that today, when a grave illness warns me of the approaching end, I can think with a quiet mind of the cessation of my own labours.[1] For that very reason, however, it is impossible for me in this *Autobiographical Study* to deal as fully with the progress of psychoanalysis during the second phase as I did with its gradual rise during the first phase, which was concerned with my own activity alone. I feel that I should only be justified in mentioning here those new discoveries in which I still played a prominent part, in particular, therefore, those made in the sphere of narcissism, of the theory of the instincts, and of the application of psychoanalysis to the psychoses.

I must begin by adding that increasing experience showed more and more plainly that the Oedipus complex was the nucleus of the neurosis. It was at once the climax of infantile sexual life and the point of junction from which all of its later developments proceeded. But if so, it was no longer possible to expect analysis to discover a factor that was specific in the aetiology of the neuroses. It must be true, as Jung expressed it so well in the early days when he was still an analyst, that neuroses have no peculiar content which belongs exclusively to them but that neurotics break down at the same difficulties that are successfully overcome by normal people. This discovery was very far from being a disappointment. It was

---

1. [Freud had in fact more than a dozen years of active life before him when he wrote this.]

in complete harmony with another one: that the depth-psychology revealed by psychoanalysis was in fact the psychology of the normal mind. Our path had been like that of chemistry: the great qualitative differences between substances were traced back to quantitative variations in the proportions in which the same elements were combined.

In the Oedipus complex the libido was seen to be attached to the image of the parental figures. But earlier there was a period in which there were no such objects. There followed from this fact the concept (of fundamental importance for the libido theory) of a state in which the subject's libido filled his own ego and had that for its object. This state could be called *narcissism* or self-love. A moment's reflection showed that this state never completely ceases. All through the subject's life his ego remains the great reservoir of his libido, from which object-cathexes are sent out and into which the libido can stream back again from the objects.[1] Thus narcissistic libido is constantly being transformed into object-libido, and *vice versa*. An excellent instance of the length to which this transformation can go is afforded by the state of being in love, whether in a sexual or sublimated manner, which goes so far as involving a sacrifice of the self. Whereas hitherto in considering the process of repression attention had only been paid to what was repressed, these ideas made it possible to form a correct estimate of the repressing forces too. It had been said that repression was set in action by the instincts of self-preservation operating in the ego (the 'ego instincts') and that it was brought to bear upon the libidinal instincts. But since the instincts of self-preservation were now recognized as also being of a libidinal nature, as being narcissistic libido, the process of repression was seen to be a process occurring within the libido itself; narcissistic libido was opposed to object-libido, the interest of self-preservation was defending itself against the demands of object-love, and therefore against the demands of sexuality in the narrower sense as well.

1. [A discussion of this will be found in Appendix B to *The Ego and the Id* (1923*b*), *P.F.L.*, **11**, 404 ff.]

There is no more urgent need in psychology than for a securely founded theory of the instincts on which it might then be possible to build further.[1] Nothing of the sort exists, however, and psychoanalysis is driven to making tentative efforts towards some such theory. It began by drawing a contrast between the ego-instincts (the instinct of self-preservation, hunger) and the libidinal instincts (love), but later replaced it by a new contrast between narcissistic and object-libido. This was clearly not the last word on the subject; biological considerations seemed to make it impossible to remain content with assuming the existence of only a single class of instincts.

In the works of my later years (*Beyond the Pleasure Principle* [1920g], *Group Psychology and the Analysis of the Ego* [1912c], and *The Ego and the Id* [1923b]), I have given free rein to the inclination, which I kept down for so long, to speculation, and I have also contemplated a new solution of the problem of the instincts. I have combined the instincts for self-preservation and for the preservation of the species under the concept of *Eros* and have contrasted with it an *instinct of death* or *destruction* which works in silence. Instinct in general is regarded as a kind of elasticity of living things, an impulsion towards the restoration of a situation which once existed but was brought to an end by some external disturbance. This essentially conservative character of instincts is exemplified by the phenomena of the *compulsion to repeat*. The picture which life presents to us is the result of the concurrent and mutually opposing action of Eros and the death instinct.

It remains to be seen whether this construction will turn out to be serviceable. Although it arose from a desire to fix some of the most important theoretical ideas of psychoanalysis, it goes far beyond psychoanalysis. I have repeatedly heard it said contemptuously that it is impossible to take a science seriously

---

1. [Some account of the development of Freud's views on the instincts will be found in the Editor's Note to 'Instincts and their Vicissitudes' (1915c), *P.F.L.*, **11**, 105 ff.]

whose most general concepts are as lacking in precision as those of libido and of instinct in psychoanalysis. But this reproach rests on a complete misconception of the facts. Clear basic concepts and sharply drawn definitions are only possible in the mental sciences in so far as the latter seek to fit a region of facts into the frame of a logical system. In the natural sciences, of which psychology is one, such clear-cut general concepts are superfluous and indeed impossible. Zoology and botany did not start from correct and adequate definitions of an animal and a plant; to this very day biology has been unable to give any certain meaning to the concept of life. Physics itself, indeed, would never have made any advance if it had had to wait until its concepts of matter, force, gravitation, and so on, had reached the desirable degree of clarity and precision. The basic ideas or most general concepts in any of the disciplines of science are always left indeterminate at first and are only explained to begin with by reference to the realm of phenomena from which they were derived; it is only by means of a progressive analysis of the material of observation that they can be made clear and can find a significant and consistent meaning.[1] I have always felt it as a gross injustice that people have refused to treat psychoanalysis like any other science. This refusal found an expression in the raising of the most obstinate objections. Psychoanalysis was constantly reproached for its incompleteness and insufficiencies; though it is plain that a science based upon observation has no alternative but to work out its findings piecemeal and to solve its problems step by step. Again, when I endeavoured to obtain for the sexual function the recognition which had so long been withheld from it, psychoanalytic theory was branded as 'pan-sexualism'. And when I laid stress on the hitherto neglected importance of the part played by the accidental impressions of early youth, I was told that psychoanalysis was denying constitutional and hereditary factors – a thing which I had never dreamt of doing. It was a case of contradiction at any price and by any methods.

1. [The whole of the remainder of this paragraph was added in 1935.]

I had already made attempts at earlier stages of my work to arrive at some more general points of view on the basis of psychoanalytic observation. In a short essay, 'Formulations on the Two Principles of Mental Functioning',[1] I drew attention (and there was, of course, nothing original in this) to the domination of the *pleasure–unpleasure principle* in mental life and to its displacement by what is called the *reality principle*. Later on [in 1915] I made an attempt to produce a 'Meta-psychology'. By this I meant a method of approach according to which every mental process is considered in relation to three co-ordinates, which I described as *dynamic*, *topographical* and *economic* respectively; and this seemed to me to represent the furthest goal that psychology could attain. The attempt remained no more than a torso; after writing two or three papers – 'Instincts and their Vicissitudes' [1915*c*], 'Repression' [1915*d*], 'The Unconscious' [1915*e*], 'Mourning and Melancholia' [1917*e*], etc. – I broke off, wisely perhaps, since the time for theoretical predications of this kind had not yet come.[2] In my latest speculative works I have set about the task of dissecting our mental apparatus on the basis of the analytic view of pathological facts and have divided it into an *ego*, an *id* and a *super-ego*.[3] The super-ego is the heir of the Oedipus complex and represents the ethical standards of mankind.

I should not like to create an impression that during this last period of my work I have turned my back upon patient observation and have abandoned myself entirely to speculation. I have on the contrary always remained in the closest touch with the analytic material and have never ceased working at detailed points of clinical or technical importance. Even when I have moved away from observation, I have carefully avoided any contact with philosophy proper. This avoidance has been greatly facilitated by constitutional incapacity. I was always

1. [(1911*b*), *P.F.L.*, **11**, 29 ff.]

2. [As has been shown by Ernest Jones (1955, 209), all these papers were in fact written in 1915, together with seven others which have disappeared. See the Editor's Introduction to *Papers on Metapsychology*, *P.F.L.*, **11**, 101 ff.]

3. [*The Ego and the Id* [(1923*b*), ibid., 339 ff.]

open to the ideas of G. T. Fechner and have followed that thinker upon many important points.[1] The large extent to which psychoanalysis coincides with the philosophy of Schopenhauer – not only did he assert the dominance of the emotions and the supreme importance of sexuality but he was even aware of the mechanism of repression – is not to be traced to my acquaintance with his teaching. I read Schopenhauer very late in my life.[2] Nietzsche, another philosopher whose guesses and intuitions often agree in the most astonishing way with the laborious findings of psychoanalysis, was for a long time avoided by me on that very account; I was less concerned with the question of priority than with keeping my mind unembarrassed.

The neuroses were the first subject of analysis, and for a long time they were the only one. No analyst could doubt that medical practice was wrong in separating these disorders from the psychoses and in attaching them to the organic nervous diseases. The theory of the neuroses belongs to psychiatry and is indispensable as an introduction to it. It would seem, however, that the analytic study of the *psychoses* is impracticable owing to its lack of therapeutic results. Mental patients are as a rule without the capacity for forming a positive transference, so that the principal instrument of analytic technique is inapplicable to them. There are nevertheless a number of methods of approach to be found. Transference is often not so completely absent but that it can be used to a certain extent; and analysis has achieved undoubted successes with cyclical depressions, light paranoic modifications and partial schizophrenias. It has at least been a benefit to science that in many cases the diagnosis can oscillate for quite a long time between assuming the presence of a psychoneurosis or of a dementia praecox; for therapeutic attempts initiated in

1. [In particular, Fechner's influence appears in the 'principle of constancy', cf. *Beyond the Pleasure Principle* (1920g), ibid., **11**, 269 ff., and in the concept of mental topography, cf. *The Interpretation of Dreams* (1900a), ibid., **4**, 684. See also Freud's book on jokes (1905c), ibid., **6**, 219, 221, 234 and *n*.]

2. [Cf. p. 274 f. below.]

such cases have resulted in valuable discoveries before they have had to be broken off. But the chief consideration in this connection is that so many things that in the neuroses have to be laboriously fetched up from the depths are found in the psychoses on the surface, visible to every eye. For that reason the best subjects for the demonstration of many of the assertions of analysis are provided by the psychiatric clinic. It was thus bound to happen before long that analysis would find its way to the objects of psychiatric observation. I was able very early (1896) to establish in a case of paranoid dementia the presence of the same aetiological factors and the same emotional complexes as in the neuroses.[1] Jung [1907] explained some most puzzling stereotypies in dements by bringing them into relation with the patients' life-histories; Bleuler [1906b] demonstrated the existence in various psychoses of mechanisms like those which analysis had discovered in neurotics. Since then analysts have never relaxed their efforts to come to an understanding of the psychoses. Especially since it has been possible to work with the concept of narcissism, they have managed, now in this place and now in that, to get a glimpse beyond the wall. Most of all, no doubt, was achieved by Abraham [1912] in his elucidation of the melancholias. It is true that in this sphere all our knowledge is not yet converted into therapeutic power; but the mere theoretical gain is not to be despised, and we may be content to wait for its practical application. In the long run even the psychiatrists cannot resist the convincing force of their own clinical material. At the present time German psychiatry is undergoing a kind of 'peaceful penetration' by analytic views. While they continually declare that they will never be psychoanalysts, that they do not belong to the 'orthodox' school or agree with its exaggerations, and in particular that they do not believe in the predominance of the sexual factor, nevertheless the majority of the younger workers take over one piece or another of analytic theory and

1. [In Section III of Freud's second paper on 'The Neuro-Psychoses of Defence' (1896b).]

apply it in their own fashion to the material. All the signs point to the proximity of further developments in the same direction.

VI

I now watch from a distance the symptomatic reactions that are accompanying the introduction of psychoanalysis into the France which was for so long refractory. It seems like a reproduction of something I have lived through before, and yet it has peculiarities of its own. Objections of incredible simplicity are raised, such as that French sensitiveness is offended by the pedantry and crudity of psychoanalytic terminology. (One cannot help being reminded of Lessing's immortal Chevalier Riccaut de la Marlinière.[1]) Another comment has a more serious ring (a Professor of Psychology at the Sorbonne did not think it beneath him): the whole mode of thought of psychoanalysis, so he declared, is inconsistent with the *génie latin*. Here the Anglo-Saxon allies of France, who count as supporters of analysis, are explicitly thrown over. Anyone hearing the remark would suppose that psychoanalysis had been the favourite child of the *génie teutonique* and had been clasped to its heart from the moment of birth.

In France the interest in psychoanalysis began among the men of letters. To understand this, it must be borne in mind that from the time of the writing of *The Interpretation of Dreams* psychoanalysis ceased to be a purely medical subject. Between its appearance in Germany and in France lies the history of its numerous applications to departments of literature and of aesthetics, to the history of religions and to prehistory, to mythology, to folklore, to education, and so on. None of these

---

1. [The comic French soldier of fortune in *Minna von Barnhelm* who is amazed when his sharp practice at cards is described as cheating: 'Comment, Mademoiselle? Vous appelez cela "cheating"? Corriger la fortune, l'enchaîner sous ses doigts, être sûr de son fait – ('What, Mademoiselle? You call that "cheating"? Correcting Fortune, having it at one's finger ends, knowing just what one is about) – do the Germans call that "cheating"? Cheating! Oh, what a poor language, what a crude language German must be!']

things have much to do with medicine; in fact it is only through psychoanalysis that they are connected with it. I have no business, therefore, to go into them in detail in these pages. I cannot pass them over completely in silence, however, for on the one hand they are essential to a correct appreciation of the nature and value of psychoanalysis, and on the other hand I have, after all, undertaken to give an account of my life-work. The beginnings of the majority of these applications of psychoanalysis will be found in my works. Here and there I have gone a little way along the path in order to gratify my non-medical interests. Later on, others (not only doctors, but specialists in the various fields as well) have followed in my tracks and penetrated far into the different subjects. But since my programme limits me to a mention of my own share in these applications of psychoanalysis, I can only give a quite inadequate picture of their extent and importance.

A number of suggestions came to me out of the Oedipus complex, the ubiquity of which gradually dawned on me. The poet's choice, or his invention, of such a terrible subject seemed puzzling; and so too did the overwhelming effect of its dramatic treatment, and the general nature of such tragedies of destiny. But all of this became intelligible when one realized that a universal law of mental life had here been captured in all its emotional significance. Fate and the oracle were no more than materializations of an internal necessity; and the fact of the hero's sinning without his knowledge and against his intentions was evidently a right expression of the *unconscious* nature of his criminal tendencies. From understanding this tragedy of destiny it was only a step further to understanding a tragedy of character – *Hamlet*, which had been admired for three hundred years without its meaning being discovered or its author's motives guessed. It could scarcely be a chance that this neurotic creation of the poet should have come to grief, like his numberless fellows in the real world, over the Oedipus complex. For Hamlet was faced with the task of taking vengeance on another for the two deeds which are the subject of the Oedipus desires; and before that task his arm was paralysed by his own obscure sense of guilt. Shakespeare wrote *Hamlet* very soon after his father's death.[1] The suggestions made by me for the analysis of this tragedy[2] were fully worked out later on by Ernest Jones [1911b]. And the same example was afterwards used by Otto Rank as the starting-point for his investigation of the choice of material made by dramatists. In his large volume on the incest theme (Rank, 1912a) he was able to show how often imaginative writers have taken as their subject the themes of the Oedipus situation, and traced in the different literatures of the world the way in which the material has been transformed, modified and softened.

It was tempting to go on from there to an attempt at an analysis of poetic and artistic creation in general. The realm of imagination was seen to be a 'reservation' made during the

1. [*Footnote added* 1935:] This is a construction which I should like explicitly to withdraw. I no longer believe that William Shakespeare the actor from Stratford was the author of the works which have so long been attributed to him. Since the publication of J. T. Looney's volume '*Shakespeare' Identified* [1920], I am almost convinced that in fact Edward de Vere, Earl of Oxford, is concealed behind this pseudonym. – [When, in 1935, the English translator received the draft of this additional footnote, he was so much taken aback that he wrote to Freud asking him to reconsider it – not on the ground of the truth or otherwise of the theory, but of the effect the note was likely to have on the average English reader, particularly in view of the unfortunate name of the author of the book referred to. Freud's reply was most forbearing, as an excerpt from a translation of his letter will show. The letter is dated 29 August 1935. '. . . As regards the Shakespeare-Oxford note, your proposal puts me in the unusual situation of showing myself as an opportunist. I cannot understand the English attitude to this question: Edward de Vere was certainly as good an Englishman as Will Shakspere. But since the matter is so remote from analytic interest, and since you set so much store on my being reticent, I am ready to cut out the note, or merely to insert a sentence such as "For particular reasons I no longer wish to lay emphasis on this point". Decide on this yourself. On the other hand, I should be glad to have the whole note retained in the American edition. The same sort of narcissistic defence need not be feared over there. . . .' Accordingly in the English edition of 1935 the footnote reads: 'I have particular reasons for no longer wishing to lay any emphasis upon this point.']

2. [Freud put them forward in the first edition of *The Interpretation of Dreams* (1900a), *P.F.L.*, **4**, 366–8. Cf. p. 427 *n.* 1 below, where further references are given.]

painful transition from the pleasure principle to the reality principle in order to provide a substitute for instinctual satisfactions which had to be given up in real life. The artist, like the neurotic, had withdrawn from an unsatisfying reality into this world of imagination; but, unlike the neurotic, he knew how to find a way back from it and once more to get a firm foothold in reality. His creations, works of art, were the imaginary satisfactions of unconscious wishes, just as dreams are; and like them they were in the nature of compromises, since they too were forced to avoid any open conflict with the forces of repression. But they differed from the asocial, narcissistic products of dreaming in that they were calculated to arouse sympathetic interest in other people and were able to evoke and to satisfy the same unconscious wishful impulses in them too. Besides this, they made use of the perceptual pleasure of formal beauty as what I have called an 'incentive bonus'. What psychoanalysis was able to do was to take the interrelations between the impressions of the artist's life, his chance experiences, and his works, and from them to construct his [mental] constitution and the instinctual impulses at work in it – that is to say, that part of him which he shared with all men.[1] With this aim in view, for instance, I made Leonardo da Vinci the subject of a study [1910c], which is based on a single memory of childhood related by him and which aims chiefly at explaining his picture of 'The Madonna and Child with St Anne'. Since then my friends and pupils have undertaken numerous analyses of artists and their works. It does not appear that the enjoyment of a work of art is spoiled by the knowledge gained from such an analysis. The layman may perhaps expect too much from analysis in this respect, for it must be admitted that it throws no light on the two problems which probably interest him the most. It can do nothing towards elucidating the nature of the artistic gift, nor can it explain the means by which the artist works – artistic technique.

1. [Cf. 'Creative Writers and Day-Dreaming' (1908e), *P.F.L.*, **14**, 141 and n., Freud's book on jokes (1905c), ibid., **6**, 187–9, as well as the *Three Essays* (1905d), ibid., **7**, 131.]

I was able to show from a short story by W. Jensen called *Gradiva* [1907a], which has no particular merit in itself, that invented dreams can be interpreted in the same way as real ones and that the unconscious mechanisms familiar to us in the 'dream-work' are thus also operative in the processes of imaginative writing. My book on *Jokes and their Relation to the Unconscious* [1905c] was a side-issue directly derived from *The Interpretation of Dreams*. The only friend of mine who was at that time interested in my work remarked to me that my interpretations of dreams often impressed him as being like jokes.[1] In order to throw some light on this impression, I began to investigate jokes and found that their essence lay in the technical methods employed in them, and that these were the same as the means used in the 'dream-work' – that is to say, condensation, displacement, the representation of a thing by its opposite or by something very small, and so on. This led to an economic inquiry into the origin of the high degree of pleasure obtained from hearing a joke. And to this the answer was that it was due to the momentary suspension of the expenditure of energy upon maintaining repression, owing to the attraction exercised by the offer of a bonus of pleasure (*fore-pleasure*).

I myself set a higher value on my contributions to the psychology of religion, which began with the establishment of a remarkable similarity between obsessive actions and religious practices or ritual (1907b).[2] Without as yet understanding the deeper connections, I described the obsessional neurosis as a distorted private religion and religion as a kind of universal obsessional neurosis. Later on, in 1912, Jung's forcible indication of the far-reaching analogies between the mental products of neurotics and of primitive peoples led me to turn my attention to that subject. In four essays, which were collected into a book with the title of *Totem and Taboo* [1912–13],[3] I

1. [This was Wilhelm Fliess. See a footnote added in 1909 to *The Interpretation of Dreams* (1900a), ibid., **4**, 406 *n*.]

2. [*P.F.L.*, **13**, 27 ff.]

3. [*Ibid.*, **13**, 43 ff.]

showed that the horror of incest was even more marked among primitive than among civilized races and had given rise to very special measures of defence against it. I examined the relations between taboo prohibitions (the earliest form in which moral restrictions make their appearance) and emotional ambivalence; and I discovered under the primitive scheme of the universe known as 'animism' the principle of the over estimation of the importance of psychical reality – the belief in 'the omnipotence of thoughts'[1] – which lies at the root of magic as well. I developed the comparison with the obsessional neurosis at every point, and showed how many of the postulates of primitive mental life are still in force in that remarkable illness. Above all, however, I was attracted by totemism, the first system of organization in primitive tribes, a system in which the beginnings of social order are united with a rudimentary religion and the implacable domination of a small number of taboo prohibitions. The being that is revered is ultimately always an animal, from which the clan also claims to be descended. Many indications pointed to the conclusion that every race, even the most highly developed, had once passed through the stage of totemism.

The chief literary sources of my studies in this field were the well-known works of J. G. Frazer (*Totemism and Exogamy* and *The Golden Bough*), a mine of valuable facts and opinions. But Frazer effected little towards elucidating the problems of totemism; he had several times fundamentally altered his views on the subject, and the other ethnologists and prehistorians seemed in equal uncertainty and disagreement. My starting-point was the striking correspondence between the two taboo ordinances of totemism (not to kill the totem and not to have sexual relations with any woman of the same totem clan) and the two elements of the Oedipus complex (getting rid of the father and taking the mother to wife). I was therefore tempted to equate the totem animal with the father; and in fact primitive people themselves do this explicitly, by honouring it as the forefather of the clan. There next came to my help two facts

1. [Ibid., 13, 143 f.]

from psychoanalysis, a lucky observation of a child made by Ferenczi [1913a], which enabled me to speak of an 'infantile return of totemism', and the analysis of early animal phobias in children, which so often showed that the animal was a substitute for the father, a substitute on to which the fear of the father derived from the Oedipus complex had been displaced. Not much was lacking to enable me to recognize the killing of the father as the nucleus of totemism and the starting-point in the formation of religion.

This missing element was supplied when I became acquainted with W. Robertson Smith's work, *The Religion of the Semites* [1894]. Its author (a man of genius who was both a physicist and an expert in Biblical researches) introduced the so-called 'totem meal' as an essential part of the totemic religion. Once a year the totem animal, which was at other times regarded as sacred, was solemnly killed in the presence of all the members of the clan, was devoured and was then mourned over. The mourning was followed by a great festival. When I further took into account Darwin's conjecture that men originally lived in hordes, each under the domination of a single powerful, violent and jealous male, there rose before me out of all these components the following hypothesis, or, I would rather say, vision. The father of the primal horde, since he was an unlimited despot, had seized all the women for himself; his sons, being dangerous to him as rivals, had been killed or driven away. One day, however, the sons came together and united to overwhelm, kill and devour their father, who had been their enemy but also their ideal. After the deed they were unable to take over their heritage since they stood in one another's way. Under the influence of failure and remorse they learned to come to an agreement among themselves; they banded themselves into a clan of brothers by the help of the ordinances of totemism, which aimed at preventing a repetition of such a deed, and they jointly undertook to forgo the possession of the women on whose account they had killed their father. They were then driven to finding strange women, and this was the origin of the exogamy which is so closely bound up with totemism. The totem meal was the festival commemorating the fearful deed from which sprang man's sense of guilt (or 'original sin') and which was the beginning at once of social organization, of religion and of ethical restrictions.

Now whether we suppose that such a possibility was a historical event or not, it brings the formation of religion within the circle of the father-complex and bases it upon the ambivalence which dominates that complex. After the totem animal had ceased to serve as a substitute for him, the primal father, at once feared and hated, revered and envied, became the prototype of God himself. The son's rebelliousness and his affection for his father struggled against each other through a constant succession of compromises, which sought on the one hand to atone for the act of parricide and on the other to consolidate the advantages it had brought. This view of religion throws a particularly clear light upon the psychological basis of Christianity, in which, as we know, the ceremony of the totem meal still survives, with but little distortion, in the form of Communion. I should like explicitly to mention that this last observation was not made by me but is to be found in the works of Robertson Smith [1894] and Frazer [1912].

Theodor Reik and G. Róheim, the ethnologist, have taken up the line of thought which I developed in *Totem and Taboo* and, in a series of important works, have extended it, deepened it, or corrected it. I myself have since returned to it more than once, in the course of my investigations into the 'unconscious sense of guilt' (which also plays such an important part among the motives of neurotic suffering) and in my attempts at forming a closer connection between social psychology and the psychology of the individual.[1] I have moreover made use of the idea of an archaic heritage from the 'primal horde' epoch of mankind's development in explaining susceptibility to hypnosis.[2]

I have taken but little direct part in certain other applications

---

1. *The Ego and the Id* [1923*b*; P.F.L., **11**, 339 ff.] and *Group Psychology and the Analysis of the Ego* [1921*c*; ibid., **12**, 91.]

2. [*Group Psychology* (1921*c*), ibid., **12**, 157 ff.]

of psychoanalysis, though they are none the less of general interest. It is only a step from the fantasies of individual neurotics to the imaginative creations of groups and peoples as we find them in myths, legends, and fairy tales. Mythology became the special province of Otto Rank [cf. 1909, 1911, 1912a]; the interpretation of myths, the tracing of them back to the familiar unconscious complexes of early childhood, the replacing of astral explanations by a discovery of human motives, all of this is to a large extent due to his analytic efforts. The subject of symbolism, too, has found many students among my followers. Symbolism has brought psychoanalysis many enemies; many inquirers with unduly prosaic minds have never been able to forgive it the recognition of symbolism, which followed from the interpretation of dreams. But analysis is guiltless of the discovery of symbolism, for it had long been known in other regions of thought (such as folklore, legends and myths) and plays an even larger part in them than in the 'language of dreams'.

I myself have contributed nothing to the application of analysis to education. It was natural, however, that the analytic discoveries about the sexual life and mental development of children should attract the attention of educators and make them see their problems in a new light. Dr Oskar Pfister, a Protestant pastor at Zurich, led the way as a tireless pioneer along these lines, nor did he find the practice of analysis incompatible with the retention of his religion, though it is true that this was of a sublimated kind. Among the many others who worked alongside of him I may mention Frau Dr Hug-Hellmuth and Dr S. Bernfeld, both of Vienna.[1] The application of analysis to the prophylactic upbringing of healthy children and to the correcting of those who, though not actually neurotic, have deviated from the normal course of development has led to one consequence which is of practical importance. It is no longer possible to restrict the practice of psychoanalysis

1. [*Footnote added* 1935:] Since these words were written child analysis in particular has gained a powerful momentum owing to the work of Mrs Melanie Klein and of my daughter, Anna Freud.

to doctors and to exclude laymen from it. In fact, a doctor who has not been through a special training is, in spite of his diploma, a layman in analysis, and a non-doctor who has been suitably trained can, with occasional reference to a doctor, carry out the analytic treatment not only of children but also of neurotics.[1]

By a process of development against which it would have been useless to struggle, the word 'psychoanalysis' has itself become ambiguous. While it was originally the name of a particular therapeutic method, it has now also become the name of a science – the science of unconscious mental processes. By itself this science is seldom able to deal with a problem completely, but it seems destined to give valuable contributory help in the most varied regions of knowledge. The sphere of application of psychoanalysis extends as far as that of psychology, to which it forms a complement of the greatest moment.

Looking back, then, over the patchwork of my life's labours, I can say that I have made many beginnings and thrown out many suggestions. Something will come of them in the future, though I cannot myself tell whether it will be much or little. I can, however, express a hope that I have opened up a pathway for an important advance in our knowledge.[2]

1. [See *The Question of Lay Analysis* (1926e), below, p. 283 ff.]
2. [This last sentence was added in 1935.]

POSTSCRIPT
(1935)

THE editor of this series of autobiographical studies did not, so far as I know, consider the possibility that after a certain lapse of time a sequel might be written to any of them; and it may be that such an event has occurred only in the present instance. I am undertaking the task since my American publisher [W. W. Norton, New York] desires to issue the little work in a new edition. It first appeared in America in 1927 (published by Brentano) under the title of *An Autobiographical Study*, but it was injudiciously brought out in the same volume as another essay of mine which gave its title, *The Problem of Lay-Analyses*, to the whole book and so obscured the present work.

Two themes run through these pages: the story of my life and the history of psychoanalysis. They are intimately interwoven. This *Autobiographical Study* shows how psycho-analysis came to be the whole content of my life and rightly assumes that no personal experiences of mine are of any interest in comparison to my relations with that science.

Shortly before I wrote this study it seemed as though my life would soon be brought to an end by the recurrence of a malignant disease; but surgical skill saved me in 1923 and I was able to continue my life and my work, though no longer in freedom from pain. In the period of more than ten years that has passed since then, I have never ceased my analytic work nor my writing – as is proved by the completion of the twelfth volume of the German edition of my collected works. But I myself find that a significant change has come about. Threads which in the course of my development had become inter-tangled have now begun to separate; interests which I had acquired in the later part of my life have receded, while the older and original ones become prominent once more. It is true that in this last decade I have carried out some important pieces of analytic work, such as the revision of the problem of anxiety in my book *Inhibitions, Symptoms and Anxiety* (1926d) [1] or the simple explanation of sexual 'fetishism' which I was able to make a year later (1927e). [2] Nevertheless it would be true to say that, since I put forward my hypothesis of the existence of two classes of instinct (Eros and the death instinct) and since I proposed a division of the mental personality into an ego, a super-ego and an id (1923b), [3] I have made no further decisive contributions to psychoanalysis: what I have written on the subject since then has been either unessential or would soon have been supplied by someone else. This circumstance is connected with an alteration in myself, with what might be described as a phase of regressive development. My interest, after making a lifelong *détour* through the natural sciences, medicine and psychotherapy, returned to the cultural problems which had fascinated me long before, when I was a youth scarcely old enough for thinking. At the very climax of my psychoanalytic work, in 1912, I had already attempted in *Totem and Taboo* [4] to make use of the newly discovered findings of analysis in order to investigate the origins of religion and morality. I now carried this work a stage further in two later essays, *The Future of an Illusion* (1927c) and *Civilization and its Discontents* (1930a). [5] I perceived ever more clearly that the events of human history, the interactions between human nature, cultural development and the precipitates of primeval experiences (the most prominent example of which is religion) are no more than a reflection of the dynamic conflicts between the ego, the id and the super-ego, which psychoanalysis studies in the individual – are the very same processes repeated upon a wider stage. In *The Future of an Illusion* I expressed an essentially negative valuation of religion. Later, I found a formula which did better justice to it: while granting that its power lies in the truth which it contains, I showed

1. [*P.F.L.*, **10**, 227 ff.]
2. ['Fetishism' (1927e), *P.F.L.*, **7**, 345 ff.]
3. [*The Ego and the Id* (1923b), ibid., **11**, 339 ff.]
4. [*Totem and Taboo* (1912–13), ibid., **13**, 43 ff.]
5. [*P.F.L.*, **12**, 179, 243.]

that that truth was not a material but a historical truth.[1]

These studies, which, though they originate in psychoanalysis, stretch far beyond it, have perhaps awakened more public sympathy than psychoanalysis itself. They may have played a part in creating the short-lived illusion that I was among the writers to whom a great nation like Germany was ready to listen. It was in 1929 that, with words no less pregnant than friendly, Thomas Mann, one of the acknowledged spokesmen of the German people, found a place for me in the history of modern thought. A little later my daughter Anna, acting as my proxy, was given a civic reception in the Rathaus at Frankfurt am Main on the occasion of my being awarded the Goethe Prize for 1930.[2] This was the climax of my life as a citizen. Soon afterwards the boundaries of our country narrowed and the nation would know no more of us.

And here I may be allowed to break off these autobiographical notes. The public has no claim to learn any more of my personal affairs – of my struggles, my disappointments and my successes. I have in any case been more open and frank in some of my writings (such as *The Interpretation of Dreams* [1900*a*] and *The Psychopathology of Everyday Life* [1901*b*] than people usually are who describe their lives for their contemporaries or for posterity. I have had small thanks for it, and from my experience I cannot recommend anyone to follow my example.

I must add a few more words on the history of psychoanalysis during the last decade. There can no longer be any doubt that it will continue; it has proved its capacity to survive and to develop both as a branch of knowledge and as a therapeutic method. The number of its supporters (organized into the International Psycho-Analytical Association) has considerably increased. In addition to the older local groups (in Vienna, Berlin, Budapest, London, Holland, Switzerland and Russia), societies have since been formed in Paris and Calcutta, two in Japan, several in the United States, and quite recently one each in Jerusalem and South Africa and two in Scandinavia. Out of

1. [See *Moses and Monotheism* (1939*a*), ibid., **13**, 378–9, 379 *n*.]
2. [Cf. Freud (1930*d*, 1930*e*), *P.F.L.*, **14**, 461 ff.]

their own funds these local societies support (or are in process of forming) training institutes, in which instruction in the practice of psychoanalysis is given according to a uniform plan, and out-patient clinics in which experienced analysts as well as students give free treatment to patients of limited means. Every other year the members of the International Psycho-Analytical Association hold a Congress at which scientific papers are read and questions of organization decided. The thirteenth of these congresses (which I myself can no longer attend) took place at Lucerne in 1934. From a core of interests that are common to all members of the Association, their work radiates in many different directions. Some lay most stress upon clarifying and deepening our knowledge of psychology, while others are concerned with keeping in contact with medicine and psychiatry. From the practical point of view, some analysts have set themselves the task of bringing about the recognition of psychoanalysis at the universities and its inclusion in the medical curriculum, whereas others are content to remain outside these institutions and will not allow that psychoanalysis is less important in the field of education than in that of medicine. It happens from time to time that an analytic worker may find himself isolated in an attempt to emphasize some single one of the findings or views of psychoanalysis at the expense of all the rest. Nevertheless, the whole impression is a satisfactory one – of serious scientific work carried on at a high level.

THE RESISTANCES
TO PSYCHOANALYSIS
(1925 [1924])

DIE WIDERSTÄNDE GEGEN
DIE PSYCHOANALYSE

(A) German Editions:

1925   *Imago*, **11** (3), 222–33.
1948   *Gesammelte Werke*, **14**, 99–110.

(B) English Translations:
'The Resistances to Psycho-Analysis'

1950   *Collected Papers*, **5**, 163–74. (Tr. James Strachey.)
1961   *Standard Edition*, **19**, 211–24. (Corrected version of above.)

The present edition is a reprint of the *Standard Edition* version, with a few editorial changes.

Freud's name was on the Editorial Committee of *La Revue Juive* (Geneva), the periodical in which this essay first appeared in a French translation in March 1925. It was written at the request of the actual editor, Albert Cohen, probably in September 1924. The German original appeared almost simultaneously in *Imago* and in the *Almanach 1926*, which was published in September 1925 – some six months after the French issue.

THE RESISTANCES
TO PSYCHOANALYSIS

A CHILD in his nurse's arms will turn away screaming at the sight of a strange face; a pious man will begin the new season with a prayer and he will also greet the first fruits of the year with a blessing; a peasant will refuse to buy a scythe unless it bears the trade-mark that was familiar to his parents. The distinction between these situations is obvious and would seem to justify one in looking for a different motive in each of them.

Nevertheless, it would be a mistake to overlook what they have in common. In each case we are dealing with unpleasure of the same kind. The child expresses it in an elementary fashion, the pious man lulls it by an artifice, while the peasant uses it as the motive for a decision. The source of this unpleasure is the demand made upon the mind by anything that is *new*, the psychical expenditure that it requires, the uncertainty, mounting up to anxious expectancy, which it brings along with it. It would be interesting to devote a whole study to mental reactions to novelty; for under certain, no longer primary, conditions we can observe behaviour of the contrary kind – a thirst for stimulation which flings itself upon anything that is new merely because it *is* new.

In scientific affairs there should be no place for recoiling from novelty. Science, in her perpetual incompleteness and insufficiency, is driven to hope for her salvation in new discoveries and new ways of regarding things. She does well, in order not to be deceived, to arm herself with scepticism and to accept nothing new unless it has withstood the strictest examination. Sometimes, however, this scepticism shows two unexpected features; it may be sharply directed against what is new while it spares what is familiar and accepted, and it may be content to reject things before it has examined them. But in behaving thus it reveals itself as a prolongation of the primitive reaction against what is new and as a cloak for the retention of that reaction. It is a matter of common knowledge how often in the history of scientific research it has happened that innovations have met with intense and stubborn resistance, while subsequent events have shown that the resistance was unjustified and that the novelty was valuable and important. What provoked the resistance was, as a rule, certain factors in the subject-matter of the novelty, while, on the other side, several factors must have combined to make the irruption of the primitive reaction possible.

A particularly bad reception was accorded to psychoanalysis, which the present writer began to develop nearly thirty years ago from the discoveries of Josef Breuer (of Vienna) on the origin of neurotic symptoms. It cannot be disputed that it possessed the quality of novelty, even though it made use of plenty of material which was well known from other sources (quite apart from Breuer's discoveries), such as the lessons from the teachings of Charcot, the great neuropathologist, and impressions derived from the sphere of hypnotic phenomena. Its original significance was purely therapeutic: it aimed at creating a new and efficient method for treating neurotic illnesses. But connections which could not be foreseen in the beginning caused psychoanalysis to reach out far beyond its original aim. It ended by claiming to have set our whole view of mental life upon a new basis and therefore to be of importance for every field of knowledge that is founded on psychology. After a decade of complete neglect it suddenly became a subject of general interest – and set loose a storm of indignant opposition.

The *forms* in which the resistance to psychoanalysis found expression need not now be considered. It is enough to say that the struggle over this innovation is by no means at an end, though it is already possible to see what direction it will take. Its opponents have not succeeded in suppressing the movement.

Psychoanalysis, of which twenty years ago I was the only spokesman, has since attracted the support of numerous valuable and active workers, medical and non-medical, who make use of it as a procedure for the treatment of nervous diseases, as a method of psychological research and as an auxiliary instrument for scientific work in the most various departments of intellectual life. In the following pages our interest will be directed only to the *motives* of the resistance to psychoanalysis, with particular stress upon the composite character of that resistance and upon the differing amount of weight carried by its components.

From a clinical standpoint the neuroses must necessarily be put alongside the intoxications and such disorders as Graves' disease. There are conditions arising from an excess or a relative lack of certain highly active substances, whether produced inside the body or introduced into it from outside – in short, they are disturbances of the chemistry of the body, toxic conditions. If someone succeeded in isolating and demonstrating the hypothetical substance or substances concerned in neuroses, he would have no need to worry about opposition from the medical profession. For the present, however, no such avenue of approach to the problem is open. At the moment we can only start from the symptoms presented by a neurosis – symptoms which in the case of hysteria, for instance, consist of a combination of somatic and mental disturbances. Now Charcot's experiments as well as Breuer's clinical observations taught us that the somatic symptoms of hysteria are psychogenic too – that is, that they are precipitates of mental processes that have run their course. By putting a subject into a state of hypnosis it was possible at will to produce the somatic symptoms of hysteria artificially.

Psychoanalysis took hold of this new realization and began to consider the problem of the nature of the psychical processes which led to these unusual consequences. But the direction taken by this inquiry was not to the liking of the contemporary generation of physicians. They had been brought up to respect only anatomical, physical and chemical factors. They were not prepared for taking psychical ones into account and therefore met them with indifference or antipathy. They obviously had doubts whether psychical events allowed of any exact scientific treatment whatever. As an excessive reaction against an earlier phase during which medicine had been dominated by what was known as the 'philosophy of Nature',[1] they regarded such abstractions as those with which psychology is obliged to work as nebulous, fantastic and mystical; while they simply refused to believe in remarkable phenomena which might have been the starting-point of research. The symptoms of hysterical neuroses were looked upon as shamming and the phenomena of hypnotism as a hoax. Even the psychiatrists, upon whose attention the most unusual and astonishing mental phenomena were constantly being forced, showed no inclination to examine their details or inquire into their connections. They were content to classify the variegated array of symptoms and trace them back, so far as they could manage, to somatic, anatomical or chemical aetiological disturbances. During this materialistic or, rather, mechanistic period, medicine made tremendous advances, but it also showed a short-sighted misunderstanding of the most important and most difficult among the problems of life.

It is easy to understand why doctors, with an attitude of this kind towards the mind, should have had no liking for psychoanalysis and should have demurred to its demand for learning many things afresh and for seeing many things in a different light. But as a compensation it might be supposed that the new theory would be all the more likely to meet with applause from philosophers. For philosophers were accustomed to putting abstract concepts (or, as unkind tongues would say, hazy words) in the forefront of their explanations of the universe, and it would be impossible that they should object to the extension of the sphere of psychology for which psycho-

---

1. [A pantheistic attitude, chiefly associated with the name of Friedrich Schelling (1775–1854), which was very prevalent in Germany during the first part of the nineteenth century.]

analysis had paved the way. But here another obstacle arose. The philosophers' idea of what is mental was not that of psychoanalysis. The overwhelming majority of philosophers regard as mental only the phenomena of consciousness. For them the world of consciousness coincides with the sphere of what is mental. Everything else that may take place in the 'mind' – an entity so hard to grasp – is relegated by them to the organic determinants of mental processes or to processes parallel to mental ones. Or, more strictly speaking, the mind has no contents other than the phenomena of consciousness, and consequently psychology, the science of the mind, has no other subject-matter. And on this point the layman's view is the same.

What, then, can a philosopher say to a theory which, like psychoanalysis, asserts that on the contrary what is mental is in itself *unconscious* and that being conscious is only a *quality*, which may or may not accrue to a particular mental act and the withholding of which may perhaps alter that act in no other respect? He will naturally say that anything both un-conscious and mental would be an impossibility, a *contradictio in adjecto*,[1] and he will fail to observe that in making this judgement he is merely repeating his own definition of what is mental, a definition which may perhaps be too narrow. It is easy for philosophers to feel this certainty, since they have no acquaintance with the material whose investigation has compelled analysts to believe in unconscious mental acts. Philosophers have never taken account of hypnosis, they have not concerned themselves with the interpreting of dreams – on the contrary, like doctors, they regard dreams as the mean-ingless products of reduced mental activity during sleep – they are scarcely aware that there are such things as obsessions and delusions and they would find themselves in a most embar-rassing situation if they were asked to explain them on the basis of their own psychological premisses. Analysts, too, refuse to say what the unconscious is, but they can indicate the domain of phenomena whose observation has obliged them to assume

1. ['A contradiction in terms.']

its existence. Philosophers, who know no kind of observation other than self-observation, cannot follow them into that domain.

So it comes about that psychoanalysis derives nothing but disadvantages from its middle position between medicine and philosophy. Doctors regard it as a speculative system and refuse to believe that, like every other natural science, it is based on a patient and tireless elaboration of facts from the world of perception; philosophers, measuring it by the standard of their own artificially constructed systems, find that it starts from impossible premises and reproach it because its most general concepts (which are only now in process of evolution) lack clarity and precision.

This state of affairs is enough to account for the reluctant and hesitant reception of analysis in scientific quarters. But it does not explain the outbursts of indignation, derision and scorn which, in disregard of every standard of logic and good taste, have characterized the controversial methods of its opponents. A reaction of such a kind suggests that resistances other than purely intellectual ones were stirred up and that powerful emotional forces were aroused. And there are indeed plenty of things to be found in the theory of psychoanalysis calculated to produce such an effect as this upon the passions of men of every kind and not of scientists alone. Above all there is the very important place in the mental life of human beings which psychoanalysis assigns to what are known as the sexual instincts. Psychoanalytic theory maintained that the symptoms of neuroses are distorted substitutive satisfactions of sexual instinctual forces, the direct satisfaction of which has been frustrated by internal resistances. Later on, when analysis had extended beyond its original field of work and began to be applied to normal mental life, it sought to show that these same sexual components, which could be diverted from their immediate aims and directed to other things, made the most important contributions to the cultural achievements of the individual and of society. These views were not entirely new. The incomparable significance of sexual life had been proclaimed by the philosopher Schopenhauer in an intensely impressive passage.[1] Moreover, what psychoanalysis called sexuality was by no means identical with the impulsion towards a union of the two sexes or towards producing a pleasurable sensation in the genitals; it had far more resemblance to the all-inclusive and all-preserving Eros of Plato's *Symposium*.

But the opponents of psychoanalysis forgot its illustrious forerunners; they fell upon it as though it had made an assault upon the dignity of the human race. They accused it of 'pan-sexualism', though the psychoanalytic theory of the instincts had always been strictly dualistic[2] and had at no time failed to recognize, alongside the sexual instincts, others to which it actually ascribed force enough to suppress the sexual instincts. (These mutually opposing forces were described to begin with as the sexual instincts and the ego instincts. A later theoretical development changed them into Eros and the instinct of death or destruction.) The suggestion that art, religion and social order originated in part in a contribution from the sexual instincts was represented by the opponents of analysis as a degradation of the highest cultural values. They emphatically declared that men have other interests besides this eternal one of sex, overlooking in their zeal the fact that animals too have other interests — indeed they are subject to sexuality, not permanently like men, but only in bouts occurring at specific periods — overlooking, too, the fact that the existence of these other interests in men had never been disputed and that nothing can be altered in the value of a cultural achievement by its being shown to have been derived from elementary animal instinctual sources.

Such a display of unfairness and lack of logic cries out for an explanation. Its origin is not hard to find. Human civilization rests upon two pillars, of which one is the control of natural forces and the other the restriction of our instincts. The ruler's throne rests upon fettered slaves. Among the instinctual

1. [See the Appendix below.]
2. [Cf. an Editor's footnote in Chapter IV of *The Ego and the Id* (1923*b*), *P.F.L.*, **11**, 387 *n.* 2.]

components which are thus brought into service, the sexual instincts, in the narrower sense of the word, are conspicuous for their strength and savagery. Woe, if they should be set loose! The throne would be overturned and the ruler trampled under foot. Society is aware of this – and will not allow the topic to be mentioned.

But why not? What harm could the discussion do? Psycho-analysis has never said a word in favour of unfettering instincts that would injure our community; on the contrary it has issued a warning and an exhortation to us to mend our ways. But society refuses to consent to the ventilation of the question, because it has a bad conscience in more than one respect. In the first place it has set up a high ideal of morality – morality being restriction of the instincts – and insists that all its members shall fulfil that ideal without troubling itself with the possibility that obedience may bear heavily upon the individual. Nor is it sufficiently wealthy or well-organized to be able to compensate the individual for the amount of his instinctual renunciation. It is consequently left to the individual to decide how he can obtain, for the sacrifice he has made, enough compensation to enable him to preserve his mental balance. On the whole, however, he is obliged to live psy-chologically beyond his means, while the unsatisfied claims of his instincts make him feel the demands of civilization as a constant pressure upon him. Thus society maintains a condition of *cultural hypocrisy* which is bound to be accompanied by a sense of insecurity and a necessity for guarding what is an undeniably precarious situation by forbidding criticism and discussion. This line of thought holds good for all the in-stinctual impulses, including, therefore, the egoistic ones. The question whether it applies to all possible forms of civilization, and not merely to those which have evolved hitherto, cannot be discussed here. As regards the sexual instincts in the narrower sense, there is the further point that in most people they are tamed insufficiently and in a manner which is psychologically wrong and are therefore readier than the rest to break loose.

Psychoanalysis has revealed the weaknesses of this system

and has recommended that it should be altered. It proposes that there should be a reduction in the strictness with which instincts are repressed and that correspondingly more play should be given to truthfulness. Certain instinctual impulses, with whose suppression society has gone too far, should be permitted a greater amount of satisfaction; in the case of certain others the inefficient method of suppressing them by means of repression should be replaced by a better and securer procedure. As a result of these criticisms psychoanalysis is regarded as 'inimical to culture' and has been put under a ban as a 'social danger'. This resistance cannot last for ever. No human institution can in the long run escape the influence of fair criticism; but men's attitude to psychoanalysis is still dominated by this fear, which gives rein to their passions and diminishes their power of logical argument.

By its theory of the instincts psychoanalysis offended the feelings of individuals in so far as they regarded themselves as members of the social community; another branch of its theory was calculated to hurt every single person at the tenderest point of his own psychical development. Psychoanalysis disposed once and for all of the fairy tale of an asexual childhood. It demonstrated the fact that sexual interests and activities occur in small children from the beginning of their lives. It showed what transformations those activities pass through, how at about the age of five they succumb to inhibition and how from puberty onwards they enter the service of the reproductive function. It recognized that early infantile sexual life reaches its peak in what is known as the Oedipus complex (an emotional attachment of the child to the parent of the opposite sex accompanied by an attitude of rivalry to the parent of the same sex) and that at that period of life this impulsion extends uninhibited into a straightforward sexual desire. This can be confirmed so easily that only the greatest efforts could make it possible to overlook it. Every individual has in fact gone through this phase but has afterwards energetically repressed its purport and succeeded in forgetting it. A horror of incest and an enormous sense of guilt are left over from this prehistoric epoch of the individual's existence. It may be that something quite similar occurred in the prehistoric epoch of the human species as a whole and that the beginnings of morality, religion and social order were intimately connected with the surmounting of that primeval era. To adults their prehistory seems so inglorious that they refuse to allow themselves to be reminded of it: they were infuriated when psychoanalysis tried to lift the veil of amnesia from their years of childhood. There was only one way out: what psychoanalysis asserted must be false and what posed as a new science must be a tissue of fancies and distortions.

Thus the strongest resistances to psychoanalysis were not of an intellectual kind but arose from emotional sources. This explained their passionate character as well as their poverty in logic. The situation obeyed a simple formula: men in the mass behaved to psychoanalysis in precisely the same way as individual neurotics under treatment for their disorders. It is possible, however, by patient work to convince these latter individuals that everything happened as we maintained it did: we had not invented it ourselves but had arrived at it from a study of other neurotics covering a period of twenty or thirty years. The position was at once alarming and consoling: alarming because it was no small thing to have the whole human race as one's patient, and consoling because after all everything was taking place as the hypotheses of psychoanalysis declared that it was bound to.

If we cast our eyes once again over the various resistances to psychoanalysis that have been enumerated, it is evident that only a minority of them are of the kind which habitually arise against most scientific innovations of any considerable importance. The majority of them are due to the fact that powerful human feelings are hurt by the subject-matter of the theory. Darwin's theory of descent met with the same fate, since it tore down the barrier that had been arrogantly set up between men and beasts. I drew attention to this analogy in an earlier paper [1917a], in which I showed how the psychoanalytic view of the relation of the conscious ego to an overpowering unconscious was a severe blow to human self-love. I described this as the *psychological* blow to men's narcissism, and compared it with the *biological* blow delivered by the theory of descent and the earlier *cosmological* blow aimed at it by the discovery of Copernicus.

Purely external difficulties have also contributed to strengthen the resistance to psychoanalysis. It is not easy to arrive at an independent judgement upon matters to do with analysis without having experienced it oneself or practised it on someone else. Nor can one do the latter without having acquired a specific and decidedly delicate technique, while until recently there was no easily accessible means of learning psychoanalysis and its technique. This position has now been improved by the foundation (in 1920) of the Berlin Psycho-Analytic Clinic and Training Institute, and soon afterwards (in 1922) of an exactly similar institute in Vienna.

Finally, with all reserve, the question may be raised whether the personality of the present writer as a Jew who has never sought to disguise the fact that he is a Jew may not have had a share in provoking the antipathy of his environment to psychoanalysis. An argument of this kind is not often uttered aloud. But we have unfortunately grown so suspicious that we cannot avoid thinking that this factor may not have been quite without its effect. Nor is it perhaps entirely a matter of chance that the first advocate of psychoanalysis was a Jew. To profess belief in this new theory called for a certain degree of readiness to accept a situation of solitary opposition – a situation with which no one is more familiar than a Jew.

APPENDIX

EXTRACT FROM SCHOPENHAUER'S
THE WORLD AS WILL AND IDEA[1]

In his later works, Freud made several references to the emphasis which Schopenhauer laid on the importance of sexuality. As well as mentioning the subject above, he also referred to it in the closing paragraph of 'A Difficulty in the Path of Psycho-Analysis' (1917*a*), and in the preface (written in 1920) to the fourth edition of the *Three Essays* (1905*d*), *P.F.L.*, **7**, 43. It appears again in Chapter VI of *Beyond the Pleasure Principle* (1920*g*), ibid., **11**, 322 – a work which Freud was revising at about the same time as he wrote the preface just mentioned – and yet again in Chapter V of the *Autobiographical Study* (1925*d*), p. 244 above.

Freud sometimes alluded specifically to 'an intensely impressive passage' or 'words of unforgettable impressiveness', though he nowhere quoted the passage or indicated its source in Schopenhauer's writings. It seems highly likely, however, that the extract printed here is from the passage Freud had in mind, and it is, therefore, perhaps of interest to reproduce it. This paragraph occurs in the Supplements to the Fourth Book of *The World as Will and Idea*, Chapter XLII, 'The Life of the Species' ['*Leben der Gattung*']. Immediately before this point, Schopenhauer has been discussing the character of sexual desire, which he declares is different from every other desire: '. . . it is not only the strongest but even specifically of a more powerful kind than any other.' He gives examples of the recognition accorded in antiquity to this power and continues as follows:

'To all this corresponds the important *rôle* which the relation of the sexes plays in the world of men, where it is really the invisible central point of all action and conduct, and peeps out

1. Translated by R. B. Haldane and J. Kemp, 1886, **3**, 313–14. The extract is printed by arrangement with Messrs George Allen & Unwin.

everywhere in spite of all veils thrown over it. It is the cause of war and the end of peace, the basis of what is serious, and the aim of the jest, the inexhaustible source of wit, the key to all allusions, and the meaning of all mysterious hints, of all unspoken offers and all stolen glances, the daily meditation of the young, and often also of the old, the hourly thought of the unchaste, and even against their will the constantly recurring imagination of the chaste, the ever ready material of a joke, just because the profoundest seriousness lies at its foundation. It is, however, the piquant element and the joke of life that the chief concern of all men is secretly pursued and ostensibly ignored as much as possible. But, in fact, we see it every moment seat itself, as the true hereditary lord of the world, out of the fulness of its own strength, upon the ancestral throne, and looking down from thence with scornful glances, laugh at the preparations which have been made to bind it, imprison it, or at least to limit it and wherever it is possible to keep it concealed, or even so to master it that it shall only appear as a subordinate, secondary concern of life. But all this agrees with the fact that the sexual passion [1] is the kernel of the will to live, and consequently the concentration of all desire; therefore in the text I have called the genital organs the focus of the will. Indeed, one may say man is concrete sexual desire; [1] for his origin is an act of copulation and his wish of wishes is an act of copulation, and this tendency alone perpetuates and holds together his whole phenomenal existence. The will to live manifests itself indeed primarily as an effort to sustain the individual, yet this is only a step to the effort to sustain the species, and the latter endeavour must be more powerful in proportion as the life of the species surpasses that of the individual in duration, extension and value. Therefore sexual passion [1] is the most perfect manifestation of the will to live, its most distinctly expressed type; and the origin of the individual in it, and its primacy over all other desires of the natural man, are both in complete agreement with this.'

1. ['*Geschlechstrieb*' in the original – a word which, when used by Freud, is translated 'sexual instinct' in the *Standard Edition*.]

THE QUESTION
OF LAY ANALYSIS
Conversations with an Impartial Person
(1926)

EDITOR'S NOTE

DIE FRAGE DER LAIENANALYSE
Unterredungen mit einem Unparteiischen

(A) GERMAN EDITIONS:

1926   Leipzig, Vienna and Zurich: Internationaler Psycho-
      analytischer Verlag.

1948   *Gesammelte Werke*, **14**, 209–86.

'Nachwort zur *Frage der Laienanalyse*'

1927   *Internationale Zeitschrift für Psychoanalyse*, **13** (3), 326–32.

1948   *Gesammelte Werke*, **14**, 287–96.

(B) ENGLISH TRANSLATIONS:
The Problem of Lay-Analyses

1927   In *The Problem of Lay-Analyses*, New York: Brentano.
      (Tr. A. P. Maerker-Branden; preface S. Ferenczi;
      includes *An Autobiographical Study*.)

The Question of Lay-Analysis: an Introduction to Psycho-Analysis

1947   London: Imago Publishing Co. (Tr. N. Procter-Gregg;
      preface Ernest Jones.)

1950   New York: Norton. (Reissue of above.)

1959   *Standard Edition*, **20**, 177–250. (Tr. James Strachey; with
      different subtitle)

'Concluding Remarks on the Question of Lay Analysis'

1927   *International Journal of Psycho-Analysis*, **8** (3), 392–8. (Tr.
      unspecified.)

1950   *Collected Papers*, **5**, 205–14. (Tr. James Strachey; with
          changed title.)
1959   *Standard Edition*, **20**, 251–8. (Revised reprint of above.)

The present edition is a reprint of the *Standard Edition* version, with some editorial modifications.

An extract from the original German, under the title 'Psychoanalyse und Kurpfuscherei' ('Psychoanalysis and Quackery'), was included in *Almanach 1927*, 47–59, published in September 1926 at about the same time as the volume itself.

In the late spring of 1926 proceedings were begun in Vienna against Theodor Reik, a prominent non-medical member of the Vienna Psycho-Analytical Society. He was charged, on information laid by someone whom he had been treating analytically, with a breach of an old Austrian law against 'quackery' – a law which made it illegal for a person without a medical degree to treat patients. Freud at once intervened energetically. He argued the position privately with an official of high standing, and went on to compose the present pamphlet for immediate publication. He began writing it at the end of June; it was in print before the end of July, and was published in September. Partly, perhaps, as a result of his intervention, but partly because the evidence was unsatisfactory, the Public Prosecutor stopped the proceedings after a preliminary investigation.

The matter, however, did not rest there. The publication of Freud's booklet brought into the foreground the strong differences of opinion on the permissibility of non-medical psychoanalysis which existed within the psychoanalytic societies themselves. It was therefore considered advisable to ventilate the question, and a long series of reasoned statements (28 in all) by analysts from various countries were published in 1927 in the two official periodicals – the *Internationale Zeitschrift*, **13** (1–3) and the *International Journal*, **8** (2–3). The series was brought to an end by Freud himself in a postscript (see below) in which he replied to the arguments of his opponents and restated his own case.

A very full account of Freud's views on the subject will be

found in Chapter IX ('Lay Analysis') of the third volume of Ernest Jones's Freud biography (1957, 309 ff.). From early times he held strongly to the opinion that psychoanalysis was not to be regarded as purely a concern of the medical profession. His first published expression on the subject seems to have been in his preface contributed in 1913 to a book by Pfister (Freud, 1913b); and in a letter (quoted by Jones, ibid., 323), written at the very end of his life in 1938, he declared that 'I have never repudiated these views and I insist on them even more intensely than before'. But it was in the work that follows that he argued the matter most closely and fully.

Apart, however, from the discussion of the question of lay analysis Freud presented in the following pages what was perhaps his most successful non-technical account of the theory and practice of psychoanalysis, written in his liveliest and lightest style. The theoretical part in particular has the advantage over his earlier expository works of having been composed after the great clarification of his views on the structure of the mind in *The Ego and the Id* (1923b), *P.F.L.*, **11**, 339 ff.

THE QUESTION
OF LAY ANALYSIS

CONVERSATIONS WITH AN IMPARTIAL PERSON

INTRODUCTION

THE title of this small work is not immediately intelligible. I will therefore explain it. 'Layman' = 'non-doctor'; and the question is whether non-doctors as well as doctors are to be allowed to practise analysis. This question has its limitations both in time and place. In *time*, because up to now no one has been concerned as to *who* practises analysis. Indeed, people have been much too little concerned about it – the one thing they were agreed on was a wish that *no one* should practise it. Various reasons were given for this, but they were based on the same underlying distaste. Thus the demand that only doctors should analyse corresponds to a new and apparently more friendly attitude to analysis – if, that is, it can escape the suspicion of being after all only a slightly modified derivative of the earlier attitude. It is conceded that in some circumstances an analytic treatment shall be undertaken; but, if so, only doctors are to undertake it. The reason for this restriction then becomes a matter for inquiry.

The question is limited in *place* because it does not arise in all countries with equal significance. In Germany and America it would be no more than an academic discussion; for in those countries every patient can have himself treated how and by whom he chooses, and anyone who chooses can, as a 'quack', handle any patients, provided only that he undertakes the responsibility for his actions.[1] The law does not intervene until it is called in to expiate some injury done to the patient. But in

1. [This is actually true only of certain of the United States. It is also true of Great Britain.]

283

Austria, in which and for which I am writing, there is a preventive law, which forbids non-doctors from undertaking the treatment of patients, without waiting for its outcome.[1] So here the question whether laymen (= non-doctors) may treat patients by psychoanalysis has a practical sense. As soon as it is raised, however, it appears to be settled by the wording of the law. Neurotics are patients, laymen are non-doctors, psychoanalysis is a procedure for curing or improving nervous disorders, and all such treatments are reserved to doctors. It follows that laymen are not permitted to practise analysis on neurotics, and are punishable if they nevertheless do so. The position being so simple, one hardly ventures to take up the question of lay analysis. All the same, there are some complications, which the law does not trouble about, but which nevertheless call for consideration. It may perhaps turn out that in this instance the patients are not like other patients, that the laymen are not really laymen, and that the doctors have not exactly the qualities which one has a right to expect of doctors and on which their claims should be based. If this can be proved, there will be justifiable grounds for demanding that the law shall not be applied without modification to the instance before us.

I

Whether this happens will depend on people who are not obliged to be familiar with all the peculiarities of an analytic treatment. It is our task to give information on the subject to these impartial persons, whom we shall assume to be, at the moment, still in ignorance. It is to be regretted that we cannot let them be present as an audience at a treatment of this kind. But the 'analytic situation' allows of the presence of no third person. Moreover the different sessions are of very unequal value. An unauthorized listener who hit upon a chance one of them would as a rule form no useful impression; he would be in danger of not understanding what was passing between the

1. The same holds good in France.

analyst and the patient, or he would be bored. For good or ill, therefore, he must be content with our information, which we shall try to make as trustworthy as possible.

A patient, then, may be suffering from fluctuations in his moods which he cannot control, or from a sense of despondency by which his energy feels paralysed because he thinks he is incapable of doing anything properly, or from a nervous embarrassment among strangers. He may perceive, without understanding the reason for it, that he has difficulties in carrying out his professional work, or indeed any comparatively important decision or any undertaking. He may one day have suffered from a distressing attack – unknown in its origin – of feelings of anxiety, and since then have been unable, without a struggle, to walk along the street alone, or to travel by train; he may perhaps have had to give up both entirely. Or, a very remarkable thing, his thoughts may go their own way and refuse to be directed by his will. They pursue problems that are quite indifferent to him, but from which he cannot get free. Quite ludicrous tasks, too, are imposed on him, such as counting up the windows on the fronts of houses. And when he has performed simple actions such as posting a letter or turning off a gas-jet, he finds himself a moment later doubting whether he has really done so. This may be no more than an annoyance and a nuisance. But his state becomes intolerable if he suddenly finds he is unable to fend off the idea that he has pushed a child under the wheels of a car or has thrown a stranger off the bridge into the water, or if he has to ask himself whether he is not the murderer whom the police are looking for in connection with a crime that was discovered that day. It is obvious nonsense, as he himself knows; he has never done any harm to anyone; but if he were really the murderer who is being looked for, his feeling – his sense of guilt – could not be stronger.

Or again our patient – and this time let us make her a woman – may suffer in another way and in a different field. She is a pianist, but her fingers are overcome by cramp and refuse to serve her. Or when she thinks of going to a party she promptly becomes aware of a call of nature the satisfaction of which would be incompatible with a social gathering. She has therefore given up going to parties, dances, theatres or concerts. She is overcome by violent headaches or other painful sensations at times when they are most inconvenient. She may even be unable to keep down any meal she eats – which can become dangerous in the long run. And, finally, it is a lamentable fact that she cannot tolerate any agitations, which after all are inevitable in life. On such occasions she falls in a faint, often accompanied by muscular spasms that recall sinister pathological states.

Other patients, again, suffer from disturbances in a particular field in which emotional life converges with demands of a bodily sort. If they are men, they find they are incapable of giving physical expression to their tenderest feelings towards the opposite sex, while towards less loved objects they may perhaps have every reaction at their command. Or their sensual feelings attach them to people whom they despise and from whom they would like to get free; or those same feelings impose requirements on them whose fulfilment they themselves find repulsive. If they are women, they feel prevented by anxiety or disgust or by unknown obstructions from meeting the demands of sexual life; or, if they have surrendered to love, they find themselves cheated of the enjoyment which nature has provided as a reward for such compliance.

All these people recognize that they are ill and go to doctors, by whom people expect nervous disorders like these to be removed. The doctors, too, lay down the categories into which these complaints are divided. They diagnose them, each according to his own standpoint, under different names: neurasthenia, psychasthenia, phobias, obsessional neurosis, hysteria. They examine the organs which produce the symptoms, the heart, the stomach, the bowels, the genitals, and find them healthy. They recommend interruptions in the patient's accustomed mode of life, holidays, strengthening exercises, tonics, and by these means bring about temporary improvements – or no result at all. Eventually the patients hear that there are people who are concerned quite specially with the treatment of such complaints and start an analysis with them.

During this disquisition on the symptoms of neurotics, the Impartial Person, whom I imagine as being present, has been showing signs of impatience. At this point, however, he becomes attentive and interested. 'So now', he says, 'we shall learn what the analyst does with the patient whom the doctor has not been able to help.'

Nothing takes place between them except that they talk to each other. The analyst makes use of no instruments – not even for examining the patient – nor does he prescribe any medicines. If it is at all possible, he even leaves the patient in his environment and in his usual mode of life during the treatment. This is not a necessary condition, of course, and may not always be practicable. The analyst agrees upon a fixed regular hour with the patient, gets him to talk, listens to him, talks to him in his turn and gets him to listen.

The Impartial Person's features now show signs of un-mistakable relief and relaxation, but they also clearly betray some contempt. It is as though he were thinking: 'Nothing more than that? Words, words, words, as Prince Hamlet says.' And no doubt he is thinking too of Mephistopheles' mocking speech on how comfortably one can get along with words [1] – lines that no German will ever forget.

'So it is a kind of magic,' he comments: 'you talk, and blow away his ailments.'

Quite true. It *would* be magic if it worked rather quicker. An essential attribute of a magician is speed – one might say suddenness – of success. But analytic treatments take months and even years: magic that is so slow loses its miraculous character. And incidentally do not let us despise the *word*. After all it is a powerful instrument; it is the means by which we convey our feelings to one another, our method of influencing other people. Words can do unspeakable good and cause terrible wounds. No doubt 'in the beginning was the deed' [2] and the

1. [In the scene with the student in *Faust*, Part I, Scene 4.]
2. ['Im Anfang war die Tat.' (Goethe, *Faust*, Part I, Scene 3.)]

word came later; in some circumstances it meant an advance in civilization when deeds were softened into words. But originally the word was magic – a magical act; and it has retained much of its ancient power.

The Impartial Person proceeds: 'Let us suppose that the patient is no better prepared to understand analytic treatment than I am; then how are you going to make him believe in the magic of the word or of the speech that is to free him from his sufferings?'

Some preparation must of course be given to him; and there is a simple way of doing it. We call on him to be completely straightforward with his analyst, to keep nothing back intentionally that comes into his head, and then to put aside *every* reservation that might prevent his reporting certain thoughts or memories. Everyone is aware that there are some things in himself that he would be very unwilling to tell other people or that he considers it altogether out of the question to tell. These are his 'intimacies'. He has a notion too – and this represents a great advance in psychological self-knowledge – that there are other things that one would not care to admit *to oneself*: things that one likes to conceal from oneself and which for that reason one breaks off short and drives out of one's thoughts if, in spite of everything, they turn up. Perhaps he may himself notice that a very remarkable psychological problem begins to appear in this situation – of a thought of his own being kept secret from his own self. It looks as though his own self were no longer the unity which he had always considered it to be, as though there were something else as well in him that could confront that self. He may become obscurely aware of a contrast between a self and a mental life in the wider sense. If now he accepts the demand made by analysis that he shall say everything, he will easily become accessible to an expectation that to have relations and exchanges of thought with someone under such unusual conditions might also lead to peculiar results.

'I understand,' says our Impartial Person. 'You assume that every neurotic has something oppressing him, some secret.

And by getting him to tell you about it you relieve his op-
pression and do him good. That, of course, is the principle of
confession, which the Catholic Church has used from time
immemorial in order to make secure its dominance over
people's minds.'

We must reply: 'Yes and no!' Confession no doubt plays a
part in analysis – as an introduction to it, we might say. But it
is very far from constituting the essence of analysis or from
explaining its effects. In confession the sinner tells what he
knows; in analysis the neurotic has to tell more. Nor have we
heard that confession has ever developed enough power to get
rid of actual pathological symptoms.

'Then, after all, I do not understand,' comes the rejoinder.
'What can you possibly mean by "telling more than he
knows"? But I can well believe that as an analyst you gain a
stronger influence over your patients than a father-confessor
over his penitents, since your contacts with him are so much
longer, more intensive and also more individual, and since you
use this increased influence to divert him from his sick
thoughts, to talk him out of his fears, and so on. It would
certainly be strange if it were possible by such means to control
purely physical phenomena as well, such as vomiting, diarr-
hoea, convulsions; but I know that influence like that is in fact
quite possible if a person is put into a state of hypnosis. By the
trouble you take with the patient you probably succeed in
bringing about a hypnotic relation of that sort with him – a
suggestive attachment to yourself – even though you may not
intend to; and in that case the miraculous results of your
treatment are the effect of hypnotic suggestion. But, so far as
I know, hypnotic treatment works much faster than your
analysis, which, as you tell me, lasts for months and years.'

Our Impartial Person cannot be either so ignorant or so
perplexed as we thought to begin with. There are unmistakable
signs that he is trying to understand psychoanalysis with the
help of his previous knowledge, that he is trying to link it up
with something he already knows. The difficult task now lies
ahead of us of making it clear to him that he will not succeed

in this: that analysis is a procedure *sui generis*, something novel and special, which can only be understood with the help of *new* insights — or hypotheses, if that sounds better. But he is still waiting for our answer to his last remarks.

What you say about the special personal influence of the analyst certainly deserves great attention. An influence of the kind exists and plays a large part in analysis — but not the same part as in hypnotism. It ought to be possible to convince you that the situations in the two cases are quite different. It may be enough to point out that we do not use this personal influence, the factor of 'suggestion', to suppress the symptoms of the illness, as happens with *hypnotic* suggestion. Further, it would be a mistake to believe that this factor is the vehicle and promoter of the treatment throughout its length. At its beginning, no doubt. But later on it opposes our analytic intentions and forces us to adopt the most far-reaching counter-measures. And I should like to show by an example how far diverting a patient's thoughts and talking him out of things are from the technique of analysis. If a patient of ours is suffering from a sense of guilt, as though he had committed a serious crime, we do not recommend him to disregard his qualms of conscience and do not emphasize his undoubted innocence; he himself has often tried to do so without success. What we do is to remind him that such a strong and persistent feeling must after all be based on something real, which it may perhaps be possible to discover.

'It would surprise me', comments the Impartial Person, 'if you were able to soothe your patients by agreeing with their sense of guilt in that way. But what *are* your analytic intentions? and what *do* you do with your patients?'

II

If I am to say anything intelligible to you, I shall no doubt have to tell you something of a psychological theory which is not known or not appreciated outside analytic circles. It will be easy to deduce from this theory what we want from our patients and how we obtain it. I shall expound it to you dogmatically, as though it were a complete theoretical structure. But do not suppose that it came into being as such a structure, like a philosophical system. We have developed it very slowly, we have wrestled over every small detail of it, we have unceasingly modified it, keeping a continuous contact with observation, till it has finally taken a shape in which it seems to suffice for our purposes. Only a few years ago I should have had to clothe this theory in other terms. Nor, of course, can I guarantee to you that the form in which it is expressed today will remain the final one. Science, as you know, is not a revelation; long after its beginnings it still lacks the attributes of definiteness, immutability and infallibility for which human thought so deeply longs. But such as it is, it is all that we can have. If you will further bear in mind that our science is very young, scarcely as old as the century, and that it is concerned with what is perhaps the most difficult material that can be the subject of human research, you will easily be able to adopt the correct attitude towards my exposition. But interrupt me whenever you feel inclined, if you cannot follow me or if you want further explanations.

'I will interrupt you before you have even begun. You say that you intend to expound a new psychology to me; but I should have thought that psychology was no new science. There have been psychologies and psychologists enough; and I heard of great achievements in that field while I was at college.'

I should not dream of disputing them. But if you look into the matter more closely you will have to class these great achievements as belonging rather to the physiology of the sense organs. The theory of mental life could not be developed, because it was inhibited by a single essential misunderstanding. What does it comprise today, as it is taught at college? Apart from those valuable discoveries in the physiology of the senses, a number of classifications and definitions of our mental processes which, thanks to linguistic usage, have become the common property of every educated person. That is clearly not enough to give a view of our mental life. Have you not noticed that every philosopher, every imaginative writer, every historian and every biographer makes up his own psychology for himself, brings forward his own particular hypotheses concerning the interconnections and aims of mental acts – all more or less plausible and all equally untrustworthy? There is an evident lack of any common foundation. And it is for that reason too that in the field of psychology there is, so to speak, no respect and no authority. In that field everyone can 'run wild' as he chooses. If you raise a question in physics or chemistry, anyone who knows he possesses no 'technical knowledge' will hold his tongue. But if you venture upon a psychological assertion, you must be prepared to meet judgements and contradictions from every quarter. In this field, apparently, there is no 'technical knowledge'. Everyone has a mental life, so everyone regards himself as a psychologist. But that strikes me as an inadequate legal title. The story is told of how someone who applied for a post as a children's nurse was asked if she knew how to look after babies. 'Of course,' she replied, 'why, after all, I was a baby once myself.'

'And you claim that you have discovered this "common foundation" of mental life, which has been overlooked by every psychologist, from observations on *sick people*?'

The source of our findings does not seem to me to deprive them of their value. Embryology, to take an example, would not deserve to be trusted if it could not give a plain explanation of the origin of innate malformations. I have told you of people whose thoughts go their own way, so that they are obliged to worry over problems to which they are perfectly indifferent. Do you think that academic psychology could ever make the smallest contribution towards explaining an abnormality such as that? And, after all, we all of us have the experience at night-time of our thoughts going their own way and creating things which we do not understand, which puzzle us, and which are suspiciously reminiscent of pathological products. Our dreams, I mean. The common people have always firmly believed that dreams have a sense and a value – that they mean something. Academic psychology has never been able to inform us what this meaning is. It could make nothing of dreams. If it attempted to produce explanations, they were non-psychological – such as tracing them to sensory stimuli, or to an unequal depth of sleep in different portions of the brain, and so on. But it is fair to say that a psychology which cannot explain dreams is also useless for an understanding of normal mental life, that it has no claim to be called a science.

'You are becoming aggressive; so you have evidently got on to a sensitive spot. I have heard, it is true, that in analysis great value is attached to dreams, that they are interpreted, and that memories of real events are looked for behind them, and so on. But I have heard as well that the interpretation of dreams is left to the caprice of analysts, and that they themselves have never ceased disputing over the way of interpreting dreams and the justification for drawing conclusions from them. If that is so, you ought not to underline so heavily the advantage that analysis has won over academic psychology.'

There is really a great deal of truth in what you say. It is true that the interpretation of dreams has come to have unequalled importance both for the theory and the practice of analysis. If I seem to be aggressive, that is only a way of defending myself. And when I think of all the mischief some analysts have done with the interpretation of dreams I might lose heart and echo the pessimistic pronouncement of our great satirist Nestroy[1] when he says that every step forward is only half as big as it looks at first. But have you ever found that men do anything but confuse and distort what they get hold of? By the help of a little foresight and self-discipline most of the dangers of dream interpretation can be avoided with certainty. But you will agree that I shall never come to my exposition if we let ourselves be led aside like this.

'Yes. If I understood rightly, you wanted to tell me about the fundamental postulate of the new psychology.'

1. [Johann Nestroy (1801–62), famous in Vienna as a writer of comedies and farces.]

That was not what I wanted to begin with. My purpose is to let you hear what pictures we have formed of the structure of the mental apparatus in the course of our analytic studies.

'What do you mean by the "mental apparatus"? and what, may I ask, is it constructed of?'

It will soon be clear what the mental apparatus is; but I must beg you not to ask what material it is constructed of. That is not a subject of psychological interest. Psychology can be as indifferent to it as, for instance, optics can be to the question of whether the walls of a telescope are made of metal or cardboard. We shall leave entirely on one side the *material* line of approach,[1] but not so the *spatial* one. For we picture the unknown apparatus which serves the activities of the mind as being really like an instrument constructed of several parts (which we speak of as 'agencies'), each of which performs a particular function and which have a fixed spatial relation to one another: it being understood that by spatial relation – 'in front of' and 'behind', 'superficial' and 'deep' – we merely mean in the first instance a representation of the regular succession of the functions. Have I made myself clear?

'Scarcely. Perhaps I shall understand it later. But, in any case, here is a strange anatomy of the soul – a thing which, after all, no longer exists at all for the scientists.'

What do you expect? It is a hypothesis like so many others in the sciences: the very earliest ones have always been rather rough. 'Open to revision' we can say in such cases. It seems to me unnecessary for me to appeal here to the 'as if' which has become so popular. The value of a 'fiction' of this kind (as the philosopher Vaihinger[2] would call it) depends on how much one can achieve with its help.

---

1. [The question of what *material* the mental apparatus is constructed of.]
2. [Hans Vaihinger (1852–1933). His philosophical system was enunciated in *Die Philosophie des Als Ob* (1911). The work had a considerable vogue in German-speaking countries, especially after the First World War. It was discussed by Freud at some length in *The Future of an Illusion* (1927c), *P.F.L.*, **12**, 210–11.]

But to proceed. Putting ourselves on the footing of everyday knowledge, we recognize in human beings a mental organization which is interpolated between their sensory stimuli and the perception of their somatic needs on the one hand and their motor acts on the other, and which mediates between them for a particular purpose. We call this organization their *'Ich'* ['ego'; literally, 'I']. Now there is nothing new in this. Each one of us makes this assumption without being a philosopher, and some people even in spite of being philosophers. But this does not, in our opinion, exhaust the description of the mental apparatus. Besides this 'I', we recognize another mental region, more extensive, more imposing and more obscure than the 'I', and this we call the *'Es'* ['id'; literally, 'it']. The relation between the two must be our immediate concern.

You will probably protest at our having chosen simple pronouns to describe our two agencies or provinces instead of giving them orotund Greek names. In psychoanalysis, however, we like to keep in contact with the popular mode of thinking and prefer to make its concepts scientifically serviceable rather than to reject them. There is no merit in this; we are obliged to take this line; for our theories must be understood by our patients, who are often very intelligent, but not always learned. The impersonal 'it' is immediately connected with certain forms of expression used by normal people. 'It shot through me,' people say; 'there was something in me at that moment that was stronger than me.' *'C'était plus fort que moi.'*

In psychology we can only describe things by the help of analogies. There is nothing peculiar in this; it is the case elsewhere as well. But we have constantly to keep changing these analogies, for none of them lasts us long enough. Accordingly, in trying to make the relation between the ego and the id clear, I must ask you to picture the ego as a kind of façade of the id, as a frontage, like an external, cortical, layer of it. We can hold on to this last analogy. We know that cortical layers owe their peculiar characteristics to the modifying influence of the external medium on which they abut. Thus we suppose that the ego is the layer of the mental apparatus (of the id) which has been modified by the influence of the external world (of reality). This will show you how in psychoanalysis we take spatial ways of looking at things seriously. For us the ego is really something superficial and the id something deeper – looked at from outside, of course. The ego lies between reality and the id, which is what is truly mental.

'I will not ask any questions yet as to how all this can be known. But tell me first what you gain from this distinction between an ego and an id? What leads you to make it?'

Your question shows me the right way to proceed. For the important and valuable thing is to know that the ego and the id differ greatly from each other in several respects. The rules governing the course of mental acts are different in the ego and the id; the ego pursues different purposes and by other methods. A great deal could be said about this; but perhaps you will be content with a fresh analogy and an example. Think of the difference between 'the front' and 'behind the lines', as things were during the war. We were not surprised then that some things were different at the front from what they were behind the lines, and that many things were permitted behind the lines which had to be forbidden at the front. The determining influence was, of course, the proximity of the enemy; in the case of mental life it is the proximity of the external world. There was a time when 'outside', 'strange' and 'hostile' were identical concepts. And now we come to the example. In the id there are no conflicts; contradictions and antitheses persist side by side in it unconcernedly, and are often adjusted by the formation of compromises. In similar circumstances the ego feels a conflict which must be decided; and the decision lies in one urge being abandoned in favour of the other. The ego is an organization characterized by a very remarkable trend towards unification, towards synthesis. This characteristic is lacking in the id; it is, as we might say, 'all to pieces'; its different urges pursue their own purposes independently and regardless of one another.

'And if such an important mental region "behind the lines"

exists, how can you explain its having been overlooked till the time of analysis?'

That brings us back to one of your earlier questions [p. 291]. Psychology had barred its own access to the region of the id by insisting on a postulate which is plausible enough but untenable: namely, that all mental acts are conscious to us – that being conscious[1] is the criterion of what is mental, and that, if there are processes in our brain which are not conscious, they do not deserve to be called mental acts and are no concern of psychology.

'But I should have thought that was obvious.'

Yes, and that is what psychologists think. Nevertheless it can easily be shown to be false – that is, to be a quite inexpedient distinction. The idlest self-observation shows that ideas may occur to us which cannot have come about without preparation. But you experience nothing of these preliminaries of your thought, though they too must certainly have been of a mental nature; all that enters your consciousness is the ready-made result. Occasionally you can make these preparatory thought structures conscious *in retrospect*, as though in a re-construction.

'Probably one's attention was distracted, so that one failed to notice the preparations.'

Evasions! You cannot in that way get around the fact that acts of a mental nature, and often very complicated ones, can take place in you, of which your consciousness learns nothing and of which you know nothing. Or are you prepared to suppose that a greater or smaller amount of your 'attention' is enough to transform a non-mental act into a mental one? But what is the use of disputing? There are hypnotic experiments in which the existence of such non-conscious thoughts are irrefutably demonstrated to anyone who cares to learn.

1. [Here written '*Bewusst-sein*': literally, 'being conscioused'. This word (the ordinary word for 'consciousness') is of course normally written without a hyphen. The hyphen is inserted here to emphasize the underlying passive sense of the word '*bewusst*'. Cf. the similar cases in 'The Unconscious' (1915*e*) *P.F.L.*, **11**, 165 *n*.1, and *The Ego and the Id* (1923*b*), ibid., **11**, 351.]

'I shall not retract; but I believe I understand you at last. What you call "ego" is consciousness; and your "id" is the so-called subconscious that people talk about so much nowadays. But why the masquerading with the new names?'

It is not masquerading. The other names are of no use. And do not try to give me literature instead of science. If someone talks of subconsciousness, I cannot tell whether he means the term topographically – to indicate something lying in the mind beneath consciousness – or qualitatively – to indicate another consciousness, a subterranean one, as it were. He is probably not clear about any of it. The only trustworthy antithesis is between conscious and unconscious. But it would be a serious mistake to think that this antithesis coincides with the distinction between ego and id. Of course it would be delightful if it were as simple as that: our theory would have a smooth passage. But things are not so simple. All that is true is that everything that happens in the id is and remains unconscious, and that processes in the ego, and they alone, *can* become conscious. But not all of them are, nor always, nor necessarily; and large portions of the ego can remain permanently unconscious.

The becoming conscious of a mental process is a complicated affair. I cannot resist telling you – once again, dogmatically – our hypotheses about it. The ego, as you will remember, is the external, peripheral layer of the id. Now, we believe that on the outermost surface of this ego there is a special agency directed immediately to the external world, a system, an organ, through the excitation of which alone the phenomenon that we call consciousness comes about. This organ can be equally well excited from outside – thus receiving (with the help of the sense-organs) the stimuli from the external world – and from inside – thus becoming aware, first, of the sensations in the id, and then also of the processes in the ego.

'This is getting worse and worse and I can understand it less and less. After all, what you invited me to was a discussion of the question whether laymen (= non-doctors) ought to undertake analytic treatments. What is the point, then, of all these disquisitions on daring and obscure theories which you cannot convince me are justified?'

I know I cannot convince you. That is beyond any possibility and for that reason beyond my purpose. When we give our pupils theoretical instruction in psychoanalysis, we can see how little impression we are making on them to begin with. They take in the theories of analysis as coolly as other abstractions with which they are nourished. A few of them may perhaps *wish* to be convinced, but there is not a trace of their being so. But we also require that everyone who wants to practise analysis on other people shall first himself submit to an analysis. It is only in the course of this 'self-analysis' (as it is misleadingly termed),[1] when they actually experience as affecting their own person − or rather, their own mind − the processes asserted by analysis, that they acquire the convictions by which they are later guided as analysts. How then could I expect to convince you, the Impartial Person, of the correctness of our theories, when I can only put before you an abbreviated and therefore unintelligible account of them, without confirming them from your own experiences?

I am acting with a different purpose. The question at issue between us is not in the least whether analysis is sensible or nonsensical, whether it is right in its hypotheses or has fallen into gross errors. I am unrolling our theories before you since that is the best way of making clear to you what the range of ideas is that analysis embraces, on the basis of what hypotheses it approaches a patient and what it does with him. In this way a quite definite light will be thrown on the question of lay analysis. And do not be alarmed. If you have followed me so far you have got over the worst. Everything that follows will be easier for you. − But now, with your leave, I will pause to take breath.

III

'I expect you will want to tell me how, on the basis of the theories of psychoanalysis, the origin of a neurotic illness can be pictured.'

1. [This is now usually described as a 'training analysis'. 'Self-analysis', in the literal sense, is mentioned on p. 78 and *n*. above.]

I will try to. But for that purpose we must study our ego and our id from a fresh angle, from the *dynamic* one – that is to say, having regard to the forces at work in them and between them. Hitherto we have been content with a *description* of the mental apparatus.

'My only fear is that it may become unintelligible again!'

I hope not. You will soon find your way about in it. Well then, we assume that the forces which drive the mental apparatus into activity are produced in the bodily organs as an expression of the major somatic needs. You will recollect the words of our poet-philosopher: 'Hunger and love [are what moves the world].'[1] Incidentally, quite a formidable pair of forces! We give these bodily needs, in so far as they represent an instigation to mental activity, the name of '*Triebe*' [instincts], a word for which we are envied by many modern languages.[2] Well, these instincts fill the id: all the energy in the id, as we may put it briefly, originates from them. Nor have the forces in the ego any other origin; they are derived from those in the id. What, then, do these instincts want? Satisfaction – that is, the establishment of situations in which the bodily needs can be extinguished. A lowering of the tension of need is felt by our organ of consciousness as pleasurable; an increase of it is soon felt as unpleasure. From these oscillations arises the series of feelings of pleasure–unpleasure, in accordance with which the whole mental apparatus regulates its activity. In this connection we speak of a 'dominance of the pleasure principle'.

If the id's instinctual demands meet with no satisfaction, intolerable conditions arise. Experience soon shows that these situations of satisfaction can only be established with the help of the external world. At that point the portion of the id which is directed towards the external world – the ego – begins to function. If all the driving force that sets the vehicle

1. [Schiller, 'Die Weltweisen'.]

2. [Various translations have been adopted for the word '*Trieb*', the most literal being 'drive'. The reasons for using 'instinct' are given in the Editor's Note to 'Instincts and their Vicissitudes' (1915c), *P.F.L.*, **11**, 107–8. Cf. also the General Preface to the *Standard Edition*, **1**, xxiv–xxvi.]

in motion is derived from the id, the ego, as it were, undertakes the steering, without which no goal can be reached. The instincts in the id press for immediate satisfaction at all costs, and in that way they achieve nothing or even bring about appreciable damage. It is the task of the ego to guard against such mishaps, to mediate between the claims of the id and the objections of the external world. It carries on its activity in two directions. On the one hand, it observes the external world with the help of its sense-organ, the system of consciousness, so as to catch the favourable moment for harmless satisfaction; and on the other hand it influences the id, bridles its 'passions', induces its instincts to postpone their satisfaction, and indeed, if the necessity is recognized, to modify its aims, or, in return for some compensation, to give them up. In so far as it tames the id's impulses in this way, it replaces the pleasure principle, which was formerly alone decisive, by what is known as the 'reality principle', which, though it pursues the same ultimate aims, takes into account the conditions imposed by the real external world. Later, the ego learns that there is yet another way of securing satisfaction besides the *adaptation* to the external world which I have described. It is also possible to intervene in the external world by *changing* it, and to establish in it intentionally the conditions which make satisfaction possible. This activity then becomes the ego's highest function; decisions as to when it is more expedient to control one's passions and bow before reality, and when it is more expedient to side with them and to take arms against the external world – such decisions make up the whole essence of worldly wisdom.

'And does the id put up with being dominated like this by the ego, in spite of being, if I understand you aright, the stronger party?'

Yes, all will be well if the ego is in possession of its whole organization and efficiency, if it has access to all parts of the id and can exercise its influence on them. For there is no natural opposition between ego and id; they belong together, and under healthy conditions cannot in practice be distinguished from each other.

'That sounds very pretty; but I cannot see how in such an ideal relation there can be the smallest room for a pathological disturbance.'

You are right. So long as the ego and its relations to the id fulfil these ideal conditions, there will be no neurotic disturbance. The point at which the illness makes its breach is an unexpected one, though no one acquainted with general pathology will be surprised to find a confirmation of the principle that it is precisely the most important developments and differentiations that carry in them the seeds of illness, of failure of function.

'You are becoming too learned. I cannot follow you.'

I must go back a little bit further. A small living organism is a truly miserable, powerless thing, is it not? compared with the immensely powerful external world, full as it is of destructive influences. A primitive organism, which has not developed any adequate ego organization, is at the mercy of all these 'traumas'. It lives by the 'blind' satisfaction of its instinctual wishes and often perishes in consequence. The differentiation of an ego is above all a step towards self-preservation. Nothing, it is true, can be learnt from being destroyed; but if one has luckily survived a trauma one takes notice of the approach of similar situations and signalizes the danger by an abbreviated repetition of the impressions one has experienced in connection with the trauma – by an *affect of anxiety*. This reaction to the perception of the danger now introduces an attempt at flight, which can have a life-saving effect till one has grown strong enough to meet the dangers of the external world in a more active fashion – even aggressively, perhaps.

'All this is very far away from what you promised to tell me.'

You have no notion how close I am to fulfilling my promise. Even in organisms which later develop an efficient ego organization, their ego is feeble and little differentiated from their id to begin with, during their first years of childhood. Imagine now what will happen if this powerless ego experiences an instinctual demand from the id which it would already like to resist (because it senses that to satisfy it is dangerous and would conjure up a traumatic situation, a collision with the external world) but which it cannot control, because it does not yet possess enough strength to do so. In such a case the ego treats the instinctual danger as if it was an external one; it makes an attempt at flight, draws back from this portion of the id and leaves it to its fate, after withholding from it all the contributions which it usually makes to instinctual impulses. The ego, as we put it, institutes a *repression* of these instinctual impulses. For the moment this has the effect of fending off the danger; but one cannot confuse the inside and the outside with impunity. One cannot run away from oneself. In repression the ego is following the pleasure principle, which it is usually in the habit of correcting; and it is bound to suffer damage in revenge. This lies in the ego's having permanently narrowed its sphere of influence. The repressed instinctual impulse is now isolated, left to itself, inaccessible, but also uninfluence-able. It goes its own way. Even later, as a rule, when the ego has grown stronger, it still cannot lift the repression; its syn-thesis is impaired, a part of the id remains forbidden ground to the ego. Nor does the isolated instinctual impulse remain idle; it understands how to make up for being denied normal satisfac-tion; it produces psychical derivatives which take its place; it links itself to other processes which by its influence it likewise tears away from the ego; and finally it breaks through into the ego and into consciousness in the form of an unrecognizably distorted substitute, and creates what we call a symptom. All at once the nature of a neurotic disorder becomes clear to us: on the one hand an ego which is inhibited in its synthesis, which has no influence on parts of the id, which must renounce some of its activities in order to avoid a fresh collision with what has been repressed, and which exhausts itself in what are for the most part vain acts of defence against the symptoms, the derivatives of the repressed impulses; and on the other hand an id in which individual instincts have made themselves independent, pursue their aims regardless of the interests of the person as a whole and henceforth obey the laws only of the primitive psychology that rules in the depths of the id. If we survey the whole situation we arrive at a simple formula for the origin of a neurosis: the ego has made an attempt to suppress certain portions of the id *in an inappropriate manner*, this attempt has failed and the id has taken its revenge. A neurosis is thus the result of a conflict between the ego and the id, upon which the ego has embarked because, as careful investigation shows, it wishes at all costs to retain its adaptability in relation to the real external world. The disagreement is between the external world and the id; and it is because the ego, loyal to its inmost nature, takes sides with the external world that it becomes involved in a conflict with its id. But please observe that what creates the determinant for the illness is not the fact of this conflict – for disagreements of this kind between reality and the id are unavoidable and it is one of the ego's standing tasks to mediate in them – but the circumstance that the ego has made use of the inefficient instrument of repression for dealing with the conflict. But this in turn is due to the fact that the ego, at the time at which it was set the task, was undeveloped and powerless. The decisive repressions all take place in early childhood.

'What a remarkable business! I shall follow your advice and not make criticisms, since you only want to show me what psychoanalysis believes about the origin of neurosis so that you can go on to say how it sets about combating it. I should have various questions to ask and later on I shall raise some of them. But at the moment I myself feel tempted for once to carry your train of thought further and to venture upon a theory of my own. You have expounded the relation between external world, ego and id, and you have laid it down as the determinant of a neurosis that the ego in its dependence on the external world struggles against the id. Is not the opposite case conceivable of the ego in a conflict of this kind allowing itself to be dragged away by the id and disavowing its regard for the external world? What happens in a case like that? From my lay notions of the nature of insanity I should say that such a decision on the part of the ego might be the determinant of insanity. After all, a turning away of that kind from reality seems to be the essence of insanity.'

Yes, I myself have thought of that possibility,[1] and indeed I

1. [Cf. Freud, 'Neurosis and Psychosis' (1924b), *P.F.L.*, **10**, 213.]

believe it meets the facts – though to prove the suspicion true would call for a discussion of some highly complicated considerations. Neuroses and psychoses are evidently intimately related, but they must nevertheless differ in some decisive respect. That might well be the side taken by the ego in a conflict of this kind. In both cases the id would retain its characteristic of blind inflexibility.

'Well, go on! What hints on the treatment of neurotic illnesses does your theory give?'

It is easy now to describe our therapeutic aim. We try to restore the ego, to free it from its restrictions, and to give it back the command over the id which it has lost owing to its early repressions. It is for this one purpose that we carry out analysis, our whole technique is directed to this aim. We have to seek out the repressions which have been set up and to urge the ego to correct them with our help and to deal with conflicts better than by an attempt at flight. Since these repressions belong to the very early years of childhood, the work of analysis leads us, too, back to that period. Our path to these situations of conflict, which have for the most part been forgotten and which we try to revive in the patient's memory, is pointed out to us by his symptoms, dreams and free associations. These must, however, first be interpreted – translated – for, under the influence of the psychology of the id, they have assumed forms of expression that are strange to our comprehension. We may assume that whatever associations, thoughts and memories the patient is unable to communicate to us without internal struggles are in some way connected with the repressed material or are its derivatives. By encouraging the patient to disregard his resistances to telling us these things, we are educating his ego to overcome its inclination towards attempts at flight and to tolerate an approach to what is repressed. In the end, if the situation of the repression can be successfully reproduced in his memory, his compliance will be brilliantly rewarded. The whole difference between his age then and now works in his favour; and the thing from which his childish ego fled in terror will often seem to his adult and strengthened ego no more than child's play.

IV

'Everything you have told me so far has been psychology. It has often sounded strange, difficult, or obscure; but it has always been – if I may put it so – "pure". I have known very little hitherto, no doubt, about your psychoanalysis; but the rumour has nevertheless reached my ears that you are principally occupied with things that have no claim to that predicate. The fact that you have not yet touched on anything of the kind makes me feel that you are deliberately keeping something back. And there is another doubt that I cannot suppress. After all, as you yourself say, neuroses are disturbances of mental life. Is it possible, then, that such important things as our ethics, our conscience, our ideals, play no part at all in these profound disturbances?'

So you feel that a consideration both of what is lowest and of what is highest has been missing from our discussions up till now? The reason for that is that we have not yet considered the *contents* of mental life at all. But allow me now for once myself to play the part of an interrupter who holds up the progress of the conversation. I have talked so much psychology to you because I wanted you to get the impression that the work of analysis is a part of applied psychology – and, moreover, of a psychology that is unknown outside analysis. An analyst must therefore first and foremost have learnt this psychology, this depth-psychology or psychology of the unconscious, or as much of it at least as is known today. We shall need this as a basis for our later conclusions. But now, what was it you meant by your allusion to 'purity'?

'Well, it is generally reported that in analyses the most intimate – and the nastiest – events in sexual life come up for discussion in every detail. If that is so – I have not been able to gather from your psychological discussions that it is necessarily so – it would be a strong argument in favour of restricting these treatments to doctors. How could one dream of allowing such dangerous liberties to people of whose discretion one was not sure and of whose character one had no guarantee?'

It is true that doctors enjoy certain privileges in the sphere of sex: they are even allowed to inspect people's genitals – though they were not allowed to in the East and though some idealistic reformers (you know whom I have in mind)[1] have disputed this privilege. But you want to know in the first place whether it is so in analysis and why it must be so. – Yes, it is so.

And it must be so, firstly, because analysis is entirely founded on complete candour. Financial circumstances, for instance, are discussed with equal detail and openness: things are said that are kept back from every fellow-citizen, even if he is not a competitor or a tax-collector. I will not dispute – indeed, I will myself insist with energy – that this obligation to candour puts a grave moral responsibility on the analyst as well. And it must be so, secondly, because factors from sexual life play an extremely important, a dominating, perhaps even a *specific* part among the causes and precipitating factors of neurotic illnesses. What else can analysis do but keep close to its subject-matter, to the material brought up by the patient? The analyst never entices his patient on to the ground of sex. He does not say to him in advance: 'We shall be dealing with the intimacies of your sexual life!' He allows him to begin what he has to say wherever he pleases, and quietly waits until the patient himself touches on sexual things. I used always to warn my pupils: 'Our opponents have told us that we shall come upon cases in which the factor of sex plays no part. Let us be careful not to introduce it into our analyses and so spoil our chance of finding such a case.' But so far none of us has had that good fortune.

I am aware, of course, that our recognition of sexuality has become – whether admittedly or not – the strongest motive for other people's hostility to analysis. Can that shake our confidence? It merely shows us how neurotic our whole civilized life is, since ostensibly normal people do not behave very differently from neurotics. At a time when psychoanalysis was solemnly put on its trial before the learned societies of Germany

1. [No doubt Tolstoy and his followers.]

– today things have grown altogether quieter – one of the speakers claimed to possess peculiar authority because, so he said, he even allowed his patients to talk: for diagnostic purposes, clearly, and to test the assertions of analysts. 'But,' he added, 'if they begin to talk about sexual matters I shut their mouths.' What do you think of that as a method of demonstration? The learned society applauded the speaker to the echo instead of feeling suitably ashamed on his account. Only the triumphant certainty afforded by the consciousness of prejudices held in common can explain this speaker's want of logical thought. Years later a few of those who had at that time been my followers gave in to the need to free human society from the yoke of sexuality which psychoanalysis was seeking to impose on it. One of them explained that what is sexual does not mean sexuality at all, but something else, something abstract and mystical. And another actually declared that sexual life is merely one of the spheres in which human beings seek to put in action their driving need for power and domination. They have met with much applause, for the moment at least.

'I shall venture, for once in a way, to take sides on that point. It strikes me as extremely bold to assert that sexuality is not a natural, primitive need of living organisms, but an expression of something else. One need only take the example of animals.'

That makes no difference. There is no mixture, however absurd, that society will not willingly swallow down if it is advertised as an antidote to the dreaded predominance of sexuality.

I confess, moreover, that the dislike that you yourself have betrayed of assigning to the factor of sexuality so great a part in the causation of neurosis – I confess that this scarcely seems to me consistent with your task as an Impartial Person. Are you not afraid that this antipathy may interfere with your passing a just judgement?

'I am sorry to hear you say that. Your reliance on me seems to be shaken. But in that case why not have chosen someone else as your Impartial Person?'

Because that someone else would not have thought any differently from you. But if he had been prepared from the first to recognize the importance of sexual life, everyone would have exclaimed: 'Why, that is no Impartial Person, he is one of your supporters?' No, I am far from abandoning the expectation of being able to influence your opinions. I must admit, however, that from my point of view this situation is different from the one we dealt with earlier. As regards our psychological discussions it is a matter of indifference to me whether you believe me or not, provided only that you get an impression that what we are concerned with are purely psychological problems. But here, as regards the question of sexuality, I should nevertheless be glad if you were accessible to the realization that your strongest motive for contradiction is precisely the ingrained hostility which you share with so many other people.

'But after all I am without the experience that has given you your unshakable certainty.'

Very well. I can now proceed with my exposition. Sexual life is not simply something spicy; it is also a serious scientific problem. There was much that was novel to be learnt about it, many strange things to be explained. I told you just now that analysis has to go back into the early years of the patient's childhood, because the decisive repressions have taken place then, while his ego was feeble. But surely in childhood there is no sexual life? Surely it only starts at puberty? On the contrary. We have to learn that sexual instinctual impulses accompany life from birth onwards, and that it is precisely in order to fend off those instincts that the infantile ego institutes repressions. A remarkable coincidence, is it not, that small children should already be struggling against the power of sexuality, just as the speaker in the learned society was to do later, and later still my followers who have set up their own theories? How does that come about? The most general explanation would be that our civilization is built up entirely at the expense of sexuality; but there is much more to be said on the subject.

The discovery of infantile sexuality is one of those of which we have reason to feel ashamed [because of its obviousness].[1] A few paediatricians have, it seems, always known about it, and a few children's nurses. Clever men, who call themselves child psychologists, have thereupon spoken in tones of reproach of a 'desecration of the innocence of childhood'. Once again, sentiment instead of argument! Events of that kind are of daily occurrence in political bodies. A member of the Opposition rises and denounces some piece of maladministration in the Civil Service, in the Army, in the Judiciary and so on. Upon this another member, preferably one of the Government, declares that such statements are an affront to the sense of honour of the body politic, of the Army, of the dynasty, or even of the nation. So they are as good as untrue. Feelings such as these can tolerate no affronts.

The sexual life of children is of course different from that of adults. The sexual function, from its beginnings to the definitive form in which it is so familiar to us, undergoes a complicated process of development. It grows together from numerous component instincts with different aims and passes through several phases of organization till at last it comes into the service of reproduction. Not all the component instincts are equally serviceable for the final outcome; they must be diverted, remodelled and in part suppressed. Such a far-reaching course of development is not always passed through without a flaw; inhibitions in development take place, partial fixations at early stages of development. If obstacles arise later on to the exercise of the sexual function, the sexual urge – the libido, as we call it – is apt to hark back to these earlier points of fixation. The study of the sexuality of children and its transformations up to maturity has also given us the key to an understanding of what are known as the sexual perversions, which people used always to describe with all the requisite indications of disgust but whose origin they were never able to explain. The whole topic is of uncommon interest, but for the

1. [Cf. a similar passage in 'The History of the Psychoanalytic Movement' (1914*d*), p. 76 above.]

purposes of our conversation there is not much sense in telling you more about it. To find one's way about in it one of course needs anatomical and physiological knowledge, all of which is unfortunately not to be acquired in medical schools. But a familiarity with the history of civilization and with mythology is equally indispensable.

'After all that, I still cannot form any picture of the sexual life of children.'

Then I will pursue the subject further; in any case it is not easy for me to get away from it. I will tell you, then, that the most remarkable thing about the sexual life of children seems to me that it passes through the whole of its very far-reaching development in the first five years of life. From then onwards until puberty there stretches what is known as the period of latency. During it sexuality normally advances no further; on the contrary, the sexual urges diminish in strength and many things are given up and forgotten which the child did and knew. During that period of life, after the early efflorescence of sexuality has withered, such attitudes of the ego as shame, disgust and morality arise, which are destined to stand up against the latest tempest of puberty and to lay down the path of the freshly awakening sexual desires. This 'diphasic onset', as it is named, of sexual life has a great deal to do with the genesis of neurotic illnesses. It seems to occur only in human beings, and it is perhaps one of the determinants of the human privilege of becoming neurotic. The prehistory of sexual life was just as much overlooked before psychoanalysis as, in another department, the background to conscious mental life. You will rightly suspect that the two are intimately connected.

There is much to be told, for which our expectations have not prepared us, about the contents, manifestations and achievements of this early period of sexuality. For instance, you will no doubt be surprised to hear how often little boys are afraid of being eaten up by their father. (And you may also be surprised at my including this fear among the phenomena of sexual life.) But I may remind you of the mythological tale which you may still recall from your schooldays of how the

311

god Kronos swallowed his children. How strange this must have sounded to you when you first heard it! But I suppose none of us thought about it at the time. Today we can also call to mind a number of fairy tales in which some ravenous animal like a wolf appears, and we shall recognize it as a disguise of the father. And this is an opportunity of assuring you that it was only through the knowledge of infantile sexuality that it became possible to understand mythology and the world of fairy tales. Here then something has been gained as a by-product of analytic studies.

You will be no less surprised to hear that male children suffer from a fear of being robbed of their sexual organ by their father, so that this fear of being castrated has a most powerful influence on the development of their character and in deciding the direction to be followed by their sexuality. And here again mythology may give you the courage to believe psychoanalysis. The same Kronos who swallowed his children also emasculated his father Uranus, and was afterwards himself emasculated in revenge by his son Zeus, who had been rescued through his mother's cunning. If you have felt inclined to suppose that all that psychoanalysis reports about the early sexuality of children is derived from the disordered imagination of the analysts, you must at least admit that their imagination has created the same product as the imaginative activities of primitive man, of which myths and fairy tales are the precipitate. The alternative friendlier, and probably also the more pertinent view would be that in the mental life of children today we can still detect the same archaic factors which were once dominant generally in the primeval days of human civilization. In his mental development the child would be repeating the history of his race in an abbreviated form, just as embryology long since recognized was the case with somatic development.

Another characteristic of early infantile sexuality is that the female sexual organ proper as yet plays no part in it: the child has not yet discovered it. Stress falls entirely on the male organ, all the child's interest is directed towards the question of whether it is present or not. We know less about the sexual life of little girls than of boys. But we need not feel ashamed of this distinction; after all, the sexual life of adult women is a 'dark continent' for psychology. But we have learnt that girls feel deeply their lack of a sexual organ that is equal in value to the male one; they regard themselves on that account as inferior, and this 'envy for the penis' is the origin of a whole number of characteristic feminine reactions.

It is also characteristic of children that their two excretory needs are cathected [charged] with sexual interest. Later on, education draws a sharp distinction here, which is once more obliterated in the practice of joking. It may seem to us an unsavoury fact, but it takes quite a long time for children to develop feelings of disgust. This is not disputed even by people who insist otherwise on the seraphic purity of the child's mind.

Nothing, however, deserves more notice than the fact that children regularly direct their sexual wishes towards their nearest relatives – in the first place, therefore, towards their father and mother, and afterwards towards their brothers and sisters. The first object of a boy's love is his mother, and of a girl's her father (except in so far as an innate bisexual disposition favours the simultaneous presence of the contrary attitude). The other parent is felt as a disturbing rival and not infrequently viewed with strong hostility. You must understand me aright. What I mean to say is not that the child wants to be treated by its favourite parent merely with the kind of affection which we adults like to regard as the essence of the parent–child relation. No, analysis leaves us in no doubt that the child's wishes extend beyond such affection to all that we understand by sensual satisfaction – so far, that is, as the child's powers of imagination allow. It is easy to see that the child never guesses the actual facts of sexual intercourse; he replaces them by other notions derived from his own experience and feelings. As a rule his wishes culminate in the intention to bear, or in some indefinable way, to procreate a baby. Boys, too, in their ignorance, do not exclude themselves from the wish to bear a baby. We give the whole of this mental structure the name of 'Oedipus complex', after the familiar Greek legend. With the end of the early sexual period it should normally be given up, should radically disintegrate and become transformed; and the results of this transformation are destined for important functions in later mental life. But as a rule this is not effected radically enough, in which case puberty brings about a revival of the complex, which may have serious consequences.

I am surprised that you are still silent. That can scarcely mean consent. – In asserting that a child's first choice of an object is, to use the technical term, an incestuous one, analysis no doubt once more hurt the most sacred feelings of humanity, and might well be prepared for a corresponding amount of disbelief, contradiction and attack. And these it has received in abundance. Nothing has damaged it more in the good opinion of its contemporaries than its hypothesis of the Oedipus complex as a structure universally bound to human destiny. The Greek myth, incidentally, must have had the same meaning; but the majority of men today, learned and unlearned alike, prefer to believe that Nature has laid down an innate abhorrence in us as a guard against the possibility of incest.

But let us first summon history to our aid. When Caius Julius Caesar landed in Egypt, he found the young Queen Cleopatra (who was soon to become so important to him) married to her still younger brother Ptolemy. In an Egyptian dynasty there was nothing peculiar in this; the Ptolemies, who were of Greek origin, had merely carried on the custom which had been practised by their predecessors, the ancient Pharaohs, for a few thousand years. This, however, was merely brother-and-sister incest, which even at the present time is not judged so harshly. So let us turn to our chief witness in matters concerning primeval times – mythology. It informs us that the myths of every people, and not only of the Greeks, are filled with examples of love-affairs between fathers and daughters and even between mothers and sons. Cosmology, no less than the genealogy of royal races, is founded upon incest. For what purpose do you suppose these legends were created? To brand gods and kings as criminals? To fasten on them the abhorrence of the human race? Rather, surely, because incestuous wishes are a primordial human heritage and have never been fully overcome, so that their fulfilment was still granted to gods and their descendants when the majority of common humans were already obliged to renounce them. It is in complete harmony with these lessons of history and mythology that we find incestuous wishes still present and operative in the childhood of the individual.

'I might take it amiss that you tried to keep back all this about infantile sexuality from me. It seems to me most interesting, particularly on account of its connection with human prehistory.'

I was afraid it might take us too far from our purpose. But perhaps after all it will be of use.

'Now tell me, though, what certainty can you offer for your analytic findings on the sexual life of children? Is your conviction based solely on points of agreement with mythology and history?'

Oh, by no means. It is based on direct observation. What happened was this. We had begun by inferring the content of sexual childhood from the analysis of adults – that is to say, some twenty to forty years later. Afterwards, we undertook analyses on children themselves, and it was no small triumph when we were thus able to confirm in them everything that we had been able to divine, in spite of the amount to which it had been overlaid and distorted in the interval.

'What? You have had small children in analysis – children of less than six years? *Can* that be done? And is it not most risky for the children?'

It can be done very well. It is hardly to be believed what goes on in a child of four or five years old. Children are very active-minded at that age; their early sexual period is also a period of intellectual flowering. I have an impression that with the onset of the latency period they become mentally inhibited as well, stupider. From that time on, too, many children lose their physical charm. And, as regards the damage done by early analysis, I may inform you that the first child on whom the experiment was ventured, nearly twenty years ago, has since then grown into a healthy and capable young man, who has passed through his puberty irreproachably, in spite of some severe psychical traumas. It may be hoped that things will turn out no worse for the other 'victims' of early analysis. Much that is of interest attaches to these child analyses; it is possible that in the future they will become still more important. From the point of view of theory, their value is beyond question. They give unambiguous information on problems which remain unsolved in the analyses of adults; and they thus protect the analyst from errors that might have momentous consequences for him. One surprises the factors that lead to the formation of a neurosis while they are actually at work and one cannot then mistake them. In the child's interest, it is true, analytic influence must be combined with educational measures. The technique has still to receive its shaping. But practical interest is aroused by the observation that a very large number of our children pass through a plainly neurotic phase in the course of their development. Since we have learnt how to look more sharply, we are tempted to say that neurosis in children is not the exception but the rule, as though it could scarcely be avoided on the path from the innate disposition of infancy to civilized society. In most cases this neurotic phase in childhood is overcome spontaneously. But may it not also regularly leave its traces in the average healthy adult? On the other hand, in those who are neurotics in later life we never fail to find links with the illness in childhood, though at the time it need not have been very noticeable. In a precisely analogous way physicians today, I believe, hold the view that each one of us has gone through an attack of tuberculosis in his childhood. It is true that in the case of the neuroses the factor of immunization does not operate, but only the factor of predisposition.

Let me return to your question about certainty. We have become quite generally convinced from the direct analytic examination of children that we were right in our interpretation of what adults told us about their childhood. In a number of cases, however, another sort of confirmation has become possible. The material of the analysis of some patients has enabled us to reconstruct certain external happenings, certain impressive events of their childhood years, of which they have preserved no conscious memory. Lucky accidents, information from parents or nurses, have afterwards provided irrefutable evidence that these occurrences which we had inferred really did take place. This, of course, has not happened often, but when it has it has made an overwhelming impression. The correct reconstruction, you must know, of such forgotten experiences of childhood always has a great therapeutic effect, whether they permit of objective confirmation or not.[1] These events owe their importance, of course, to their having occurred at such an early age, at a time when they could still produce a traumatic effect on the feeble ego.

'And what sort of events can these be, that have to be discovered by analysis?'

Various sorts. In the first place, impressions capable of permanently influencing the child's budding sexual life – such as observations of sexual activities between adults, or sexual experiences of his own with an adult or another child (no rare events); or, again, overhearing conversations, understood either at the time or retrospectively, from which the child thought it could draw conclusions about mysterious or uncanny matters; or again, remarks or actions by the child himself which give evidence of significant attitudes of affection or enmity towards other people. It is of special importance in an analysis to induce a memory of the patient's own forgotten sexual activity as a child and also of the intervention by the adults which brought it to an end.

'That gives me an opportunity of bringing up a question that I have long wanted to ask. What, then, is the nature of this "sexual activity" of children at an early age, which, as you say, was overlooked before the days of analysis?'

It is an odd thing that the regular and essential part of this sexual activity was *not* overlooked. Or rather, it is by no means odd; for it was impossible to overlook it. Children's sexual impulses find their main expressions in self-gratification by

1. [Cf. Freud's later paper on this subject (1937*d*).]

friction of their own genitals, or, more precisely, of the male portion of them. The extraordinarily wide distribution of this form of childish 'naughtiness' was always known to adults, and it was regarded as a grave sin and severely punished. But please do not ask me how people could reconcile these observations of the immoral inclinations of children – for children do it, as they themselves say, because it gives them pleasure – with the theory of their innate purity and non-sensuality. You must get our opponents to solve this riddle. *We* have a more important problem before us. What attitude should we adopt towards the sexual activity of early childhood? We know the responsibility we are incurring if we suppress it; but we do not venture to let it take its course without restriction. Among races at a low level of civilization, and among the lower strata of civilized races, the sexuality of children seems to be given free rein. This probably provides a powerful protection against the subsequent development of neuroses in the individual. But does it not at the same time involve an extraordinary loss of the aptitude for cultural achievements? There is a good deal to suggest that here we are faced by a new Scylla and Charybdis.

But whether the interests which are stimulated by the study of the sexual life of neurotics create an atmosphere favourable to the encouragement of lasciviousness – *that* is a question which I venture to leave to your own judgement.

V

'I believe I understand your purpose. You want to show me what kind of knowledge is needed in order to practise analysis, so that I may be able to judge whether only doctors should have a right to do so. Well, so far very little to do with medicine has turned up: a great deal of psychology and a little biology or sexual science. But perhaps we have not got to the end?'

Decidedly not. There are still gaps to be filled. May I make a request? Will you describe how you now picture an analytic treatment? – Just as though you had to undertake one yourself.

'A fine idea, to be sure! No, I have not the least intention of settling our controversy by an experiment of that sort. But just to oblige, I will do what you ask – the responsibility will be yours. Very well. I will suppose that the patient comes to me and complains of his troubles. I promise him recovery or improvement if he will follow my directions. I call on him to tell me with perfect candour everything that he knows and that occurs to him, and not to be deterred from that intention even if some things are disagreeable to say. Have I taken in the rule properly?'

Yes. You should add: 'even if what occurs to him seems unimportant or senseless.'

'I will add that. Thereupon he begins to talk and I listen. And what then? I infer from what he tells me the kind of impressions, experiences and wishes which he has repressed because he came across them at a time when his ego was still feeble and was afraid of them instead of dealing with them. When he has learnt this from me, he puts himself back in the old situations and with my help he manages better. The limitations to which his ego was tied then disappear, and he is cured. Is that right?'

Bravo! bravo! I see that once again people will be able to accuse me of having made an analyst of someone who is not a doctor. You have mastered it all admirably.

'I have done no more than repeat what I have heard from you – as though it was something I had learnt by heart. All the same, I cannot form any picture of how I should do it, and I am quite at a loss to understand why a job like that should take an hour a day for so many months. After all, an ordinary person has not as a rule experienced such a lot, and what was repressed in childhood is probably in every case the same.'

When one really practises analysis one learns all kinds of things besides. For instance: you would not find it at all such a simple matter to deduce from what the patient tells you the experiences he has forgotten and the instinctual impulses he has repressed. He says something to you which at first means as little to you as it does to him. You will have to make up your mind to look at the material which he delivers to you in obedience to the rule in a quite special way: as though it were ore, perhaps, from which its content of precious metal has to be extracted by a particular process. You will be prepared, too, to work over many tons of ore which may contain but little of the valuable material you are in search of. Here we should have a first reason for the prolonged character of the treatment.

'But how does one work over this raw material – to keep to your simile?'

By assuming that the patient's remarks and associations are only distortions of what you are looking for – allusions, as it were, from which you have to guess what is hidden behind them. In a word, this material, whether it consists of memories, associations or dreams, has first to be *interpreted*. You will do this, of course, with an eye to the expectations you have formed as you listened, thanks to your special knowledge.

' "Interpret!" A nasty word! I dislike the sound of it; it robs me of all certainty. If everything depends on my interpretation who can guarantee that I interpret right? So after all everything *is* left to my caprice.'

Just a moment! Things are not quite as bad as that. Why do you choose to except your own mental processes from the rule of law which you recognize in other people's? When you have attained some degree of self-discipline and have certain knowledge at your disposal, your interpretations will be independent of your personal characteristics and will hit the mark. I am not saying that the analyst's personality is a matter of indifference for this portion of his task. A kind of sharpness of hearing for what is unconscious and repressed, which is not possessed equally by everyone, has a part to play. And here, above all, we are brought to the analyst's obligation to make himself capable, by a deep-going analysis of his own, of the unprejudiced reception of the analytic material. Something, it is true, still remains over: something comparable to the 'personal equation' in astronomical observations. This individual factor will always play a larger part in psychoanalysis than elsewhere. An abnormal person can become an accurate physicist; as an analyst he will be hampered by his own abnormality from seeing the pictures of mental life undistorted. Since it is impossible to demonstrate to anyone his own abnormality, gen-

eral agreement in matters of depth-psychology will be particularly hard to reach. Some psychologists, indeed, think it is
quite impossible and that every fool has an equal right to give
out his folly as wisdom. I confess that I am more of an optimist
about this. After all, our experiences show that fairly satisfactory agreements can be reached even in psychology. Every
field of research has its particular difficulty which we must try
to eliminate. And, moreover, even in the interpretative art of
analysis there is much that can be learnt like any other material
of study: for instance, in connection with the peculiar method
of indirect representation through symbols.

'Well, I no longer have any desire to undertake an analytic
treatment even in my imagination. Who can say what other
surprises I might meet with?'

You are quite right to give up the notion. You see how
much more training and practice would be needed. When
you have found the right interpretation, another task lies ahead.
You must wait for the right moment at which you can
communicate your interpretation to the patient with some
prospect of success.

'How can one always tell the right moment?'

That is a question of tact, which can become more refined
with experience. You will be making a bad mistake if, in an
effort, perhaps, at shortening the analysis, you throw your
interpretations at the patient's head as soon as you have found
them. In that way you will draw expressions of resistance,
rejection and indignation from him; but you will not enable
his ego to master his repressed material. The formula is: to
wait till he has come so near to the repressed material that he
has only a few more steps to take under the lead of the interpretation you propose.

'I believe I should never learn to do that. And if I carry out
these precautions in making my interpretation, what next?'

It will then be your fate to make a discovery for which you
were not prepared.

'And what may that be?'

That you have been deceived in your patient; that you

cannot count in the slightest on his collaboration and compliance; that he is ready to place every possible difficulty in the way of your common work – in a word, that he has no wish whatever to be cured.

'Well! That is the craziest thing you have told me yet. And I do not believe it either. The patient who is suffering so much, who complains so movingly about his troubles, who is making so great a sacrifice for the treatment – you say he has no wish to be cured! But of course you do not mean what you say.'

Calm yourself! I *do* mean it. What I said was the truth – not the whole truth, no doubt, but a very noteworthy part of it. The patient wants to be cured – but he also wants not to be. His ego has lost its unity, and for that reason his will has no unity either. If that were not so, he would be no neurotic.

' "Were I sagacious, I should not be Tell!" ' [1]

The derivatives of what is repressed have broken into his ego and established themselves there; and the ego has as little control over trends from that source as it has over what is actually repressed, and as a rule it knows nothing about them. These patients, indeed, are of a peculiar nature and raise difficulties with which we are not accustomed to reckon. All our social institutions are framed for people with a united and normal ego, which one can classify as good or bad, which either fulfils its function or is altogether eliminated by an overpowering influence. Hence the juridical alternative: responsible or irresponsible. None of these distinctions apply to neurotics. It must be admitted that there is difficulty in adapting social demands to their psychological condition. This was experienced on a large scale during the last war. Were the neurotics who evaded service malingerers or not? They were both. If they were treated as malingerers and if their illness was made highly uncomfortable, they recovered; if after being ostensibly restored they were sent back into service, they promptly took flight once more into illness. Nothing could be done with them. And the same is true of neurotics in civil life.

1. ['Wär' ich besonnen, hiess ich nicht der Tell.' Schiller, *Wilhelm Tell*, Act III, Scene 3.]

They complain of their illness but exploit it with all their strength; and if someone tries to take it away from them they defend it like the proverbial lioness with her young. Yet there would be no sense in reproaching them for this contradiction.

'But would not the best plan be not to give these difficult people any treatment at all, but to leave them to themselves? I cannot think it is worthwhile to expend such great efforts over each of them as you lead me to suppose that you make.'

I cannot approve of your suggestion. It is undoubtedly a more proper line to accept the complications of life rather than struggle against them. It may be true that not every neurotic whom we treat is worth the expenditure of an analysis; but there are some very valuable individuals among them as well. We must set ourselves the goal of bringing it about that as few human beings as possible enter civilized life with such a defective mental equipment. And for that purpose we must collect much experience and learn to understand many things. Every analysis can be instructive and bring us a yield of new understanding quite apart from the personal value of the individual patient.

'But if a volitional impulse has been formed in the patient's ego which wishes to retain the illness, it too must have its reasons and motives and be able in some way to justify itself. But it is impossible to see why anyone should want to be ill or what he can get out of it.'

Oh, that is not so hard to understand. Think of the war neurotics, who do not have to serve, precisely because they are ill. In civil life illness can be used as a screen to gloss over incompetence in one's profession or in competition with other people; while in the family it can serve as a means for sacrificing the other members and extorting proofs of their love or for imposing one's will upon them. All of this lies fairly near the surface; we sum it up in the term 'gain from illness'.[1] It is curious, however, that the patient – that is, his ego – nevertheless knows nothing of the whole concatenation of these motives and the actions which they involve. One combats the

1. [See above, p. 113 n.]

influence of these trends by compelling the ego to take cognizance of them. But there are other motives, that lie still deeper, for holding on to being ill, which are not so easily dealt with. But these cannot be understood without a fresh journey into psychological theory.

'Please go on. A little more theory will make no odds now.'

When I described the relation between the ego and the id to you, I suppressed an important part of the theory of the mental apparatus. For we have been obliged to assume that within the ego itself a particular agency has become differentiated, which we name the super-ego. This super-ego occupies a special position between the ego and the id. It belongs to the ego and shares its high degree of psychological organization; but it has a particularly intimate connection with the id. It is in fact a precipitate of the first object-cathexes of the id and is the heir to the Oedipus complex after its demise. This super-ego can confront the ego and treat it like an object; and it often treats it very harshly. It is as important for the ego to remain on good terms with the super-ego as with the id. Estrangements between the ego and the super-ego are of great significance in mental life. You will already have guessed that the super-ego is the vehicle of the phenomenon that we call conscience. Mental health very much depends on the super-ego's being normally developed – that is, on its having become sufficiently impersonal. And that is precisely what it is not in neurotics, whose Oedipus complex has not passed through the correct process of transformation. Their super-ego still confronts their ego as a strict father confronts a child; and their morality operates in a primitive fashion in that the ego gets itself punished by the super-ego. Illness is employed as an instrument for this 'self-punishment', and neurotics have to behave as though they were governed by a sense of guilt which, in order to be satisfied, needs to be punished by illness.

'That really sounds most mysterious. The strangest thing about it is that apparently even this mighty force of the patient's conscience does not reach his consciousness.'

Yes, we are only beginning to appreciate the significance of all these important circumstances. That is why my description was bound to turn out so obscure. But now I can proceed. We describe all the forces that oppose the work of recovery as the patient's 'resistances'. The gain from illness is one such resistance. The 'unconscious sense of guilt' represents the super-ego's resistance; it is the most powerful factor, and the one most dreaded by us. We meet with still other resistances during the treatment. If the ego during the early period has set up a repression out of fear, then the fear still persists and manifests itself as a resistance if the ego approaches the repressed material. And finally, as you can imagine, there are likely to be diffi-culties if an instinctual process which has been going along a particular path for whole decades is suddenly expected to take a new path that has just been made open for it. That might be called the id's resistance. The struggle against all these resist-ances is our main work during an analytic treatment; the task of making interpretations is nothing compared to it. But as a result of this struggle and of the overcoming of the resistances, the patient's ego is so much altered and strengthened that we can look forward calmly to his future behaviour when the treatment is over. On the other hand, you can understand now why we need such long treatments. The length of the path of development and the wealth of the material are not the decisive factors. It is more a question of whether the path is clear. An army can be held up for weeks on a stretch of country which in peacetime an express train crosses in a couple of hours – if the army has to overcome the enemy's resistance there. Such battles call for time in mental life too. I am unfortunately obliged to tell you that every effort to hasten analytic treatment appreciably has hitherto failed. The best way of shortening it seems to be to carry it out according to the rules.

'If I ever felt any desire to poach on your preserves and try my hand at analysing someone else, what you tell me about the resistances would have cured me of it. But how about the special personal influence that you yourself have after all admitted? Does not that come into action against the resist-ances?'

It is a good thing you have asked me about that. This personal influence is our most powerful dynamic weapon. It is the new element which we introduce into the situation and by means of which we make it fluid. The intellectual content of our explanations cannot do it, for the patient, who shares all the prejudices of the world around him, need believe us as little as our scientific critics do. The neurotic sets to work because he has faith in the analyst, and he believes him because he acquires a special emotional attitude towards the figure of the analyst. Children, too, only believe people they are attached to. I have already told you [p. 290] what use we make of this particularly large 'suggestive' influence. Not for suppressing the symptoms – this distinguishes the analytic method from other psychotherapeutic procedures – but as a motive force to induce the patient to overcome his resistances.

'Well, and if that succeeds, does not everything then go smoothly?'

Yes, it ought to. But there turns out to be an unexpected complication. It was perhaps the greatest of the analyst's surprises to find that the emotional relation which the patient adopts towards him is of a quite peculiar nature. The very first doctor who attempted an analysis – it was not myself – came up against this phenomenon and did not know what to make of it. For this emotional relation is, to put it plainly, in the nature of falling in love. Strange, is it not? Especially when you take into account that the analyst does nothing to provoke it but on the contrary rather keeps at a distance from the patient, speaking humanly, and surrounds himself with some degree of reserve – when you learn besides that this odd love-relationship disregards anything else that is really propitious and every variation in personal attraction, age, sex or class. This love is of a positively compulsive kind. Not that that characteristic need be absent from spontaneous falling in love. As you know, the contrary is often the case. But in the analytic situation it makes its appearance with complete regularity without there being any rational explanation for it. One would have thought that the patient's relation to the analyst called for no more than a certain amount of respect, trust, gratitude and human sympathy. Instead, there is this falling in love, which itself gives the impression of being a pathological phenomenon.

'I should have thought all the same that it would be favourable for your analytic purposes. If someone is in love, he is amenable, and he will do anything in the world for the sake of the other person.'

Yes. It *is* favourable to start with. But when this falling in love has grown deeper, its whole nature comes to light, much of which is incompatible with the task of analysis. The patient's love is not satisfied with being obedient; it grows exacting, calls for affectionate and sensual satisfactions, it demands exclusiveness, it develops jealousy, and it shows more and more clearly its reverse side, its readiness to become hostile and revengeful if it cannot obtain its ends. At the same time, like all falling in love, it drives away all other mental material; it extinguishes interest in the treatment and in recovery – in short, there can be no doubt that it has taken the place of the neurosis and that our work has had the result of driving out one form of illness with another.

'That does sound hopeless! What can be done about it? The analysis would have to be given up. But if, as you say, the same thing happens in every case, it would be impossible to carry through any analyses at all.'

We will begin by using the situation in order to learn something from it. What we learn may then perhaps help us to master it. Is it not an extremely noteworthy fact that we succeed in transforming every neurosis, whatever its content, into a condition of pathological love?

Our conviction that a portion of erotic life that has been abnormally employed lies at the basis of neuroses must be unshakably strengthened by this experience. With this discovery we are once more on a firm footing and can venture to make this love itself the object of analysis. And we can make another observation. Analytic love is not manifested in every case as clearly and blatantly as I have tried to depict it. Why not? We can soon see. In proportion as the purely sensual and the hostile sides of his love try to show themselves, the patient's opposition to them is aroused. He struggles against them and tries to repress them before our very eyes. And now we understand what is happening. The patient is *repeating* in the form of falling in love with the analyst mental experiences which he has already been through once before; he has *transferred* on to the analyst mental attitudes that were lying ready in him and were intimately connected with his neurosis. He is also repeating before our eyes his old defensive actions; he would like best to repeat in his relation to the analyst *all* the history of that forgotten period of his life. So what he is showing us is the kernel of his intimate life history: *he is reproducing it tangibly, as though it were actually happening, instead of remembering it*. In this way the riddle of the transference-love is solved and the analysis can proceed on its way – with the *help* of the new situation which had seemed such a menace to it.

'That is very cunning. And is the patient so easy to convince that he is not in love but only obliged to stage a revival of an old piece?'

Everything now depends on that. And the whole skill in handling the 'transference' is devoted to bringing it about. As you see, the requirements of analytic technique reach their maximum at this point. Here the gravest mistakes can be made or the greatest successes be registered. It would be folly to attempt to evade the difficulties by suppressing or neglecting the transference; whatever else had been done in the treatment, it would not deserve the name of an analysis. To send the patient away as soon as the inconveniences of his transference neurosis make their appearance would be no more sensible, and would moreover be cowardly. It would be as though one had conjured up spirits and run away from them as soon as they appeared. Sometimes, it is true, nothing else is possible. There are cases in which one cannot master the unleashed transference and the analysis has to be broken off; but one must at least have struggled with the evil spirits to the best of one's strength. To yield to the demands of the transference, to fulfil the patient's wishes for affectionate and sensual satisfaction, is not only justly forbidden by moral considerations but is also completely ineffective as a technical method for attaining the purpose of the analysis. A neurotic cannot be cured by being enabled to reproduce uncorrected an unconscious stereotype plate that is ready to hand in him. If one engages in compromises with him by offering him partial satisfactions in exchange for his further collaboration in the analysis, one must beware of falling into the ridiculous situation of the cleric who was supposed to convert a sick insurance agent. The sick man remained unconverted but the cleric took his leave insured. The only possible way out of the transference situation is to trace it back to the patient's past, as he really experienced it or as he pictured it through the wish-fulfilling activity of his imagination. And this demands from the analyst much skill, patience, calm and self-abnegation.

'And where do you suppose the neurotic experienced the prototype of his transference-love?'

In his childhood: as a rule in his relation with one of his parents. You will remember what importance we had to attribute to these earliest emotional ties. So here the circle closes.

'Have you finished at last? I am feeling just a little bewildered with all I have heard from you. Only tell me one thing more: how and where can one learn what is necessary for practising analysis?'

There are at the moment two institutes at which instruction in psychoanalysis is given. The first has been founded in Berlin by Dr Max Eitingon, who is a member of the Society there. The second is maintained by the Vienna Psycho-Analytical Society at its own expense and at considerable sacrifice. The part played by the authorities is at present limited to the many difficulties which they put in the way of the young undertaking. A third training institute is at this moment being opened in London by the Society there, under the direction of Dr Ernest Jones. At these institutes the candidates themselves are taken into analysis, receive theoretical instruction by lectures on all the subjects that are important for them, and enjoy the supervision of older and more experienced analysts when they are allowed to make their first trials with comparatively slight cases. A period of some two years is calculated for this training. Even after this period, of course, the candidate is only a beginner and not yet a master. What is still needed must be acquired by practice and by an exchange of ideas in the psychoanalytical societies in which young and old members meet together. Preparation for analytic activity is by no means so easy and simple. The work is hard, the responsibility great. But anyone who has passed through such a course of instruction, who has been analysed himself, who has mastered what can be taught today of the psychology of the unconscious, who is at home in the science of sexual life, who has learnt the delicate technique of psychoanalysis, the art of interpretation, of fighting resistances and of handling the transference – anyone who has accomplished all this *is no longer a layman in the field of psychoanalysis*. He is capable of undertaking the treatment of neurotic disorders, and will be able in time to achieve in that field whatever can be required from this form of therapy.

VI

'You have expended a great deal of effort on showing me what psychoanalysis is and what sort of knowledge is needed in order to practise it with some prospect of success. Very well. Listening to you can have done me no harm. But I do not know what influence on my judgement you expect your explanations to have. I see before me a case which has nothing unusual about it. The neuroses are a particular kind of illness and analysis is a particular method of treating them – a specialized branch of medicine. It is the rule in other cases as well for a doctor who has chosen a special branch of medicine not to be satisfied with the education that is confirmed by his diploma: particularly if he intends to set up in a fairly large town, such as can alone offer a livelihood to specialists. Anyone who wants to be a surgeon tries to work for a few years at a surgical clinic, and similarly with oculists, laryngologists and so on – to say nothing of psychiatrists, who are perhaps never able to get away from a state institution or a sanatorium. And the same will happen in the case of psychoanalysts: anyone who decides in favour of this new specialized branch of medicine will, when his studies are completed, take on the two years' training you spoke of in a training institute, if it really requires so much time. He will realize afterwards, too, that it is to his advantage to keep up his contact with his colleagues in a psychoanalytical society, and everything will go along swimmingly. I cannot see where there is a place in this for the question of lay analysis.'

A doctor who does what you have promised on his behalf will be welcome to all of us. Four-fifths of those whom I recognize as my pupils are in any case doctors. But allow me to point out to you how the relations of doctors to analysis have really developed and how they will probably continue to develop. Doctors have no historical claim to the sole possession of analysis. On the contrary, until recently they have met it with everything possible that could damage it, from the shallowest ridicule to the gravest calumny. You will justly reply that that belongs to the past and need not affect the future. I agree, but I fear the future will be different from what you have foretold.

Permit me to give the word 'quack' the meaning it ought to have instead of the legal one. According to the law a quack is anyone who treats patients without possessing a state diploma to prove he is a doctor. I should prefer another definition: a quack is anyone who undertakes a treatment without possessing the knowledge and capacities necessary for it. Taking my stand on this definition, I venture to assert that – not only in European countries – doctors form a preponderating contingent of quacks in analysis. They very frequently practise analytic treatment without having learnt it and without understanding it.

It is no use your objecting that that is unconscientious and that you cannot believe doctors capable of it; that after all a doctor knows that a medical diploma is not a letter of marque [1] and that a patient is not an outlaw; and that one must always grant to a doctor that he is acting in good faith even if he may perhaps be in error.

The facts remain; we will hope that they can be accounted for as you think. I will try to explain to you how it becomes possible for a doctor to act in connection with psychoanalysis in a manner which he would carefully avoid in every other field.

The first consideration is that in his medical school a doctor receives a training which is more or less the opposite of what he would need as a preparation for psychoanalysis. His attention has been directed to objectively ascertainable facts of anatomy, physics and chemistry, on the correct appreciation and suitable influencing of which the success of medical treatment depends. The problem of life is brought into his field of vision so far as it has hitherto been explained to us by the play of forces which can also be observed in inanimate nature. His interest is not aroused in the mental side of vital phenomena; medicine is not concerned with the study of the higher intellectual functions, which lies in the sphere of another faculty. Only psychiatry is supposed to deal with the disturbances of mental functions; but we know in what manner and with what aims it does so. It looks for the somatic determinants of mental disorders and treats them like other causes of illness.

Psychiatry is right to do so and medical education is clearly excellent. If it is described as one-sided, one must first discover the standpoint from which one is making that characteristic into a reproach. In itself every science is one-sided. It must be so, since it restricts itself to particular subjects, points of view and methods. It is a piece of nonsense in which I would take no part to play off one science against another. After all, physics does not diminish the value of chemistry; it cannot take its place but on the other hand cannot be replaced by it. Psychoanalysis is certainly quite particularly one-sided, as being the science of

1. [I.e. does not give him a privateer's licence.]

the mental unconscious. We must not therefore dispute to the medical sciences their right to be one-sided.

We shall only find the standpoint we are in search of if we turn from scientific medicine to practical therapeutics. A sick person is a complicated organism. He may remind us that even the mental phenomena which are so hard to grasp should not be effaced from the picture of life. Neurotics, indeed, are an undesired complication, an embarrassment as much to therapeutics as to jurisprudence and to military service. But they exist and are a particular concern of medicine. Medical education, however, does nothing, literally nothing, towards their understanding and treatment. In view of the intimate connection between the things that we distinguish as physical and mental, we may look forward to a day when paths of knowledge and, let us hope, of influence will be opened up, leading from organic biology and chemistry to the field of neurotic phenomena. That day still seems a distant one, and for the present these illnesses are inaccessible to us from the direction of medicine.

It would be tolerable if medical education merely failed to give doctors any orientation in the field of the neuroses. But it does more: it gives them a false and detrimental attitude. Doctors whose interest has not been aroused in the psychical factors of life are all too ready to form a low estimate of them and to ridicule them as unscientific. For that reason they are unable to take anything really seriously which has to do with them and do not recognize the obligations which derive from them. They therefore fall into the layman's lack of respect for psychological research and make their own task easy for themselves. – No doubt neurotics have to be treated, since they are sick people and come to the doctor; and one must always be ready to experiment with something new. But why burden oneself with a tedious preparation? We shall manage all right; who can tell if what they teach in the analytic institutes is any good? – The less such doctors understand about the matter, the more venturesome they become. Only a man who really knows is modest, for he knows how insufficient his knowledge is.

The comparison which you brought up to pacify me, between specialization in analysis and in other branches of medicine, is thus not applicable. For surgery, ophthalmology, and so on, the medical school itself offers an opportunity for further education. The analytic training institutes are few in number, young in years, and without authority. The medical schools have not recognized them and take no notice of them. The young doctor, who has had to take so much on trust from his teachers that he has had little occasion for educating his judgement, will gladly seize an occasion for playing the part of a critic for once in a field in which there is as yet no recognized authority.

There are other things too that favour his appearing as an analytic quack. If he tried to undertake eye operations without sufficient preparation, the failure of his cataract extractions and iridectomies and the absence of patients would soon bring his hazardous enterprise to an end. The practice of analysis is comparatively safe for him. The public is spoilt by the average successful outcome of eye operations and expects cure from the surgeon. But if a 'nerve specialist' fails to restore his patients no one is surprised. People have not been spoilt by successes in the therapy of the neuroses; the nerve specialist has at least 'taken a lot of trouble with them'. Indeed, there is not much that can be done; nature must help, or time. With women there is first menstruation, then marriage, and later on the menopause. Finally death is a real help. Moreover, what the medical analyst has done with his neurotic patient is so inconspicuous that no reproach can attach to it. He has made use of no instruments or medicines; he has merely conversed with him and tried to talk him into or out of something. Surely that can do no harm, especially if he avoids touching on distressing or agitating subjects. The medical analyst, who has avoided any strict teaching, will, no doubt, not have omitted an attempt to improve analysis, to pull out its poison fangs and make it pleasant for the patient. And it will be wise for him to stop there; for if he really ventures to call up resistances and then does not know how to meet them, he may in true earnest make himself unpopular.

Honesty compels me to admit that the activity of an untrained analyst does less harm to his patients than that of an unskilled surgeon. The possible damage is limited to the patient having been led into useless expenditure and having his chances of recovery removed or diminished. Furthermore, the reputation of analytic therapy has been lowered. All this is most undesirable, but it bears no comparison with the dangers that threaten from the knife of a surgical quack. In my judgement, severe or permanent aggravations of a pathological condition are not to be feared even with an unskilled use of analysis. The unwelcome reactions cease after a while. Compared with the traumas of life which have provoked the illness, a little mishandling by the doctor is of no account. It is simply that the unsuitable attempt at a cure has done the patient no good.

'I have listened to your account of the medical quack in analysis without interrupting you, though I formed an impression that you are dominated by a hostility against the medical profession to the historical explanation of which you yourself have pointed the way. But I will grant you one thing: if analyses are to be carried out, it should be by people who have been thoroughly trained for it. And do you not think that with time the doctors who turn to analysis will do everything to obtain that training?'

I fear not. So long as the attitude of the medical school to the analytic training institute remains unaltered, doctors will find the temptation to make things easier for themselves too great.

'But you seem to be consistently evading any direct pronouncement on the question of lay analysis. What I guess now is that, because it is impossible to keep a check on doctors who want to analyse, you are proposing, out of revenge, as it were, to punish them by depriving them of their monopoly in analysis and by throwing open this medical activity to laymen as well.'

I cannot say whether you have guessed my motives correctly. Perhaps I shall be able later on to put evidence before you of a less partial attitude. But I lay stress on the demand that *no one should practise analysis who has not acquired the right to do so by a particular training*. Whether such a person is a doctor or not seems to me immaterial.

'Then what definite proposals have you to make?'

I have not got so far as that yet; and I cannot tell whether I shall get there at all. I should like to discuss another question with you, and first of all to touch on one special point. It is said that the authorities, at the instigation of the medical profession, want to forbid the practice of analysis by laymen altogether. Such a prohibition would also affect the non-medical members of the Psycho-Analytical Society, who have enjoyed an excellent training and have perfected themselves greatly by practice. If the prohibition were enacted, we should find ourselves in a position in which a number of people are prevented from carrying out an activity which one can safely feel convinced they can perform very well, while the same activity is opened to other people for whom there is no question of a similar guarantee. That is not precisely the sort of result to which legislation should lead. However, this special problem is neither very important nor difficult to solve. Only a handful of people are concerned, who cannot be seriously damaged. They will probably emigrate to Germany where no legislation will prevent them from finding recognition for their proficiency. If it is desired to spare them this and to mitigate the law's severity, that can easily be done on the basis of some well-known precedents. Under the Austrian monarchy it repeatedly happened that permission was given to notorious quacks, *ad personam* [personally], to carry out medical activities in certain fields, because people were convinced of their real ability. Those concerned were for the most part peasant healers, and their recommendation seems regularly to have been made by one of the archduchesses who were once so numerous; but it ought to be possible for it also to be done in the case of town-dwellers and on the basis of a different and merely expert guarantee. Such a prohibition would have more important effects on the Vienna analytic training institute, which would thenceforward be unable to accept any candidates for training from non-medical circles. Thus once again in our country a line of intellectual activity would be suppressed which is allowed to develop freely elsewhere. I am the last person to claim any competence in judging laws and regulations. But this much I can see: that to lay emphasis on our quackery law does not lead in the direction of the approach to conditions in Germany which is so much aimed at today,[1] and that the application of that law to the case of psychoanalysis has something of an anachronism about it, since at the time of its enactment there was as yet no such thing as analysis and the peculiar nature of neurotic illnesses was not yet recognized.

I come now to a question the discussion of which seems to me more important. Is the practice of psychoanalysis a matter which should in general be subject to official interference, or would it be more expedient to leave it to follow its natural development? I shall certainly not come to any decision on this point here and now, but I shall take the liberty of putting the problem before you for your consideration. In our country from of old a positive *furor prohibendi* [passion for prohibitions] has been the rule, a tendency to keep people under tutelage, to interfere and to forbid, which, as we all know, has not borne particularly good fruit. In our new republican Austria, it seems, things have not yet changed very much. I fancy you will have an important word to say in deciding the case of psychoanalysis which we are now considering; I do not know whether you have the wish or the influence with which to oppose these bureaucratic tendencies. At all events, I shall not spare you my unauthoritative thoughts on the subject. In my opinion a superabundance of regulations and prohibitions injures the authority of the law. It can be observed that where only a few prohibitions exist they are carefully observed, but where one is accompanied by prohibitions at every step, one feels definitely tempted to disregard them. Moreover, it does not mean one is quite an anarchist if one is prepared to realize that laws and

1. [This of course was in the days of the Weimar Republic.]

regulations cannot from their origin claim to possess the attribute of being sacred and untransgressable, that they are often inadequately framed and offend our sense of justice, or will do so after a time, and that, in view of the sluggishness of the authorities, there is often no other means of correcting such inexpedient laws than by boldly violating them. Furthermore, if one desires to maintain respect for laws and regulations it is advisable not to enact any where a watch cannot easily be kept on whether they are obeyed or transgressed. Much of what I have quoted above on the practice of analysis by doctors could be repeated here in regard to genuine analysis by laymen which the law is seeking to suppress. The course of an analysis is most inconspicuous, it employs neither medicines nor instruments and consists only in talking and an exchange of information; it will not be easy to prove that a layman is practising 'analysis', if he asserts that he is merely giving encouragement and explanations and trying to establish a healthy human influence on people who are in search of mental assistance. It would surely not be possible to forbid that merely because doctors sometimes do the same thing. In English-speaking countries the practices of Christian Science have become very widespread: a kind of dialectical denial of the evils in life, based on an appeal to the doctrines of the Christian religion. I do not hesitate to assert that that procedure represents a regrettable aberration of the human spirit; but who in America or England would dream of forbidding it and making it punishable? Are the authorities so certain of the right path to salvation that they venture to prevent each man from trying 'to be saved after his own fashion'?[1] And granted that many people if they are left to themselves run into danger and come to grief, would not the authorities do better carefully to mark the limits of the regions which are to be regarded as not to be trespassed upon, and for the rest, so far as possible, to allow human beings to be educated by experience and mutual influence? Psychoanalysis

1. ['*Nach seiner Façon selig zu werden.*' The saying, '*In meinem Staate kann jeder nach seiner Façon selig werden*' ('In my State every man can be saved after his own fashion'), is attributed to Frederick the Great.]

is something so new in the world, the mass of mankind is so little instructed about it, the attitude of official science to it is still so vacillating, that it seems to me over-hasty to intervene in its development with legislative regulations. Let us allow patients themselves to discover that it is damaging to them to look for mental assistance to people who have not learnt how to give it. If we explain this to them and warn them against it, we shall have spared ourselves the need to forbid it. On the main roads of Italy the pylons that carry high-tension cables bear the brief and impressive inscription: '*Chi tocca, muore* [He who touches will die].' This is perfectly calculated to regulate the behaviour of passers-by to any wires that may be hanging down. The corresponding German notices exhibit an unnecessary and offensive verbosity: '*Das Berühren der Leitungsdrähte ist, weil lebensgefährlich, strengstens verboten* [Touching the transmission cables is, since it is dangerous to life, most strictly prohibited].' Why the prohibition? Anyone who holds his life dear will make the prohibition for himself; and anyone who wants to kill himself in that way will not ask for permission.

'But there are instances that can be quoted as legal precedents against allowing lay analysis; I mean the prohibition against laymen practising hypnotism and the recently enacted prohibition against holding spiritualist séances or founding spiritualist societies.'

I cannot say that I am an admirer of these measures. The second one is a quite undisguised encroachment of police supervision to the detriment of intellectual freedom. I am beyond suspicion of having much belief in what are known as 'occult phenomena' or of feeling any desire that they should be recognized. But prohibitions like these will not stifle people's interest in that supposedly mysterious world. They may on the contrary have done much harm and have closed the door to an impartial curiosity which might have arrived at a judgement that would have set us free from these harassing possibilities. But once again this only applies to Austria. In other countries 'parapsychical' researches are not met by any legal obstacles.

The case of hypnotism is somewhat different from that of analysis. Hypnotism is the evoking of an abnormal mental state and is used by laymen today only for the purpose of public shows. If hypnotic therapy had maintained its very promising beginnings, a position would have been arrived at similar to that of analysis. And incidentally the history of hypnotism provides a precedent for that of analysis in another direction. When I was a young lecturer in neuropathology, the doctors inveighed passionately against hypnotism, declared that it was a swindle, a deception of the Devil's and a highly dangerous procedure. Today they have monopolized this same hypnotism and they make use of it unhesitatingly as a method of examination; for some nerve specialists it is still their chief therapeutic instrument.

But I have already told you that I have no intention of making proposals which are based on the decision as to whether legal control or letting things go is to be preferred in the matter of analysis. I know this is a question of principle on the reply to which the inclinations of persons in authority will probably have more influence than arguments. I have already set out what seems to me to speak in favour of a policy of *laissez faire*. If the other decision is taken – for a policy of active intervention – then it seems to me that in any case a lame and unjust measure of ruthlessly forbidding analysis by non-doctors will be an insufficient outcome. More will have to be considered in that case: the conditions will have to be laid down under which the practice of analysis shall be permitted to all those who seek to make use of it, an authority will have to be set up from whom one can learn what analysis is and what sort of preparation is needed for it, and the possibilities for instruction in analysis will have to be encouraged. We must therefore either leave things alone or establish order and clarity; we must not rush into a complicated situation with a single isolated prohibition derived mechanically from a regulation that has become inadequate.

VII

'Yes, but the doctors! the doctors! I cannot induce you to go into the real subject of our conversations. You still keep on evading me. It is a question of whether we should not give doctors the exclusive right of practising analysis – for all I care, after they have fulfilled certain conditions. The majority of doctors are certainly not quacks in analysis as you have represented them. You say yourself that the great majority of your pupils and followers are doctors. It has come to my ears that they are far from sharing your point of view on the question of lay analysis. I may no doubt assume that your pupils agree with your demands for sufficient preparation and so on; and yet these pupils think it consistent to close the practice of analysis to laymen. Is that so? and if so, how do you explain it?'

I see you are well informed. Yes, it is so. Not all, it is true, but a good proportion of my medical colleagues do not agree with me over this, and are in favour of doctors having an exclusive right to the analytic treatment of neurotics. This will show you that differences of opinion are allowed even in our camp. The side I take is well known and the contradiction on the subject of lay analysis does not interfere with our good understanding. How can I explain the attitude of these pupils of mine to you? I do not know for certain; I think it must be the power of professional feeling. The course of their development has been different from mine, they still feel uncomfortable in their isolation from their colleagues, they would like to be accepted by the 'profession' as having plenary rights, and are prepared, in exchange for that tolerance, to make a sacrifice at a point whose vital importance is not obvious to them. Perhaps it may be otherwise; to impute motives of competition to them would be not only to accuse them of base sentiments but also to attribute a strange shortsightedness to them. They are always ready to introduce other doctors into analysis, and from a material point of view it must be a matter of indifference to them whether they have to share the available patients with medical colleagues or with laymen. But something different probably plays a part. These pupils of mine may be influenced by certain factors which guarantee a doctor an undoubted advantage over a layman in analytic practice.

'Guarantee him an advantage? There we have it. So you are admitting the advantage at last? This should settle the question.'

The admission is not hard for me to make. It may show you that I am not so passionately prejudiced as you suppose. I have put off mentioning these things because their discussion will once again make theoretical considerations necessary.

'What are you thinking of now?'

First, there is the question of diagnosis. When one takes into analysis a patient suffering from what are described as nervous disorders, one wishes beforehand to be certain – so far, of course, as certainty can be attained – that he is suited for this kind of treatment, that one can help him, that is to say, by this method. That, however, is only the case if he really has a neurosis.

'I should have thought that would be recognizable from the phenomena, the symptoms, of which he complains.'

This is where a fresh complication arises. It cannot always be recognized with complete certainty. The patient may exhibit the external picture of a neurosis, and yet it may be something else – the beginning of an incurable mental disease or the preliminary of a destructive process in the brain. The distinction – the differential diagnosis – is not always easy and cannot be made immediately in every phase. The responsibility for such a decision can of course only be undertaken by a doctor. As I have said, it is not always easy for him. The illness may have an innocent appearance for a considerable time, till in the end it after all displays its evil character. Indeed, it is one of the regular fears of neurotics that they may become insane. However, if a doctor has been mistaken for a time over a case of this sort or has been in uncertainty about it, no harm has been caused and nothing unnecessary has been done. Nor indeed would the analytic treatment of this case have done any harm, though it would have been exposed as an unnecessary waste. And moreover there would certainly be enough people who would blame the analysis for the unfortunate outcome. Unjustly, no doubt, but such occasions ought to be avoided.

'But that sounds hopeless. It strikes at the roots of everything you have told me about the nature and origin of a neurosis.'

Not at all. It merely confirms once again the fact that neurotics are a nuisance and an embarrassment for all concerned – including the analysts. But perhaps I shall clear up your confusion if I state my new information in more correct terms. It would probably be more correct to say of the cases we are now dealing with that they have really developed a neurosis, but that it is not psychogenic but somatogenic – that its causes are not mental but physical. Do you understand?

'Oh, yes, I understand. But I cannot bring it into harmony with the other side, the psychological one.'

That can be managed, though, if one bears in mind the complexities of living substance. In what did we find the essence of a neurosis? In the fact that the ego, the higher organization of the mental apparatus (elevated through the influence of the external world), is not able to fulfil its function of mediating between the id and reality, that in its feebleness it draws back from some instinctual portions of the id and, to make up for this, has to put up with the consequences of its renunciation in the form of restrictions, symptoms and unsuccessful reaction formations.

A feebleness of the ego of this sort is to be found in all of us in childhood; and that is why the experiences of the earliest years of childhood are of such great importance for later life. Under the extraordinary burden of this period of childhood – we have in a few years to cover the enormous developmental distance between stone-age primitive men and the participants in contemporary civilization, and, at the same time and in particular, we have to fend off the instinctual impulses of the early sexual period – under this burden, then, our ego takes refuge in repression and lays itself open to a childhood neurosis, the precipitate of which it carries with it into maturity as a disposition to a later nervous illness. Everything now depends on how the growing organism is treated by fate. If life becomes too hard, if the gulf between instinctual claims and the demands of reality becomes too great, the ego may fail in its efforts to reconcile the two, and the more readily, the more it is inhibited by the disposition carried over by it from infancy. The process of repression is then repeated, the instincts tear themselves away from the ego's domination, find their substitutive satisfactions along the paths of regression, and the poor ego has become helplessly neurotic.

Only let us hold fast to this: the nodal point and pivot of the whole situation is the relative strength of the ego organization. We shall then find it easy to complete our aetiological survey. As what may be called the normal causes of neurotic illness we already know the feebleness of the childhood ego, the task of dealing with the early sexual impulses and the effects of the more or less chance experiences of childhood. Is it not possible, however, that yet other factors play a part, derived from the time before the beginning of the child's life? For instance, an innate strength and unruliness of the instinctual life in the id, which from the outset sets the ego tasks too hard for it? Or a special developmental feebleness of the ego due to unknown reasons? Such factors must of course acquire an aetiological importance, in some cases a transcendent one. We have invariably to reckon with the instinctual strength of the id; if it has developed to excess, the prospects of our therapy are poor. We still know too little of the causes of a developmental inhibition of the ego. These then would be the cases of neurosis with an essentially constitutional basis. Without some such constitutional, congenital favouring factors a neurosis can, no doubt, scarcely come about.

But if the relative feebleness of the ego is the decisive factor for the genesis of a neurosis, it must also be possible for a later physical illness to produce a neurosis, provided that it can bring about an enfeeblement of the ego. And that, once again, is very frequently found. A physical disorder of this kind can affect the instinctual life in the id and increase the strength of the instincts beyond the limit up to which the ego is capable of coping with them. The normal model of such processes is perhaps the alteration in women caused by the disturbances of menstruation and the menopause. Or again, a general somatic illness, indeed an organic disease of the nervous central organ, may attack the nutritional conditions of the mental apparatus and compel it to reduce its functioning and to bring to a halt its more delicate workings, one of which is the maintenance of the ego organization. In all these cases approximately the same picture of neurosis emerges; neurosis always has the same psychological mechanism, but, as we see, a most varied and often very complex aetiology.

'You please me better now. You have begun talking like a doctor at last. And now I expect you to admit that such a complicated medical affair as a neurosis can only be handled by a doctor.'

I fear you are overshooting the mark. What we have been discussing was a piece of pathology, what we are concerned with in analysis is a therapeutic procedure. I allow – no, I insist – that in every case which is under consideration for analysis the diagnosis shall be established first by a doctor. Far the greater number of neuroses which occupy us are fortunately of a psychogenic nature and give no grounds for pathological suspicions. Once the doctor has established this, he can confidently hand over the treatment to a lay analyst. In our analytical societies matters have always been arranged in that way. Thanks to the intimate contact between medical and non-medical members, mistakes such as might be feared have been as good as completely avoided. There is a further contingency, again, in which the analyst has to ask the doctor's help. In the course of an analytic treatment, symptoms – most often physical symptoms – may appear about which one is doubtful whether they should be regarded as belonging to the neurosis or whether they should be related to an independent organic illness that has intervened. The decision on this point must once again be left to a doctor.

'So that even during the course of an analysis a lay analyst cannot do without a doctor. A fresh argument against their fitness.'

No. No argument against lay analysts can be manufactured out of this possibility, for in such circumstances a medical analyst would not act differently.

'I do not understand that.'

There is a technical rule that an analyst, if dubious symptoms like this emerge during the treatment, shall not submit them to his own judgement but shall get them reported upon by a doctor who is not connected with analysis – a consultant physician perhaps – even if the analyst himself is a doctor and still well versed in his medical knowledge.

'And why should a rule be made that seems to me so uncalled for?'

It is not uncalled for; in fact, there are several reasons for it. In the first place it is not a good plan for a combination of organic and psychical treatment to be carried out by one and the same person. Secondly, the relation in the transference may make it inadvisable for the analyst to examine the patient physically. And thirdly, the analyst has every reason for doubting whether he is unprejudiced, since his interests are directed so intensely to the psychical factors.

'I now understand your attitude to lay analysis quite clearly. You are determined that there must be lay analysts. And since you cannot dispute their inadequacy for their task, you are scraping together everything you can to excuse them and make their existence easier. But I cannot in the least see why there should be lay analysts, who, after all, can only be therapists of the second class. I am ready, so far as I am concerned, to make an exception in the case of the few laymen who have already been trained as analysts; but no fresh ones should be created and the training institutes should be put under an obligation to take no more laymen into training.'

I am at one with you, if it can be shown that all the interests involved will be served by this restriction. You will agree that these interests are of three sorts: that of the patients, that of the doctors and – last not least – that of science, which indeed comprises the interests of all future patients. Shall we examine these three points together?

For the patient, then, it is a matter of indifference whether the analyst is a doctor or not, provided only that the danger of his condition being misunderstood is excluded by the necessary medical report before the treatment begins and on some possible occasions during the course of it. For him it is incomparably more important that the analyst should possess personal qualities that make him trustworthy, and that he should have acquired the knowledge and understanding as well as the experience which alone can make it possible for him to fulfil his task. It might be thought that it would damage an analyst's authority if the patient knows that he is not a doctor and cannot in some situations do without a doctor's support. We have, of course, never omitted to inform patients of their analyst's qualification, and we have been able to convince ourselves that professional prejudices find no echo in them and that they are ready to accept a cure from whatever direction it is offered them – which, incidentally, the medical profession discovered long ago to its deep mortification. Nor are the lay analysts who practise analysis today any chance collection of riff-raff, but people of academic education, doctors of philosophy, educationists, together with a few women of great experience in life and outstanding personality. The analysis, to which all the candidates in an analytic training institute have to submit, is at the same time the best means of forming an opinion of their personal aptitude for carrying out their exacting occupation.

Now as to the interest of the doctors. I cannot think that it would gain by the incorporation of psychoanalysis into medicine. The medical curriculum already lasts for five years and the final examinations extend well into a sixth year. Every few years fresh demands are made on the student, without the fulfilment of which his equipment for the future would have to be declared insufficient. Access to the medical profession is very difficult and its practice neither very satisfying nor very remunerative. If one supports what is certainly a fully justified demand that doctors should also be familiar with the mental side of illness, and if on that account one extends medical education to include some preparation for analysis, that implies a further increase in the curriculum and a corresponding prolongation of the period of study. I do not know whether the doctors will be pleased by this consequence of their claim upon analysis. But it can scarcely be escaped. And this at a period in which the conditions of material existence have so greatly deteriorated for the classes from which doctors are recruited, a period in which the younger generation sees itself compelled to make itself self-supporting as early in life as possible.

But perhaps you will choose not to burden medical studies with the preparations for analytic practice but think it more expedient for future analysts to take up their necessary training only after the end of their medical studies. You may say the loss of time involved in this is of no practical account, since after all a young man of less than thirty will never enjoy his patients' confidence, which is a *sine qua non* of giving mental assistance. It might no doubt be said in reply that a newly fledged physician for physical illnesses cannot count upon being treated by his patients with very great respect either, and that a young analyst might very well fill in his time by working in a psychoanalytic out-patient clinic under the supervision of experienced practitioners.

But what seems to me more important is that with this proposal of yours you are giving support to a waste of energy for which, in these difficult times, I can really find no economic justification. Analytic training, it is true, cuts across the field of medical education, but neither includes the other. If – which may sound fantastic today – one had to found a college of psychoanalysis, much would have to be taught in it which is also taught by the medical faculty: alongside depth-psychology, which would always remain the principal subject, there would be an introduction to biology, as much as possible of the science of sexual life, and familiarity with the symptomatology of psychiatry. On the other hand, analytic instruction would include branches of knowledge which are remote from medicine and which the doctor does not come across in his practice: the history of civilization, mythology, the psychology of religion and the science of literature. Unless he is well at home in these subjects, an analyst can make nothing of a large amount of his material. By way of compensation, the great mass of what is taught in medical schools is of no use to him for his purposes. A knowledge of the anatomy of the tarsal bones, of the constitution of the carbohydrates, of the course of the cranial nerves, a grasp of all that medicine has brought to light on bacillary exciting causes of disease and the means of combating them, on serum reactions and on neoplasms – all of this knowledge, which is undoubtedly of the highest value in itself, is nevertheless of no consequence to him; it does not concern him; it neither helps him directly to understand a neurosis and to cure it nor does it contribute to a sharpening of those intellectual capacities on which his occupation makes the greatest demands. It cannot be objected that the case is much the same when a doctor takes up some other special branch of medicine – dentistry, for instance: in that case, too, he may not need some of what he has to pass examinations in, and he will have to learn much in addition, for which his schooling has not prepared him. But the two cases cannot be put on a par. In dentistry the great principles of pathology – the theories of inflammation, suppuration, necrosis, and of the metabolism of the bodily organs – still retain their importance. But the experience of an analyst lies in another world, with other phenomena and other laws. However much philosophy may ignore the gulf between the physical and the mental, it still exists for our immediate experience and still more for our practical endeavours.

It is unjust and inexpedient to try to compel a person who wants to set someone else free from the torment of a phobia or an obsession to take the roundabout road of the medical curriculum. Nor will such an endeavour have any success, unless it results in suppressing analysis entirely. Imagine a landscape in which two paths lead to a hilltop with a view – one short and straight, the other long, winding and circuitous. You try to stop up the short path by a prohibitory notice, perhaps because it passes by some flower-beds that you want to protect. The only chance you have of your prohibition being respected is if the short path is steep and difficult while the longer one leads gently up. If, however, that is not so, and the roundabout path is on the contrary the harder, you may imagine the use of your prohibition and the fate of your flower-beds! I fear you will succeed in compelling the laymen to study medicine just as little as I shall be able to induce doctors to learn analysis. For you know human nature as well as I do.

'If you are right, that analytic treatment cannot be carried out without special training, but that the medical curriculum cannot bear the further burden of a preparation for it, and that medical knowledge is to a great extent unnecessary for an analyst, how shall we achieve the ideal physician who shall be equal to all the tasks of his calling?'

I cannot foresee the way out of these difficulties, nor is it my business to point it out. I see only two things, first that analysis is an embarrassment to you and that the best thing would be for it not to exist – though neurotics, no doubt, are an embarrassment too; and secondly, that the interests of everyone concerned would for the time being be met if the doctors could make up their minds to tolerate a class of therapists which would relieve them of the tedium of treating the enormously common psychogenic neuroses while remaining in constant touch with them to the benefit of the patients.

'Is that your last word on the subject? or have you something more to say?'

Yes indeed. I wanted to bring up a third interest – the interest of science. What I have to say about that will concern you little; but, by comparison, it is of all the more importance to me.

For we do not consider it at all desirable for psychoanalysis to be swallowed up by medicine and to find its last resting-place in a textbook of psychiatry under the heading 'Methods of Treatment', alongside of procedures such as hypnotic sugges-tion, autosuggestion and persuasion, which, born from our ignorance, have to thank the laziness and cowardice of mankind for their short-lived effects. It deserves a better fate and, it may be hoped, will meet with one. As a 'depth-psychology', a theory of the mental unconscious, it can become indispensable to all the sciences which are concerned with the evolution of human civilization and its major institutions such as art, religion and the social order. It has already, in my opinion, afforded these sciences considerable help in solving their problems. But these are only small contributions compared with what might be achieved if historians of civilization, psychologists of re-ligion, philologists and so on would agree themselves to handle the new instrument of research which is at their service. The use of analysis for the treatment of the neuroses is only one of its applications; the future will perhaps show that it is not the most important one. In any case it would be wrong to sacrifice all the other applications to this single one, just because it touches on the circle of medical interests.

For here a further prospect stretches ahead, which cannot be encroached upon with impunity. If the representatives of the various mental sciences are to study psychoanalysis so as to be able to apply its methods and angles of approach to their own material, it will not be enough for them to stop short at the findings which are laid down in analytic literature. They must learn to understand analysis in the only way that is possible – by themselves undergoing an analysis. The neurotics who need analysis would thus be joined by a second class of persons, who accept analysis from intellectual motives, but who will no doubt also welcome the increase in their capacities which they will incidentally achieve. To carry out these analyses a number of analysts will be needed, for whom any medical knowledge will have particularly little importance. But these 'teaching analysts' – let us call them – will require to have had a par-ticularly careful education. If this is not to be stunted, they must be given an opportunity of collecting experience from instructive and informative cases; and since healthy people who also lack the motive of curiosity do not present themselves for analysis, it is once more only upon neurotics that it will be possible for the teaching analysts – under careful supervision – to be educated for their subsequent non-medical activity. All this, however, requires a certain amount of freedom of movement, and is not compatible with petty restrictions.

Perhaps you do not believe in these purely theoretical interests of psychoanalysis or cannot allow them to affect the practical question of lay analysis. Then let me advise you that psychoanalysis has yet another sphere of application, which is outside the scope of the quackery law and to which the doctors will scarcely lay claim. Its application, I mean, to the bringing-up of children. If a child begins to show signs of an undesirable development, if it grows moody, refractory and inattentive, the paediatrician and even the school doctor can do nothing for it, even if the child produces clear neurotic symptoms, such as nervousness, loss of appetite, vomiting or insomnia. A treatment that combines analytic influence with educational measures, carried out by people who are not ashamed to concern themselves with the affairs in a child's world, and who understand how to find their way into a child's mental life, can bring about two things at once: the removal of the neurotic symptoms and the reversal of the change in character which had begun. Our recognition of the importance of these inconspicuous neuroses of children as laying down the disposition for serious illnesses in later life points to these child analyses as an excellent method of prophylaxis. Analysis undeniably still has its enemies. I do not know whether they have means at their command for stopping the activities of these educational analysts or analytic educationalists. I do not think it very likely; but one can never feel too secure.

Moreover, to return to our question of the analytic treatment of adult neurotics, even there we have not yet exhausted every line of approach. Our civilization imposes an almost intolerable pressure on us and it calls for a corrective. Is it too fantastic to expect that psychoanalysis in spite of its difficulties may be destined to the task of preparing mankind for such a corrective? Perhaps once more an American may hit on the idea of spending a little money to get the 'social workers' of his country trained analytically and to turn them into a band of helpers for combating the neuroses of civilization.

'Aha! a new kind of Salvation Army!'

Why not? Our imagination always follows patterns. The stream of eager learners who will then flow to Europe will be obliged to pass Vienna by, for here the development of analysis may have succumbed to a premature trauma of prohibition. You smile? I am not saying this as a bribe for your support. Not in the least. I know you do not believe me; nor can I guarantee that it will happen. But one thing I do know. It is by no means so important what decision you give on the question of lay analysis. It may have a local effect. But the things that really matter – the possibilities in psychoanalysis for *internal* development – can never be affected by regulations and prohibitions.

POSTSCRIPT
(1927)

THE immediate occasion of my writing the small volume which was the starting-point of the present discussion was a charge of quackery brought against a non-medical member of our Society, Dr Theodor Reik, in the Vienna courts. It is generally known, I think, that after all the preliminary proceedings had been completed and a number of expert opinions had been received, the charge was dropped. I do not believe that this was a result of my book. No doubt the prosecution's case was too weak, and the person who brought the charge as an aggrieved party proved an untrustworthy witness. So that the quashing of the proceedings against Dr Reik is probably not to be regarded as a considered judgement of the Vienna courts on the general question of lay analysis. When I drew the figure of the 'Impartial Person' who was my interlocutor in my tract, I had before my mind one of our high officials. This was a man with a friendly attitude and a mind of unusual integrity, to whom I had myself talked about Reik's case and for whom I had, at his request, written a confidential opinion on the subject. I knew I had not succeeded in converting him to my views, and that was why I made my dialogue with the Impartial Person end without agreement too.

Nor did I expect that I should succeed in bringing about unanimity in the attitude of analysts themselves towards the problem of lay analysis. Anyone who compares the views expressed by the Hungarian Society in this discussion with those of the New York group will perhaps conclude that my book has produced no effect whatever and that everyone persists in his former opinion. But I do not believe this either. I think that many of my colleagues have modified their extreme *parti pris* and that the majority have accepted my view that the problem of lay analysis ought not to be decided along the lines of traditional usage but that it arises from a novel situation and therefore demands a fresh judgement.

Again, the turn which I gave to the whole discussion seems to have met with approval. My main thesis was that the important question is not whether an analyst possesses a medical diploma but whether he has had the special training necessary for the practice of analysis. This served as the starting-point for a discussion, which was eagerly embarked upon, as to what is the training most suitable for an analyst. My own view was and still remains that it is not the training prescribed by the university for future doctors. What is known as medical education appears to me to be an arduous and circuitous way of approaching the profession of analysis. No doubt it offers an analyst much that is indispensable to him. But it burdens him with too much else of which he can never make use, and there is a danger of its diverting his interest and his whole mode of thought from the understanding of psychical phenomena. A scheme of training for analysts has still to be created. It must include elements from the mental sciences, from psychology, the history of civilization and sociology, as well as from anatomy, biology and the study of evolution. There is so much to be taught in all this that it is justifiable to omit from the curriculum anything which has no direct bearing on the practice of analysis and only serves indirectly (like any other study) as a training for the intellect and for the powers of observation. It is easy to meet this suggestion by objecting that analytic colleges of this kind do not exist and that I am merely setting up an ideal. An ideal, no doubt. But an ideal which can and must be realized. And in our training institutes, in spite of all their youthful insufficiencies, that realization has already begun.

It will not have escaped my readers that in what I have said I have assumed as axiomatic something that is still violently disputed in the discussion. I have assumed, that is to say, that psychoanalysis is not a specialized branch of medicine. I cannot see how it is possible to dispute this. Psychoanalysis is a part of psychology; not of medical psychology in the old sense, nor of the psychology of morbid processes, but simply of psychology. It is certainly not the whole of psychology, but its substructure and perhaps even its entire foundation. The possibility of its application to medical purposes must not lead us astray. Electricity and radiology also have their medical application, but the science to which they both belong is none the less physics. Nor can their situation be affected by historical arguments. The whole theory of electricity had its origin in an observation of a nerve-muscle preparation; yet no one would dream today of regarding it as a part of physiology. It is argued that psychoanalysis was after all discovered by a physician in the course of his efforts to assist his patients. But that is clearly neither here nor there. Moreover, the historical argument is double-edged. We might pursue the story and recall the unfriendliness and indeed the animosity with which the medical profession treated analysis from the very first. That would seem to imply that it can have no claims over analysis today. And though I do not accept that implication, I still feel some doubts as to whether the present wooing of psychoanalysis by the doctors is based, from the point of view of the libido theory, upon the first or upon the second of Abraham's sub-stages [1] – whether they wish to take possession of their object for the purpose of destroying or of preserving it.

I should like to consider the historical argument a moment longer. Since it is with me personally that we are concerned, I can throw a little light, for anyone who may be interested, on my own motives. After forty-one years of medical activity, my self-knowledge tells me that I have never really been a doctor in the proper sense. I became a doctor through being compelled to deviate from my original purpose; and the triumph of my life lies in my having, after a long and roundabout journey, found my way back to my earliest path. I have no knowledge of having had any craving in my early childhood to help suffering humanity. My innate sadistic disposition was not a very strong one, so that I had no need to develop this one

1. [Cf. Abraham (1924). See also Lecture 32 in the *New Introductory Lectures* (1933a), *P.F.L.*, **2**, 132.]

of its derivatives. Nor did I ever play the 'doctor game'; my infantile curiosity evidently chose other paths. In my youth I felt an overpowering need to understand something of the riddles of the world in which we live and perhaps even to contribute something to their solution. The most helpful means of achieving this end seemed to be to enrol myself in the medical faculty; but even after that I experimented – unsuccessfully – with zoology and chemistry, till at last, under the influence of Brücke, who carried more weight with me than anyone else in my whole life, I settled down to physiology, though in those days it was too narrowly restricted to histology. By that time I had already passed all my medical examinations; but I took no interest in anything to do with medicine till the teacher whom I so deeply respected warned me that in view of my impoverished material circumstances I could not possibly take up a theoretical career. Thus I passed from the histology of the nervous system to neuropathology and then, prompted by fresh influences, I began to be concerned with the neuroses. I scarcely think, however, that my lack of a genuine medical temperament has done much damage to my patients. For it is not greatly to the advantage of patients if their doctor's therapeutic interest has too marked an emotional emphasis. They are best helped if he carries out his task coolly and keeping as closely as possible to the rules.

No doubt what I have just said throws little light on the problem of lay analysis; it was only intended to exhibit my personal credentials as being myself a supporter of the inherent value of psychoanalysis and of its independence of its application to medicine. But it will be objected at this point that whether psychoanalysis, regarded as a science, is a subdivision of medicine or of psychology is a purely academic question and of no practical interest. The real point at issue, it will be said, is a different one, namely the application of analysis to the treatment of patients; in so far as it claims to do this it must be content, the argument will run, to be accepted as a specialized branch of medicine, like radiology, for instance, and to submit to the rules laid down for all therapeutic methods. I recognize that that is so; I admit it. I only want to feel assured that the therapy will not destroy the science. Unluckily analogies never carry one more than a certain distance; a point is soon reached at which the subjects of the comparison take divergent paths. The case of analysis differs from that of radiology. A physicist does not require to have a patient in order to study the laws that govern X-rays. But the only subject-matter of psycho-analysis is the mental processes of human beings and it is only in human beings that it can be studied. For reasons which can easily be understood, neurotic human beings offer far more instructive and accessible material than normal ones, and to withhold that material from anyone who wishes to study and apply analysis is to dock him of a good half of his training possibilities. I have, of course, no intention of asking that the interests of neurotic patients should be sacrificed to those of instruction and scientific research. The aim of my small volume on the question of lay analysis was precisely to show that, if certain precautions are observed, the two interests can quite easily be brought into harmony and that the interests of medicine, as rightly understood, will not be the last to profit by such a solution.

I myself brought forward all the necessary precautions and I can safely say that the discussion added nothing on this point. But I should like to remark that the emphasis was often placed in a manner which did not do justice to the facts. What was said about the difficulties of differential diagnosis and the uncer-tainty in many cases in deciding about somatic symptoms – situations, that is, in which medical knowledge and medical intervention are necessary – this is all of it perfectly true. Nevertheless, the number of cases in which doubts of this kind never arise at all and in which a doctor is *not* required is surely incomparably greater. These cases may be quite uninteresting scientifically, but they play an important enough part in life to justify the activity of lay analysts, who are perfectly competent to deal with them. Some time ago I analysed a colleague who gave evidence of a particularly strong dislike of the idea of anyone being allowed to engage in a medical activity who was not himself a medical man. I was in a position to say to him: 'We have now been working for more than three months. At what point in our analysis have I had occasion to make use of my medical knowledge?' He admitted that I had had no such occasion.

Again, I attach no great importance to the argument that a lay analyst, because he must be prepared to consult a doctor, will have no authority in the eyes of his patients and will be treated with no more respect than such people as bone-setters or masseurs. Once again, the analogy is an imperfect one – quite apart from the fact that what governs patients in their recognition of authority is usually their emotional transference and that the possession of a medical diploma does not impress them nearly so much as doctors believe. A professional lay analyst will have no difficulty in winning as much respect as is due to a secular pastoral worker.[1] Indeed, the words, 'secular pastoral worker', might well serve as a general formula for describing the function which the analyst, whether he is a doctor or a layman, has to perform in his relation to the public. Our friends among the Protestant clergy, and more recently among the Catholic clergy as well, are often able to relieve their parishioners of the inhibitions of their daily life by confirming their faith – after having first offered them a little analytic information about the nature of their conflicts. Our opponents, the Adlerian 'individual psychologists',[2] endeavour to produce a similar result in people who have become unstable and inefficient by arousing their interest in the social community – after having first thrown some light upon a single corner of their mental life and shown them the part played in their illness by their egoistic and distrustful impulses. Both of these procedures, which derive their power from being based on analysis, have their place in psychotherapy. We who are analysts set before us as our aim the most complete and pro-

1. ['Seelsorger.' Freud had already referred to the work performed in this capacity in Protestant countries in his preface to a book of Pfister's (1913b).]
2. [See pp. 60, 112 and 114 above.]

foundest possible analysis of whoever may be our patient. We do not seek to bring him relief by receiving him into the Catholic, Protestant or socialist community. We seek rather to enrich him from his own internal sources, by putting at the disposal of his ego those energies which, owing to repression, are inaccessibly confined in his unconscious, as well as those which his ego is obliged to squander in the fruitless task of maintaining these repressions. Such activity as this is pastoral work in the best sense of the words. Have we set ourselves too high an aim? Are the majority of our patients worth the pains that this work requires of us? Would it not be more economical to prop up their weaknesses from without rather than to re-build them from within? I cannot say; but there is something else that I *do* know. In psychoanalysis there has existed from the very first an inseparable bond between cure and research. Knowledge brought therapeutic success. It was impossible to treat a patient without learning something new; it was im-possible to gain fresh insight without perceiving its beneficent results. Our analytic procedure is the only one in which this precious conjunction is assured. It is only by carrying on our analytic pastoral work that we can deepen our dawning comprehension of the human mind. This prospect of scientific gain has been the proudest and happiest feature of analytic work. Are we to sacrifice it for the sake of any considerations of a practical sort?

Some remarks that have been made in the course of this discussion have led me to suspect that, in spite of everything, my book on lay analysis has been misunderstood in one respect. The doctors have been defended against me, as though I had declared that they were in general incompetent to practise analysis and as though I had given it out as a password that medical reinforcements were to be rejected. That was not my intention. The idea probably arose from my having been led to declare in the course of my observations (which had a con-troversial end in view) that untrained medical analysts were even more dangerous than laymen. I might make my true opinion on this question clear by echoing a cynical remark about women that once appeared in *Simplicissimus*.[1] One man was complaining to another about the weaknesses and troublesome nature of the fair sex. 'All the same,' replied his companion, 'women are the best thing we have of the kind.' I am bound to admit that, so long as schools such as we desire for the training of analysts are not yet in existence, people who have had a preliminary education in medicine are the best material for future analysts. We have a right to demand, however, that they should not mistake their preliminary education for a complete training, that they should overcome the one-sidedness that is fostered by instruction in medical schools and that they should resist the temptation to flirt with endocrinology and the autonomic nervous system, when what is needed is an apprehension of psychological facts with the help of a framework of psychological concepts. I also share the view that all those problems which relate to the connection between psychical phenomena and their organic, anatomical and chemical foundations can be approached only by those who have studied both, that is, by medical analysts. It should not be forgotten, however, that this is not the whole of psychoanalysis, and that for its other aspect we can never do without the co-operation of people who have had a preliminary education in the *mental* sciences. For practical reasons we have been in the habit – and this is true, incidentally, of our publications as well – of distinguishing between medical and applied analysis. But that is not a logical distinction. The true line of division is between *scientific* analysis and its *applications* alike in medical and non-medical fields.

In these discussions the bluntest rejection of lay analysis has been expressed by our American colleagues. A few words to them in reply will, I think, not be out of place. I can scarcely be accused of making a misuse of analysis for controversial purposes if I express an opinion that their resistance is derived wholly from practical factors. They see how in their own country lay analysts put analysis to all kinds of mischievous and illegitimate purposes and in consequence cause injury both

1. [The satirical Munich periodical.]

to their patients and to the good name of analysis. It is therefore not to be wondered at if in their indignation they give the widest possible berth to such unscrupulous mischief-makers and try to prevent any laymen from having a share in analysis. But these facts are already enough to diminish the significance of the American position; for the question of lay analysis must not be decided on practical considerations alone, and local conditions in America cannot be the sole determining influence on our views.

The resolution passed by our American colleagues against lay analysts, based as it essentially is upon practical reasons, appears to me nevertheless to be unpractical; for it cannot affect any of the factors which govern the situation. It is more or less equivalent to an attempt at repression. If it is impossible to prevent the lay analysts from pursuing their activities and if the public does not support the campaign against them, would it not be more expedient to recognize the fact of their existence by offering them opportunities for training? Might it not be possible in this way to gain some influence over them? And, if they were offered as an inducement the possibility of receiving the approval of the medical profession and of being invited to co-operate, might they not have some interest in raising their own ethical and intellectual level?

VIENNA, *June* 1927

DR REIK AND THE PROBLEM OF QUACKERY
(1926)

DR REIK AND THE PROBLEM
OF QUACKERY [1]

A LETTER TO THE *NEUE FREIE PRESSE*
(1926)

Dear Sir,

In an article in your issue of July 15 dealing with the case of my pupil, Dr Theodor Reik, or, more precisely, in a section of it headed 'Information from Psychoanalytic Circles', there is a passage on which I should like to make a few remarks by way of correction.

The passage runs: '... during the last few years he has become convinced that Dr Reik, who has gained a wide reputation from his philosophical and psychological writings, possesses a far greater gift for psychoanalysis than the physicians attached to the Freudian school; and he has entrusted the most difficult cases only to him and to his daughter Anna, who has proved quite specially adept in the difficult technique of psychoanalysis.'

Dr Reik himself would, I think, be the first to reject any such account of the basis of our relations. It is true, however, that I have availed myself of his skill in particularly difficult cases, but this has only been where the symptoms lay in a sphere far removed from the physical one. And I have never

---

1. ['Dr Reik und die Kurpfuschereifrage.' This letter was published in the *Neue Freie Presse* of Sunday, 18 July 1926, p. 12. A translation appeared in the *Bulletin of the American Psychoanalytic Association*, **4** (1948), 56, and a further translation by James Strachey was published in the *Standard Edition*, **21** (1961), 247–8. The present edition is a reprint of the *Standard Edition* version. An account of the circumstances which led Freud to write the letter is given in the Editor's Note on p. 280 above.]

failed to inform a patient that he is not a physician but a psychologist.

My daughter Anna has devoted herself to the pedagogic analysis of children and adolescents. I have never yet referred to her a case of severe neurotic illness in an adult. Incidentally, the only case with moderately severe symptoms verging on the psychiatric which she has hitherto treated repaid the physician who referred it to her by its complete success.

I take the opportunity of informing you that I have just sent to press a small work on *The Question of Lay Analysis* [1926*e*; p. 277 ff. above]. In it I have tried to show what a psycho-analysis is and what demands it makes on the analyst. I have considered the far from simple relations between psycho-analysis and medicine, and have drawn the conclusion that any mechanical application to trained analysts of the section against quackery [in the criminal code] is open to grave doubts.

Since I have given up my Vienna practice and have cut down my activity to the treatment of a very few foreigners, I trust that this announcement will not involve me too in a prosecution for unprofessional advertisement.

Yours &c.,
Professor Freud

AN OUTLINE
OF PSYCHOANALYSIS
(1940 [1938])

EDITOR'S NOTE

ABRISS DER PSYCHOANALYSE

(A) GERMAN EDITIONS:

1940   *Internationale Zeitschrift für Psychoanalyse und Imago*, **25** (1), 7–67.

1941   *Gesammelte Werke*, **17**, 63–138.

(B) ENGLISH TRANSLATION:
An Outline of Psychoanalysis

1940   *International Journal of Psycho-Analysis*, **21** (1), 27–82. (Tr. James Strachey.)

1949   London: Hogarth Press and Institute of Psycho-Analysis; New York: Norton.
      (Revised reprint of above in book form)

1964   *Standard Edition*, **23**, 139–207. (Considerably revised version of the 1949 translation.)

The present edition is a reprint of the *Standard Edition* version, with some editorial modifications.

When this work was first published, both in German and English, it was accompanied by two long extracts from Freud's contemporary fragment 'Some Elementary Lessons in Psycho-Analysis (1940*b*). These extracts appeared as a footnote in Chapter IV of the German version and as an appendix in the English one. The fragment from which the extracts were drawn was published in full soon afterwards, and the footnote and appendix were consequently omitted in the subsequent reprints.

The manuscript of this whole work is written out in an

unusually abbreviated form. In particular, the third chapter ('The Development of the Sexual Function') is for the most part greatly abbreviated, with the omission, for instance, of definite and indefinite articles and of many principal verbs – in what may be described as a telegraphic style. The German editors have, as they tell us, expanded these abbreviations. The general sense is not in doubt and, although the editing is at certain points a little free, it has seemed simplest to accept it and to translate the version supplied in the *Gesammelte Werke*.

It is not certain when Freud began writing the *Outline*. According to Ernest Jones (1957, 255) 'he began it during the waiting time in Vienna' – which would mean April or May 1938. The manuscript, however, bears on its opening page the date '22 July', which confirms the statement of the German editors that the work was begun in July 1938 – that is to say, soon after Freud's arrival in London at the beginning of June. By early September he had written sixty-three sheets of the *Outline*, when his work on it was interrupted by his having to undergo a very serious operation, and he did not return to it again, though he began shortly afterwards on another expository work, 'Some Elementary Lessons in Psycho-Analysis' (1940b), but very soon broke this off as well.

Thus the *Outline* must be described as unfinished, but it is difficult to regard it as incomplete. The last chapter, it is true, is shorter than the rest and might well have gone on to a discussion of such things as the sense of guilt, though this had already been touched on in Chapter VI. In general, however, the question of how far and in what direction Freud would have proceeded with the book is an intriguing one, for the programme laid down by the author in his preface seems already to be reasonably well carried out.

In the long succession of Freud's expository works the *Outline* exhibits a unique character. The others are without exception aimed at explaining psychoanalysis to an outside public, a public with very varying degrees and types of general approach to Freud's subject, but always a relatively ignorant public. This cannot be said of the *Outline*. It should clearly be understood that this is not a book for beginners; it is something much more like a 'refresher course' for advanced students. The reader is everywhere expected to be familiar not only with Freud's general approach to psychology but with his findings and theories on quite detailed points. For instance, a couple of very short allusions to the part played by the memory-traces of verbal sense impressions (pp. 394 and 435) would scarcely be intelligible to anyone unacquainted with a number of difficult arguments in the last chapter of *The Interpretation of Dreams* (1900*a*), *P.F.L.*, **4**, 652 ff., and in the final section of the metapsychological paper on 'The Unconscious' (1915*e*), ibid., **11**, 206–10. And again, the very scanty remarks on identification and its relation to abandoned love-objects (pp. 428 and 441) imply a knowledge at least of Chapter III of *The Ego and the Id* (1923*b*), ibid., **11**, 367–79. But those who are already at home in Freud's writings will find this a most fascinating epilogue. New light is thrown on whatever he touches – the most fundamental theories or the most detailed clinical observations – and everything is discussed in the vocabulary of his very latest terminology. There are even occasional hints at entirely new developments, particularly in the later part of Chapter VIII, where the question of the splitting of the ego and its disavowal of portions of the external world as exemplified in the case of fetishism receives an enlarged consideration. All of this shows that at the age of 82 Freud still possessed an astonishing gift for making a fresh approach to what might have seemed well-worn topics. Nowhere else, perhaps, does his style reach a higher level of succinctness and lucidity. The whole work gives us a sense of freedom in its presentation which is perhaps to be expected in a master's last account of the ideas of which he was the creator.

AN OUTLINE
OF PSYCHOANALYSIS

[PREFACE]

THE aim of this brief work is to bring together the tenets of psychoanalysis and to state them, as it were, dogmatically – in the most concise form and in the most unequivocal terms. Its intention is naturally not to compel belief or to arouse conviction.

The teachings of psychoanalysis are based on an incalculable number of observations and experiences, and only someone who has repeated those observations on himself and on others is in a position to arrive at a judgement of his own upon it.

PART I
[THE MIND AND ITS WORKINGS][1]

CHAPTER I
THE PSYCHICAL APPARATUS

Psychoanalysis makes a basic assumption, the discussion of which is reserved to philosophical thought but the justification for which lies in its results. We know two kinds of things about what we call our psyche (or mental life): firstly,

1. [Title added by the translator.]

375

its bodily organ and scene of action, the brain (or nervous system) and, on the other hand, our acts of consciousness, which are immediate data and cannot be further explained by any sort of description. Everything that lies between is unknown to us, and the data do not include any direct relation between these two terminal points of our knowledge. If it existed, it would at the most afford an exact localization of the processes of consciousness and would give us no help towards understanding them.

Our two hypotheses start out from these ends or beginnings of our knowledge. The first is concerned with localization. We assume that mental life is the function of an apparatus to which we ascribe the characteristics of being extended in space and of being made up of several portions – which we imagine, that is, as resembling a telescope or microscope or something of the kind. Notwithstanding some earlier attempts in the same direction, the consistent working-out of a conception such as this is a scientific novelty.

We have arrived at our knowledge of this psychical apparatus by studying the individual development of human beings. To the oldest of these psychical provinces or agencies we give the name of *id*. It contains everything that is inherited, that is present at birth, that is laid down in the constitution – above all, therefore, the instincts, which originate from the somatic organization and which find a first psychical expression here [in the id] in forms unknown to us.[1]

Under the influence of the real external world around us, one portion of the id has undergone a special development. From what was originally a cortical layer, equipped with the organs for receiving stimuli and with arrangements for acting as a protective shield against stimuli, a special organization has arisen which henceforward acts as an intermediary between the id and the external world. To this region of our mind we have given the name of *ego*.

Here are the principal characteristics of the ego. In consequence

1. This oldest portion of the psychical apparatus remains the most important throughout life; moreover, the investigations of psychoanalysis started with it.

of the pre-established connection between sense perception and muscular action, the ego has voluntary movement at its command. It has the task of self-preservation. As regards *external* events, it performs that task by becoming aware of stimuli, by storing up experiences about them (in the memory), by avoiding excessively strong stimuli (through flight), by dealing with moderate stimuli (through adaptation) and finally by learning to bring about expedient changes in the external world to its own advantage (through activity). As regards *internal* events, in relation to the id, it performs that task by gaining control over the demands of the instincts, by deciding whether they are to be allowed satisfaction, by postponing that satisfaction to times and circumstances favourable in the external world or by suppressing their excitations entirely. It is guided in its activity by consideration of the tensions produced by stimuli, whether these tensions are present in it or introduced into it. The raising of these tensions is in general felt as *unpleasure* and their lowering as *pleasure*. It is probable, however, that what is felt as pleasure or unpleasure is not the *absolute* height of this tension but something in the rhythm of the changes in them. The ego strives after pleasure and seeks to avoid unpleasure. An increase in unpleasure that is expected and foreseen is met by a *signal of anxiety*; the occasion of such an increase, whether it threatens from without or within, is known as a *danger*. From time to time the ego gives up its connection with the external world and withdraws into the state of sleep, in which it makes far-reaching changes in its organization. It is to be inferred from the state of sleep that this organization consists in a particular distribution of mental energy.

The long period of childhood, during which the growing human being lives in dependence on his parents, leaves behind it as a precipitate the formation in his ego of a special agency in which this parental influence is prolonged. It has received the name of *super-ego*. In so far as this super-ego is differentiated from the ego or is opposed to it, it constitutes a third power which the ego must take into account.

An action by the ego is as it should be if it satisfies simultaneously the demands of the id, of the super-ego and of reality – that is to say, if it is able to reconcile their demands with one another. The details of the relation between the ego and the super-ego become completely intelligible when they are traced back to the child's attitude to its parents. This parental influence of course includes in its operation not only the personalities of the actual parents but also the family, racial and national traditions handed on through them, as well as the demands of the immediate social *milieu* which they represent. In the same way, the super-ego, in the course of an individual's development, receives contributions from later successors and substitutes of his parents, such as teachers and models in public life of admired social ideals. It will be observed that, for all their fundamental difference, the id and the super-ego have one thing in common: they both represent the influences of the past – the id the influence of heredity, the super-ego the influence, essentially, of what is taken over from other people – whereas the ego is principally determined by the individual's own experience, that is by accidental and contemporary events.

This general schematic picture of a psychical apparatus may be supposed to apply as well to the higher animals which resemble man mentally. A super-ego must be presumed to be present wherever, as is the case with man, there is a long period of dependence in childhood. A distinction between ego and id is an unavoidable assumption. Animal psychology has not yet taken in hand the interesting problem which is here presented.

CHAPTER II

THE THEORY OF THE INSTINCTS

The power of the id expresses the true purpose of the individual organism's life. This consists in the satisfaction of its innate needs. No such purpose as that of keeping itself alive or of protecting itself from dangers by means of anxiety can be attributed to the id. That is the task of the ego, whose business it also is to discover the most favourable and least perilous method of obtaining satisfaction, taking the external world into account. The super-ego may bring fresh needs to the fore, but its main function remains the limitation of satisfactions.

The forces which we assume to exist behind the tensions caused by the needs of the id are called *instincts*. They represent the somatic demands upon the mind. Though they are the ultimate cause of all activity, they are of a conservative nature; the state, whatever it may be, which an organism has reached gives rise to a tendency to re-establish that state so soon as it has been abandoned. It is thus possible to distinguish an indeterminate number of instincts, and in common practice this is in fact done. For us, however, the important question arises whether it may not be possible to trace all these numerous instincts back to a few basic ones. We have found that instincts can change their aim (by displacement) and also that they can replace one another – the energy of one instinct passing over to another. This latter process is still insufficiently understood. After long hesitancies and vacillations we have decided to assume the existence of only two basic instincts, *Eros* and *the destructive instinct*. (The contrast between the instincts of self-preservation and the preservation of the species, as well as the contrast between ego-love and object-love, falls within Eros.) The aim of the first of these basic instincts is to establish ever greater unities and to preserve them thus – in short, to bind together; the aim of the second is, on the contrary, to undo connections and so to destroy things. In the case of the destructive instinct we may suppose that its final aim is to lead what is living into an inorganic state. For this reason we also call it the *death instinct*. If we assume that living things came later than inanimate ones and arose from them, then the death instinct fits in with the formula we have proposed to the effect that instincts tend towards a return to an earlier state. In the case of Eros (or the love instinct) we cannot apply this formula. To do so would presuppose that living substance was once a unity which had later been torn apart and was now striving towards reunion.[1]

In biological functions the two basic instincts operate against each other or combine with each other. Thus, the act of eating is a destruction of the object with the final aim of incorporating it, and the sexual act is an act of aggression with the purpose of the most intimate union. This concurrent and mutually opposing action of the two basic instincts gives rise to the whole variegation of the phenomena of life. The analogy of our two basic instincts extends from the sphere of living things to the pair of opposing forces – attraction and repulsion – which rule in the inorganic world.[2]

Modifications in the proportions of the fusion between the instincts have the most tangible results. A surplus of sexual aggressiveness will turn a lover into a sex-murderer, while a sharp diminution in the aggressive factor will make him bashful or impotent.

1. Creative writers have imagined something of the sort, but nothing like it is known to us from the actual history of living substance. [Freud no doubt had in mind among other writings Plato's *Symposium*, which he had quoted in this connection in *Beyond the Pleasure Principle* (1920g), *P.F.L.*, **11**, 331, and had alluded to earlier in the *Three Essays on the Theory of Sexuality* (1905d), ibid., **7**, 46.]

2. This picture of the basic forces or instincts, which still arouses much opposition among analysts, was already familiar to the philosopher Empedocles of Acragas. [Freud had discussed Empedocles and his theories at some length in Section VI of his paper on 'Analysis Terminable and Interminable' (1937c). He had included a reference to the dual forces operating in physics in his open letter to Einstein, *Why War?* (1933b), *P.F.L.*, **12**, 356, as well as in Lecture 32 of the *New Introductory Lectures* (1933a), ibid., **2**, 136].

There can be no question of restricting one or the other of the basic instincts to one of the provinces of the mind. They must necessarily be met with everywhere. We may picture an initial state as one in which the total available energy of Eros, which henceforward we shall speak of as 'libido', is present in the still undifferentiated ego-id [1] and serves to neutralize the destructive tendencies which are simultaneously present. (We are without a term analogous to 'libido' for describing the energy of the destructive instinct.) At a later stage it becomes relatively easy for us to follow the vicissitudes of the libido, but this is more difficult with the destructive instinct.

So long as that instinct operates internally, as a death instinct, it remains silent; it only comes to our notice when it is diverted outwards as an instinct of destruction. It seems to be essential for the preservation of the individual that this diversion should occur; the muscular apparatus serves this purpose. When the super-ego is established, considerable amounts of the aggressive instinct are fixated in the interior of the ego and operate there self-destructively. This is one of the dangers to health by which human beings are faced on their path to cultural development. Holding back aggressiveness is in general unhealthy and leads to illness (to mortification [2]). A person in a fit of rage will often demonstrate how the transition from aggressiveness that has been prevented to self-destructiveness is brought about by diverting the aggressiveness against himself: he tears his hair or beats his face with his fists, though he would evidently have preferred to apply this treatment to someone else. Some portion of self-destructiveness remains within, whatever the circumstances; till at last it succeeds in killing the individual, not, perhaps, until his libido has been used up or fixated in a disadvantageous way. Thus it may in general be suspected that the *individual* dies of his internal conflicts but that the *species* dies of its unsuccessful struggle against the external world if

1. [See footnote on p. 382 below.]

2. ['*Kränkung*' means literally 'making ill'. This same point, including the verbal one, was made by Freud in a lecture on hysteria delivered forty-five years previously (Freud, 1893*h*).]

the latter changes in a fashion which cannot be adequately dealt with by the adaptations which the species has acquired.

It is hard to say anything of the behaviour of the libido in the id and in the super-ego. All that we know about it relates to the ego, in which at first the whole available quota of libido is stored up. We call this state absolute, primary *narcissism*. It lasts till the ego begins to cathect the ideas of objects with libido, to transform narcissistic libido into object-libido. Throughout the whole of life the ego remains the great reservoir from which libidinal cathexes are sent out to objects and into which they are also once more withdrawn, just as an amoeba behaves with its pseudopodia.[1] It is only when a person is completely in love that the main quota of libido is transferred on to the object and the object to some extent takes the place of the ego. A characteristic of the libido which is important in life is its *mobility*, the facility with which it passes from one object to another. This must be contrasted with the *fixation* of the libido to particular objects, which often persists throughout life.

There can be no question but that the libido has somatic sources, that it streams to the ego from various organs and parts of the body. This is most clearly seen in the case of that portion of the libido which, from its instinctual aim, is described as sexual excitation. The most prominent of the parts of the body from which this libido arises are known by the name of '*erotogenic zones*', though in fact the whole body is an erotogenic zone of this kind. The greater part of what we know about Eros — that is to say, about its exponent, the libido — has been gained from a study of the sexual function, which, indeed, on the prevailing view, even if not according to our theory, coincides with Eros. We have been able to form a picture of the way in which the sexual urge, which is destined to exercise a decisive influence on our life, gradually develops out of successive contributions from a number of component instincts, which represent particular erotogenic zones.

1. [Some discussion of this passage will be found in Appendix B to *The Ego and the Id* (1923*b*), *P.F.L.*, **11**, 405, 407.]

CHAPTER III
THE DEVELOPMENT OF THE SEXUAL FUNCTION

ACCORDING to the prevailing view human sexual life consists essentially in an endeavour to bring one's own genitals into contact with those of someone of the opposite sex. With this are associated, as accessory phenomena and introductory acts, kissing this extraneous body, looking at it and touching it. This endeavour is supposed to make its appearance at puberty – that is, at the age of sexual maturity – and to serve the purposes of reproduction. Nevertheless, certain facts have always been known which do not fit into the narrow framework of this view. (1) It is a remarkable fact that there are people who are only attracted by individuals of their own sex and by their genitals. (2) It is equally remarkable that there are people whose desires behave exactly like sexual ones but who at the same time entirely disregard the sexual organs or their normal use; people of this kind are known as 'perverts'. (3) And lastly it is a striking thing that some children (who are on that account regarded as degenerate) take a very early interest in their genitals and show signs of excitation in them.

It may well be believed that psychoanalysis provoked astonishment and denials when, partly on the basis of these three neglected facts, it contradicted all the popular opinions on sexuality. Its principal findings are as follows:

(a) Sexual life does not begin only at puberty, but starts with plain manifestations soon after birth.

(b) It is necessary to distinguish sharply between the concepts of 'sexual' and 'genital'. The former is the wider concept and includes activities that have nothing to do with the genitals.

(c) Sexual life includes the function of obtaining pleasure from zones of the body – a function which is subsequently brought into the service of reproduction. The two functions often fail to coincide completely.

The chief interest is naturally focused on the first of these assertions, the most unexpected of all. It has been found that in early childhood there are signs of bodily activity to which only an ancient prejudice could deny the name of sexual and which are linked to psychical phenomena that we come across later in adult erotic life – such as fixation to particular objects, jealousy, and so on. It is further found, however, that these phenomena which emerge in early childhood form part of an ordered course of development, that they pass through a regular process of increase, reaching a climax towards the end of the fifth year, after which there follows a lull. During this lull progress is at a standstill and much is unlearnt and there is much recession. After the end of this period of latency, as it is called, sexual life advances once more with puberty; we might say that it has a second efflorescence. And here we come upon the fact that the onset of sexual life is *diphasic*, that it occurs in two waves – something that is unknown except in man and evidently has an important bearing on hominization.[1] It is not a matter of indifference that the events of this early period, except for a few residues, fall a victim to *infantile amnesia*. Our views on the aetiology of the neuroses and our technique of analytic therapy are derived from these conceptions; and our tracing of the developmental processes in this early period has also provided evidence for yet other conclusions.

1. Cf. the suggestion that man is descended from a mammal which reached sexual maturity at the age of five, but that some major external influence was brought to bear on the species and at that point interrupted the straight course of development of sexuality. Other transformations in the sexual life of man as compared with that of animals might be connected with this – such as the abolition of the periodicity of the libido and the exploitation of the part played by menstruation in the relation between the sexes. [The idea of there being a connection between the latency period and the glacial epoch was first made many years earlier by Ferenczi (1913b). Freud referred to it with a good deal of caution in *The Ego and the Id* (1923b), P.F.L., **11**, 375, and again, with rather greater acquiescence, in *Inhibitions, Symptoms and Anxiety* (1926d), ibid., **10**, 314. The question of the cessation of periodicity in the sexual function was discussed by Freud at some length in two footnotes to Chapter IV of *Civilization and its Discontents* (1930a), ibid., **12**, 288–9, 295–7. On hominization, see *Moses and Monotheism* (1939a), ibid., **13**, 318.]

III. THE SEXUAL FUNCTION

The first organ to emerge as an erotogenic zone and to make libidinal demands on the mind is, from the time of birth onwards, the mouth. To begin with, all psychical activity is concentrated on providing satisfaction for the needs of that zone. Primarily, of course, this satisfaction serves the purpose of self-preservation by means of nourishment; but physiology should not be confused with psychology. The baby's obstinate persistence in sucking gives evidence at an early stage of a need for satisfaction which, though it originates from and is instigated by the taking of nourishment, nevertheless strives to obtain pleasure independently of nourishment and for that reason may and should be termed *sexual*.

During this oral phase sadistic impulses already occur sporadically along with the appearance of the teeth. Their extent is far greater in the second phase, which we describe as the sadistic-anal one, because satisfaction is then sought in aggression and in the excretory function. Our justification for including aggressive urges under the libido is based on the view that sadism is an instinctual fusion of purely libidinal and purely destructive urges, a fusion which thenceforward persists uninterruptedly.[1]

The third phase is that known as the phallic one, which is, as it were, a forerunner of the final form taken by sexual life and already much resembles it. It is to be noted that it is not the genitals of both sexes that play a part at this stage, but only the male ones (the phallus). The female genitals long remain unknown: in children's attempts to understand the sexual processes they pay homage to the venerable cloacal theory – a theory which has a genetic justification.[2]

1. The question arises whether the satisfaction of purely destructive instinctual impulses can be felt as pleasure, whether pure destructiveness without any libidinal admixture occurs. Satisfaction of the death instinct remaining in the ego seems not to produce feelings of pleasure, though masochism represents a fusion which is entirely analogous to sadism.

2. The occurrence of early vaginal excitations is often asserted. But it is most probable that what is in question are excitations in the clitoris – that is, in an organ analogous to the penis. This does not invalidate our right to describe the phase as phallic.

With the phallic phase and in the course of it the sexuality of early childhood reaches its height and approaches its dissolution. Thereafter boys and girls have different histories. Both have begun to put their intellectual activity at the service of sexual researches; both start off from the premiss of the universal presence of the penis. But now the paths of the sexes diverge. The boy enters the Oedipus phase; he begins to manipulate his penis and simultaneously has fantasies of carrying out some sort of activity with it in relation to his mother, till, owing to the combined effect of a threat of castration and the sight of the absence of a penis in females, he experiences the greatest trauma of his life and this introduces the period of latency with all its consequences. The girl, after vainly attempting to do the same as the boy, comes to recognize her lack of a penis or rather the inferiority of her clitoris, with permanent effects on the development of her character; as a result of this first disappointment in rivalry, she often begins by turning away altogether from sexual life.

It would be a mistake to suppose that these three phases succeed one another in a clear-cut fashion. One may appear in addition to another; they may overlap one another, may be present alongside of one another. In the early phases the different component instincts set about their pursuit of pleasure independently of one another; in the phallic phase there are the beginnings of an organization which subordinates the other urges to the primacy of the genitals and signifies the start of a co-ordination of the general urge towards pleasure into the sexual function. The complete organization is only achieved at puberty, in a fourth, genital phase. A state of things is then established in which (1) some earlier libidinal cathexes are retained, (2) others are taken into the sexual function as preparatory, auxiliary acts, the satisfaction of which produces what is known as fore-pleasure, and (3) other urges are excluded from the organization, and are either suppressed altogether (repressed) or are employed in the ego in another way, forming character-traits or undergoing sublimation with a displacement of their aims.

This process is not always performed faultlessly. Inhibitions in its development manifest themselves as the many sorts of disturbance in sexual life. When this is so, we find fixations of the libido to conditions in earlier phases, whose urge, which is independent of the normal sexual aim, is described as *perversion*. One such developmental inhibition, for instance, is homosexuality when it is manifest. Analysis shows that in every case a homosexual object-tie was present and in most cases persisted in a *latent* condition. The situation is complicated by the fact that as a rule the processes necessary for bringing about a normal outcome are not completely present or absent, but *partially* present, so that the final result remains dependent on these *quantitative* relations. In these circumstances the genital organization is, it is true, attained, but it lacks those portions of the libido which have not advanced with the rest and have remained fixated to pregenital objects and aims. This weakening shows itself in a tendency, if there is an absence of genital satisfaction or if there are difficulties in the real external world, for the libido to hark back to its earlier pregenital cathexes (*regression*).

During the study of the sexual functions we have been able to gain a first, preliminary conviction, or rather a suspicion, of two discoveries which will later be found to be important over the whole of our field. Firstly, the normal and abnormal manifestations observed by us (that is, the phenomenology of the subject) need to be described from the point of view of their dynamics and economics (in our case, from the point of view of the quantitative distribution of the libido). And secondly, the aetiology of the disorders which we study is to be looked for in the individual's developmental history – that is to say, in his early life.

CHAPTER IV
PSYCHICAL QUALITIES

I HAVE described the structure of the psychical apparatus and the energies or forces which are active in it, and I have traced in a prominent example the way in which these energies (in the main, the libido) organize themselves into a physiological function which serves the purpose of the preservation of the species. There was nothing in all this to demonstrate the quite peculiar characteristic of what is psychical, apart, of course, from the empirical fact that this apparatus and these energies are the basis of the functions which we describe as our mental life. I will now turn to something which is uniquely characteristic of what is psychical, and which, indeed, according to a very widely held opinion, coincides with it to the exclusion of all else.

The starting-point for this investigation is provided by a fact without parallel, which defies all explanation or description – the fact of consciousness. Nevertheless, if anyone speaks of consciousness we know immediately and from our most personal experience what is meant by it.[1] Many people, both inside and outside [psychological] science, are satisfied with the assumption that consciousness alone is psychical; in that case nothing remains for psychology but to discriminate among psychical phenomena between perceptions, feelings, thought-processes and volitions. It is generally agreed, however, that these conscious processes do not form unbroken sequences which are complete in themselves; there would thus be no alternative left to assuming that there are physical or somatic processes which are concomitant with the psychical ones and which we should necessarily have to recognize as more complete than the psychical sequences, since some of

1. One extreme line of thought, exemplified in the American doctrine of behaviourism, thinks it possible to construct a psychology which disregards this fundamental fact!

them would have conscious processes parallel to them but others would not. If so, it of course becomes plausible to lay the stress in psychology on these somatic processes, to see in *them* the true essence of what is psychical and to look for some other assessment of the conscious processes. The majority of philosophers, however, as well as many other people, dispute this and declare that the idea of something psychical being unconscious is self-contradictory.

But this is precisely what psychoanalysis is obliged to assert, and this is its second fundamental hypothesis [p. 376]. It explains the supposedly somatic concomitant phenomena as being what is truly psychical, and thus in the first instance disregards the quality of consciousness. It is not alone in doing this. Some thinkers (such as Theodor Lipps,[1] for instance) have asserted the same thing in the same words; and the general dissatisfaction with the usual view of what is psychical has resulted in an increasingly urgent demand for the inclusion in psychological thought of a concept of the unconscious, though this demand has taken such an indefinite and obscure form that it could have no influence on science.[2]

Now it would look as though this dispute between psychoanalysis and philosophy is concerned only with a trifling matter of definition – the question whether the name 'psychical' should be applied to one or another sequence of phenomena. In fact, however, this step has become of the highest significance. Whereas the psychology of consciousness never went beyond the broken sequences which were obviously dependent on something else, the other view, which held that the psychical is unconscious in itself, enabled psychology to take its place as a natural science like any other. The processes with which it is concerned are in themselves just as unknowable

1. [Some account of Lipps (1851–1914) and Freud's relations with him is given in the Editor's Introduction to Freud's book on jokes (1905*c*), *P.F.L.*, 6, 32.]

2. [When this work was first published in 1940, a long footnote was inserted at this point in the German version. See the Editor's Note, p. 371 above.]

as those dealt with by other sciences, by chemistry or physics, for example; but it is possible to establish the laws which they obey and to follow their mutual relations and interdependences unbroken over long stretches – in short, to arrive at what is described as an 'understanding' of the field of natural phenomena in question. This cannot be effected without framing fresh hypotheses and creating fresh concepts; but these are not to be despised as evidence of embarrassment on our part but deserve on the contrary to be appreciated as an enrichment of science. They can lay claim to the same value as approximations that belong to the corresponding intellectual scaffolding found in other natural sciences, and we look forward to their being modified, corrected and more precisely determined as further experience is accumulated and sifted. So too it will be entirely in accordance with our expectations if the basic concepts and principles of the new science (instinct, nervous energy, etc.) remain for a considerable time no less indeterminate than those of the older sciences (force, mass, attraction, etc.).

Every science is based on observations and experiences arrived at through the medium of our psychical apparatus. But since *our* science has as its subject that apparatus itself, the analogy ends here. We make our observations through the medium of the same perceptual apparatus, precisely with the help of the breaks in the sequence of 'psychical' events: we fill in what is omitted by making plausible inferences and translating it into conscious material. In this way we construct, as it were, a sequence of conscious events complementary to the unconscious psychical processes. The relative certainty of our psychical science is based on the binding force of these inferences. Anyone who enters deeply into our work will find that our technique holds its ground against any criticism.

In the course of this work the distinctions which we describe as psychical qualities force themselves on our notice. There is no need to characterize what we call 'conscious': it is the same as the consciousness of philosophers and of everyday opinion. Everything else psychical is in our view 'the unconscious'. We are soon led to make an important division in this unconscious.

Some processes become conscious easily; they may then cease to be conscious, but can become conscious once more without any trouble: as people say, they can be reproduced or re-membered. This reminds us that consciousness is in general a highly fugitive state. What is conscious is conscious only for a moment. If our perceptions do not confirm this, the con-tradiction is only an apparent one; it is explained by the fact that the stimuli which lead to perception may persist for con-siderable periods, so that meanwhile the perception of them may be repeated. The whole position is made clear in con-nection with the conscious perception of our thought-pro-cesses: these too may persist for some time, but they may just as well pass in a flash. Everything unconscious that behaves in this way, that can thus easily exchange the unconscious state for the conscious one, is therefore preferably described as 'capable of becoming conscious' or as *preconscious*. Experience has taught us that there is hardly a psychical process, however complicated it may be, which cannot on occasion remain preconscious, even though as a rule it will, as we say, push its way forward into consciousness. There are other psychical processes and psychical material which have no such easy access to becoming conscious but must be inferred, recognized and translated into conscious form in the manner described. For such material we reserve the name of the unconscious proper.

Thus we have attributed three qualities to psychical pro-cesses: they are either conscious, preconscious or unconscious. The division between the three classes of material which possess these qualities is neither absolute nor permanent. What is preconscious becomes conscious, as we have seen, without any assistance from us; what is unconscious can, through our efforts, be made conscious, and in the process we may have a feeling that we are often overcoming very strong resistances. When we attempt to do this with someone else, we should not forget that the conscious filling-in of the gaps in his perceptions – the construction we are presenting him with – does not mean as yet that we have made the unconscious material in question conscious to him. All that is true so far is that the material is present in him in two records, once in the conscious reconstruction he has been given, and besides this in its original unconscious state. Our continued efforts usually succeed eventually in making this unconscious material conscious to him himself, as a result of which the two records are brought to coincide. The amount of effort we have to use, by which we estimate the resistance against the material becoming conscious, varies in magnitude in individual cases. For instance, what comes about in an analytic treatment as a result of our efforts can also occur spontaneously: material which is ordinarily unconscious can transform itself into preconscious material and then becomes conscious – a thing that happens to a large extent in psychotic states. From this we infer that the maintenance of certain internal resistances is a *sine qua non* of normality. A relaxation of resistances such as this, with a consequent pushing forward of unconscious material, takes place regularly in the state of sleep, and thus brings about a necessary precondition for the construction of dreams. Conversely, preconscious material can become temporarily inaccessible and cut off by resistances, as happens when something is temporarily forgotten or escapes the memory; or a preconscious thought can even be temporarily put back into the unconscious state, as seems to be a precondition in the case of jokes. We shall see that a similar transformation back of preconscious material or processes into the unconscious state plays a great part in the causation of neurotic disorders.

The theory of the three qualities of what is psychical, as described in this generalized and simplified manner, seems likely to be a source of limitless confusion rather than a help towards clarification. But it should not be forgotten that in fact it is not a theory at all but a first stock-taking of the facts of our observations, that it keeps as close to those facts as possible and does not attempt to explain them. The complications which it reveals may bring into relief the peculiar difficulties with which our investigations have to contend. It may be suspected, however, that we shall come to a closer understanding of this theory itself if we trace out the relations between the psychical qualities and the provinces or agencies of the psychical apparatus which we have postulated – though these relations too are far from being simple.

The process of something becoming conscious is above all linked with the perceptions which our sense-organs receive from the external world. From the topographical point of view, therefore, it is a phenomenon which takes place in the outermost cortex of the ego. It is true that we also receive conscious information from the inside of the body – the feelings, which actually exercise a more peremptory influence on our mental life than external perceptions; moreover, in certain circumstances the sense-organs themselves transmit feelings, sensations of pain, in addition to the perceptions specific to them. Since, however, these sensations (as we call them in contrast to conscious perceptions) also emanate from the terminal organs and since we regard all these as prolongations or offshoots of the cortical layer, we are still able to maintain the assertion made above [at the beginning of this paragraph]. The only distinction would be that, as regards the terminal organs of sensation and feeling, the body itself would take the place of the external world.

Conscious processes on the periphery of the ego and everything else in the ego unconscious – such would be the simplest state of affairs that we might picture. And such may in fact be the state that prevails in animals. But in men there is an added complication through which internal processes in the ego may also acquire the quality of consciousness. This is the work of the function of speech, which brings material in the ego into a firm connection with mnemic residues of visual, but more particularly of auditory, perceptions. Thenceforward the perceptual periphery of the cortical layer can be excited to a much greater extent from inside as well, internal events such as passages of ideas and thought processes can become conscious, and a special device is called for in order to distinguish between the two possibilities – a device known as *reality-testing*. The equation 'perception = reality (external world)' no longer holds. Errors, which can now easily arise and do so regularly in dreams, are called *hallucinations*.

The inside of the ego, which comprises above all the thought processes, has the quality of being preconscious. This is characteristic of the ego and belongs to it alone. It would not be correct, however, to think that connection with the mnemic residues of speech is a necessary precondition of the preconscious state. On the contrary, that state is independent of a connection with them, though the presence of that connection makes it safe to infer the preconscious nature of a process. The preconscious state, characterized on the one hand by having access to consciousness and on the other hand by its connection with the speech residues, is nevertheless something peculiar, the nature of which is not exhausted by these two characteristics. The evidence for this is the fact that large portions of the ego, and particularly of the super-ego, which cannot be denied the characteristic of preconsciousness, none the less remain for the most part unconscious in the phenomenological sense of the word. We do not know why this must be so. We shall attempt presently to attack the problem of the true nature of the preconscious.

The sole prevailing quality in the id is that of being unconscious. Id and unconscious are as intimately linked as ego and preconscious: indeed, in the former case the connection is even more exclusive. If we look back at the developmental history of an individual and of his psychical apparatus, we shall be able to perceive an important distinction in the id. Originally, to be sure, everything was id; the ego was developed out of the id by the continual influence of the external world. In the course of this slow development certain of the contents of the id were transformed into the preconscious state and so taken into the ego; others of its contents remained in the id unchanged, as its scarcely accessible nucleus. During this development, however, the young and feeble ego put back into the unconscious state some of the material it had already taken in, dropped it, and behaved in the same way to some fresh impressions which it *might* have taken in, so that these, having been rejected, could leave a trace only in the id. In consideration of its origin we speak of this latter portion of the id as *the repressed*. It is of little importance that we are not always able to draw a sharp line between these two categories of contents in the id. They coincide approximately with the distinction between what was innately present originally and what was acquired in the course of the ego's development.

Having now decided upon the topographical dissection of the psychical apparatus into an ego and an id, with which the difference in quality between preconscious and unconscious runs parallel, and having agreed that this quality is to be regarded only as an *indication* of the difference and not as its essence, a further question faces us. What, if this is so, is the true nature of the state which is revealed in the id by the quality of being unconscious and in the ego by that of being preconscious and in what does the difference between them consist?

But of that we know nothing. And the profound obscurity of the background of our ignorance is scarcely illuminated by a few glimmers of insight. Here we have approached the still-shrouded secret of the nature of the psychical. We assume, as other natural sciences have led us to expect, that in mental life some kind of energy is at work; but we have nothing to go upon which will enable us to come nearer to a knowledge of it by analogies with other forms of energy. We seem to recognize that nervous or psychical energy occurs in two forms, one freely mobile and another, by comparison, bound; we speak of cathexes and hypercathexes of psychical material, and even venture to suppose that a hypercathexis brings about a kind of synthesis of different processes – a synthesis in the course of which free energy is transformed into bound energy. Further than this we have not advanced. At any rate, we hold firmly to the view that the distinction between the unconscious and the preconscious state lies in dynamic relations of this kind, which would explain how it is that, whether spontaneously or with our assistance, the one can be changed into the other.

Behind all these uncertainties, however, there lies one new

fact, whose discovery we owe to psychoanalytic research. We have found that processes in the unconscious or in the id obey different laws from those in the preconscious ego. We name these laws in their totality the *primary process*, in contrast to the *secondary process* which governs the course of events in the preconscious, in the ego. In the end, therefore, the study of psychical qualities has after all proved not unfruitful.

Chapter V
DREAM INTERPRETATION
AS AN ILLUSTRATION

An investigation of normal, stable states, in which the frontiers of the ego are safeguarded against the id by resistances (anti-cathexes) and have held firm, and in which the super-ego is not distinguished from the ego, because they work together harmoniously – an investigation of that kind would teach us little. The only thing that can help us are states of conflict and uproar, when the contents of the unconscious id have a prospect of forcing their way into the ego and into consciousness and the ego puts itself once more on the defensive against this invasion. It is only under these conditions that we can make such observations as will confirm or correct our statements about the two partners. Now, our nightly sleep is precisely a state of this sort, and for that reason psychical activity during sleep, which we perceive as dreams, is our most favourable object of study. In that way, too, we avoid the familiar reproach that we base our constructions of normal mental life on pathological findings; for dreams are regular events in the life of a normal person, however much their characteristics may differ from the productions of our waking life. Dreams, as everyone knows, may be confused, unintelligible or positively nonsensical, what they say may contradict all that we know of reality, and we behave in them like insane people, since, so long as we are dreaming, we attribute objective reality to the contents of the dream.

We find our way to the understanding ('interpretation') of a dream by assuming that what we recollect as the dream after we have woken up is not the true dream process but only a *façade* behind which that process lies concealed. Here we have our distinction between the *manifest* content of a dream and the *latent* dream-thoughts. The process which produces the former out of the latter is described as the *dream-work*. The study of the dream-work teaches us by an excellent example the way in which unconscious material from the id (originally unconscious and repressed unconscious alike) forces its way into the ego, becomes preconscious and, as a result of the ego's opposition, undergoes the changes which we know as *dream distortion*. There are no features of a dream which cannot be explained in this way.

It is best to begin by pointing out that the formation of a dream can be provoked in two different ways. Either, on the one hand, an instinctual impulse which is ordinarily suppressed (an unconscious wish) finds enough strength during sleep to make itself felt by the ego, or, on the other hand, an urge left over from waking life, a preconscious train of thought with all the conflicting impulses attached to it, finds reinforcement during sleep from an unconscious element. In short, dreams may arise either from the id or from the ego. The mechanism of dream formation is in both cases the same and so also is the necessary dynamic precondition. The ego gives evidence of its original derivation from the id by occasionally ceasing its functions and allowing a reversion to an earlier state of things. This is logically brought about by its breaking off its relations with the external world and withdrawing its cathexes from the sense organs. We are justified in saying that there arises at birth an instinct to return to the intra-uterine life that has been abandoned – an instinct to sleep. Sleep is a return of this kind to the womb. Since the waking ego governs motility, that function is paralysed in sleep, and accordingly a good part of the inhibitions imposed on the unconscious id become superfluous. The withdrawal or reduction of these 'anticathexes' thus allows the id what is now a harmless amount of liberty.

The evidence of the share taken by the unconscious id in the formation of dreams is abundant and convincing. (*a*) Memory is far more comprehensive in dreams than in waking life. Dreams bring up recollections which the dreamer has forgotten, which are inaccessible to him when he is awake. (*b*) Dreams make an unrestricted use of linguistic symbols, the meaning of which is for the most part unknown to the dreamer.

Our experience, however, enables us to confirm their sense. They probably originate from earlier phases in the development of speech. (c) Memory very often reproduces in dreams impressions from the dreamer's early childhood of which we can definitely assert not only that they had been forgotten but that they had become unconscious owing to repression. That explains the help — usually indispensable — given us by dreams in the attempts we make during the analytic treatment of neuroses to reconstruct the dreamer's early life. (d) Furthermore, dreams bring to light material which cannot have originated either from the dreamer's adult life or from his forgotten childhood. We are obliged to regard it as part of the *archaic heritage* which a child brings with him into the world, before any experience of his own, influenced by the experiences of his ancestors. We find the counterpart of this phylogenetic material in the earliest human legends and in surviving customs. Thus dreams constitute a source of human prehistory which is not to be despised.

But what makes dreams so invaluable in giving us insight is the circumstance that, when the unconscious material makes its way into the ego, it brings its own modes of working along with it. This means that the preconscious thoughts in which the unconscious material has found its expression are handled in the course of the dream-work as though they were unconscious portions of the id; and, in the case of the alternative method of dream formation, the preconscious thoughts which have obtained reinforcement from an unconscious instinctual impulse are brought down to the unconscious state. It is only in this way that we learn the laws which govern the passage of events in the unconscious and the respects in which they differ from the rules that are familiar to us in waking thought. Thus the dream-work is essentially an instance of the unconscious working-over of preconscious thought processes. To take an analogy from history: invading conquerors govern a conquered country, not according to the judicial system which they find in force there, but according to their own. It is, however, an unmistakable fact that the outcome of the dream-work is a compromise. The ego organization is not yet paralysed, and its influence is to be seen in the distortion imposed on the unconscious material and in what are often very ineffective attempts at giving the total result a form not too unacceptable to the ego (*secondary revision*). In our analogy this would be an expression of the continued resistance of the defeated people.

The laws that govern the passage of events in the unconscious, which come to light in this manner, are remarkable enough and suffice to explain most of what seems strange to us about dreams. Above all there is a striking tendency to *condensation*, an inclination to form fresh unities out of elements which in our waking thought we should certainly have kept separate. As a consequence of this, a single element of the manifest dream often stands for a whole number of latent dream-thoughts as though it were a combined allusion to all of them; and in general the compass of the manifest dream is extraordinarily small in comparison with the wealth of material from which it has sprung. Another peculiarity of the dream-work, not entirely independent of the former one, is the ease with which psychical intensities [1] (cathexes) are *displaced* from one element to another, so that it often happens that an element which was of little importance in the dream-thoughts appears as the clearest and accordingly most important feature of the manifest dream, and, *vice versa*, that essential elements of the dream-thoughts are represented in the manifest dream only by slight allusions. Moreover, as a rule the existence of quite insignificant points in common between two elements is enough to allow the dream-work to replace one by the other in all further operations. It will easily be imagined how greatly these mechanisms of condensation and displacement can increase the difficulty of interpreting a dream and of revealing the relations between the manifest dream and the latent dream-thoughts. From the evidence of the existence of these two tendencies to

1. [A term very often used by Freud from the earliest times as an equivalent to psychical energy. See the Editor's footnote in the paper on 'Female Sexuality' (1931*b*), *P.F.L.*, **7**, 391.]

condensation and displacement our theory infers that in the unconscious id the energy is in a freely mobile state and that the id sets more store by the possibility of discharging quantities of excitation than by any other consideration;[1] and our theory makes use of these two peculiarities in defining the character of the primary process we have attributed to the id.

The study of the dream-work has taught us many other characteristics of the processes in the unconscious which are as remarkable as they are important; but we must only mention a few of them here. The governing rules of logic carry no weight in the unconscious; it might be called the Realm of the Illogical. Urges with contrary aims exist side by side in the unconscious without any need arising for an adjustment between them. Either they have no influence whatever on each other, or, if they have, no decision is reached, but a compromise comes about which is nonsensical since it embraces mutually incompatible details. With this is connected the fact that contraries are not kept apart but treated as though they were identical, so that in the manifest dream any element may also have the meaning of its opposite. Certain philologists have found that the same held good in the most ancient languages and that contraries such as 'strong-weak', 'light-dark' and 'high-deep' were originally expressed by the same roots, until two different modifications of the primitive word distinguished between the two meanings. Residues of this original double meaning seem to have survived even in a highly developed language like Latin in its use of words such as *altus* ('high' and 'deep') and *sacer* ('sacred' and 'infamous').[2]

In view of the complication and ambiguity of the relations between the manifest dream and the latent content lying behind

---

1. An analogy may be seen in the behaviour of a non-commissioned officer who accepts a reprimand from his superior in silence but vents his anger on the first innocent private he comes across. [In this insistence by the id on discharging quantities of excitation we have an exact replica of what Freud in his *Project* of 1895 (Part I, Section 1) had described in quasi-neurological terms as the primary principle of neuronal activity: 'neurones tend to divest themselves of quantity.' (1950a, *Standard Ed.*, **1**, 296.)]

2. [Cf. *Moses and Monotheism* (1939a), *P.F.L.*, **13**, 369.]

it, it is of course justifiable to ask how it is at all possible to deduce the one from the other and whether all we have to go on is a lucky guess, assisted perhaps by a translation of the symbols that occur in the manifest dream. It may be said in reply that in the great majority of cases the problem can be satisfactorily solved, but only with the help of the associations provided by the dreamer himself to the elements of the manifest content. Any other procedure is arbitrary and can yield no certain result. But the dreamer's associations bring to light intermediate links which we can insert in the gap between the two [between the manifest and latent content] and by aid of which we can reinstate the latent content of the dream and 'interpret' it. It is not to be wondered at if this work of interpretation (acting in a direction opposite to the dream-work) fails occasionally to arrive at complete certainty.

It remains for us to give a dynamic explanation of why the sleeping ego takes on the task of the dream-work at all. The explanation is fortunately easy to find. With the help of the unconscious, every dream that is in process of formation makes a demand upon the ego – for the satisfaction of an instinct, if the dream originates from the id; for the solution of a conflict, the removal of a doubt or the forming of an intention, if the dream originates from a residue of preconscious activity in waking life. The sleeping ego, however, is focused on the wish to maintain sleep; it feels this demand as a disturbance and seeks to get rid of the disturbance. The ego succeeds in doing this by what appears to be an act of compliance: it meets the demand with what is in the circumstances a harmless *fulfilment of a wish* and so gets rid of it. This replacement of the demand by the fulfilment of a wish remains the essential function of the dream-work. It may perhaps be worth while to illustrate this by three simple examples – a hunger dream, a dream of convenience and a dream prompted by sexual desire. A need for food makes itself felt in a dreamer during his sleep: he has a dream of a delicious meal and sleeps on. The choice, of course, was open to him either of waking up and eating something or of continuing his sleep. He decided in favour of the latter and satisfied his hunger by means of the dream – for the time being, at all events, for if his hunger had persisted he would have had to wake up nevertheless. Here is the second example. A sleeper had to wake up so as to be in time for his work at the hospital. But he slept on, and had a dream that he was already at the hospital – but as a patient, who has no need to get up. Or again, a desire becomes active during the night for the enjoyment of a forbidden sexual object, the wife of a friend of the sleeper. He has a dream of sexual intercourse – not, indeed, with this person but with someone else of the same name to whom he is in fact indifferent; or his struggle against the desire may find expression in his mistress remaining altogether anonymous.

Naturally, every case is not so simple. Especially in dreams which have originated from undealt-with residues of the previous day, and which have only obtained an unconscious reinforcement during the state of sleep, it is often no easy task to uncover the unconscious motive force and its wish-fulfilment; but we may assume that it is always there. The thesis that dreams are the fulfilments of wishes will easily arouse scepticism when it is remembered how many dreams have an actually distressing content or even wake the dreamer in anxiety, quite apart from the numerous dreams without any definite feeling-tone. But the objection based on anxiety dreams cannot be sustained against analysis. It must not be forgotten that dreams are invariably the product of a conflict, that they are a kind of compromise structure. Something that is a satisfaction for the unconscious id may for that very reason be a cause of anxiety for the ego.

As the dream-work proceeds, sometimes the unconscious will press forward more successfully and sometimes the ego will defend itself with greater energy. Anxiety dreams are mostly those whose content has undergone the least distortion. If the demand made by the unconscious is too great for the sleeping ego to be in a position to fend it off by the means at its disposal, it abandons the wish to sleep and returns to waking life. We shall be taking every experience into account if we say that a dream is invariably an *attempt* to get rid of a disturbance of sleep by means of a wish-fulfilment, so that the dream is a guardian of sleep. The attempt may succeed more or less completely; it may also fail, and in that case the sleeper wakes up, apparently woken precisely by the dream. So, too, there are occasions when that excellent fellow the night-watchman, whose business it is to guard the little township's sleep, has no alternative but to sound the alarm and waken the sleeping townspeople.

I will close this discussion with a comment which will justify the length of time I have spent on the problem of the interpretation of dreams. Experience has shown that the unconscious mechanisms which we have come to know from our study of the dream-work and which gave us the explanation of the formation of dreams also help us to understand the puzzling symptoms which attract our interest to neuroses and psychoses. A conformity of such a kind cannot fail to excite high hopes in us.

PART II
THE PRACTICAL TASK

CHAPTER VI
THE TECHNIQUE OF PSYCHOANALYSIS

A DREAM, then, is a psychosis, with all the absurdities, delusions and illusions of a psychosis. A psychosis of short duration, no doubt, harmless, even entrusted with a useful function, introduced with the subject's consent and terminated by an act of his will. None the less it is a psychosis, and we learn from it that even so deep-going an alteration of mental life as this can be undone and can give place to the normal function. Is it too bold, then, to hope that it must also be possible to submit the dreaded spontaneous illnesses of mental life to our influence and bring about their cure?

We already know a number of things preliminary to such an undertaking. According to our hypothesis it is the ego's task to meet the demands raised by its three dependent relations – to reality, to the id and to the super-ego – and nevertheless at the same time to preserve its own organization and maintain its own autonomy. The necessary precondition of the pathological states under discussion can only be a relative or absolute weakening of the ego which makes the fulfilment of its tasks impossible. The severest demand on the ego is probably the keeping down of the instinctual claims of the id, to accomplish which it is obliged to maintain large expenditures of energy on anticathexes. But the demands made by the super-ego too may become so powerful and so relentless that the ego may be paralysed, as it were, in the face of its other tasks. We may suspect that, in the economic conflicts which arise at this point, the id and the super-ego often make common cause against the hard-pressed ego which tries to cling to reality in order to retain its normal state. If the other two become too strong, they succeed in loosening and altering the ego's organization, so that its proper relation to reality is disturbed or even brought to an end. We have seen it happen in dreaming: when the ego is detached from the reality of the external world, it slips down, under the influence of the internal world, into psychosis.

Our plan of cure is based on these discoveries. The ego is weakened by the internal conflict and we must go to its help. The position is like that in a civil war which has to be decided by the assistance of an ally from outside. The analytic physician and the patient's weakened ego, basing themselves on the real external world, have to band themselves together into a party against the enemies, the instinctual demands of the id and the conscientious demands of the super-ego. We form a pact with each other. The sick ego promises us the most complete candour — promises, that is, to put at our disposal all the material which its self-perception yields it; we assure the patient of the strictest discretion and place at his service our experience in interpreting material that has been influenced by the unconscious. Our knowledge is to make up for his ignorance and to give his ego back its mastery over lost provinces of his mental life. This pact constitutes the analytic situation.

No sooner have we taken this step than a first disappointment awaits us, a first warning against over-confidence. If the patient's ego is to be a useful ally in our common work, it must, however hard it may be pressed by the hostile powers, have retained a certain amount of coherence and some fragment of understanding for the demands of reality. But this is not to be expected of the ego of a psychotic; it cannot observe a pact of this kind, indeed it can scarcely enter into one. It will very soon have tossed us away and the help we offer it and sent us to join the portions of the external world which no longer mean anything to it. Thus we discover that we must renounce the idea of trying our plan of cure upon psychotics — renounce it perhaps for ever or perhaps only for the time being, till we have found some other plan better adapted for them.

There is, however, another class of psychical patients who clearly resemble the psychotics very closely – the vast number of people suffering severely from neuroses. The determinants of their illness as well as its pathogenic mechanisms must be the same or at least very similar. But their ego has proved more resistant and has become less disorganized. Many of them, in spite of their maladies and the inadequacies resulting from them, have been able to maintain themselves in real life. These neurotics may show themselves ready to accept our help. We will confine our interest to *them* and see how far and by what methods we are able to 'cure' them.

With the neurotics, then, we make our pact: complete candour on one side and strict discretion on the other. This looks as though we were only aiming at the post of a secular father-confessor. But there is a great difference, for what we want to hear from our patient is not only what he knows and conceals from other people; he is to tell us too what he does *not* know. With this end in view we give him a more detailed definition of what we mean by candour. We pledge him to obey the *fundamental rule* of analysis, which is henceforward to govern his behaviour towards us. He is to tell us not only what he can say intentionally and willingly, what will give him relief like a confession, but everything else as well that his self-observation yields him, everything that comes into his head, even if it is *disagreeable* for him to say it, even if it seems to him *unimportant* or actually *nonsensical*. If he can succeed after this injunction in putting his self-criticism out of action, he will present us with a mass of material – thoughts, ideas, recollections – which are already subject to the influence of the unconscious, which are often its direct derivatives, and which thus put us in a position to conjecture his repressed unconscious material and to extend, by the information we give him, his ego's knowledge of his unconscious.

But it is far from being the case that his ego is content to play the part of passively and obediently bringing us the material we require and of believing and accepting our translation of it. A number of other things happen, a few of which we might have foreseen but others of which are bound to surprise us. The most remarkable thing is this. The patient is not satisfied with regarding the analyst in the light of reality as a helper and adviser who, moreover, is remunerated for the trouble he takes and who would himself be content with some such role as that of a guide on a difficult mountain climb. On the contrary, the patient sees in him the return, the reincarnation, of some important figure out of his childhood or past, and consequently transfers on to him feelings and reactions which undoubtedly applied to this prototype. This fact of transference soon proves to be a factor of undreamt-of importance, on the one hand an instrument of irreplaceable value and on the other hand a source of serious dangers. This transference is *ambivalent*: it comprises positive (affectionate) as well as negative (hostile) attitudes towards the analyst, who as a rule is put in the place of one or other of the patient's parents, his father or mother. So long as it is positive it serves us admirably. It alters the whole analytic situation; it pushes to one side the patient's rational aim of becoming healthy and free from his ailments. Instead of it there emerges the aim of pleasing the analyst and of winning his applause and love. It becomes the true motive force of the patient's collaboration; his weak ego becomes strong; under its influence he achieves things that would ordinarily be beyond his power; he leaves off his symptoms and seems apparently to have recovered – merely for the sake of the analyst. The analyst may shamefacedly admit to himself that he set out on a difficult undertaking without any suspicion of the extraordinary powers that would be at his command.

Moreover, the relation of transference brings with it two further advantages. If the patient puts the analyst in the place of his father (or mother), he is also giving him the power which his super-ego exercises over his ego, since his parents were, as we know, the origin of his super-ego. The new super-ego now has an opportunity for a sort of *after-education* of the neurotic; it can correct mistakes for which his parents were responsible in educating him. But at this point a warning must be given against misusing this new influence. However much the analyst may be tempted to become a teacher, model and ideal for other people and to create men in his own image, he should not forget that that is not his task in the analytic relationship, and indeed that he will be disloyal to his task if he allows himself to be led on by his inclinations. If he does, he will only be repeating a mistake of the parents who crushed their child's independence by their influence, and he will only be replacing the patient's earlier dependence by a new one. In all his attempts at improving and educating the patient the analyst should respect his individuality. The amount of influence which he may legitimately allow himself will be determined by the degree of developmental inhibition present in the patient. Some neurotics have remained so infantile that in analysis too they can only be treated as children.

Another advantage of transference, too, is that in it the patient produces before us with plastic clarity an important part of his life-story, of which he would otherwise have probably given us only an insufficient account. He acts it before us, as it were, instead of reporting it to us.

And now for the other side of the situation. Since the transference reproduces the patient's relation with his parents, it takes over the ambivalence of that relation as well. It almost inevitably happens that one day his positive attitude towards the analyst changes over into the negative, hostile one. This too is as a rule a repetition of the past. His obedience to his father (if it is his father that is in question), his courting of his father's favour, had its roots in an erotic wish directed towards him. Some time or other that demand will press its way forward in the transference as well and insist on being satisfied. In the analytic situation it can only meet with frustration. Real sexual relations between patients and analysts are out of the question, and even the subtler methods of satisfaction, such as the giving of preference, intimacy and so on, are only sparingly granted by the analyst. A rejection of this kind is taken as the occasion for the change-over; probably things happened in the same way in the patient's childhood.

The therapeutic successes that occurred under the sway of the positive transference are open to the suspicion of being of a *suggestive* nature. If the negative transference gains the upper hand, they are blown away like chaff before the wind. We observe with horror that all our trouble and labour hitherto have been in vain. Indeed, what we might have regarded as a permanent intellectual gain by the patient, his understanding of psychoanalysis and his reliance on its efficacy, suddenly vanish. He behaves like a child who has no power of judgement of his own but blindly believes anyone whom he loves and no one who is a stranger to him. The danger of these states of transference evidently lies in the patient's misunderstanding their nature and taking them for fresh real experiences instead of reflections of the past. If he (or she) becomes aware of the strong erotic desire that lies concealed behind the positive transference, he believes that he has fallen passionately in love; if the transference changes over, then he feels insulted and neglected, he hates the analyst as his enemy and is ready to abandon the analysis. In both these extreme cases he has forgotten the pact that he made at the beginning of the treatment and has become useless for continuing the common work. It is the analyst's task constantly to tear the patient out of his menacing illusion and to show him again and again that what he takes to be new real life is a reflection of the past. And lest he should fall into a state in which he is inaccessible to all evidence, the analyst takes care that neither the love nor the hostility reach an extreme height. This is effected by preparing him in good time for these possibilities and by not overlooking the first signs of them. Careful handling of the transference on these lines is as a rule richly rewarded. If we succeed, as we usually can, in enlightening the patient on the true nature of the phenomena of transference, we shall have struck a powerful weapon out of the hand of his resistance and shall have converted dangers into gains. For a patient never forgets again what he has experienced in the form of transference; it carries a greater force of conviction than anything he can acquire in other ways.

We think it most undesirable if the patient *acts* outside the transference instead of remembering. The ideal conduct for our purposes would be that he should behave as normally as possible outside the treatment and express his abnormal reactions only in the transference.

The method by which we strengthen the weakened ego has as a starting-point an extending of its self-knowledge. That is not, of course, the whole story but it is a first step. The loss of such knowledge signifies for the ego a surrender of power and influence; it is the first tangible sign that it is being hemmed in and hampered by the demands of the id and the super-ego. Accordingly, the first part of the help we have to offer is intellectual work on our side and encouragement to the patient to collaborate in it. This first kind of activity, as we know, is intended to pave the way to another, more difficult, task. We shall not lose sight of the dynamic element in this task, even during its preliminary stage. We gather the material for our work from a variety of sources – from what is conveyed to us by the information given us by the patient and by his free associations, from what he shows us in his transferences, from what we arrive at by interpreting his dreams and from what he betrays by his slips or *parapraxes*. All this material helps us to make constructions about what happened to him and has been forgotten as well as about what is happening in him now without his understanding it. But in all this we never fail to make a strict distinction between *our* knowledge and *his* knowledge. We avoid telling him at once things that we have often discovered at an early stage, and we avoid telling him the whole of what we think we have discovered. We reflect carefully over when we shall impart the knowledge of one of our constructions to him and we wait for what seems to us the suitable moment – which it is not always easy to decide. As a rule we put off telling him of a construction or explanation till he himself has so nearly arrived at it that only a single step remains to be taken, though that step is in fact the decisive synthesis. If we proceeded in another way and overwhelmed him with our interpretations before he was prepared for them, our information would either produce no effect or it would provoke a violent outbreak of *resistance* which would make the progress of our work more difficult or might even threaten to stop it altogether. But if we have prepared everything properly, it often happens that the patient will at once confirm our construction and himself recollect the internal or external event which he had forgotten. The more exactly the construction coincides with the details of what has been forgotten the easier will it be for him to assent. On that particular matter *our* knowledge will then have become *his* knowledge as well.

With the mention of resistance we have reached the second and more important part of our task. We have already learnt that the ego protects itself against the invasion of undesired elements from the unconscious and repressed id by means of anticathexes, which must remain intact if it is to function normally. The more hard-pressed the ego feels, the more convulsively it clings (as though in a fright) to these anticathexes, in order to protect what remains of itself from further irruptions. But this defensive purpose does not by any means accord with the aims of our treatment. What we desire, on the contrary, is that the ego, emboldened by the certainty of our help, shall dare to take the offensive in order to reconquer what has been lost. And it is here that we become aware of the strength of these anticathexes in the form of *resistances* to our work. The ego draws back in alarm from such undertakings, which seem dangerous and threaten unpleasure; it must be constantly encouraged and soothed if it is not to fail us. This resistance, which persists throughout the whole treatment and is renewed at every fresh piece of work, is known, not quite correctly, as the *resistance due to repression*. We shall find that it is not the only one that faces us. It is interesting to notice that in this situation the party divisions are to some extent reversed: for the ego struggles against our instigation, while the unconscious, which is ordinarily our opponent, comes to our help, since it has a natural 'upward drive' and desires nothing better than to press forward across its settled frontiers into the ego and so to consciousness. The struggle which develops, if we gain our end and can induce the ego to overcome its resistances, is carried through under our direction and with our assistance. Its outcome is a matter of indifference: whether it results in the ego accepting, after a fresh examination, an instinctual demand which it has hitherto rejected, or whether it dismisses it once more, this time for good and all. In either case a permanent danger has been disposed of, the compass of the ego has been extended and a wasteful expenditure of energy has been made unnecessary.

The overcoming of resistances is the part of our work that requires the most time and the greatest trouble. It is worthwhile, however, for it brings about an advantageous alteration of the ego which will be maintained independently of the outcome of the transference and will hold good in life. We have also worked simultaneously at getting rid of the alteration of the ego which had been brought about under the influence of the unconscious; for whenever we have been able to detect any of its derivatives in the ego we have pointed out their illegitimate origin and have instigated the ego to reject them. It will be remembered that it was one of the necessary preconditions of our pact of assistance that any such alteration of the ego due to the intrusion of unconscious elements should not have gone beyond a certain amount.

The further our work proceeds and the more deeply our insight penetrates into the mental life of neurotics, the more clearly two new factors force themselves on our notice, which demand the closest attention as sources of resistance. Both of them are completely unknown to the patient, neither of them could be taken into account when our pact was made; nor do they arise from the patient's ego. They may both be embraced under the single name of 'need to be ill or to suffer', but they have different origins though in other respects they are of a kindred nature. The first of these two factors is the sense of guilt or consciousness of guilt, as it is called, though the patient does not feel it and is not aware of it. It is evidently the portion of the resistance contributed by a super-ego that has become particularly severe and cruel. The patient must not become well but must remain ill, for he deserves no better. This resistance does not actually interfere with our intellectual work, but it makes it inoperative; indeed, it often allows us to remove one form of neurotic suffering, but is ready at once to replace it by another, or perhaps by some somatic illness. The sense of guilt also explains the cure or improvement of severe neuroses which we occasionally observe after real misfortunes: all that matters is that the patient should be miserable – in what way is of no consequence. The uncomplaining resignation with which such people often put up with their hard fate is most remarkable, but also revealing. In warding off this resistance we are obliged to restrict ourselves to making it conscious and attempting to bring about the slow demolition of the hostile super-ego.

It is less easy to demonstrate the existence of another resistance, our means of combating which are specially inadequate. There are some neurotics in whom, to judge by all their reactions, the instinct of self-preservation has actually been reversed. They seem to aim at nothing other than self-injury and self-destruction. It is possible too that the people who in fact do in the end commit suicide belong to this group. It is to be assumed that in such people far-reaching defusions of instinct have taken place, as a result of which there has been a liberation of excessive quantities of the destructive instinct directed inwards. Patients of this kind are not able to tolerate recovery through our treatment and fight against it with all their strength. But we must confess that this is a case which we have not yet succeeded in completely explaining.

Let us once more glance over the situation which we have reached in our attempt at bringing help to the patient's neurotic ego. That ego is no longer able to fulfil the task set it by the external world (including human society). Not all of its experiences are at its disposal, a large proportion of its store of memories have escaped it. Its activity is inhibited by strict prohibitions from the super-ego, its energy is consumed in vain attempts at fending off the demands of the id. Beyond this, as a result of continuous irruptions by the id, its organization is impaired, it is no longer capable of any proper synthesis, it is torn by mutually opposed urges, by unsettled conflicts and by unsolved doubts. To start with, we get the patient's thus weakened ego to take part in the purely intellectual work of interpretation, which aims at provisionally filling the gaps in his mental assets, and to transfer to us the authority of his super-ego; we encourage it to take up the struggle over each individual demand made by the id and to conquer the resistances which arise in connection with it. At the same time we restore order in the ego by detecting the material and urges which have forced their way in from the unconscious, and expose them to criticism by tracing them back to their origin. We serve the patient in various functions, as an authority and a substitute for his parents, as a teacher and educator; and we have done the best for him if, as analysts, we raise the mental processes in his ego to a normal level, transform what has become unconscious and repressed into preconscious material and thus return it once more to the possession of his ego. On the patient's side a few rational factors work in our favour, such as the need for recovery which has its motive in his sufferings, and the intellectual interest that we may awaken in him in the theories and revelations of psychoanalysis; but of far greater force is the positive transference with which he meets us. Fighting against us, on the other hand, are the negative transference, the ego's resistance due to repression (that is, its unpleasure at having to lay itself open to the hard work imposed on it), the sense of guilt arising from its relation to the super-ego and the need to be ill due to deep-going changes in the economics of his instincts. The share taken by the last two factors decides whether the case is to be regarded as slight or severe. Apart from these, a few other factors may be discerned as having a favourable or unfavourable bearing. A certain psychical inertia,[1] a sluggishness of the libido, which is un-

1. [Cf. Freud (1915*f*), *P.F.L.*, **10**, 158 and *n*. 1.]

willing to abandon its fixations, cannot be welcome to us; the patient's capacity of sublimating his instincts plays a large part and so does his capacity for rising above the crude life of the instincts; so, too, does the relative power of his intellectual functions.

We shall not be disappointed, but, on the contrary, we shall find it entirely intelligible, if we reach the conclusion that the final outcome of the struggle we have engaged in depends on *quantitative* relations – on the quota of energy we are able to mobilize in the patient to our advantage as compared with the sum of energy of the powers working against us. Here once again God is on the side of the big battalions. It is true that we do not always succeed in winning, but at least we can usually recognize why we have not won. Those who have been following our discussion only out of therapeutic interest will perhaps turn away in contempt after this admission. But here we are concerned with therapy only in so far as it works by psychological means; and for the time being we have no other. The future may teach us to exercise a direct influence, by means of particular chemical substances, on the amounts of energy and their distribution in the mental apparatus. It may be that there are other still undreamt-of possibilities of therapy. But for the moment we have nothing better at our disposal than the technique of psychoanalysis, and for that reason, in spite of its limitations, it should not be despised.

Chapter VII
AN EXAMPLE OF PSYCHOANALYTIC WORK

WE have arrived at a general acquaintance with the psychical apparatus, with the parts, organs and agencies of which it is composed, with the forces which operate in it and with the functions allotted to its parts. The neuroses and psychoses are the states in which disturbances in the functioning of the apparatus come to expression. We have chosen the neuroses as the subjects of our study because they alone seem accessible to the psychological methods of our intervention. While we are trying to influence them, we collect observations which give us a picture of their origin and of the manner in which they arise.

I will state in advance one of our chief findings before proceeding with my description. The neuroses (unlike infectious diseases, for instance) have no specific determinants. It would be idle to seek in them for pathogenic excitants. They shade off by easy transitions into what is described as the normal; and, on the other hand, there is scarcely any state recognized as normal in which indications of neurotic traits could not be pointed out. Neurotics have approximately the same innate dispositions as other people, they have the same experiences and they have the same tasks to perform. Why is it, then, that they live so much worse and with so much greater difficulty and, in the process, suffer more feelings of unpleasure, anxiety and pain?

We need not be at a loss to find an answer to this question. Quantitative *disharmonies* are what must be held responsible for the inadequacy and sufferings of neurotics. The determining cause of all the forms taken by human mental life, is, indeed, to be sought in the reciprocal action between innate dispositions and accidental experiences. Now a particular instinct may be too strong or too weak innately, or a particular capacity may be stunted or insufficiently developed in life. On the other hand, external impressions and experiences may make demands of differing strength on different people; and what one person's constitution can deal with may prove an unmanageable task for another's. These quantitative differences will determine the variety of the results.

We shall very soon feel, however, that this explanation is unsatisfactory: it is too general, it explains too much. The aetiology put forward applies to every case of mental suffering, misery and disablement, but not every such state can be termed neurotic. The neuroses have specific characteristics, they are miseries of a particular kind. So we must after all expect to find particular causes for them. Or we may adopt the supposition that, among the tasks with which mental life has to deal, there are a few on which it can especially easily come to grief; so that the peculiarity of the phenomena of neurosis, which are often so very remarkable, would follow from this without our needing to withdraw our earlier assertions. If it remains true that the neuroses do not differ in any essential respect from the normal, their study promises to yield us valuable contributions to our knowledge of the normal. It may be that we shall thus discover the 'weak points' in a normal organization.

The supposition we have just made finds confirmation. Analytic experiences teach us that there is in fact one instinctual demand, attempts to deal with which most easily fail or succeed imperfectly, and that there is one period of life which comes in question exclusively or predominantly in connection with the generation of a neurosis. These two factors – the nature of the instinct and the period of life concerned – call for separate consideration, although they are closely enough connected.

We can speak with a fair degree of certainty about the part played by the period of life. It seems that neuroses are acquired only in early childhood (up to the age of six), even though their symptoms may not make their appearance till much later. The childhood neurosis may become manifest for a short time or may even be overlooked. In every case the later neurotic illness links up with the prelude in childhood. It is possible that what are known as traumatic neuroses (due to excessive fright or severe somatic shocks, such as railway collisions, burial under falls of earth, and so on) are an exception to this: their relations to determinants in childhood have hitherto eluded investigation. There is no difficulty in accounting for this aetiological preference for the first period of childhood. The neuroses are, as we know, disorders of the ego; and it is not to be wondered at if the ego, so long as it is feeble, immature and incapable of resistance, fails to deal with tasks which it could cope with later on with the utmost ease. In these circumstances instinctual demands from within, no less than excitations from the external world, operate as 'traumas', particularly if they are met half-way by certain innate dispositions. The helpless ego fends them off by means of attempts at flight (*repressions*), which later turn out to be inefficient and which involve permanent restrictions on further development. The damage inflicted on the ego by its first experiences gives us the appearance of being disproportionately great; but we have only to take as an analogy the differences in the results produced by the prick of a needle into a mass of cells in the act of cell division (as in Roux's experiments) and into the fully grown animal which eventually develops out of them.[1] No human individual is spared such traumatic experiences; none escapes the repressions to which they give rise. These questionable reactions on the part of the ego may perhaps be indispensable for the attainment of another aim which is set for the same period of life: in the space of a few years the little primitive creature must turn into a civilized human being; he must pass through an immensely long stretch of human cultural development in an almost uncannily abbreviated form. This is made possible by hereditary disposition; but it can almost never be achieved without the additional help of upbringing, of parental influence, which, as a precursor of the super-ego, restricts the ego's activity by prohibitions and punishments, and encourages or compels the setting-up of repressions. We must therefore not forget to include the in-

1. [Wilhelm Roux (1850–1924) was one of the founders of experimental embryology.]

fluence of civilization among the determinants of neurosis. It is easy, as we can see, for a barbarian to be healthy; for a civilized man the task is hard. The desire for a powerful, uninhibited ego may seem to us intelligible; but, as we are taught by the times we live in, it is in the profoundest sense hostile to civilization. And since the demands of civilization are represented by family upbringing, we must bear in mind the part played by this biological characteristic of the human species – the prolonged period of its childhood dependence – in the aetiology of the neuroses.

As regards the other point – the specific instinctual factor – we come upon an interesting discrepancy between theory and experience. Theoretically there is no objection to supposing that any sort of instinctual demand might occasion the same repressions and their consequences; but our observation shows us invariably, so far as we can judge, that the excitations that play this pathogenic part arise from the component instincts of sexual life. The symptoms of neuroses are, it might be said, without exception either a substitutive satisfaction of some sexual urge or measures to prevent such a satisfaction; and as a rule they are compromises between the two, of the kind that come about in accordance with the laws operating between contraries in the unconscious. The gap in our theory cannot at present be filled; our decision is made more difficult by the fact that most of the urges of sexual life are not of a purely erotic nature but have arisen from alloys of the erotic instinct with portions of the destructive instinct. But it cannot be doubted that the instincts which manifest themselves physiologically as sexuality play a prominent, unexpectedly large part in the causation of the neuroses – whether it is an exclusive one remains to be decided. It must also be borne in mind that in the course of cultural development no other function has been so energetically and extensively repudiated as precisely the sexual one. Theory must rest satisfied with a few hints that betray a deeper connection: the fact that the first period of childhood, during which the ego begins to be differentiated from the id, is also the period of the early sexual efflorescence which is brought to an end by the period of latency; that it can hardly be a matter of chance that this momentous early period subsequently falls a victim to infantile amnesia; and lastly, that biological changes in sexual life (such as the function's diphasic onset which we have already mentioned, the disappearance of the periodic character of sexual excitation and the transformation in the relation between female menstruation and male excitation) – that these innovations in sexuality must have been of high importance in the evolution of animals into man. It is left for the science of the future to bring these still isolated data together into a new understanding. It is not in psychology but in biology that there is a gap here. We shall not be wrong, perhaps, in saying that the weak point in the ego's organization seems to lie in its attitude to the sexual function, as though the biological antithesis between self-preservation and the preservation of the species had found a psychological expression at that point.

Analytic experience has convinced us of the complete truth of the assertion so often to be heard that the child is psychologically father to the adult and that the events of his first years are of paramount importance for his whole later life. It will thus be of special interest to us if there is something that may be described as the central experience of this period of childhood. Our attention is first attracted by the effects of certain influences which do not apply to all children, though they are common enough – such as the sexual abuse of children by adults, their seduction by other children (brothers or sisters) slightly their seniors, and, what we should not expect, their being deeply stirred by seeing or hearing at first hand sexual behaviour between adults (their parents) mostly at a time at which one would not have thought they could either be interested in or understand any such impressions, or be capable of remembering them later. It is easy to confirm the extent to which such experiences arouse a child's susceptibility and force his own sexual urges into certain channels from which they cannot afterwards depart. Since these impressions are subjected to repression either at once or as soon as they seek to return as memories, they constitute the determinant for the neurotic compulsion which will subsequently make it impossible for the ego to control the sexual function and will probably cause it to turn away from that function permanently. If this latter reaction occurs, the result will be a neurosis; if it is absent, a variety of perversions will develop, or the function, which is of immense importance not only for reproduction but also for the entire shaping of life, will become totally unmanageable.

However instructive cases of this kind may be, a still higher degree of interest must attach to the influence of a situation which every child is destined to pass through and which follows inevitably from the factor of the prolonged period during which a child is cared for by other people and lives with his parents. I am thinking of the *Oedipus complex*, so named because its essential substance is to be found in the Greek legend of King Oedipus, which has fortunately been preserved for us in a version by a great dramatist. The Greek hero killed his father and took his mother to wife. That he did so unwittingly, since he did not know them as his parents, is a deviation from the analytic facts which we can easily understand and which, indeed, we shall recognize as inevitable.

At this point we must give separate accounts of the development of boys and girls (of males and females), for it is now that the difference between the sexes finds psychological expression for the first time. We are faced here by the great enigma of the biological fact of the duality of the sexes: it is an ultimate fact for our knowledge, it defies every attempt to trace it back to something else. Psychoanalysis has contributed nothing to clearing up this problem, which clearly falls wholly within the province of biology. In mental life we only find reflections of this great antithesis; and their interpretation is made more difficult by the fact, long suspected, that no individual is limited to the modes of reaction of a single sex but always finds some room for those of the opposite one, just as his body bears, alongside of the fully developed organs of one sex, atrophied and often useless rudiments of those of the other. For distinguishing between male and female in mental life we make use of what is obviously an inadequate empirical and conventional equation: we call everything that is strong and active male, and everything that is weak and passive female. This fact of psychological bisexuality, too, embarrasses all our inquiries into the subject and makes them harder to describe.

A child's first erotic object is the mother's breast that nourishes it; love has its origin in attachment to the satisfied need for nourishment. There is no doubt that, to begin with, the child does not distinguish between the breast and its own body; when the breast has to be separated from the body and shifted to the '*outside*' because the child so often finds it absent, it carries with it as an '*object*' a part of the original narcissistic libidinal cathexis. This first object is later completed into the person of the child's mother, who not only nourishes it but also looks after it and thus arouses in it a number of other physical sensations, pleasurable and unpleasurable. By her care of the child's body she becomes its first seducer. In these two relations lies the root of a mother's importance, unique, without parallel, established unalterably for a whole lifetime as the first and strongest love-object and as the prototype of all later love relations – for both sexes. In all this the phylogenetic foundation has so much the upper hand over personal accidental experience that it makes no difference whether a child has really sucked at the breast or has been brought up on the bottle and never enjoyed the tenderness of a mother's care. In both cases the child's development takes the same path; it may be that in the second case its later longing grows all the greater. And for however long it is fed at its mother's breast, it will always be left with a conviction after it has been weaned that its feeding was too short and too little.

This preface is not superfluous, for it can heighten our realization of the intensity of the Oedipus complex. When a boy (from the age of two or three) has entered the phallic phase of his libidinal development, is feeling pleasurable sensations in his sexual organ and has learnt to procure these at will by manual stimulation, he becomes his mother's lover. He wishes to possess her physically in such ways as he has divined from his observations and intuitions about sexual life, and he tries to seduce her by showing her the male organ which he is proud to own. In a word, his early awakened masculinity seeks to take his father's place with her; his father has hitherto in any case been an envied model to the boy, owing to the physical strength he perceives in him and the authority with which he finds him clothed. His father now becomes a rival who stands in his way and whom he would like to get rid of. If while his father is away he is allowed to share his mother's bed and if when his father returns he is once more banished from it, his satisfaction when his father disappears and his disappointment when he emerges again are deeply felt experiences. This is the subject of the Oedipus complex, which the Greek legend has translated from the world of a child's fantasy into pretended reality. Under the conditions of our civilization it is invariably doomed to a frightening end.

The boy's mother has understood quite well that his sexual excitation relates to herself. Sooner or later she reflects that it is not right to allow it to continue. She thinks she is doing the correct thing in forbidding him to handle his genital organ. Her prohibition has little effect; at the most it brings about some modification in his method of obtaining satisfaction. At last his mother adopts the severest measures; she threatens to take away from him the thing he is defying her with. Usually, in order to make the threat more frightening and more credible, she delegates its execution to the boy's father, saying that she will tell him and that he will cut the penis off. Strange to say, this threat operates only if another condition is fulfilled before or afterwards. In itself it seems too inconceivable to the boy that such a thing could happen. But if at the time of the threat he can recall the appearance of female genitals or if shortly afterwards he has a sight of them – of genitals, that is to say, which really lack this supremely valued part, then he takes what he has heard seriously and, coming under the influence of the *castration complex*, experiences the severest trauma of his young life.[1]

1. Castration has a place too in the Oedipus legend, for the blinding with

The results of the threat of castration are multifarious and incalculable; they affect the whole of a boy's relations with his father and mother and subsequently with men and women in general. As a rule the child's masculinity is unable to stand up to this first shock. In order to preserve his sexual organ he renounces the possession of his mother more or less completely; his sexual life often remains permanently encumbered by the prohibition. If a strong feminine component, as we call it, is present in him, its strength is increased by this intimidation of his masculinity. He falls into a passive attitude to his father, such as he attributes to his mother. It is true that as a result of the threat he has given up masturbation, but not the activities of his imagination accompanying it. On the contrary, since these are now the only form of sexual satisfaction remaining to him, he indulges in them more than before and in these fantasies, though he still continues to identify himself with his father, he also does so, simultaneously and perhaps predominantly, with his mother. Derivatives and modified products of these early masturbatory fantasies usually make their way into his later ego and play a part in the formation of his character. Apart from this encouragement of his femininity, fear and hatred of his father gain greatly in intensity. The boy's masculinity withdraws, as it were, into a defiant attitude towards his father, which will dominate his later behaviour in human society in a compulsive fashion. A residue of his erotic fixation to his mother is often left in the form of an excessive dependence on her, and this persists as a kind of bondage to

---

which Oedipus punishes himself after the discovery of his crime is, by the evidence of dreams, a symbolic substitute for castration. The possibility cannot be excluded that a phylogenetic memory-trace may contribute to the extraordinarily terrifying effect of the threat – a memory-trace from the prehistory of the primal family, when the jealous father actually robbed his son of his genitals if the latter became troublesome to him as a rival with a woman. The primeval custom of circumcision, another symbolic substitute for castration, can only be understood as an expression of submission to the father's will. (Cf. the puberty rites of primitive peoples.) No investigation has yet been made of the form taken by the events described above among peoples and in civilizations which do not suppress masturbation in children.

women.[1] He no longer ventures to love his mother, but he cannot risk not being loved by her, for in that case he would be in danger of being betrayed by her to his father and handed over to castration. The whole experience, with all its antecedents and consequences, of which my account has only been able to give a selection, is subjected to a highly energetic repression, and, as is made possible by the laws operating in the unconscious id, all the mutually contending emotional impulses and reactions which are set going at that time are preserved in the unconscious and ready to disturb the later development of the ego after puberty. When the somatic process of sexual maturation puts fresh life into the old libidinal fixations which had apparently been surmounted, sexual life will turn out to be inhibited, without homogeneity and fallen apart into mutually conflicting urges.

It is no doubt true that the impact of the threat of castration upon a boy's budding sexual life does not always have these dreaded consequences. It will depend once again on *quantitative* relations how much damage is done and how much avoided. The whole occurrence, which may probably be regarded as the central experience of the years of childhood, the greatest problem of early life and the strongest source of later inadequacy, is so completely forgotten that its reconstruction during the work of analysis is met in adults by the most decided disbelief. Indeed, aversion to it is so great that people try to silence any mention of the proscribed subject and the most obvious reminders of it are overlooked by a strange intellectual blindness. One may hear it objected, for instance, that the legend of King Oedipus has in fact no connection with the construction made by analysis: the cases are quite different, since Oedipus did not know that it was his father that he killed and his mother that he married. What is overlooked in this is that a distortion of this kind is inevitable if an attempt is made at a poetic handling of the material, and that there is no introduction of extraneous material but only a skilful employment of the factors presented by the theme. The ignorance of Oedipus

1. [Cf. 'The Taboo of Virginity' (1918a), *P.F.L.*, **7**, 265–6.]

is a legitimate representation of the unconscious state into which, for adults, the whole experience has fallen; and the coercive power of the oracle, which makes or should make the hero innocent, is a recognition of the inevitability of the fate which has condemned every son to live through the Oedipus complex. Again it was pointed out from psychoanalytic quarters how easily the riddle of another dramatic hero, Shakespeare's procrastinator, Hamlet, can be solved by reference to the Oedipus complex, since the prince came to grief over the task of punishing someone else for what coincided with the substance of his own Oedipus wish – whereupon the general lack of understanding on the part of the literary world showed how ready is the mass of mankind to hold fast to its infantile repressions.[1]

Yet more than a century before the emergence of psychoanalysis the French philospher Diderot bore witness to the importance of the Oedipus complex by expressing the difference between the primitive and civilized worlds in this sentence: 'Si le petit sauvage était abandonné à lui-même, qu'il conservât toute son imbécillité, et qu'il réunît au peu de raison de l'enfant au berceau la violence des passions de l'homme de trente ans, il tordrait le col à son père et coucherait avec sa mère.'[2] I venture

---

1. The name 'William Shakespeare' is very probably a pseudonym behind which a great unknown lies concealed. Edward de Vere, Earl of Oxford, a man who has been thought to be identifiable with the author of Shakespeare's works, lost a beloved and admired father while he was still a boy and completely repudiated his mother, who contracted a new marriage very soon after her husband's death. – [Freud's first mention of this view was in a sentence added in 1930 to a footnote to Chapter V (D) of *The Interpretation of Dreams* (1900a), *P.F.L.*, 4, 368 n. He enlarged on the point in his 'Address in the Goethe House' (1930e), ibid., 14, 470–71 and n., and in the *Autobiographical Study* (1925d), p. 248 n. above. He referred to it once more in *Moses and Monotheism* (1939a), ibid., 13, 307 n. A letter from Freud arguing in favour of his opinion is included in the third volume of Jones's biography (1957, 487–8).]

2. ['If the little savage were left to himself, preserving all his foolishness and adding to the small sense of a child in the cradle the violent passions of a man of thirty, he would strangle his father and lie with his mother.' From *Le neveu de Rameau*.]

to say that if psychoanalysis could boast of no other achievement than the discovery of the repressed Oedipus complex, that alone would give it a claim to be included among the precious new acquisitions of mankind.

The effects of the castration complex in little girls are more uniform and no less profound. A female child has, of course, no need to fear the loss of a penis; she must, however, react to the fact of not having received one. From the very first she envies boys its possession; her whole development may be said to take place under the colours of envy for the penis. She begins by making vain attempts to do the same as boys and later, with greater success, makes efforts to compensate for her defect – efforts which may lead in the end to a normal feminine attitude. If during the phallic phase she tries to get pleasure like a boy by the manual stimulation of her genitals, it often happens that she fails to obtain sufficient satisfaction and extends her judgement of inferiority from her stunted penis to her whole self. As a rule she soon gives up masturbating, since she has no wish to be reminded of the superiority of her brother or playmate, and turns away from sexuality altogether.

If a little girl persists in her first wish – to grow into a boy – in extreme cases she will end as a manifest homosexual, and otherwise she will exhibit markedly masculine traits in the conduct of her later life, will choose a masculine vocation, and so on. The other path leads by way of abandoning the mother she has loved: the daughter, under the influence of her envy for the penis, cannot forgive her mother for having sent her into the world so insufficiently equipped. In her resentment over this she gives up her mother and puts someone else in her place as the object of her love – her father. If one has lost a love-object, the most obvious reaction is to identify oneself with it, to replace it from within, as it were, by identification. This mechanism now comes to the little girl's help. Identification with her mother can take the place of attachment to her mother. The little daughter puts herself in her mother's place, as she has always done in her games; she tries to take her mother's place with her father, and begins to hate the mother she used to love, and from two motives: from jealousy as well as from mortification over the penis she has been denied. Her new relation to her father may start by having as its content a wish to have his penis at her disposal, but it culminates in another wish – to have a baby from him as a gift. The wish for a baby has thus taken the place of the wish for a penis, or has at all events split off from it.

It is an interesting thing that the relation between the Oedipus complex and the castration complex should take such a different shape – an opposite one, in fact – in the case of females as compared to that of males. In males, as we have seen, the threat of castration brings the Oedipus complex to an end; in females we find that, on the contrary, it is their lack of a penis that forces them into their Oedipus complex. It does little harm to a woman if she remains in her feminine Oedipus attitude. (The term 'Electra complex' has been proposed for it.[1]) She will in that case choose her husband for his paternal characteristics and be ready to recognize his authority. Her longing to possess a penis, which is in fact unappeasable, may find satisfaction if she can succeed in completing her love for the organ by extending it to the bearer of the organ, just as happened earlier when she progressed from her mother's breast to her mother as a whole person.

If we ask an analyst what his experience has shown to be the mental structures least accessible to influence in his patients, the answer will be: in a woman her wish for a penis, in a man his feminine attitude towards his own sex, a precondition of which would, of course, be the loss of his penis.[2]

1. [The term seems to have been used first by Jung (1913, 370). Freud argued against its introduction in his paper on 'Female Sexuality' (1931*b*), *P.F.L.*, **7**, 375.]

2. [Freud had discussed this at much greater length in Section VIII of 'Analysis Terminable and Interminable' (1937*c*). Cf. also Ferenczi (1928).]

PART III
THE THEORETICAL YIELD

CHAPTER VIII
THE PSYCHICAL APPARATUS
AND THE EXTERNAL WORLD

ALL of the general discoveries and hypotheses which I brought forward in the first chapter were, of course, arrived at by laborious and patient detailed work of the kind of which I have given an example in the previous chapter. We may now feel tempted to make a survey of the increases in knowledge that we have achieved by work such as this and to consider what paths we have opened for further advances. In this connection we may be struck by the fact that we have so often been obliged to venture beyond the frontiers of the science of psychology. The phenomena with which we were dealing do not belong to psychology alone; they have an organic and biological side as well, and accordingly in the course of our efforts at building up psychoanalysis we have also made some important biological discoveries and have not been able to avoid framing new biological hypotheses.

But let us for the moment keep to psychology. We have seen that it is not scientifically feasible to draw a line of demarcation between what is psychically normal and abnormal; so that that distinction, in spite of its practical importance, possesses only a conventional value. We have thus established a right to arrive at an understanding of the normal life of the mind from a study of its disorders — which would not be admissible if these pathological states, neuroses and psychoses, had specific causes operating in the manner of foreign bodies.

The study of a mental disorder occurring during sleep, which is transient and harmless and which, indeed, performs a useful

430

function, has given us a key to the understanding of the mental diseases which are permanent and injurious to life. And we may now venture on the assertion that the psychology of consciousness was no better capable of understanding the normal functioning of the mind than of understanding dreams. The data of conscious self-perception, which alone were at its disposal, have proved in every respect inadequate to fathom the profusion and complexity of the processes of the mind, to reveal their interconnections and so to recognize the determinants of their disturbances.

The hypothesis we have adopted of a psychical apparatus extended in space, expediently put together, developed by the exigencies of life, which gives rise to the phenomena of consciousness only at one particular point and under certain conditions – this hypothesis has put us in a position to establish psychology on foundations similar to those of any other science, such, for instance, as physics. In our science as in the others the problem is the same: behind the attributes (qualities) of the object under examination which are presented directly to our perception, we have to discover something else which is more independent of the particular receptive capacity of our sense-organs and which approximates more closely to what may be supposed to be the real state of affairs. We have no hope of being able to reach the latter itself, since it is evident that everything new that we have inferred must nevertheless be translated back into the language of our perceptions, from which it is simply impossible for us to free ourselves. But herein lies the very nature and limitation of our science. It is as though we were to say in physics: 'If we could see clearly enough we should find that what appears to be a solid body is made up of particles of such and such a shape and size and occupying such and such relative positions.' In the meantime we try to increase the efficiency of our sense-organs to the furthest possible extent by artificial aids; but it may be expected that all such efforts will fail to affect the ultimate outcome. Reality will always remain 'unknowable'. The yield brought to light by scientific work from our primary sense perceptions will consist in an insight into connections and dependent relations which are present in the external world, which can somehow be reliably reproduced or reflected in the internal world of our thought and a knowledge of which enables us to 'understand' something in the external world, to foresee it and possibly to alter it. Our procedure in psychoanalysis is quite similar. We have discovered technical methods of filling up the gaps in the phenomena of our consciousness, and we make use of those methods just as a physicist makes use of experiment. In this manner we infer a number of processes which are in themselves 'unknowable' and interpolate them in those that are conscious to us. And if, for instance, we say: 'At this point an unconscious memory intervened', what that means is: 'At this point something occurred of which we are totally unable to form a conception, but which, if it had entered our consciousness, could only have been described in such and such a way.'

Our justification for making such inferences and interpolations and the degree of certainty attaching to them of course remain open to criticism in each individual instance; and it cannot be denied that it is often extremely difficult to arrive at a decision – a fact which finds expression in the lack of agreement among analysts. The novelty of the problem is to blame for this – that is to say, a lack of training. But there is besides this a special factor inherent in the subject itself; for in psychology, unlike physics, we are not always concerned with things which can only arouse a cool scientific interest. Thus we shall not be very greatly surprised if a woman analyst who has not been sufficiently convinced of the intensity of her own wish for a penis also fails to attach proper importance to that factor in her patients. But such sources of error, arising from the personal equation, have no great importance in the long run. If one looks through old textbooks on the use of the microscope, one is astonished to find the extraordinary demands which were made on the personality of those who made observations with that instrument while its technique was still young – of all of which there is no question today.

I cannot undertake to attempt a complete picture here of the psychical apparatus and its activities; I should find myself hindered, among other things, by the circumstance that psychoanalysis has not yet had time to study all those functions equally. I shall therefore content myself with a detailed recapitulation of the account in my opening chapter.

The core of our being, then, is formed by the obscure *id*, which has no direct communication with the external world and is accessible even to our own knowledge only through the medium of another agency. Within this id the organic *instincts* operate, which are themselves compounded of fusions of two primal forces (Eros and destructiveness) in varying proportions and are differentiated from one another by their relation to organs or systems of organs. The one and only urge of these instincts is towards satisfaction, which is expected to arise from certain changes in the organs with the help of objects in the external world. But immediate and unheeding satisfaction of the instincts, such as the id demands, would often lead to perilous conflicts with the external world and to extinction. The id knows no solicitude about ensuring survival and no anxiety; or it would perhaps be more correct to say that, though it can generate the sensory elements of anxiety, it cannot make use of them. The processes which are possible in and between the assumed psychical elements in the id (the *primary process*) differ widely from those which are familiar to us through conscious perception in our intellectual and emotional life; nor are they subject to the critical restrictions of logic, which repudiates some of these processes as invalid and seeks to undo them.

The id, cut off from the external world, has a world of perception of its own. It detects with extraordinary acuteness certain changes in its interior, especially oscillations in the tension of its instinctual needs, and these changes become conscious as feelings in the pleasure–unpleasure series. It is hard to say, to be sure, by what means and with the help of what sensory terminal organs these perceptions come about. But it is an established fact that self-perceptions – coenaesthetic feelings and feelings of pleasure–unpleasure – govern the passage of events in the id with despotic force. The id obeys the inexorable pleasure principle. But not the id alone. It seems that the activity of the other psychical agencies too is able only to modify the pleasure principle but not to nullify it; and it remains a question of the highest theoretical importance, and one that has not yet been answered, when and how it is ever possible for the pleasure principle to be overcome. The consideration that the pleasure principle demands a reduction, at bottom the extinction perhaps, of the tensions of instinctual needs (that is, *Nirvana*) leads to the still unassessed relations between the pleasure principle and the two primal forces, Eros and the death instinct.

The other agency of the mind, which we believe we know best and in which we recognize ourselves most easily – what is known as the *ego* – has been developed out of the id's cortical layer, which, through being adapted to the reception and exclusion of stimuli, is in direct contact with the external world (*reality*). Starting from conscious perception it has subjected to its influence ever larger regions and deeper strata of the id, and, in the persistence with which it maintains its dependence on the external world, it bears the indelible stamp of its origin (as it might be 'Made in Germany'). Its psychological function consists in raising the passage [of events] in the id to a higher dynamic level (perhaps by transforming freely mobile energy into bound energy, such as corresponds to the preconscious state); its constructive function consists in interpolating, between the demand made by an instinct and the action that satisfies it, the activity of thought which, after taking its bearings in the present and assessing earlier experiences, endeavours by means of experimental actions to calculate the consequences of the course of action proposed. In this way the ego comes to a decision on whether the attempt to obtain satisfaction is to be carried out or postponed or whether it may not be necessary for the demand by the instinct to be suppressed altogether as being dangerous. (Here we have the *reality principle*.) Just as the id is directed exclusively to obtaining pleasure, so the ego is governed by considerations of safety. The ego has set itself the task of self-preservation, which the id appears to neglect. It [the ego] makes use of the sensations of anxiety as a signal to give a warning of dangers that threaten its integrity. Since memory-traces can become conscious just as perceptions do, especially through their association with residues of speech, the possibility arises of a confusion which would lead to a mistaking of reality. The ego guards itself against this possibility by the institution of *reality-testing*, which is allowed to fall into abeyance in dreams on account of the conditions prevailing in the state of sleep. The ego, which seeks to maintain itself in an environment of overwhelming mechanical forces, is threatened by dangers which come in the first instance from external reality; but dangers do not threaten it from there alone. Its own id is a source of similar dangers, and that for two different reasons. In the first place, an excessive strength of instinct can damage the ego in a similar way to an excessive 'stimulus' from the external world. It is true that the former cannot destroy it; but it can destroy its characteristic dynamic organization and change the ego back into a portion of the id. In the second place, experience may have taught the ego that the satisfaction of some instinctual demand which is not in itself intolerable would involve dangers in the external world, so that an instinctual demand of that kind itself becomes a danger. Thus the ego is fighting on two fronts: it has to defend its existence against an external world which threatens it with annihilation as well as against an internal world that makes excessive demands. It adopts the same methods of defence against both, but its defence against the internal enemy is particularly inadequate. As a result of having originally been identical with this latter enemy and of having lived with it since on the most intimate terms, it has great difficulty in escaping from the internal dangers. They persist as threats, even if they can be temporarily held down.

We have heard how the weak and immature ego of the first period of childhood is permanently damaged by the stresses put upon it in its efforts to fend off the dangers that are peculiar to that period of life. Children are protected against the dangers that threaten them from the external world by the solicitude of their parents; they pay for this security by a fear of *loss of love* which would deliver them over helpless to the dangers of the external world. This factor exerts a decisive influence on the outcome of the conflict when a boy finds himself in the situation of the Oedipus complex, in which the threat to his narcissism by the danger of castration, reinforced from primeval sources, takes possession of him. Driven by the combined operation of these two influences, the contemporary real danger and the remembered one with its phylogenetic basis, the child embarks on his attempts at defence – repressions – which are effective for the moment but nevertheless turn out to be psychologically inadequate when the later reanimation of sexual life brings a reinforcement to the instinctual demands which have been repudiated in the past. If this is so, it would have to be said from a biological standpoint that the ego comes to grief over the task of mastering the excitations of the early sexual period, at a time when its immaturity makes it incompetent to do so. It is in this lagging of ego development behind libidinal development that we see the essential precondition of neurosis; and we cannot escape the conclusion that neuroses could be avoided if the childish ego were spared this task – if, that is to say, the child's sexual life were allowed free play, as happens among many primitive peoples. It may be that the aetiology of neurotic illnesses is more complicated than we have here described it; if so, we have at least brought out one essential part of the aetiological complex. Nor should we forget the phylogenetic influences, which are represented in some way in the id in forms that we are not yet able to grasp, and which must certainly act upon the ego more powerfully in that early period than later. On the other hand, the realization dawns on us that such an early attempt at damming up the sexual instinct, so decided a partisanship by the young ego in favour of the external as opposed to the internal world, brought about by the prohibition of infantile sexuality, cannot be without its effect on the individual's later readiness for culture.[1]

[1]. [The similar concept of 'susceptibility to culture' is discussed by Freud in 'Thoughts for the Times on War and Death' (1915b), *P.F.L.*, **12**, 70, and is also mentioned in *The Future of an Illusion* (1927c), ibid., **12**, 220. Freud made no distinction between the use of the words 'culture' and 'civilization'.]

The instinctual demands forced away from direct satisfaction are compelled to enter on new paths leading to substitutive satisfaction, and in the course of these *détours* they may become desexualized and their connection with their original instinctual aims may become looser. And at this point we may anticipate the thesis that many of the highly valued assets of our civilization were acquired at the cost of sexuality and by the restriction of sexual motive forces.

We have repeatedly had to insist on the fact that the ego owes its origin as well as the most important of its acquired characteristics to its relation to the real external world. We are thus prepared to assume that the ego's pathological states, in which it most approximates once again to the id, are founded on a cessation or slackening of that relation to the external world. This tallies very well with what we learn from clinical experience – namely, that the precipitating cause of the outbreak of a psychosis is either that reality has become intolerably painful or that the instincts have become extraordinarily intensified – both of which, in view of the rival claims made on the ego by the id and the external world, must lead to the same result. The problem of psychoses would be simple and perspicuous if the ego's detachment from reality could be carried through completely. But that seems to happen only rarely or perhaps never. Even in a state so far removed from the reality of the external world as one of hallucinatory confusion,[1] one learns from patients after their recovery that at the time in some corner of their mind (as they put it) there was a normal person hidden, who, like a detached spectator, watched the hubbub of illness go past him. I do not know if we may assume that this is so in general, but I can report the same of other psychoses with a less tempestuous course. I call to mind a case of chronic paranoia in which after each attack of jealousy a dream conveyed to the analyst a correct picture of the precipitating cause, free from any delusion.[2] An interest-

1. [Freud adds the term 'amentia', used by Meynert in this sense.]
2. [This case is reported at some length in Freud's paper 'Some Neurotic Mechanisms' (1922*b*), *P.F.L.*, **10**, 195.]

ing contrast was thus brought to light: while we are accustomed to discover from the dreams of neurotics jealousies which are alien to their waking lives, in this psychotic case the delusion which dominated the patient in the daytime was corrected by his dream. We may probably take it as being generally true that what occurs in all these cases is a psychical *split*. Two psychical attitudes have been formed instead of a single one – one, the normal one, which takes account of reality, and another which under the influence of the instincts detaches the ego from reality. The two exist alongside of each other. The issue depends on their relative strength. If the second is or becomes the stronger, the necessary precondition for a psychosis is present. If the relation is reversed, then there is an apparent cure of the delusional disorder. Actually it has only retreated into the unconscious – just as numerous observations lead us to believe that the delusion existed ready-made for a long time before its manifest irruption.

The view which postulates that in all psychoses there is a *splitting of the ego* could not call for so much notice if it did not turn out to apply to other states more like the neuroses and, finally, to the neuroses themselves. I first became convinced of this in cases of *fetishism*. This abnormality, which may be counted as one of the perversions, is, as is well known, based on the patient (who is almost always male) not recognizing the fact that females have no penis – a fact which is extremely undesirable to him since it is a proof of the possibility of his being castrated himself. He therefore disavows his own sense perception which showed him that the female genitals lack a penis and holds fast to the contrary conviction. The disavowed perception does not, however, remain entirely without influence for, in spite of everything, he has not the courage to assert that he actually saw a penis. He takes hold of something else instead – a part of the body or some other object – and assigns it the role of the penis which he cannot do without. It is usually something that he in fact saw at the moment at which he saw the female genitals, or it is something that can suitably serve as a symbolic substitute for the penis. Now it would be incorrect to describe this process when a fetish is constructed as a splitting of the ego; it is a compromise formed with the help of displacement, such as we have been familiar with in dreams. But our observations show us still more. The creation of the fetish was due to an intention to destroy the evidence for the possibility of castration, so that fear of castration could be avoided. If females, like other living creatures, possess a penis, there is no need to tremble for the continued possession of one's own penis. Now we come across fetishists who have developed the same fear of castration as non-fetishists and react in the same way to it. Their behaviour is therefore simultaneously expressing two contrary premises. On the one hand they are disavowing the fact of their perception – the fact that they saw no penis in the female genitals; and on the other hand they are recognizing the fact that females have no penis and are drawing the correct conclusions from it. The two attitudes persist side by side throughout their lives without influencing each other. Here is what may rightly be called a splitting of the ego. This circumstance also enables us to understand how it is that fetishism is so often only partially developed. It does not govern the choice of object exclusively but leaves room for a greater or lesser amount of normal sexual behaviour; sometimes, indeed, it retires into playing a modest part or is limited to a mere hint. In fetishists, therefore, the detachment of the ego from the reality of the external world has never succeeded completely.

It must not be thought that fetishism presents an exceptional case as regards a splitting of the ego; it is merely a particularly favourable subject for studying the question. Let us return to our thesis that the childish ego, under the domination of the real world, gets rid of undesirable instinctual demands by what are called repressions. We will now supplement this by further asserting that, during the same period of life, the ego often enough finds itself in the position of fending off some demand from the external world which it feels distressing and that this is effected by means of a *disavowal* of the perceptions which bring to knowledge this demand from reality. Disavowals of this kind occur very often and not only with fetishists; and whenever we are in a position to study them they turn out to be half-measures, incomplete attempts at detachment from reality. The disavowal is always supplemented by an acknowledgement; two contrary and independent attitudes always arise and result in the situation of there being a splitting of the ego. Once more the issue depends on which of the two can seize hold of the greater intensity.[1]

The facts of this splitting of the ego, which we have just described, are neither so new nor so strange as they may at first appear. It is indeed a universal characteristic of neuroses that there are present in the subject's mental life, as regards some particular behaviour, two different attitudes, contrary to each other and independent of each other. In the case of neuroses, however, one of these attitudes belongs to the ego and the contrary one, which is repressed, belongs to the id. The difference between this case and the other [discussed in the previous paragraph] is essentially a topographical or structural one, and it is not always easy to decide in an individual instance with which of the two possibilities one is dealing. They have, however, the following important characteristic in common. Whatever the ego does in its efforts of defence, whether it seeks to disavow a portion of the real external world or whether it seeks to reject an instinctual demand from the internal world, its success is never complete and unqualified. The outcome always lies in two contrary attitudes, of which the defeated, weaker one, no less than the other, leads to psychical complications. In conclusion, it is only necessary to point out how little of all these processes becomes known to us through our conscious perception.[2]

1. [I.e., the greater psychical energy.]

2. [The account of fetishism in this chapter is mainly derived from Freud's paper on the subject written some ten years before (1927e), where an early reference to a splitting of the ego will also be found. Cf. P.F.L., **7**, 345 ff. Both these questions had also been approached in an unfinished paper 'Splitting of the Ego in the Process of Defence' (1940e), ibid., **11**, 457 ff., which Freud had begun a few months before he wrote the present work. A discussion of the position appears in the Editor's Note to that paper.]

CHAPTER IX
THE INTERNAL WORLD

WE have no way of conveying knowledge of a complicated set of simultaneous events except by describing them successively; and thus it happens that all our accounts are at fault to begin with owing to one-sided simplification and must wait till they can be supplemented, built on to, and so set right.

The picture of an ego which mediates between the id and the external world, which takes over the instinctual demands of the former in order to lead them to satisfaction, which derives perceptions from the latter and uses them as memories, which, intent on its self-preservation, puts itself in defence against excessively strong claims from both sides and which, at the same time, is guided in all its decisions by the injunctions of a modified pleasure principle – this picture in fact applies to the ego only up to the end of the first period of childhood, till about the age of five. At about that time an important change has taken place. A portion of the external world has, at least partially, been abandoned as an object and has instead, by identification, been taken into the ego and thus become an integral part of the internal world. This new psychical agency continues to carry on the functions which have hitherto been performed by the people [the abandoned objects] in the external world: it observes the ego, gives it orders, judges it and threatens it with punishments, exactly like the parents whose place it has taken. We call this agency the *super-ego* and are aware of it in its judicial functions as our *conscience*. It is a remarkable thing that the super-ego often displays a severity for which no model has been provided by the real parents, and moreover that it calls the ego to account not only for its deeds but equally for its thoughts and unexecuted intentions, of which the super-ego seems to have knowledge. This reminds us that the hero of the Oedipus legend too felt guilty for his deeds and submitted himself to self-punishment, although the coercive power of the oracle should have acquitted him of guilt in our judgement and his own. The super-ego is in fact the heir to the Oedipus complex and is only established after that complex has been disposed of. For that reason its excessive severity does not follow a real model but corresponds to the strength of the defence used against the temptation of the Oedipus complex. Some suspicion of this state of things lies, no doubt, at the bottom of the assertion made by philosophers and believers that the moral sense is not instilled into men by education or acquired by them in their social life but is implanted in them from a higher source.

So long as the ego works in full harmony with the super-ego it is not easy to distinguish between their manifestations; but tensions and estrangements between them make themselves very plainly visible. The torments caused by the reproaches of conscience correspond precisely to a child's fear of loss of love, a fear the place of which has been taken by the moral agency. On the other hand, if the ego has successfully resisted a temptation to do something which would be objectionable to the super-ego, it feels raised in its self-esteem and strengthened in its pride, as though it had made some precious acquisition. In this way the super-ego continues to play the part of an external world for the ego, although it has become a portion of the internal world. Throughout later life it represents the influence of a person's childhood, of the care and education given him by his parents and of his dependence on them – a childhood which is prolonged so greatly in human beings by a family life in common. And in all this it is not only the personal qualities of these parents that is making itself felt, but also everything that had a determining effect on them themselves, the tastes and standards of the social class in which they lived and the innate dispositions and traditions of the race from which they sprang. Those who have a liking for generalizations and sharp distinctions may say that the external world, in which the individual finds himself exposed after being detached from his parents, represents the power of the present; that his id, with its inherited trends, represents the organic past; and that the super-ego, which comes to join them later, represents more than anything the cultural past, which a child has, as it were, to repeat as an after-experience during the few years of his early life. It is unlikely that such generalizations can be universally correct. Some portion of the cultural acquisitions have undoubtedly left a precipitate behind them in the id; much of what is contributed by the super-ego will awaken an echo in the id; not a few of the child's new experiences will be intensified because they are repetitions of some primeval phylogenetic experience.

> 'Was du ererbt von deinen Vätern hast,
> Erwirb es, um es zu besitzen.' [1]

Thus the super-ego takes up a kind of intermediate position between the id and the external world; it unites in itself the influences of the present and the past. In the establishment of the super-ego we have before us, as it were, an example of the way in which the present is changed into the past. . . .

1. ['What thou hast inherited from thy fathers, acquire it to make it thine.' Goethe, *Faust*, Part I, Scene 1.]

BIBLIOGRAPHY
AND AUTHOR INDEX

Titles of books and periodicals are in italics, titles of papers are in inverted commas. Abbreviations are in accordance with the *World List of Scientific Periodicals* (London, 1963–5). Further abbreviations used in this volume will be found in the List at the end of this bibliography. Numerals in bold type refer to volumes, ordinary numerals refer to pages. The figures in round brackets at the end of each entry indicate the page or pages of this volume on which the work in question is mentioned.

In the case of the Freud entries, only English translations are given. The initial dates are those of the German, or other, original publications. (The date of writing is added in square brackets where it differs from the latter.) The letters attached to the dates of publication are in accordance with the corresponding entries in the complete bibliography of Freud's writings included in Volume 24 of the *Standard Edition*. Details of the original publications, including the original German (or other) title, are given in the editorial introduction to each work included in the *Pelican Freud Library*.

For non-technical authors, and for technical authors where no specific work is mentioned, see the General Index.

ABEL, K. (1884) *Über den Gegensinn der Urworte*, Leipzig. (41, 178)

ABRAHAM, K. (1907) 'Das Erleiden sexueller Traumen als Form infantiler Sexualbetätigung', *Zentbl. Nervenheilk. Psychiat.*, N.F., **18**, 854. (34, 75)

    [*Trans.*: 'The Experiencing of Sexual Traumas as a Form of Sexual Activity', *Selected Papers*, London, 1927; New York, 1953, Chap. I.]

  (1909) *Trauma und Mythus: eine Studie zur Völkerpsychologie*, Leipzig and Vienna. (50, 94, 106)

    [*Trans.*: 'Dreams and Myth: A Study in Folk-Psychology',

Clinical Papers and Essays on Psycho-Analysis, London and New York, 1955; Part III: Essays, I.]

(1911) *Giovanni Segantini: ein psychoanalytischer Versuch*, Leipzig and Vienna. (86, 95, 106)

[*Trans.*: 'Giovanni Segantini: A Psycho-Analytical Study', *Clinical Papers and Essays on Psycho-Analysis*, London and New York, 1955; Part III: Essays, II.]

(1912) 'Ansätze zur psychoanalytischen Erforschung und Behandlung des manisch-depressiven Irreseins und verwandter Zustände', *Zentbl. Psychoanal.*, **2**, 302. (87, 245)

[*Trans.*: 'Notes on the Psycho-Analytical Investigation and Treatment of Manic-Depressive Insanity and Allied Conditions', *Selected Papers*, London, 1927; New York, 1953, Chap. VI.]

(1924) *Versuch einer Entwicklungsgeschichte der Libido*, Leipzig, Vienna and Zurich. (357)

[*Trans.*: 'A Short Study of the Development of the Libido', *Selected Papers*, London, 1927; New York, 1953; Chap. XXVI.]

(1965) With FREUD, S. *See* FREUD, S. (1965*a*)

ADLER, A. (1907) *Studie über Minderwertigkeit von Organen*, Berlin and Vienna. (110)

[*Trans.*: *Study of Organ-Inferiority and its Psychical Compensation*, New York, 1917.]

(1910) 'Der psychische Hermaphroditismus im Leben und in der Neurose', *Fortschr. Med.*, **28**, 486. (114)

(1911*a*) Review of C. G. Jung's 'Über Konflikte der kindlichen Seele', *Zentbl. Psychoanal.*, **1**, 122. (116)

(1911*b*) 'Beitrag zur Lehre vom Widerstand', *Zentbl. Psychoanal.*, **1**, 214. (117)

(1911*c*) 'Der männliche Protest, seine Rolle und Bedeutung in der Neurose' (Abstract), *Zentbl. Psychoanal.*, **1**, 371. (117)

(1912) *Über den nervösen Charakter*, Wiesbaden. (117)

[*Trans.*: *The Neurotic Constitution*, New York, 1916; London, 1918.]

(1914) With FURTMÜLLER, C. (eds.), *Heilen und Bilden*, Munich. (97)

ANDREAS-SALOMÉ, L., and FREUD, S. (1966), *See* FREUD, S. (1966*a*)

BLEULER, E. (1906*a*) *Affektivität, Suggestibilität, Paranoia*, Halle. (100)

[*Trans.*: *Affectivity, Suggestibility, Paranoia*, New York, 1912.]

(1906*b*) 'Freudsche Mechanismen in der Symtomatologie von Psychosen', *Psychiat.-neurol. Wschr.*, **8**, 323, 338. (176, 245)

(1910) 'Die Psychoanalyse Freuds', *Jb. psychoanalyt. psychopath. Forsch.*, **2**, 623. (99, 234)

(1911) *Dementia Praecox, oder Gruppe der Schizophrenien*, Leipzig and Vienna. (176, 234)

[*Trans.*: *Dementia Praecox, or the Group of Schizophrenias*, New York, 1950.]

(1913) 'Kritik der Freudschen Theorien', *Allg. Z. Psychiat.*, **70**, 665. (100)

(1914) 'Die Kritiken der Schizophrenien', *Z. ges. Neurol. Psychiat.*, **22**, 19. (100)

BREUER, J., and FREUD, S. (1893). *See* FREUD, S. (1893*a*)

(1895) *See* FREUD, S. (1895*d*)

BRILL, A. A. (1912) *Psychoanalysis: its Theories and Practical Application*, Philadelphia. (32, 94, 90)

DARKSCHEWITSCH, L. O. VON, and FREUD, S. (1886). *See* FREUD, S. (1886*b*)

ELLIS, HAVELOCK (1898) 'Hysteria in Relation to the Sexual Emotions', *Alien. & Neurol.*, **19**, 599. (207)

(1911) 'Die Lehren der Freud-Schule', *Zentbl. Psychoanal.*, **2**, 61. (88)

ERB, W. (1882) *Handbuch der Elektrotherapie*, Leipzig. (65, 162, 199)

[*Trans.*: *Handbook of Electro-Therapeutics*, London, 1883.]

FEDERN, E., and NUNBERG, H. *See* NUNBERG, H., and FEDERN, E.

FERENCZI, S. (1910) 'Die Psychoanalyse der Träume', *Psychiat.-neurol. Wschr.*, **12**, 114, 125. (34)

[*Trans.*: 'The Psychological Analysis of Dreams', *First Contributions to Psycho-Analysis*, London, 1952, Chap. III.]

(1911) 'Über lenkbare Träume', *Zentbl. Psychoanal.*, **2**, 31. (34)

[*Trans.*: 'Dirigible Dreams', *Final Contributions to the Problems and Methods of Psycho-Analysis*, London, 1955, Chap. XXVII.]

(1913*a*) 'Ein kleiner Hahnemann', *Int. Z. ärztl. Psychoanal.*, **1**, 240. (252)

[*Trans.*: 'A Little Chanticleer', *First Contributions to Psycho-Analysis*, London, 1952, Chap. IX.]

(1913*b*) 'Entwicklungsstufen des Wirklichkeitssinnes', *Int. Z. ärztl. Psychoanal.*, **1**, 124. (52, 384)

[*Trans.*: 'Stages in the Development of the Sense of Reality', *First Contributions to Psycho-Analysis*, London, 1952, Chap. VIII.]

(1928) 'Das Problem der Beendigung der Analysen', *Int. Z. Psychoanal.*, **14**, 1. (429)

[*Trans.*: 'The Problem of the Termination of Analyses', *Final Contributions to the Problems and Methods of Psycho-Analysis*, London, 1955, Chap. VII]

FRAZER, J. G. (1910) *Totemism and Exogamy* (4 vols), London. (251)

(1911, 1912, 1914) *The Golden Bough* (3rd ed.) London. (251, 253)

FREUD, M. (1957) *Glory Reflected*, London. (22)

FREUD, S. (1877a) 'Über den Ursprung der hinteren Nervenwurzeln im Rückenmarke von Amnocoetes (*Petromyzon Planeri*), *S.B. Akad. Wiss. Wien* (Math.-Naturwiss. Kl.), III. Abt., **75**, 15. (193)

(1878a) 'Über Spinalganglien und Rückenmark des Petromyzon', *S.B. Akad. Wiss. Wien* (Math.-Naturwiss. Kl.), III. Abt., **78**, 81. (193)

(1884e) 'Über Coca', *Zentbl. ges. Ther.*, **2**, 289. (197)

[*Trans.*: 'On Coca', in S. Freud, *The Cocaine Papers*, Vienna and Zurich.]

(1885d) 'Zur Kenntnis der Olivenzwischenschicht', *Neurol. Zentbl.*, **4**, Nr. 12, 268. (193)

(1886b) With DARKSCHEWITSCH, L. O. VON, 'Über die Beziehung des Strickkörpers zum Hinterstrang und Hinterstrangskern nebst Bemerkungen über zwei Felder der Oblongata', *Neurol. Zentbl.*, **5** (6), 121. (193)

(1886c) 'Über den Ursprung des Nervus acusticus', *Mschr. Ohrenheilk.*, N.F., **20** (8), 245; (9), 277. (193)

(1886d) 'Beobachtung einer hochgradigen Hemianästhesie bei einem hysterischen Manne (Beiträge zur Kasuistik der Hysterie, I)', *Wien. med. Wschr.*, **36** (49), 1633. (198)

(1888b) 'Hysteria' and 'Hystero-Epilepsy', *Standard Ed.*, **1**, 39, 58. (201)

(1888–89) 'Preface to the Translation of Bernheim's *Suggestion*', *Standard Ed.*, **1**, 73. (201)

(1889a) Review of August Forel's *Der Hypnotismus*, *Standard Ed.*, **1**, 91. (162)

(1891a) With RIE, O., *Klinische Studie über die halbseitige Cerebrallähmung der Kinder* (Beiträge zur Kinderheilkunde, Heft III, ed. Kassowitz), Vienna. (197, 201)

(1891b) *On Aphasia*, London and New York, 1953. (14, 24, 201)

(1891c) 'Kinderlähmung' and 'Lähmung' in Villaret's *Handwörterbuch der gesamten Medizin*, Vol. 2, Stuttgart. (201)

(1892a) Translation of Bernheim's *Hypnotisme, suggestion et psycho-thérapie: études nouvelles* with title, *Neue Studien über Hypnotismus, Suggestion und Psychotherapie*, Vienna. (201)

(1892–94) 'Preface and Footnotes to the Translation of Charcot's *Tuesday Lectures*', *Standard Ed.*, **1**, 131. (196)

(1893a) With BREUER, J., 'On the Psychical Mechanism of Hysterical Phenomena: Preliminary Communication', in *Studies on Hysteria*, *Standard Ed.*, **2**, 3; *P.F.L.*, **3**, 53. (25, 132, 204)

(1893b) *Zur Kenntnis der cerebralen Diplegien des Kindesalters (im Anschluss an die Little'sche Krankheit)* (Beiträge zur Kinderheilkunde, Heft III, ed. Kassowitz), Vienna. (197)

(1893c) 'Some Points for a Comparative Study of Organic and Hysterical Motor Paralyses', *Standard Ed.*, **1**, 157. (196)

(1893f) 'Charcot', *Standard Ed.*, **3**, 9. (29)

(1893h) 'On the Psychical Mechanism of Hysterical Phenomena', *Int. J. Psycho-Analysis*, **37** (1956), 8; *Standard Ed.*, **3**, 27. (381)

(1894a) 'The Neuro-Psychoses of Defence', *Standard Ed.*, **3**, 43. (65)

(1895b [1894]) 'On the Grounds for Detaching a Particular Syndrome from Neurasthenia under the Description "Anxiety Neurosis"', *Standard Ed.*, **3**, 87; *P.F.L.*, **10**, 31. (153, 208)

(1895d) With BREUER, J., *Studies on Hysteria*, London, 1956; *Standard Ed.*, **2**; *P.F.L.*, **3**. (25, 65, 87, 132, 164, 204)

(1896a) 'Heredity and the Aetiology of the Neuroses', *Standard Ed.*, **3**, 143. (135)

(1896b) 'Further Remarks on the Neuro-Psychoses of Defence', *Standard Ed.*, **3**, 159. (86, 176, 245)

(1896c) 'The Aetiology of Hysteria', *Standard Ed.*, **3**, 189. (78)

(1897a) *Die infantile Cerebrallähmung*, in Nothnagel's *Specielle Pathologie und Therapie*, Vol. 9, Vienna. (197)

(1900a) *The Interpretation of Dreams*, London and New York, 1955; *Standard Ed.*, **4–5**; *P.F.L.*, **4**. (25, 34, 77, 80, 83, 112, 118, 126, 138, 161, 171, 192, 198, 227, 230 ff., 246 ff., 250, 258, 373, 427)

(1901a) *On Dreams*, London and New York, 1951; *Standard Ed.*, **5**., 633. (34)

(1901b) *The Psychopathology of Everyday Life*, *Standard Ed.*, **6**; *P.F.L.*, **5**.(25, 32, 170, 258)

(1905c) *Jokes and their Relation to the Unconscious*, *Standard Ed.*, **8**; *P.F.L.*, **6**. (53, 83, 96, 127, 244, 249, 389)

(1905*d*) *Three Essays on the Theory of Sexuality*, London, 1962; *Standard Ed.*, **7**, 125; *P.F.L.*, **7**, 31. (25, 45, 115 f., 168, 208, 217, 221, 249, 274, 380)

(1905*e* [1901]) 'Fragment of an Analysis of a Case of Hysteria', *Standard Ed.*, **7**, 3; *P.F.L.*, **8**, 29. (67, 80, 113)

(1906*a* [1905]) 'My Views on the Part played by Sexuality in the Aetiology of the Neuroses', *Standard Ed.*, **7**, 271; *P.F.L.*, **10**, 67. (217)

(1906*c*) 'Psycho-Analysis and the Establishment of the Facts in Legal Proceedings', *Standard Ed.*, **9**, 99. (87)

(1907*a*) *Delusions and Dreams in Jensen's 'Gradiva'*, *Standard Ed.*, **9**, 3; *P.F.L.*, **14**, 27. (95, 106, 250)

(1907*b*) 'Obsessive Actions and Religious Practices', *Standard Ed.*, **9**, 116; *P.F.L.*, **13**, 27. (95, 178, 250)

(1908*e* [1907]) 'Creative Writers and Day-Dreaming', *Standard Ed.*, **9**, 143; *P.F.L.*, **14**, 129. (249)

(1909*b*) 'Analysis of a Phobia in a Five-Year-Old Boy', *Standard Ed.*, **10**, 3; *P.F.L.*, **8**, 165. (25, 223)

(1910*a* [1909]) *Five Lectures on Psycho-Analysis*, *Standard Ed.*, **11**, 3; in *Two Short Accounts of Psycho-Analysis*, Penguin Books, Harmondsworth, 1962. (29, 64, 88, 172, 189, 236)

(1910*c*) *Leonardo da Vinci and a Memory of his Childhood*, *Standard Ed.*, **11**, 59; *P.F.L.*, **14**, 143. (53, 95, 106, 249)

(1910*e*) 'The Antithetical Meaning of Primal Words', *Standard Ed.*, **11**, 155. (41, 178)

(1911*b*) 'Formulations on the Two Principles of Mental Functioning', *Standard Ed.*, **12**, 215; *P.F.L.*, **11**, 29. (243)

(1911*c* [1910]) 'Psycho-Analytic Notes on An Autobiographical Account of a Case of Paranoia (Dementia Paranoides)', *Standard Ed.*, **12**, 3; *P.F.L.*, **9**, 129. (25)

(1912–13) *Totem and Taboo*, London, 1950; New York, 1952; *Standard Ed.*, **13**, 1; *P.F.L.*, **13**, 43. (25, 51, 96, 179, 250 ff.)

(1913*b*) 'Introduction to Pfister's *Die psychoanalytische Methode*', *Standard Ed.*, **12**, 329. (97, 281, 360)

(1913*j*) 'The Claims of Psycho-Analysis to Scientific Interest', *Standard Ed.*, **13**, 165; *P.F.L.*, **15**, 27. (97).

(1914*b*) 'The Moses of Michelangelo', *Standard Ed.*, **13**, 211; *P.F.L.*, **14**, 249. (53)

(1914*c*) 'On Narcissism: an Introduction', *Standard Ed.*, **14**, 69; *P.F.L.*, **11**, 59. (60, 114, 209)

(1914*d*) 'On the History of the Psycho-Analytic Movement', *Standard Ed.*, **14**, 3; *P.F.L.*, **15**, 57. (26, 186, 189, 207, 231, 310)

(1915*b*) 'Thoughts for the Times on War and Death', *Standard Ed.*, **14**, 275; *P.F.L.*, **12**, 57. (233, 436)

(1915*c*) 'Instincts and their Vicissitudes', *Standard Ed.*, **14**, 111; *P.F.L.*, **11**, 105. (241, 243, 300)

(1915*d*) 'Repression', *Standard Ed.*, **14**, 143; *P.F.L.*, **11**, 139. (73, 213, 243)

(1915*e*) 'The Unconscious', *Standard Ed.*, **14**, 161; *P.F.L.*, **11**, 159. (73, 243, 297, 373)

(1915*f*) 'A Case of Paranoia Running Counter to the Psycho-Analytic Theory of the Disease', *Standard Ed.*, **14**, 263; *P.F.L.*, **10**, 145. (123, 415)

(1916–17 [1915–17]) *Introductory Lectures on Psycho-Analysis*, New York, 1966; London, 1971; *Standard Ed.*, **15–16**; *P.F.L.*, **1**. (26, 32, 34, 113, 209)

(1917*a*) 'A Difficulty in the Path of Psycho-Analysis', *Standard Ed.*, **17**, 137. (272, 274)

(1917*e* [1915]) 'Mourning and Melancholia', *Standard Ed.*, **14**, 239; *P.F.L.*, **11**, 245. (243)

(1918*a* [1917]) 'The Taboo of Virginity', *Standard Ed.*, **11**, 193; *P.F.L.*, **7**, 261. (426)

(1918*b* [1914]) 'From the History of an Infantile Neurosis', *Standard Ed.*, **17**, 3; *P.F.L.*, **9**, 225. (26, 61, 116)

(1919*b*) 'James J. Putnam', *Standard Ed.*, **17**, 271. (89)

(1919*d*) 'Introduction to *Psycho-Analysis and the War Neuroses*', London and New York, 1921; *Standard Ed.*, **17**, 207. (238)

(1919*e*) ' "A Child is Being Beaten" ', *Standard Ed.*, **17**, 177; *P.F.L.*, **10**, 159. (61,114)

(1920*b*) 'A Note on the Prehistory of the Technique of Analysis', *Standard Ed.*, **18**, 263. (73)

(1920*g*) *Beyond the Pleasure Principle*, London, 1961; *Standard Ed.*, **18**, 7; *P.F.L.*, **11**, 269. (26, 241, 244, 274, 380)

(1921*a*) 'Preface to Putnam's *Addresses on Psycho-Analysis*', London and New York, 1921; *Standard Ed.*, **18**, 269. (89)

(1921*c*) *Group Psychology and the Analysis of the Ego*, London and New York, 1959; *Standard Ed.*, **18**, 69; *P.F.L.*, **12**, 91. (26, 253)

(1922*b* [1921]) 'Some Neurotic Mechanisms in Jealousy, Paranoia and Homosexuality', *Standard Ed.*, **18**, 223; *P.F.L.*, **10**, 195. (437)

(1923*a* [1922]) 'Two Encyclopaedia Articles', *Standard Ed.*, **18**, 235; *P.F.L.*, **15**, 129.

(1923*b*) *The Ego and the Id*, London and New York, 1962; *Standard Ed.*, **19**, 3; *P.F.L.*, **11**, 339. (26, 115, 130, 157, 240 ff., 253, 257, 269, 281, 297, 373, 382, 384)

(1923*c* [1922]) 'Remarks on the Theory and Practice of Dream-Interpretation', *Standard Ed.*, **19**, 109. (126)

(1923*d* [1922]) 'A Seventeenth-Century Demonological Neurosis', *Standard Ed.*, **19**, 69; *P.F.L.*, **14**, 377. (114)

(1923*f*) 'Josef Popper-Lynkeus and the Theory of Dreams', *Standard Ed.*, **19**, 261. (77)

(1923*i*) 'Dr Sándor Ferenczi (on his 50th Birthday)', *Standard Ed.*, **19**, 267. (92)

(1924*b* [1923]) 'Neurosis and Psychosis', *Standard Ed.*, **19**, 149; *P.F.L.*, **10**, 209. (305)

(1924*d*) 'The Dissolution of the Oedipus Complex', *Standard Ed.*, **19**, 173; *P.F.L.*, **7**, 313. (220)

(1924*f* [1923]) 'A Short Account of Psycho-Analysis', *Standard Ed.*, **19**, 191; *P.F.L.*, **15**, 159. (130, 189)

(1925*d* [1924]) *An Autobiographical Study*, *Standard Ed.*, **20**, 3; *P.F.L.*, **15**, 183. (12, 37, 61, 75, 274, 427)

(1925*e* [1924]) 'The Resistances to Psycho-Analysis', *Standard Ed.*, **19**, 213; *P.F.L.*, **15**, 261.

(1925*g*) 'Josef Breuer', *Int. J. Psycho-Analysis*, **6**, 459; *Standard Ed.*, **19**, 279. (29)

(1925*j*) 'Some Psychical Consequences of the Anatomical Distinction between the Sexes', Standard Ed., **19**, 243; *P.F.L.*, **7**, 323. (116, 220)

(1926*d* [1925]) *Inhibitions, Symptoms and Anxiety*, London, 1960; *Standard Ed.*, **20**, 77; *P.F.L.*, **10**, 227. (26, 68, 209, 257, 384)

(1926*e*) *The Question of Lay-Analysis*, London, 1947; *Standard Ed.*, **20**, 179; *P.F.L.*, **15**, 227. (255, 368)

(1926*f*) 'Psycho-Analysis: Freudian School', *Encyclopaedia Britannica* (13th ed.), Vol. 3, 253; *Standard Ed.*, **20**, 261. (160)

(1926*i*) 'Dr Reik and the Problem of Quackery', *Standard Ed.*, **21**, 247; *P.F.L.*, **15**, 365.

(1927*a*) 'Postscript to *The Question of Lay Analysis*', *Standard Ed.*, **20**, 251; *P.F.L.*, **15**, 355. (12, 190)

(1927*c*) *The Future of an Illusion*, London, 1962; *Standard Ed.*, **21**, 3; *P.F.L.*, **12**, 179. (26, 257, 294, 436)

(1927e) 'Fetishism', *Standard Ed.*, **21**, 149; *P.F.L.*, **7**, 345. (257, 440)

(1930a [1929]) *Civilization and its Discontents*, New York, 1961; London, 1963; *Standard Ed.*, **21**, 59; *P.F.L.*, **12**, 243. (26, 257, 284)

(1930d) 'Letter to Dr Alfons Paquet', *Standard Ed.*, **21**, 207; *P.F.L.*, **14**, 465. (258)

(1930e) 'Address delivered in the Goethe House at Frankfurt', *Standard Ed.*, **21**, 208; *P.F.L.*, **14**, 467. (258, 427)

(1931b) 'Female Sexuality', *Standard Ed.*, **21**, 223; *P.F.L.*, **7**, 367. (217, 400, 429)

(1932c) 'My Contact with Josef Popper-Lynkeus', *Standard Ed.*, **22**, 219. (77)

(1933a [1932]) *New Introductory Lectures on Psycho-Analysis*, New York, 1966; London, 1971; *Standard Ed.*, **22**; *P.F.L.*, **2**. (61, 217, 357, 380)

(1933b [1932]) *Why War?*, Paris; *Standard Ed.*, **22**, 197; *P.F.L.*, **12**, 341. (380)

(1935a) Postscript (1935) to *An Autobiographical Study*, new ed., London and New York; *Standard Ed.*, **20**, 71; *P.F.L.*, **15**, 256. (12)

(1937c) 'Analysis Terminable and Interminable', *Standard Ed.*, **23**, 211. (429)

(1937d) 'Constructions in Analysis', *Standard Ed.*, **23**, 257. (317)

(1939a [1934–38]) *Moses and Monotheism*, *Standard Ed.*, **23**, 3; *P.F.L.*, **13**, 237. (26, 258, 384, 401, 427)

(1940a [1938]) *An Outline of Psycho-Analysis*, New York, 1968; London, 1969; Standard Ed., **23**, 141; *P.F.L.*, **15**, 369. (26)

(1940b [1938]) 'Some Elementary Lessons in Psycho-Analysis', *Standard Ed.*, **23**, 281. (371)

(1940e [1938]) 'Splitting of the Ego in the Process of Defence', *Standard Ed.*, **23**, 273; *P.F.L.*, **11**, 457. (440)

(1950a [1887–1902]) *The Origins of Psycho-Analysis*, London and New York, 1954. (Partly, including 'A Project for a Scientific Psychology', in *Standard Ed.*, **1**, 175.) (15 f., 23, 25, 63, 78, 101)

(1956a [1886]) 'Report on my Studies in Paris and Berlin', *Int. J. Psycho-Analysis*, **37**, 2; *Standard Ed.*, **1**, 3. (65, 70, 195)

(1960a) *Letters 1873–1939* (ed. E. L. Freud) (trans. T. and J. Stern), New York, 1960; London, 1961. (23)

(1963a [1909–39]) *Psycho-Analysis and Faith. The Letters of Sigmund Freud and Oskar Pfister* (ed. H. Meng and E. L. Freud) (trans. E. Mosbacher), London and New York, 1963. (23)

(1965a [1907–26]) *A Psycho-Analytic Dialogue. The Letters of Sigmund Freud and Karl Abraham* (ed. H. C. Abraham and E. L. Freud) (trans. B. Marsh and H. C. Abraham), London and New York, 1965. (23)

(1966a [1912–36]) *Sigmund Freud and Lou Andreas-Salomé: Letters* (ed. E. Pfeiffer) (trans. W. and E. Robson-Scott), London and New York, 1972. (23)

(1968a [1927–39]) *The Letters of Sigmund Freud and Arnold Zweig* (ed. E. L. Freud) (trans. W. and E. Robson-Scott), London and New York, 1970. (23)

(1970a [1919–35]) *Sigmund Freud as a Consultant. Recollections of a Pioneer in Psychoanalysis* (Letters from Freud to Edoardo Weiss, including a Memoir and Commentaries by Weiss, with Foreword and Introduction by Martin Grotjahn), New York, 1970. (23)

(1974a [1906–23]) *The Freud/Jung Letters* (ed. W. McGuire) (trans. R. Manheim and R. F. C. Hull), London and Princeton, N. J., 1974. (23, 119)

FURTMÜLLER, C., and ADLER, A. *See* ADLER, A., and FURT-MÜLLER, C.

GRAF, M. (1911) *Richard Wagner im 'Fliegenden Holländer': ein Beitrag zur Psychologie künstlerischen Schaffens*, Leipzig and Vienna. (106)

GREVE, G. (1910) 'Sobre psicologia y psicoterapia de ciertos estados angustiosos', Lecture to Neurological Section, Int. American Congress of Medicine and Hygiene, Buenos Aires. (88)

HESNARD, A., and RÉGIS, E. *See* RÉGIS, E., and HESNARD, A.

HOCHE, A. (1910) 'Eine psychische Epidemie unter Ärzten', *Med. Klin.*, **6**, 1007. (85)

HUG-HELLMUTH, H. VON (1913) *Aus dem Seelenleben des Kindes*, Leipzig and Vienna. (96, 106)
   [*Trans.*: *A Study of the Mental Life of the Child*, New York, 1919.]

JANET, P. (1913) 'Psycho-Analysis. Rapport par M. le Dr Pierre Janet', *Int. Congr. Med.*, **17**, Sect. XII (Psychiatry) (1), 13. (90, 98)

JELGERSMA, G. (1914) *Ongeweten Geestesleven*, Leyden. (91)
   [*German trans.*: *Unbewusstes Geistesleben*, Leipzig and Vienna, 1914.]

JENSEN, W. (1903) *Gradiva: ein pompejanisches Phantasiestück*, Dresden and Leipzig. (95, 250)

JONES, E. (1908) 'Rationalization in Everyday Life', *J. abnorm. Psychol.*, **3**, 161; *Papers on Psycho-Analysis*, London, 1913. (113)

(1911*a*) 'The Psychopathology of Everyday Life', *Amer. J. Psychol.*, **22**, 477; *Papers on Psycho-Analysis*, London, 1913. (32)

(1911*b* [1910]) *Das Problem des Hamlet und der Oedipus-Komplex*, Leipzig and Vienna. (106, 248)

[*English text*: 'The Oedipus Complex as an Explanation of Hamlet's Mystery', *Amer. J. Psychol.*, **21** (1910), 72.]

(1912*a*) *Der Alptraum in seiner Beziehung zu gewissen Formen des mittelalterlichen Aberglaubens* (trans. H. Sachs), Leipzig and Vienna. (34, 94, 106)

[*English text*: *On the Nightmare*, London and New York, 1931.]

(1912*b*) 'Die Bedeutung des Salzes in Sitte und Brauch der Völker', *Imago*, **1**, 361, 454. (94)

[*English text*: 'The Symbolic Significance of Salt in Folklore and Superstition', *Essays in Applied Psycho-Analysis*, Vol. 2, London, 1951.]

(1913) *Papers on Psycho-Analysis*, London and New York, 1913. (90)

(1915) 'Professor Janet on Psychoanalysis: a Rejoinder', *J. abnorm. (soc.) Psychol.*, **9**, 400; *Papers on Psycho-Analysis* (2nd ed.), London and New York, 1918. (1953–7) *Sigmund Freud: Life and Work* (3 vols), London and New York, (page references are to the English edition.) (23, 60 f., 69, 73, 160, 186 f., 197, 210, 243, 281, 372, 427)

JUNG, C. G. (1902) *Zur Psychologie und Pathologie sogenannter okkulter Phänomene*, Leipzig. (85)

[*Trans.*: 'On the Psychology and Pathology of so-called Occult Phenomena', *Collected Papers on Analytical Psychology*, London, 1916, Chap. I.]

(1906, 1909) *Diagnostische Assoziationsstudien* (2 vols), Leipzig. (87)

[*Trans.*: *Studies in Word-Association*, London, 1918; New York, 1919.]

(1907) *Über die Psychologie der Dementia Praecox*, Halle. (86, 245)

[*Trans.*: *The Psychology of Dementia Praecox*, New York, 1909.]

(1908) *Der Inhalt der Psychose*, Leipzig and Vienna. (38, 106)

(1910*a*) 'The Association Method', *Amer. J. Psychol.*, **21**, 219; *Collected Papers on Analytical Psychology*, London, 1916, Chap. II. (89)

(1910*b*) 'Über Konflikte der kindlichen Seele', *Jb. psychoanalyt. psychopath. Forsch.*, **2**, 33. (89, 116, 27)

[*Trans.*: 'Psychic Conflicts in a Child', *The Collected Works of C. G. Jung*, Vol. 17, London, 1954.]

(1911–12) 'Wandlungen und Symbole der Libido', *Jb. psychoanalyt. psychopath. Forsch.*, **3**, 120; **4**, 162; in book form, Leipzig and Vienna, 1912. (50 f., 250)
[*Trans.*: *Psychology of the Unconscious*, New York, 1916; London, 1917.]

(1913) 'Versuch einer Darstellung der psychoanalytischen Theorie', *Jb. psychoanalyt. psychopath. Forsch.*, **5**, 307; in book form, Leipzig and Vienna, 1913. (127, 429)
[*Trans.*: *The Theory of Psycho-Analysis*, New York, 1915.]

(1974) With FREUD, S. *See* FREUD, S. (1974*a*)

KIELHOLZ, A. (1919) *Jakob Böhme: ein pathographischer Beitrag zur Psychologie der Mystik*, Leipzig and Vienna. (106)

LOONEY, J. T. (1920) *'Shakespeare' Identified*, London. (248)

MAEDER, A. (1906, 1908) 'Contributions à la psychopathologie de la vie quotidienne', *Archs Psychol., Genève*, **6**, 148; **7**, 283. (32)

(1912) 'Über die Funktion des Traumes', *Jb. psychoanalyt. psychopath. Forsch.*, **4**, 692. (34, 118)

MANN, T. (1929) 'Die Stellung Freuds in der modernen Geistesgeschichte', *Psychoanal. Beweg.*, **1**, 3. (258)
[*Trans.*: 'Freud's Position in the History of Modern Culture', *Psychoanal. Rev.*, 28, (1941), 92.]

MOLL, A. (1898) *Untersuchungen über die Libido sexualis*, Vol. 1, Berlin. (153)

NELKEN, J. (1912) 'Analytische Beobachtungen über Phantasien eines Schizophrenen', *Jb. psychoanalyt. psychopath. Forsch.*, **4**, 504. (94)

NOTHNAGEL, H. (1879) *Topische Diagnostik der Gehirnkrankheiten*, Berlin. (194)

(ed.) (1897) *Specielle Pathologie und Therapie*, Vol. 9, Vienna. (197)

NUNBERG, H., and FEDERN, E. (eds) (1962, 1974) *Minutes of the Vienna Psychoanalytic Society*, Vols. 1 and 3, New York. (70, 117)

PESTALOZZI, R. (1956) 'Sigmund Freuds Berufswahl', *Neue Zürcher Zeitung*, 1 July, Fernausgabe, 179, Bl. 5. (191)

PFISTER, O. (1910) *Die Frömmigkeit des Grafen Ludwig von Zinzendorf*, Vienna. (96, 106)

(1913) *Die psychoanalytische Methode*, Leipzig and Berlin. (56, 96, 152, 181, 281, 360)
[*Trans.*: *The Psycho-Analytic Method*, New York and London, 1917.]

(1963) With FREUD, S. *See* FREUD, S. (1963*a*)

POPPER, J. ['LYNKEUS'] (1899) *Phantasien eines Realisten*, Vienna. (77)

PUTNAM, J. J. (1912) 'Über die Bedeutung philosophischer An-schauungen und Ausbildung für die weitere Entwicklung der psychoanalytischen Bewegung', *Imago*, **1**, 101. (104)
[*English text*: 'A Plea for the Study of Philosophic Methods in Preparation for Psycho-Analytic Work', *Addresses on Psycho-Analysis*, New York, 1921, Chap. IV.]

(1921) *Addresses on Psycho-Analysis*, New York. (89)

RANK, O. (1907) *Der Künstler: Ansätze zu einer Sexualpsychologie*, Leipzig and Vienna. (53, 95, 180)
[*Trans.*: *Art and the Artist: Creative Urge and Personality Development*, New York, 1932.]

(1909) *Der Mythus von der Geburt des Helden*, Leipzig and Vienna. (50, 94, 106, 254)
[*Trans.*: *The Myth of the Birth of the Hero*, New York, 1914.]

(1910a) 'Schopenhauer über den Wahnsinn', *Zentbl. Psychoanal.*, **1**, 69. (72)

(1910b) 'Ein Beispiel von poetischer Verwertung des Ver-sprechens', *Zentbl. Psychoanal.*, **1**, 109. (32)

(1910c) 'Ein Traum, der sich selbst deutet', *Jb. psychoanalyt. psycho-path. Forsch.*, **2**, 465. (34)

(1911) *Die Lohengrinsage*, Leipzig and Vienna. (50, 94, 106, 152, 254)

(1912a) *Das Inzest-Motiv in Dichtung und Sage*, Leipzig and Vienna. (53, 95, 152, 248, 254)

(1912b) 'Fehlleistungen aus dem Alltagsleben', *Zentbl. Psychoanal.*, **2**, 265. (32)

(1912c) 'Aktuelle Sexualregungen als Traumanlässe', *Zentbl. Psychoanal.*, **2**, 596. (34)

RANK, O., and SACHS, H. (1913) *Die Bedeutung der Psychoanalyse für die Geisteswissenschaften* Wiesbaden. (93, 179)
[*Trans.*: *The Significance of Psychoanalysis for the Mental Sciences*, New York, 1916.]

RÉGIS, E., and HESNARD, A. (1914) *La psychoanalyse des névroses et des psychoses*, Paris. (90)

REIK, T. (1912) *Flaubert und seine 'Versuchung des heiligen Antonius'*, Minden. (95)

(1919) *Probleme der Religionspsychologie*, Vienna. (152, 181)
[*Trans.*: *Ritual: Psycho-Analytic Studies*, London and New York, 1931.]

RENTERGHEM, A. W. VAN (1913) *Freud en zijn School*, Baarn. (91)

RIE, O., and FREUD, S. (1891). *See* FREUD, S. (1891a)

RIKLIN, F. (1908) *Wunscherfüllung und Symbolik im Märchen*, Leipzig and Vienna. (94, 106)

[*Trans.*: *Wish-fulfillment and Symbolism in Fairy Tales*, New York, 1915.]

SACHS, H., and RANK, O. *See* RANK, O., and SACHS, H.

SADGER, I. (1909) *Aus dem Liebesleben Nicolaus Lenaus*, Leipzig and Vienna. (95, 106)

(1914) *Über Nachtwandeln und Mondsucht: eine medizinisch-literarische Studie*, Leipzig. (106)

(1920) *Friedrich Hebbel: ein psychoanalytischer Versuch*, Vienna. (106)

SCHERNER, K. A. (1861) *Das Leben des Traumes*, Berlin. (77)

SCHOPENHAUER, A. (1819) *Die Welt als Wille und Vorstellung*, Leipzig. (70, 244, 274)

SILBERER, H. (1909) 'Bericht über eine Methode, gewisse symbolische Halluzinations-Erscheinungen hervorzurufen und zu beobachten', *Jb. psychoanalyt. psychopath. Forsch.*, **1**, 513. (34)

(1912) 'Symbolik des Erwachens und Schwellensymbolik überhaupt', *Jb. psychoanalyt. psychopath. Forsch.*, **3**, 621. (34)

(1914) *Probleme der Mystik und ihrer Symbolik*, Leipzig and Vienna. (123)

[*Trans.*: *Problems of Mysticism and its Symbolism*, New York, 1917.]

SIMMEL, E. (1918) *Kriegsneurosen und 'Psychisches Trauma'*, Munich. (205)

SMITH, W. ROBERTSON (1894) *Lectures on the Religion of the Semites* (2nd ed.), London. (252, 253)

SPERBER, H. (1912) 'Über den Einfluss sexueller Momente auf Entstehung und Entwicklung der Sprache', *Imago*, **1**, 405. (42)

STEKEL, W. (1911) *Die Sprache des Traumes*, Wiesbaden. (34)

STORFER, A. J. (1911) *Zur Sonderstellung des Vatermordes*, Leipzig and Vienna. (106)

(1914) *Marias jungfräuliche Mutterschaft*, Berlin. (94)

STRÜMPELL, A. VON (1896) Review of Breuer and Freud's *Studien über Hysterie*, *Dtsch. Z. Nervenheilk.*, **8**, 159. (206)

VAIHINGER, H. (1911) *Die Philosophie des Als Ob*, Berlin. (294)

[*Trans.*: *The Philosophy of 'As If'*, London, 1924.]

VILLARET, A. (ed.) (1888, 1891) *Handwörterbuch der gesamten Medizin* (2 vols), Stuttgart. (201)

VOGT, R. (1907) *Psykiatriens grundtraek*, Christiana. (91)

WEISS, E. and FREUD, S. (1970). *See* FREUD, S. (1970a)

ZWEIG, A., and FREUD, S. (1968). *See* FREUD, S. (1968a)

LIST OF ABBREVIATIONS

Gesammelte Schriften = Freud, *Gesammelte Schriften* (12 vols), 1924–34.

Gesammelte Werke = *Freud, Gesammelte Werke* (18 vols), Vols. 1–17 London, 1940–52, Vol. 18 Frankfurt am Main, 1968. From 1960 the whole edition published by S. Fischer Verlag, Frankfurt am Main.

S.K.S.N. = Freud, *Sammlung kleiner Schriften zur Neurosenlehre* (5 vols), Vienna, 1906–22.

Almanach 1926 = *Almanach für das Jahr 1926*, Internationaler Psychoanalytischer Verlag, Vienna, 1925.

Almanach 1927 = *Almanach für das Jahr 1927*, Internationaler Psychoanalytischer Verlag, Vienna, 1926.

Almanach 1936 = *Almanach der Psychoanalyse 1936*, Internationaler Psychoanalytischer Verlag, Vienna, 1935.

Collected Papers = Freud, *Collected Papers* (5 vols), London, 1924–50.

Standard Edition = *The Standard Edition of the Complete Psychological Works of Sigmund Freud* (24 vols), Hogarth Press and The Institute of Psycho-Analysis, London, 1953–74.

P.F.L. = *Pelican Freud Library* (15 vols), Penguin Books, Harmondsworth, 1973–86.

GENERAL INDEX

This index includes the names of non-technical authors as well as those of technical authors where no reference is made in the text to specific works. For references to specific technical works, the Bibliography should be consulted.

461

FOR THE BEST IN PAPERBACKS, LOOK FOR THE

In every corner of the world, on every subject under the sun, Penguins represent quality and variety – the very best in publishing today.

For complete information about books available from Penguin and how to order them, write to us at the appropriate address below. Please note that for copyright reasons the selection of books varies from country to country.

In the United Kingdom: For a complete list of books available from Penguin in the U.K., please write to *Dept EP, Penguin Books Ltd, Harmondsworth, Middlesex, UB7 0DA*

In the United States: For a complete list of books available from Penguin in the U.S., please write to *Dept BA, Viking Penguin, 299 Murray Hill Parkway, East Rutherford, New Jersey 07073*

In Canada: For a complete list of books available from Penguin in Canada, please write to *Penguin Books Canada Limited, 2801 John Street, Markham, Ontario L3R 1B4*

In Australia: For a complete list of books available from Penguin in Australia, please write to the *Marketing Department, Penguin Books Australia Ltd, P.O. Box 257, Ringwood, Victoria 3134*

In New Zealand: For a complete list of books available from Penguin in New Zealand, please write to the *Marketing Department, Penguin Books (N.Z.) Ltd, Private Bag, Takapuna, Auckland 9*

In India: For a complete list of books available from Penguin in India, please write to *Penguin Overseas Ltd, 706 Eros Apartments, 56 Nehru Place, New Delhi 110019*

FOR THE BEST IN PAPERBACKS, LOOK FOR THE

A CHOICE OF PENGUINS AND PELICANS

Adieux Simone de Beauvoir

This 'farewell to Sartre' by his life-long companion is a 'true labour of love' (the *Listener*) and 'an extraordinary achievement' (*New Statesman*).

British Society 1914–45 John Stevenson

A major contribution to the Pelican Social History of Britain, which 'will undoubtedly be the standard work for students of modern Britain for many years to come' – *The Times Educational Supplement*

The Pelican History of Greek Literature Peter Levi

A remarkable survey covering all the major writers from Homer to Plutarch, with brilliant translations by the author, one of the leading poets of today.

Art and Literature Sigmund Freud

Volume 14 of the Pelican Freud Library contains Freud's major essays on Leonardo, Michelangelo and Dostoevsky, plus shorter pieces on Shakespeare, the nature of creativity and much more.

A History of the Crusades Sir Steven Runciman

This three-volume history of the events which transferred world power to Western Europe – and founded Modern History – has been universally acclaimed as a masterpiece.

A Night to Remember Walter Lord

The classic account of the sinking of the *Titanic*. 'A stunning book, incomparably the best on its subject and one of the most exciting books of this or any year' – *The New York Times*

FOR THE BEST IN PAPERBACKS, LOOK FOR THE

A CHOICE OF PENGUINS AND PELICANS

The Literature of the United States Marcus Cunliffe

The fourth edition of a masterly one-volume survey, described by D. W. Brogan in the *Guardian* as 'a very good book indeed'.

The Sceptical Feminist Janet Radcliffe Richards

A rigorously argued but sympathetic consideration of feminist claims. 'A triumph' – *Sunday Times*

The Enlightenment Norman Hampson

A classic survey of the age of Diderot and Voltaire, Goethe and Hume, which forms part of the Pelican History of European Thought.

Defoe to the Victorians David Skilton

A 'Learned and stimulating' (*The Times Educational Supplement*) survey of two centuries of the English novel.

Reformation to Industrial Revolution Christopher Hill

This 'formidable little book' (Peter Laslett in the *Guardian*) by one of our leading historians is Volume 2 of the Pelican Economic History of Britain.

The New Pelican Guide to English Literature Boris Ford (ed.)
Volume 8: The Present

This book brings a major series up to date with important essays on Ted Hughes and Nadine Gordimer, Philip Larkin and V. S. Naipaul, and all the other leading writers of today.

A CHOICE OF PENGUINS AND PELICANS

The Second World War (6 volumes) Winston S. Churchill

The definitive history of the cataclysm which swept the world for the second time in thirty years.

1917: The Russian Revolutions and the Origins of Present-Day Communism
Leonard Schapiro

A superb narrative history of one of the greatest episodes in modern history by one of our greatest historians.

Imperial Spain 1496–1716 J. H. Elliot

A brilliant modern study of the sudden rise of a barren and isolated country to be the greatest power on earth, and of its equally sudden decline. 'Outstandingly good' – *Daily Telegraph*

Joan of Arc: The Image of Female Heroism Marina Warner

'A profound book, about human history in general and the place of women in it' – Christopher Hill

Man and the Natural World: Changing Attitudes in England 1500–1800
Keith Thomas

'A delight to read and a pleasure to own' – Auberon Waugh in the *Sunday Telegraph*

The Making of the English Working Class E. P. Thompson

Probably the most imaginative – and the most famous – post-war work of English social history.

FOR THE BEST IN PAPERBACKS, LOOK FOR THE

A CHOICE OF PENGUINS AND PELICANS

The French Revolution   Christopher Hibbert

'One of the best accounts of the Revolution that I know . . . Mr Hibbert is outstanding' – J. H. Plumb in the *Sunday Telegraph*

The Germans   Gordon A. Craig

An intimate study of a complex and fascinating nation by 'one of the ablest and most distinguished American historians of modern Germany' – Hugh Trevor-Roper

Ireland: A Positive Proposal   Kevin Boyle and Tom Hadden

A timely and realistic book on Northern Ireland which explains the historical context – and offers a practical and coherent set of proposals which could actually work.

A History of Venice   John Julius Norwich

'Lord Norwich has loved and understood Venice as well as any other Englishman has ever done' – Peter Levi in the *Sunday Times*

Montaillou: Cathars and Catholics in a French Village 1294–1324
Emmanuel Le Roy Ladurie

'A classic adventure in eavesdropping across time' – Michael Ratcliffe in *The Times*

Star Wars   E. P. Thompson and others

Is Star Wars a serious defence strategy or just a science fiction fantasy? This major book sets out all the arguments and makes an unanswerable case *against* Star Wars.

FOR THE BEST IN PAPERBACKS, LOOK FOR THE

A CHOICE OF PENGUINS AND PELICANS

The Apartheid Handbook   Roger Omond

This book provides the essential hard information about how apartheid actually works from day to day and fills in the details behind the headlines.

The World Turned Upside Down   Christopher Hill

This classic study of radical ideas during the English Revolution 'will stand as a notable monument to . . . one of the finest historians of the present age' – *The Times Literary Supplement*

Islam in the World   Malise Ruthven

'His exposition of "the Qurenic world view" is the most convincing, and the most appealing, that I have read' – Edward Mortimer in *The Times*

The Knight, the Lady and the Priest   Georges Duby

'A very fine book' (Philippe Aries) that traces back to its medieval origin one of our most important institutions, modern marriage.

A Social History of England   New Edition   Asa Briggs

'A treasure house of scholarly knowledge . . . beautifully written and full of the author's love of his country, its people and its landscape' – John Keegan in the *Sunday Times*, Books of the Year

The Second World War   A. J. P. Taylor

A brilliant and detailed illustrated history, enlivened by all Professor Taylor's customary iconoclasm and wit.

FOR THE BEST IN PAPERBACKS, LOOK FOR THE

PENGUIN REFERENCE BOOKS

The Penguin Guide to the Law

This acclaimed reference book is designed for everyday use, and forms the most comprehensive handbook ever published on the law as it affects the individual.

The Penguin Medical Encyclopedia

Covers the body and mind in sickness and in health, including drugs, surgery, history, institutions, medical vocabulary and many other aspects. 'Highly commendable' – *Journal of the Institute of Health Education*

The Penguin French Dictionary

This invaluable French-English, English-French dictionary includes both the literary and dated vocabulary needed by students, and the up-to-date slang and specialized vocabulary (scientific, legal, sporting, etc) needed in everyday life. As a passport to the French language, it is second to none.

A Dictionary of Literary Terms

Defines over 2,000 literary terms (including lesser known, foreign language and technical terms) explained with illustrations from literature past and present.

The Penguin Map of Europe

Covers all land eastwards to the Urals, southwards to North Africa and up to Syria, Iraq and Iran. Scale – 1:5,500,000, 4-colour artwork. Features main roads, railways, oil and gas pipelines, plus extra information including national flags, currencies and populations.

The Penguin Dictionary of Troublesome Words

A witty, straightforward guide to the pitfalls and hotly disputed issues in standard written English, illustrated with examples and including a glossary of grammatical terms and an appendix on punctuation.